MYSTICISM
IN SHAIVISM AND CHRISTIANITY

MYSTICISM
IN SHAIVISM AND CHRISTIANITY

Edited by
Bettina Bäumer

DK PRINTWORLD
Publishers of Indian Traditions

Cataloging in Publication Data – DK
[Courtesy: D.K. Agencies (P) Ltd. <docinfo@dkagencies.com>]

Mysticism in Shaivism and Christianity / edited by Bettina Bäumer.
pages cm
Includes bibliographical references.
ISBN 9788124600962 (hardback)

1. Mysticism – Saivism. 2. Mysticism – Christianity. I. Bäumer, Bettina, 1940- editor.

LCC BL1215.M9M97 2018 | DDC 294.5422 23

ISBN 978-81-246-0096-2
First published in India in 1997
Second impression published in 2006
Third impression published in 2019

Printed and published by:
D.K. Printworld (P) Ltd.
Regd. office : *Vedaśrī*, F-395, Sudarshan Park
(Metro Station: ESI Hospital) New Delhi - 110 015
Phones : (011) 2545 3975, 2546 6019
e-mail : indology@dkprintworld.com
Web : www.dkprintworld.com

CONTENTS

ACKNOWLEDGEMENTS

Our thanks are due to all the participants of the Rajpur Seminar, not only the authors of the papers, but also the respondents and discussants. We thank the contributors for their patience, since the publication of this Volume was delayed for several reasons.

We thank Prof. A. Haas for permitting us to include his article in this Volume, and Dr. F. Wöhrer for looking after the translation from the German.

Prof. R. Panikkar has not only taken much care in revising his contribution, but he was also guiding and encouraging me in the Rajpur Seminar, as well as with this publication.

Fr G. Gispert-Sauch has assisted me in noting down and writing summaries of the discussions.

Fr James Stuart has been kind to edit the English of most of the articles.

The Abhishiktananda Society has supported the Seminar and the preparation of the press-copy.

In the heart of every man there is something — a drive? — which is already there when he is born and will haunt him unremittingly until his last breath. It is a mystery which encompasses him on every side, but one which none of his faculties can ever attain to or, still less, lay hold of. It cannot be located in anything that can be seen, heard, touched or known in this world. There is no sign for it . . . It is a bursting asunder at the very heart of being, something utterly unbearable. But nevertheless this is the price of finding the treasure that is without name or form or sign. It is the unique splendour of the Self — but no one is left in its presence to exclaim, "How beautiful it is!"

Abhishiktananda, *The Further Shore*, p. 37

INTRODUCTION

So'ham

I am He.
Jn 4.26

In our times of narrow fundamentalism and religious conflicts, a dialogue of religions is not a luxury, but a necessity. But dialogue in the true — and etymological — sense should mean a piercing through the *logos*,[1] transcending the logical, the verbal, the social and institutional levels in order to come to a real meeting beyond the infinite differences of religious expressions. Institutional dialogues do not bring the followers of different religions closer to each other, unless a real spiritual meeting takes place. The true meeting-point is at the mystical level, "in the cave of the heart".[2] If two persons, and more so two spiritual persons, truly meet, they do not remain the same. A mutual transformation takes place which does not allow the followers of a particular tradition to remain exclusivistic, because one realizes that the spiritual reality that one aims at may also be present in another tradition, though in a different form and language. Therefore dialogue at the spiritual level is one of the most important

[1]Cf. R. Panikkar, "The Dialogical Dialogue", in F. Whaling (ed.), *The World's Religious Traditions*, Edinburgh 1984, p. 218; see also R. Panikkar, *Myth, Faith and Hermeneutics*, Bangalore, 1983, pp. 232–57, and *The Intrareligious Dialogue*, New York, The Paulist Press, 1978; Bangalore 1984.

[2]In the favourite expression of Abhishiktananda, taken from the Upaniṣads. Cp. his book *Hindu-Christian Meeting-Point — Within the Cave of the Heart*, Delhi, ISPCK, 1st edn. 1969, reprint 1983.

means of bringing about an understanding between different people, cultures and religions.

One of the etymologies of the word 'mysticism', derived from the Greek *myeo*, has also the sense of 'closing a wound which has been split open', hence healing. "Mystic then means to restore original unity, which through the embarrassing manifoldness of empirical appearances is temporarily broken or obscured."[3] Our time is in need of a mysticism of this kind, which can heal the wounds of differences, separation and alienation of human beings, Man and Nature, Man and the ultimate Reality, by whatever name we call it.

It is not a modern idea that the closer a person, a group or a tradition is to the mystical experience, the less do they feel the differences between the various religious expressions. Thus the Śaiva mystic Utpaladeva of the ninth century exclaims, after realizing his oneness with Śiva:

> Glory to you, O Śarva,
> who are the essence of the 'right-handed path',
> who are the essence of the 'left-handed path',[4]
> who belong to every tradition
> and to no tradition at all.
>
> Glory to you, O God,
> who can be worshipped in any manner,
> in any place,
> in whatever form at all.
>
> *Śivastotrāvalī* 2.19–20

The mystic is aware of the relativity of any path, and only such a person has the inner freedom to transcend the limitations of tradition.

---

[3] Betty Heimann, "Opposites: Contrasts or Complements in early Greek and Indian Philosophy?", in: *The Adyar Library Bulletin*, Vol. XXV, 1–4, 1961, pp. 226–27.

[4] *Dakṣiṇācāra* and *vāmācāra* are two Tantric traditions usually considered to be mutually exclusive.

In the Christian tradition, thinkers like Ramon Lull, Nicolas of Cusa and others have foreseen a spiritual dialogue of different religions, which may be coming true only in our days. But here the extremes have to be avoided: an indiscriminate mixing of traditions in a 'spiritual supermarket', a narrow fundamentalism fearful of losing its self-identity, and the spiritual indifference created by materialism. No doubt we have to dive deep in the existing spiritual traditions of humankind in order to overcome the spiritual crisis of our times. The saying of the great Catholic theologian Karl Rahner that 'only the mystic will survive' has almost become a common-place, and one wishes it would become a practical truth.[5]

The present book is the outcome of a spiritual dialogue between Śaivas and Christians, more than a comparative study of Śaiva and Christian mysticism, because any comparison from a one-sided perspective cannot really help to bridge the gulf between traditions. Such a comparison is not even able to clarify concepts, because those very concepts are the outcome of an experience. They can only be communicated from within a living tradition. Therefore the believers of each tradition have to speak for themselves, and the comparison will emerge in a dialogue, not in any a priori intellectual position. No preconceived ideas of either oneness or difference, *abheda* or *bheda*, are guiding the studies of these two traditions. If there is any presupposition, it is the acknowledgment of differences as well as an openness for unity. In the words of Gopinath Kaviraj, one of the greatest authorities on Tantra and Kashmir Śaivism: "There are different ways of approach to this Supreme Experience and there are infinite shades of differences among the various ways. The Supreme Experience is certainly one and the same and yet there is a characteris-

[5]Cp. Karl Rahner, *Schriften zur Theologie VII*, Einsiedeln, 2nd edn. 1971, p. 19.

tic quiddity (*viśeṣa*) in each individual, which has an abiding spiritual value."[6] We may just think of the difference between a Ramakrishna and a Ramana Maharshi, or between a Francis of Assisi and a John of the Cross. These differences attract us as much as their unity.

The second question to be clarified is: What do we understand by 'mysticism', and what are the Indian equivalents of this term? The important article by Alois Haas throws much light on the history and use of the term in the Western — mostly Christian — tradition. If we try to translate this into Indian terms — mostly based on Sanskrit — we often come across the term *rahasyavāda*, 'secret doctrine'. This is not satisfactory because our emphasis is not on the *-ism*, nor on the *-vāda*, i.e. a doctrine or theory, but on an experience, or a state of being. In this sense other words from the Indian traditions may be considered and explored: *ātmasākṣātkāra, yoga, samādhi, samāveśa, anubhava, jīvanmukti, bodhi, pratyabhijñā* and others. Of course, our *speaking about* these terms or the mystical experience should not be confused with the experience as such, and one has to remain constantly aware of the 'mystical difference'. And yet, the 'talking about' should, ideally, emerge from or lead to an experience. Alois Haas has dealt with this question not only in the present article, but in many of his writings.[7]

Another objection has often been raised, that is, if a mystic has realized something he or she should keep silence to preserve the unspeakability of the experience. But the contrary is true. Most of the mystics of whom we know have spoken, written and sung about the reality they have experienced. Meister Eckhart says that even if nobody were ready

[6] "Some salient features of Mysticism", in: *Selected Writings of MM Gopinath Kaviraj*, Varanasi 1990, p. 150.

[7] Cp. the latest publication: Alois M. Haas, *Mystik als Aussage*, Frankfurt, 1996.

to listen to his sermons, he would preach to the wooden chairs in the Church. And yet he says that nobody can receive this truth who has not become it.[8] Abhinavagupta says that he writes his works in order to enlighten his disciples. Thus a principal motivation of the mystic to speak is compassion and the desire to illuminate those who are ignorant of their own true nature. In many mystic writings we find an explanation about the expression in words of what is really beyond words. A great mystic and theologian like Gregory Palamas says:

> On this account, although we have written at length about stillness, whether enjoined to do so by the fathers, or at the request of our brethren, we have never dared to write about deification. But now, since there is need to speak, we will speak, reverently, with the Lord's grace, though to describe it is beyond our skill. For even when spoken of, deification remains unutterable: as the Fathers say, it can be identified only by those who have been blessed with it.[9]

The paradox between silence and speech or writing is a constant and inevitable topic of mysticism.

By mysticism we do not mean any extreme emotional states, nor dry intellectual convictions. There may be many phenomena associated with the mystical experience, depending often on the psychic condition of the person undergoing them, but it is not these extraordinary phenomena which are the essence of mysticism. They are only symptoms, like the five *cihnas* or signs of the *yogīn* in Krama mysticism. The essence of the mystical experience can be said to be God-realization, the attainment or recognition (*pratyabhijñā*) of

[8] See the article; pp. 203–19 by Sr. Brigitte in this volume.

[9] *Defence of the Hesychasts*, 3, 1, 32, Works 1, p. 644.

one's own true nature (*svasvarūpa*), illumination or union. However it may be termed, what is important is the attainment of a state of being which is our very own — ultimate — reality, and at the same time the reality of God or the Absolute, the Divine Love or the ultimate I. And if we speak of 'attainment', this is never automatic or the result of some human effort, it is received through grace, some unexpected, overwhelming, blissful surprise. Here again, Kashmir Śaivism has the beautiful term *vismaya*, the wonder of surprise. Ultimately it is wrong to speak of 'attaining'.

All this is implied in the word mysticism: (1) It is the attainment of a Reality which has ever been with us and which is our inmost nature, as well as that of the whole of reality. (2) It is never the result of some action, effort, ritual or even desire — though all these may be useful at a preliminary stage. It is always something happening, given, graciously bestowed and not deserved. There can be a spiritual search, but not a mystical search. (3) It is not a momentary mood or emotional extravagance: if momentary it is a moment which touches eternity, if emotional it touches the source of all emotion, the source of Love.

All the mystic has to do is to empty his mind from thoughts, images and forms, what is called *nirvikalpa* in all the traditions of Yoga. Thus we read in Evagrius Ponticus:

> When you are praying, do not shape within yourself any image of the Deity, and do not let your mind be stamped with the impress of any form; but approach the Immaterial in an immaterial manner ... Prayer means the shedding of thoughts ... Blessed is the intellect that has acquired complete freedom from sensations during prayer.[10]

---

[10] *On Prayer*, quoted from: K. Ware, "Ways of Prayer and Contemplation, I. Eastern", in *Christian Spirituality I, Origins to the Twelfth Cen-*

The mystic attains a pure state of being one with one's real nature, which is divine, where there is neither acceptance nor rejection of anything. Abhinavagupta refers to this highest state in some of his mystical hymns:

> There is no need of spiritual progress,
> nor of contemplation, disputation or discussion,
> nor meditation, concentration nor even the effort
> of prayer —
> Please tell me clearly: What is supreme Truth?
> Listen: Neither renounce nor possess anything,
> share in the joy of the total Reality
> and be as you are!
>
> *Anuttarāṣṭikā*, v.1

* * *

Most of the articles contained in this Volume were papers presented at a Seminar on "Mysticism: Śaiva and Christian", held in Rajpur, Dehra Dun, in November 1990 under the auspices of the Abhishiktananda Society. The first article by Alois Haas has been added in order to clarify the very concept of mysticism, and the last one by the editor is intended to show another aspect which is integral to Śaiva mysticism, that is its being the 'elder brother' (in the words of Abhinavagupta) of the aesthetic experience.

Raimon Panikkar's presentation on the mysticism of Jesus the Christ has been greatly enlarged for this publication, taking into account a long history and many controversies around the central figure of Christianity. His selection of few of Christ's *mahāvākyas* and their interpretation could be seen as what is now called 'intercultural exegesis', which is an important instrument for bringing about a mutual understanding in this case between Christianity and Hinduism.

---

tury, ed. by Bernard McGinn and John Meyendorff, New York, Crossroad, 1985, p. 399.

The general approach of the Seminar was that the followers of a particular tradition should speak for themselves and present their own tradition. Thus scholars as well as practitioners of Śaiva Siddhānta (Swami Nityananda Giri, T.N. Ramachandran) and Kashmir Śaivism (H.N. Chakravarty, B.N. Pandit, J.N. Kaul) have presented various aspects of the mysticism of their schools. Among the Christian mystics, the following are represented here: Meister Eckhart (Sr. Brigitte), Hadewijch (O. Baumer-Despeigne), Julian of Norwich (Murray Rogers) and Ignatius Loyola (G. Gispert-Sauch). The vast mystical traditions of Eastern Christianity have been presented in only one article (S. Descy).

The present selection is certainly far from complete, but it can still provide an insight into both major mystical traditions and lead to a mutual understanding. Corresponding to the two Christian women mystics presented here, Hadewijch and Julian, it would have been desirable to present two Śaiva women mystics, such as Lal Ded (Lalleśvarī) of Kashmir and Akkā Mahādevī of the Vīraśaiva tradition of Karnataka, but this has not been possible. No attempt has been made to develop an overall mystical theology, but the purpose of this volume is to let the various traditions speak for themselves. Besides, it has not been possible to include the summaries of the discussions and dialogues, which were most enriching, and much less to let the silence speak which was shared by the participants of different traditions in meditation.

The symbol of the intertwining of trident and cross has been drawn by Sri S. Dorai who prepared a number of versions. As any symbol, it can speak for itself.

While an attempt has been made to edit the articles in a certain uniform way, the styles and formats of the authors were so different that complete uniformity would have done violence to the articles. The different styles have therefore been respected.

*   *   *

Against the most common misunderstanding of mysticism, that it is something so sublime, transcendent and unattainable, far removed from daily life and experience, I want to conclude this introduction by a very similar injunction found in two historically unrelated texts: the *Vijñāna Bhairava Tantra* of Kashmir Śaivism, and Meister Eckhart's final words to his disciples.

The *Vijñāna Bhairava* says:

> *yatra yatra mano yāti bāhye vābhyantare'pi vā,*
> *tatra tatra śivāvasthā vyāpakatvāt kva yāsyati.*
> v.116
>
> Wherever the mind goes,
> whether outside or within,
> there itself is the state of Śiva.
> Since He is all-pervading,
> where else could the mind go?

The Master of German mysticism gives to his friends the following parting instruction as the 'master key' to mystical life:

> It often happens that what seems trivial to us is greater in God's sight than what looms large in our eyes. Therefore we should accept all things equally from God, not ever looking and wondering which is greater, or higher, or better. We should just follow where God points out for us, that is, what we are inclined to and to which we are most often directed, and where our bent is. If a man were to follow that path, God would give him the

> most in the least, and would not fail him. ... But the noblest and best thing would be this, if a man were come to such equality, with such calm and certainty that he could find God and enjoy Him in *any* way and in *all* things, without having to wait for anything or chase after anything: *that* would delight me![11]

It can be seen therefore that the authentic mystical traditions do not see mysticism as an experience alien to our common experience, but that it rather leads us to a deeper perception and to a more balanced view of reality. Thus the true encounter between two (or more) spiritual traditions can help us even in rediscovering our own, often hidden, treasures.

Since the Rajpur Seminar has been inspired by the ideas and ideals of Swami Abhishiktananda (Henri Le Saux, 1910–1973), who had devoted his life to a spiritual dialogue of Hinduism and Christianity, this book is also dedicated to his memory.

Varanasi
Mahāśivarātri
and Lent 1997

Bettina Bäumer

---

[11] Meister Eckhart, *Sermons and Treatises*, Vol. III, ed. by M.O'.C. Walshe, Element Books, 1990, pp. 147–48.

WHAT IS MYSTICISM?[1]

Alois M. Haas

With unsurpassed honesty Tauler, in Sermon 41, makes the following confession about his own efforts to gain mystical experience:

> *Kinder, kumet der mensche recht in disen grunt und in dis wesen, sint sicher, so mus dis netz von not rissen. Nut wenent, das ich mich dis ut anneme, das ich ut her zukomen si, allein enkein lerer nut ensulle leren, das er selber von lebende nut enhabe. Doch ist es ze noten gnug, das er es minne und meine und nut do wider entu. Doch wissent das es nut anders enmag sin.*
>
> Vetter 175, 3–7
>
> [My children! If man indeed should reach the ground of the soul and this core of being, heed this: this web must needs be rent. Fancy not that I claim this for myself or have partaken of such experience. Though no teacher should guide others in what he himself has not witnessed in his life. Yet for want of better it may suffice that he love and mean what he teach and undertake nothing counter to it. Know ye that it cannot be other.]

[1]This paper was first published in German in: Alois M. Haas, *Gottleiden, Gottlieben. Zur volkssprachlichen Mystik im Mittelalter*, Frankfurt a. Main 1989, pp. 23-44. Translated from the German original by Ian Mansfield (University of Edinburgh), in collaboration with Franz Wöhrer (University of Vienna).

With all due respect and with infinite deference for this modesty, I would like to use these words as the interpretational basis of my concern with mysticism. Needless to say, I have never been granted any mystical experience in my life ('von lebende'). Yet I have devoted myself to the subject of mysticism and believed in it ('minne und meine es') for decades, although I often live contrary to it. Here I would have to make a public confession, whose embarrassing and delicate aspects I would like to spare the reader. I would prefer to generalize. If it is true that man's cognitive faculty unites him with the object of cognition, all concern with mysticism must surely hinge on the unity with its object at a hidden point in mysticism's intrinsic panorama — however objective and buttressed by mere rationality mysticism may be. Otherwise there will be no possibility of interpretation. This also applies to the ever celebrated and demanded criterion of the objective nature of scientific results, which are frequently only the inadequate products of ideology anyway. This does not mean that we should abandon thinking, on the contrary, it means it should be applied rigorously and uncompromisingly.

As hardly anywhere else, the concept of mysticism seems to point to a fundamental flaw in man's ability to devise clearly defined categories. After all, the application of the concept of mysticism handed down in history and current today evinces such a wealth of possible meanings and connotations that we may despair of ever finding an appropriate and workable definition. The abundance of meanings attached to the concept of mysticism will become clear, when it is considered how one and the same subject matter has been interpreted in the most divergent ways by different disciplines, without there being any prospect of these readings ever being reconciled.

In its most general sense, mysticism can be understood as the sphere of religious experience in which an intense union occurs between the subject and the object of this experience in some or other indefinable way. The question immediately arises as to whether 'mysticism' merely implies the experience itself, or also the subsequent process of communication, i.e. its narrative or reflective reproduction. In practice, both are fused in the concept of mysticism, as experience would remain dumb if it were not conveyed. Hence 'mysticism' should be divided into two fundamentally distinct components, so that several disciplines can and must necessarily undertake to explore the phenomenon from their own specific angles.

Of course, theology — and, in particular, the department formerly called 'asceticism and mysticism', but today usually termed 'spirituality' (or the history of spirituality) — is in charge of mysticism. This explains why the profane disciplines of the philosophy of religion and the psychology of religion have likewise a legitimate interest in mystical experiences and their interpretation, as it would be a truism to say that mysticism is an essential component of all religions. Moreover, as mystical experiences are always extreme psychological phenomena, both rare and exceptional, medicine, psychology (the medical and anthropological approaches), as well as psychoanalysis display a more than average interest in the empirical dimension. This scientific approach to mysticism has gained in importance since William James,[2] presumably because an artificially induced release of para-normal psychological states — "altered states of consciousness"[3], 'cos-

---

[2]W. James, *The Varieties of Religious Experience, A Study in Human Nature*, New York 1902; E. Herms, *Radical Empiricism, Studien zur Psychologie, Metaphysik und Religionstheorie William James'*, Gütersloh 1977.

[3]Cp. *Altered States of Consciousness*, a collection of critical essays, ed. by Ch. T. Tart, New York 1969. From this has developed a separate branch of psychology: 'Transpersonal psychology'; cp. Ch. T. Tart, *Transpersonal Psychologies*, New York 1975; R. Assagioli, *Handbook of Psychosynthesis, Applied Transpersonal Psychology*, German transl.,

mic consciousness'[4] etc. — by means of psychedelic drugs or meditational techniques[5] has today become a highly acute issue in our affluent consumer society. However, on its lowest semantic level, the concept of mysticism has always been held to include the fields of occultism, magic, prophecy and astrology termed "nebbie mistiche" by Sturlese. Yet today the German language has a separate concept for these fields, 'Mystizismus', and no longer links them with the word 'Mystik'[6].

Freiburg i. Br. 1978; R.E. Ornstein, *The Psychology of Consciousness*, New York 1972; C. Naranjo/R.E. Ornstein, *On the Psychology of Meditation*, New York 1971.

[4]Anyone discussing the subject of 'mystical experience' in the USA and Canada will be immediately confronted with the study by the Canadian physician Richard Maurice Bucke (1868-1899), entitled *Cosmic Consciousness*, first published in 1901 (24th edn. 1967). See also H.J. Urban, *"Über-Bewußtsein" nach Bucke und Wehr*, Innsbruck and Vienna 1950.

[5]On the formal structure of meditational techniques, see — (in lieu of a more exhaustive survey, not to be provided in the context of this paper) — the synopsis given by R. Bleistein/H.G. Lubkoll/R.Pfützner, *Türen nach innen, Wege zur Meditation*, Munich 1974; on the evaluation of the phenomenon in terms of modern (French) philosophy, see U. Liebmann-Schaub, "Kultur und 'Subkultur', Zur Charakteristik irrationalistischer Deutungssysteme", DVJs 53 (1979), 125-62. — On 'drug-mysticism' see (a selection only!) R. Gelpke, *Vom Rausch im Orient und Okzident*, Stuttgart 1966; R.E.L. Masters/J. Houston, *The Varieties of Psychedelic Experience*, New York 1966; W.H. Clark, *Chemische Extase, Drogen und Religion*, Salzburg 1971; Josuttis/H. Leuner (eds), *Religion und Droge*, Stuttgart 1972; H. Cancik (ed.), *Rausch - Ekstase - Mystik*, Düsseldorf 1978. There is no need to draw special attention to the persevering significance of the views on drugs and mysticism expressed by Aldous Huxley, Timothy Leary and Ernst Jünger.

[6]Cp. H. Silberer, *Probleme der Mystik und Ihrer Symbolik*, Vienna 1914 (reprint: Darmstadt 1961) (alchemy as a 'mystical' art); B. Grabinski, *Neuere Mystik, Eine Darstellung und Untersuchung der übersinnlichen Phänomene*, Hildesheim 1916; M. Kemmerich, *Das Weltbild des Mystikers*, Leipzig 1926; K. Aram, *Magie und Mystik in Vergangenheit und Gegenwart*, Berlin 1929; B.H. Streeter, *Reality, A New Correlation of Science and Religion*, London 1935; P.K. Hoffmann-Reihhoff, *Versuch einer Metaphysik zum Weltbild der Mystik*, Bonn 1934; N. Fer-

The common denominator between the empirical sciences, parapsychology and PSI is the liminal psychological occurrence conveyed by 'mysticism' in the broadest sense of the term. It is true that mathematics,[7], logic[8], physics[9], (of late), ethnology,[10] and behavioural research,[11] have evinced an interest in the analysis and explanation of mystical phenomena and have done so for quite legitimate reasons; the main one being the desire to establish and elaborate more tangible categories for the understanding of contexts not readily accessi-

---

ger, *Magie und Mystik, Gegensatz und Zusammenhang,* Zurich 1935; R. Crookall, *The Interpretation of Cosmic and Mystical Experiences*, London 1969; J. Zeisel, *Entschleierte Mystik*, Freiburg i.Br. 1984; W. Loesen, *Mystiek, Mysterie en Mystificatie*, Amsterdam 1976. See also, the somewhat heterogeneous medley of information given by A. Cartel in: *A Dictionary of Esoteric Words*, New York 1967; F. Gaynor, *Dictionary of Mysticism*, London 1974. — Quotation from L. Sturlese, 'Eckhart, Teodorico e Picardi nella Summa Philosophiae di Nicola di Strasborgo', Giornale critico della Filosophia Italiana 61 (1982) 83-206, l.c.p. 198.

[7] K. Joel, *Der Ursprung der Naturphilosophie aus dem Geiste der Mystik*, 1926; F.C. Endres, *Die Zahl in Mystik und Glauben der Kulturvölker*, Zurich 1935 (re-edited by A. Schimmel, Cologne 1985).

[8] B. Russell, *Mysticism and Logic*, London 1910. 12th edn., 1963.

[9] F. Capra, *Der kosmische Reigen, Physik und östliche Mystik – ein zeitgemässes Weltbild*, Berne 6th edn. 1983; F. Capra, *Wendezeit, Bausteine für ein neues Weltbild*, Berne 2nd. edn. 1983; M. Talbot, *Mysticisme et physique nouvelle*, Paris 1984.

[10] H.P. Duerr, *Der Wissenschaftler und das Irrationale*, 2 vols, Frankfurt a.M. 1981; H.P. Duerr, *Traumzeit, Über die Grenze zwischen Wildnis und Zivilisation,* Frankfurt a.M. 1978; R. Gehlen/B. Wolf (eds), *Der gläserne Zaun, Aufsätze zu H.P. Duerrs "Traumzeit"*, Frankfurt a.M. 1983. On this see also the issues of the periodical 'Unter dem Pflaster liegt der Strand'. It does not matter to me in this context if, or to what extent, this kind of research is generally accepted or not.

[11] K. Lorenz, *Die Rückseite des Spiegels, Versuch einer Naturgeschichte des menschlichen Erkennens,* Munich 2nd edn. 1973.

ble to the natural sciences. History[12] and sociology[13] for their part have focussed their curiosity on mysticism in their endeavour to grasp its historical impact (e.g. in revolutionary ideals[14]) and social group mentalities.

Apart from the specifically epistemological concern shown by theology in mysticism, it is above all philosophy, poetry and philology that devote attention to mysticism out of a genuine awareness of affinity. I will deal with these aspects later.

A few general remarks might be apposite in view of the wide range of proposals as to what mysticism may be in terms of history, subject matter, definition and content. Every branch of science has its own heuristic methods, its *a prioris*, and its objective and methodological assumptions. Empirical psychology[15] or the psychology of consciousness,

---

[12]In particular the achievements of the history of religion should be mentioned here (e.g. the work of Mircea Eliade). — In a more restricted historical sense, the studies of Herbert Grundmann are still exemplary: *Religiöse Bewegungen im Mittelalter*, Darmstadt 2nd. edn. 1961; the same, *Ausgewählte Aufsätze*, Teil 1: Religiöse Bewegungen, Stuttgart 1976.

[13]E. Troeltsch, *Die Soziallehren der christlichen Kirchen und Gruppen*, Tübingen 1919 (=Gesammelte Schriften, 1.Bd.); M. Weber, *Gesammelte Aufsätze zur Religionssoziologie*, 3 vols., Tübingen 1972/1976.

[14]E.Topitsch, *Gottwerdung und Revolution*, Munich 1973; on Ernst Bloch's interest in mysticism see K.P. Steinacker-Berghäuser, *Das Verhältnis der Philosophie Ernst Blochs zur Mystik*, Diss. Marburg/Lahn 1973; A.F. Christen, *Ernst Blochs Metaphysik der Materie*, Bonn 1979; A. Münster, *Utopie, Messianismus und Apokalypse im Frühwerk von Ernst Bloch*, Frankfurt a.M. 1982. On this see also the secondary literature on Thomas Müntzer and his influence. Finally, see L. Rougier, *La mystique démocratique*, Paris 1983.

[15]The approach to mysticism of empirical psychology is grounded both in a general psychological interest and in a medical one. From a medical point of view cp. the studies of J. Lhermitte, *Echte und falsche Mystiker*, Lucerne 1953; H. Thurston, S.J., *The Physical Phenomena of Mysticism*, London 1952; A. Michel, *Les Pouvoirs du mysticisme*, Paris 1973. See also the relevant studies published in "Archiv für Religionspsychologie".

for instance, tend to see mystical experience as a mere psychosomatic phenomenon, whose waves and currents can be monitored by an EEG, indeed even controlled to a certain extent thanks to intentional biofeedback.[16] It will be clear that such an investigation of mystical experiences attaches less importance to their religious, ideological, social and historical dimensions than to their mental structures in an a-historical context. Hence a fundamental sense of ambiguity informs the empirical research of mysticism. Should mystical experience be explored solely as a mental state, or should it be studied in relation to its religious, theological and philosophical implications, polemically dismissed by Frits Staal[17] as mere "superstructures"? In his book *Exploring Mysticism* the Indologist Staal vehemently pleads in favour of the first alternative, by asserting that mystical research is just a variant form of the profane enquiry into the nature of consciousness. In his view, explorations of this kind should be forbidden to philologists, historians and phenomenologists of religion.

On the other hand, this new approach is opposed by a phalanx of scholars who view the contextual historical interpretation of mystical experiences as having primary significance, and legitimately refer to their foundations in religious

---

- The general psychological interest in mysticism is documented by innumerable publications ranging — from the Roman Catholic perspective — from Aug. Poulain (*Des grâces d'oraison*, Paris 11th edn. 1931), Alois Mager (*Mystik als Lehre und Leben*, Innsbruck 1934; *Mystik als seelische Wirklichkeit*, Graz 1945) and Otto Karrer (Mystik und Psychologie, Schweizer Rundschau 48 [1948] 653-66) to the comprehensive early monograph by James H. Leuba (*The Psychology of Religious Mysticism*, London 1925, 3rd edn. 1972) and more modern views based on Freud and Jung (cp. 'Résurgence et dérivés de la mystique', Nouvelle Revue de Psychoanalyse, n. 22, Automne 1980).

[16] For a short summary of recent research see W. Johnston, *Silent Music, The Science of Meditation*, London 1974.

[17] F. Staal, *Exploring Mysticism*, Harmondsworth 1975. The modern topic of mysticism and its iterpretation is discussed in R. Woods, OP (ed.), *Understanding Mysticism*, New York 1980.

traditions and doctrines.[18] Gershom Scholem puts the views of many scholars in a nutshell when he says:

> *Ich möchte... Nachdruck darauf legen, daß es... Mystik als solche, als ein Phänomen oder eine Anschauung, die unabhängig von anderem in sich selber besteht, in der Religionsgeschichte im Grund gar nicht gibt. Es gibt nicht Mystik an sich, sondern Mystik von etwas, Mystik einer bestimmten religiösen Form: Mystik des Christentums, Mystik des Islams, Mystik des Judentums und dergleichen. Gewiß, es steckt etwas Einheitliches in diesen mannigfachen historischen Phänomenen. Dies Einheitliche, dies 'Objekt' aller Mystik, zeigt sich eben in der Analyse der*

[18] In his early study *The Mystical Element of Religion* (vol. II, London 4th edn. 1961, p. 283 f.; German transl. Religion als Ganzheit, Düsseldorf, 1948, p. 185.) Baron von Hügel wrote: *Gibt es, genau gesprochen, eine besonders abgegrenzte, selbstgenügende, mystische Art der Wirklichkeitserfassung? Bestimmt nicht; und ich glaube, daß alle Irrtümer des Mystizismus [Exklusive Mystik as opposed to true mysticism, which von Hügel calls Inklusive Mystik] gerade von der Behauptung ausgehen, daß die Mystik eine ganz getrennte, vollständing selbständige Art der menschlichen Erfahrung sei. [Is there, to be precise, such a thing as a clearly delineated, self-sufficient, purely mystical manner of understanding reality? Certainly not; and I think that all the fallacies of mysticism (the 'exclusive mystic' as opposed to true mysticism, called the 'inclusive mystic' by von Hügel) proceed from the assertion that mysticism is a separate and completely autonomous mode of human experience.]* [Translators' note: This is a re-translation of the German translation, the original English text not being available.] On this see also P. Neuner, *Religion zwischen Kirche und Mystik. Friedrich von Hügel und der Modernismus*, Frankurt a.M. 1977, p. 49ff. Steven T. Katz and the group of scholars around him have put particular emphasis on the view that mystical experience is automatically determined by tradition and cannot be reasonably divorced from the historical, cultural and religious context. Cp. St. T. Katz (ed.), *Mysticism and Philosophical Analysis*, London 1978; St. T. Katz (ed.), *Mysticism and Religious Traditions*, Oxford 1983.

> *persönlichen Erfahrung der Mystiker. Aber es ist der modernen Zeit vorbehalten geblieben, so etwas wie eine abstrakte Religion der Mystik überhaupt zu erfinden.*[19]
>
> [I would like ... to stress that ... mysticism as such, as a phenomenon or philosophical outlook, just does not exist in the history of philosophy as a detached and autonomous entity. There is no such thing as mysticism in itself, but only the mysticism of something, the mysticism of a specific religious creed: the mysticism of Christianity, the mysticism of Islam, the mysticism of Judaism, etc. Admittedly, these manifold historical phenomena have something in common. This common attribute, this 'object' of all mysticism is manifested in an analysis of the personal experience of mystics. But it has been left to modern times to contrive something like an abstract religion of mysticism.]

All the same, it is confusing when the same author elsewhere[20] sees "the heterogeneous mystical experience" ("das amorphe mystische Erlebnis", p. 29) as having been realized in various stages and degrees, thus conceding "the endless possible interpretations of this experience" ("unendliche Deutungsmöglichkeiten dieser Erfahrung", p. 27), without failing to notice their unity. Scholem, who is quite willing to accept the function and obligatory nature of religious tradition in the shaping of mystical experience, envisages its 'unity' as a fact above and beyond all its historical manifestations.

[19] G. Scholem, *Die Jüdische Mystik in ihren Hauptströmungen*, Zurich 1957, p. 6f.

[20] G. Scholem, *Zur Kabbala ud ihrer Symbolik*, Zurich 1960. See also G. Scholem, 'Offenbarung und Tradition als religiöse Kategorien im Judentum', in: Judaica 4, Frankfurt a.M. 1984, pp. 189-228.

On the other hand, an author such as Robert C. Zaehner[21] insists on a clear-cut distinction. For him mystical experience is not a 'heterogeneous experience', but a spiritual process differentiated in its mental and substantial structure according to religious doctrine, a process that can be classified into three basic types. He distinguishes between (1) 'panenhenic' or 'nature mysticism' (as in Rimbaud or Jefferies); (2) 'monistic mysticism' (e.g. in the Advaita and in Saṃkhya-Yoga); and (3) 'theistic mysticism' (in Christianity, and in the *Gītā* etc.) [22]

Zaehner's distinction between monistic and theistic mysticism, and especially his verdict that monistic mysticism is not in accordance with actual reality, has often been criticized with reference to his religious bias — he was a practising Catholic. Zaehner's preconceptions were determined by the context of a theistic mystical system. This is an example of how the problems increase, the more conceptual accuracy and scholarly precision are striven for.

Although the basic distinction necessary between experience and the interpreted account of this experience has always been the source of multifarious assessments of mystical experience by the most varied disciplines, the problems of interpretation multiply when criteria have to be included that are implied in the scholars' personal religious convictions. Here the ideal of truth becomes unattainable, an ideal that scientifically orientated scholars of mysticism try to evade by

---

[21] Zaehner's major studies on Mysticism are: *Inde, Israel, Islam, Religions mystiques et révélations prophétiques*, Paris 1965; *Mysticism, Sacred and Profane, An Inquiry into some Varieties of Praeter-natural Experience*, Oxford 1957; *Concordant Discord, The Interdependence of Faiths*, Oxford 1979; *Zen, Drugs, and Mysticism*, New York 1973; *The City within the Heart*, London 1980.

[22] For a critical review of Zaehner's position see N. Smart, 'Interpretation and Mystical Experience', *Religious Studies* 1 (965), pp. 75-87, esp. p. 76f.

means of a kind of "mystical relativism".[23] They do so either by completely resorting to the medical and psychological plane of interpretation, or by elaborating with precise philological tools a mystical system in the context of its written revelations only. However, the problem of this relativist approach lies in the fact that a comparative analysis, let us say, between Christian and Buddhist mysticism, would be pointless if not exactly impossible, because the very comparability of two systems was excluded a priori for methodological reasons.[24] These difficulties aside, I am convinced that a relative approach is inevitable for a scholarly interpretation of mystical texts. For what do we have but texts? We do not possess the experiences, but only the texts relating them.[25] We must abide by these necessities. So contextuality is a methodological must. With the help of a remarkable example Hans H. Penner has recently demonstrated that such contextuality must not be confined merely to texts recording individual experiences. If they are to be comprehended, contextuality must be extended as far as possible, i.e. to include the etymological, terminological, historical, social, economic contexts and, above all, the overall religious setting. As Penner has shown, it was for this very reason that the most positive intentions of the Indian mystical way have been misunderstood in the West, particularly since the caste-system was neglected as a constituent of asceticism and mysticism.[26] But it is only this

[23] H.H. Penner, 'The Mystical Illusion', Katz (ed.) *Mysticism and Religious Tradition* [cp. note 18], pp. 89-116. Also Kurt Ruh opts for a relativism of an acceptable kind in the study of mystical texts in: 'Vorbemerkungen zu einer neuen Geschichte der abendländischen Mystik im Mittelalter', in: *Sitzungsberichte der Bayr. Akad. d.Wiss.* 1982, Heft 7, p. 8ff.

[24] Penner [see note 23], p. 94.

[25] Cp. J. Seyppel, 'Mystik als Grenzphänomen und Existenzial', in: J. Sudbrack (ed.), *Das Mysterium und die Mystik, Beiträge zu einer Theologie der christlichen Gotteserfahrung*, Würzburg 1974, pp. 111-53.

[26] Penner [see note 23], p. 104ff.

dichotomy that makes us aware of the freedom that asceticism and mystical experience can provide in India.

If one thing follows from these premises, it is surely that we must go back to mysticism's historical origins, if we want to gain even an inkling of what mysticism is or is about. As I am not remotely in a position to delineate a history of mysticism or merely of occidental mysticism, I would like to follow this postulate only by tracing the history of the word 'mysticism'. Then I will return to a more systematic approach — with undue optimism — by endeavouring to establish the status of mystical texts as compared with linguistic procedures in poetical and philosophical writings. In a final section I will come back to the Christian concept of *theologia mystica*. My restricted viewpoint is inevitably occasioned by my cultural and spiritual background, the Christian faith and its historical manifestations.

I

Although classical Greek terms are used in the entire domain of Christian mysticism, the subject does not seem to be a classical Greek phenomenon at all. There seems to be no clear evidence of mysticism in the Christian or the Indian sense of the word before Plotinus.[27] The relevant vocabulary consists of the following group of words: the noun 'mysticism' and the adjective 'mystical' (*mystikos*); the latter refers to the noun *mystes* (the initiate), and to *mysteria*, the process of initiation as a ritual act, and to *myein*, the 'act of initiation' itself, which must be kept a secret by those to be initiated. There is no direct link between the Greek mysteries, e.g. that of Eleusis, and Christian mysticism. For in the mysteries the 'mystic'

[27] In the following I gratefully make use of the suggestions made by W. Burkert, *Mysterien ohne Mystik? Antike Kultur zwischen Unsagbarkeit und Rhetorik* [manuscript], Zurich 1983, p. 1; cp. W. Burkert, *Griechische Religion der archaischen und klassischen Epoche*, Stuttgart 1977, p. 413ff.

becomes an *epoptes*, someone who sees 'the Holy' in objective shape,[28] not someone who becomes one with it. Plato became the mediator between the antique mysteries and (Western) mysticism in his dialogues *Symposion* and *Phaidros*, in which he combines the ascent of the soul to the most sublime, truly spiritual vision, with Eros,[29] at the same time according considerable space to the language of Eleusis. The absorption of the metaphorical language taken from the mysteries in the conception of a spiritual ascent resulted in a model of mystical diction, which was adopted enthusiastically by the Jew Philo, and whose attraction early Christianity was unable to resist — an influence first documented in Christian Gnosis (second century), then in Dionysius, the Areopagite (c. 500).

The fact remains, however, that the words '*mysticism*' and '*mystical*' do not appear in the Bible.[30] There is no mention of them in the *New Testament*. In the *Old Testament* the word '*mystes*' does occur, albeit only to dismiss the cults of the Canaanites.[31] The adjective *mystikos* is used to term something concerned with the *Mysterion*, which in turn designates both a human and an eschatological mystery.[32] In the *New Testament* the only passage in which the word occurs is in the Synoptic Gospels, where it refers to God's gift of grace to the faithful: "*It has been granted to you to know the secrets of the kingdom of Heaven.*" (Matth. 13, 11; cp. Lk. 8, 10; Mk. 4, 11) To quote Hans Urs von Balthasar, the following conclusion can be drawn for the *New Testament*:

Auf der Koordinate Offenbarungs-Glaube liegt im

---

[28] Burkert [see note 27], pp. 8, 13.

[29] Burkert, p. 12.

[30] H.U. von Balthasar, 'Zur Ortsbestimmung christlicher Mystik', in: *Pneuma und Institution, Skizzen zur Theologie* IV, Einsiedeln 1974, pp. 298-339; esp. p. 298.

[31] *Wisdom* 12, 6 and 8, 4.

[32] Cp. *Theologisches Wörterbuch*, IV, p. 809ff.; F. Stegmüller, in: *Wahrheit und Verkündigung*, Munich 1967, p. 599ff.

> *Neuen Testament der ganze Ton; die subjektiven Formen, in denen der entgegennehmende Glaube auftreten kann, werden zwar einigermaßen unterschieden, aber ohne daß ein Wertakzent darauf gelegt oder ein psychologisches Interesse daran bekundet wird.*[33]
>
> [In the New Testament the whole emphasis is placed on the axis between revelation and faith; the subjective forms in which the gift of faith can appear are differentiated to some extent, but without any judgement being pronounced or any psychological interest displayed.]

The Early Fathers and the whole of the Middle Ages very often used the adjectives *mystikos* or *mysticus* in direct semantic derivation from the word *mysterion*,[34] and in doing so intended not only to introduce a psychological dimension to religious practice, but also and primarily to oust prophecy — which, according to the *New Testament*, had lost its immediate function after the Saviour's coming — and subsequently to replace it with mysticism, thus ushering in a new era in Christian spirituality.[35]

It would go too far to list in detail all the different uses of the adjective *mystikos* in this restricted context. Generally speaking, three uses can be distinguished: a biblical, a litur-

---

[33] von Balthasar [see note 30], p. 300.

[34] On the patristic passages see L. Bouyer, 'Mystique, Essai sur l'histoire d'un mot', La Vie spirituelle, Suppl. N 9, 15 May 1949, pp. 3-23; in German in: J. Sudbrack (ed.), *Das Mysterium* [note 25]: "Mystisch" — Zur Geschichte eines Wortes, pp. 57-75. Cp. more recently in particular G.W.H. Lampe, *A Patristic Greek Lexicon*, Oxford, 5th edn. 1978, pp. 891-93; pp. 893-94, where the crucial passages of the patristic period are most accurately listed.

[35] H.U. von Balthasar, 'Besondere Gnadengaben und die zwei Wege des menschlichen Lebens', in: *Thomas von Aquin. Summa Theologica, Latin-German edition*, Vol. 23, Heidelberg 1954, p. 375.

gical and a spiritual one.[36] All of these three uses have more to do with the concept of mysticism than is generally thought today.

Starting with Origen in the first half of the third century, in biblical exegesis based on the Christian faith, the word 'mystical' was used to denote the textual meaning underlying the obvious literal sense and revealing itself to the inquisitive reader as the mystery and reality of Christ — living in the individual parts and the whole body of the Church. Divine Reality unfolds itself in the Gospels in its 'mystery-like' 'mystical' sense, one that can also be called the 'pneumatological' or 'spiritual', because it is revealed objectively and subjectively in the Holy Spirit; or, alternatively, the 'allegorical' sense, because it marks a transition between the old literal meaning and the new pneumatological (or christological) one.[37]

The ways leading from this doctrine of the four-fold meanings of scripture to mysticism are multifarious. The monastic reading of scripture (*lectio*),[38] in particular, and above all the meditation on the *Song of Songs*,[39] opened up an exceptionally broad scope for the imagination in which a loving soul could attain ecstatic union with Christ, her 'Bridegroom'.

The almost universal monopolization of the word 'mystical' in the liturgy demonstrates the apparently objective nature of this epithet and its continued association with the holy mysteries.[40] It is always "Christ's living and hidden

[36] Cp. Bouyer [note 34].

[37] von Balthasar [note 30], p. 301.

[38] J. Leclercq, *Wissenschaft und Gottverlangen, Zur Mönchstheologie des Mittelalters*, Düsseldorf 1963.

[39] F. Ohly, *Hohelied-Studien, Grundzüge einer Geschichte der Hoheliedauslegung des Abendlandes bis um 1200*, Wiesbaden 1958; H. Riedlinger, *Die Makellosigkeit der Kirche in den lateinischen Hoheliedkommentaren des Mittelalters*, Münster 1958.

[40] von Balthasar [note 30], p. 301.

presence"[41] what is meant and intended by the 'mystical body' of the Lord. Later, in a remarkable re-interpretation of the concept of the *corpus mysticum*, this was to be the point of departure of ecclesiology in the Middle Ages.[42] Ecclesiology was also to be a spiritual dimension which — like the liturgy — enabled union with God in our specific spiritual and mystical sense.

The all-important use of the word 'mystical' in terms of a specific "form of immediate, experiential knowledge of God"[43] — a use similarly derived from Origen — is certainly based to the extension of the mystical meaning of scripture to individual experience. "Nobody can grasp scripture who does not in his innermost soul become one with the realities it tells us of."[44] In this claim, exegesis is directly transformed into religious experience. Origen says "that in Jesus Christ we have 'the high priest according to Melchisedech's order, guide to mystical and ineffable contemplation'."[45] By taking up the concept of *theoria*, both Origen and, subsequently, the tradition of early Christianity, assumed a classical Greek ideal of a way of life that Plotinus had succinctly put as: "*toîs pratioûsin hê theôria télos*" — "the goal of all activity is theoria".[46] In Christianity, the key word *mystike theo-*

---

[41] Bouyer, "Mystisch" [note 34], p. 65.

[42] H. de Lubac, *Corpus Mysticum, Eucharistie und Kirche im Mittelalter*, Einsiedeln 1969, p. 69ff.

[43] Bouyer, "Mystisch" [note 34], p. 68.

[44] Commentary on *St. John* 13, 24; PG 14, 440 C. Quoted in Bouyer "Mystisch" [note 34], p. 69

[45] Bouyer, "Mystisch" [note 34], p. 69.

[46] *Enn.* III, 6, 1. Quoted by H.G. Beck, 'Theoria, Ein byzantinischer Traum?', in: *Sitzungsberichte der Bayer. Akad.d.Wiss. 1983* Heft 7, p. 5; cp. also F. Boll, 'Vita contemplativa' in: F. Boll, *Kleine Schriften zur Sternkunde des Altertums*, Leipzing 1950, pp. 303-31; A.J. Festugière, *Contemplation et vie contemplative selon Platon*, Paris 3rd edn. 1967; H. Rausch, *Theoria. Von ihrer sakralen zur philosophischen Bedeutung*, Munich 1982.

ria was to become generally accepted for mystical experience and found an equivalent as *contemplatio mystica* in the Latin Middle Ages.[47]

However, this terminological issue and its appropriate interpretation are of very broad scope. The Christian adaptation of the Greek, i.e. Platonic *theoria* — called by A.J. Festugière 'spiritualité philosophique'[48] — has become the cause of very divergent views and opinions. Seen by some as a Christian lapse, it is considered by others to be a necessary and inevitable form of intercultural exchange. In all discussions of the matter a certain anxious caution is always felt on the part of christian speakers, who would often render void the resulting conflation of ideas.

Nevertheless, it is an irrevocable fact in the history of spirituality that the Platonic concept of *theoria* has had a powerful impact on Christianity, indeed, it has been able to shape Christian mysticism in the most persistent manner.[49] The origin of this 'spiritualité philosophique' in Christianity must be sought in the school of Alexandria and its representatives St. Clement and Origen. It is from here that a whole series of Christian Platonic thinkers have issued: in the East, Evagrius Ponticus, St. Gregory of Nyssa, Diadochus of Photike and Pseudo-Dionysius, the Areopagite; in the West, St. Augustine, Gregory the Great, the Augustinianism of the entire Middle Ages and the Neoplatonic revival from the twelfth century onwards.

St. Clement of Alexandria once worded his Christian view

[47] Cp. "Contemplation", DSAM II (1949-1953), cols. 1643-2193; M.E. Mason, *Active Life and Contemplative Life, A Study of the Concepts from Plato to the Present*, Milwaukee, Wisc. 1961.

[48] A.J. Festugière, *L'enfant d'Agrigente suivi de Le Grec et la nature*, Paris 1950, p. 141ff.

[49] A. Louth, *The Origins of the Christian Mystical Tradition from Plato to Denys*, Oxford 1981; E. Hoffmann, *Platonismus und Mystik im Altertum*, Heidelberg 1935.

of the *theoria* in his *Stromateis* as follows:

> We shall understand the method of purification by confession, and the visionary method by analysis, attaining to the primary intelligence by analysis, beginning at its basic principles. We take away from the body its natural qualities, removing the dimension of height, and then that of breadth and then that of length. The point that remains is a unit, as it were, having position; if we take away everything concerned with bodies and the things called incorporeal, and cast ourselves into the greatness of Christ, and so advance into the immeasureable by holiness, we might perhaps attain to the conception of the Almighty, knowing not what He is but what He is not.
>
> (*Stromateis* V.11.7)[50]

These ideas were expanded by Dionysius, the Areopagite[51] and developed into a mystical theory proper. He must be accorded the title of a father of Christian mysticism, both on the grounds of his influence,[52] and his intellectual stature. He

[50] Quote in Louth [note 49], p. 194.

[51] On Dionysius, the Areopagite see R. Roques, *L'univers dionysien, Structure hiérarchique du monde selon le Pseudo-Denys*, Paris 2nd edn. 1983; R. Roques, 'Problèmes pseudodionysiens', in: R. Roques, *Structures théologiques, De la gnose à Richard de Saint-Victor*, Paris 1962, pp. 63-240; J. Vanneste, *Le Mystère de Dieu, Essai sur la structure rationnelle de la doctrine mystique du Pseudo-Denys l' Aréopagite*, Paris 1959; B. Brons, *Gott und die Seienden, Untersuchungen zum Verhältnis von neuplatonischer Metaphysik und christlicher Tradition bei Dionysius Areopagita*, Göttingen 1976; M. Schiavone, *Neoplatonismo e Christianesimo nello Pseudo Dionigi*, Milan 1963; W. Völker, *Kontemplation und Ekstase bei Pseudo-Dionysius*, Wiesbaden 1958; H.U. von Balthasar, *Herrlichkeit, Eine theologische Ästhetik, II: Fächer der Stile*, Einsiedeln 1962, pp. 147-214.

[52] H.F.Dondaine, *Le Corpus dionysien de l'université de Paris au XIIIe*

is the pivotal mediator introducing Greek thinking with its formative impact into Christianty. This is witnessed linguistically in his adoption of the diction of the Hellenistic mysteries, in terms of content, in his transposition of the biblical mysteries of salvation into an a-historical context, "timelessness and permanence".[53] The a-temporal *theoria* becomes the instrument of "a festive and ecclesiastical realization of the divine Mysteries in their trans-temporal embodiment."[54] For Dionysius, the Areopagite, 'mystical theology' is not only the title of a short treatise, but, in a deeper sense the meaning of all his theological utterances; it does not present additional guidelines for those gratified with the gift of special grace. Apart from the fact that Dionysius, the Pseudo-Areopagite, was long mistaken for the Apostle's convert, it was his first systematization of the theology of mysticism that surely explains his lasting appeal and almost boundless and fecund popularity throughout the Middle Ages. Commented on by John of Scythopolis (in the sixth century) and by Maximus the Confessor (in the seventh century), the writings of Dionysius became the main source for Eastern Christian theology and mysticism. Translated into Latin time and again (by Hilduin of St. Denis and John Scotus Eriugena in the ninth century, by John Sarracenus in the twelfth, by Robert Grossteste, Bishop of Lincoln, in the thirteenth, by Ambrogio Traversari and Marsilio Ficino in the fifteenth), and commented on by the greatest theologians (Hugh of St. Victor, Albertus Magnus and Thomas Aquinas), the Dionysian treatises exerted a major influence both on the theology and the mysticism of the Middle Ages.[55] From the reception of

---

siècle, Rome 1953; A. Combes, *Jean Gerson, Commentateur dionysien*, Paris 1973; E. von Ivanka, *Plato Christianus, Übernahme und Umgestaltung des Platonismus durch die Väter*, Einsiedeln 1964, pp. 225-89.

[53]von Balthasar [note 51], p. 156.

[54]von Balthasar, p. 156f.

[55]E. von Ivanka, *Dionysius Areopagita, Von den Namen zum Un-*

Dionysius thus originate a literary and theological genre and the doctrine of man's union with God that goes back to the Greek *theoria*.

Unlike what is often termed mysticism today, Dionysian mysticism is not the description of paranormal states of consciousness, the *gratiae gratis datae*,[56] in which experiential and sensual knowledge of God is effected by man's union with Him. Dionysius has a more fundamental approach: striving for mystical contemplation implies setting out on a path. The goal of this path is "becoming united with what is beyond all being and knowing", by unknowing. The process is described as an ecstasy detached from the self, as a radical effacement of self-awareness, and as an exclusive alertness for "the sovereign-substantial ray of Divine Darkness".[57]

The Christianity preached by Dionysius is 'mystagogical', an initiation, a *myesis*, which — in conformity with *Phaidros* — leads to the "celestial and sublime *visio Dei*".[58] Aside from the mystagogy of Proclos, Dionysius refers to Hierotheos, presumably a mystical teacher, who for him was a model as to how to experience God. For Dionysius indeed possessed wisdom, be it from scripture, be it that he was gratified with the 'wind' of the divine Spirit, so that — and here Dionysius takes up a quotation from Aristotle familiar in late antiquity (*Frag.* 15)[59] — he not only studied the Divine, but also experienced and suffered the same; and from the active compassion, *sympatheia*, with the Divine he attained the gift of mystical union, and, together with it, the ultimate goal of mystical initiation — perfection (cp. *Div. Nom.* 2, 9):[60] *Oū*

nennbaren, Einsiedeln (no date), p. 23.

[56] Thomas Aquinas, *Summa theol.* I–II q.iii, a, 4f.; cp. von Balthasar [note 35], p. 268ff.

[57] *Von der mystischen Theologie* 1 (ed. by Ivanka [note 55], p. 91).

[58] Burkert [note 27], p. 28.

[59] Cp. Beck [note 46], p. 24.

[60] Burkert [note 27], p. 19.

monon mathōn, allà kai pathōn ta theīa. In these words the elements of both experience and grace are defined as the fundamental components underlying all Christian mysticism.[61]

Quite apart from the fact that the tradition of 'symbolical theology', of which, unfortunately, nothing has survived, should present a kind of positive antithesis to the important negative theology, which existentially requires man to apply a process of abstraction, and which prepares him for mystical union with God, the process of mystical 'voiding' is by no means one that excludes philosophical reflection as something inappropriate. Discursive thinking is not a faculty that is suspended by occurrences effected by God, infused into the soul and affecting the senses. On the contrary, cognitive thought and the subtle conceptual understanding accompanying it, are means of spiritual ascent leading to a state of awareness beyond all logical reasoning or imagining. The very path leading over what is conceptual becomes a means of transcending it, of attaining knowledge in which the soul, entering the Realm of the Invisible and Unthinkable, is embraced by Divine Night and through love obtains certainty as to the Presence of Him, veiled by Darkness.[62] The soul only has awareness of what lies beyond the conceptual while passing through the conceptual. The conceptual proves inadequate to grasp what is beyond it. The very fact that all the possibilities of understanding the one and only Cause cognitively are listed at the end of the Mystical Theology clearly demonstrates that all of them were tried and tested. So, according to Dionysius, both the negative and the positive theology are resolved in the *via eminentiae*, objectively in the

[61] It is a moot point as to whether Luther's conception of the *vita passiva* can be derived from such a formulation by Dionysius. Cp. Chr. Link, 'Vita passiva, Rechtfertigung als Lebensvorgang', Evangelische Theologie 44 (1984) 315-51.

[62] Ivanka [note 55], p. 24.

"superabundance of God"[63], subjectively, for the person relating it, in a rapturous and effusive mode of speech attributing God with what he is not and cannot be. Union with God first involves this kind of negation but ultimately accompanies the movement upwards into the "sovereign-substantial realm of the Divine", as Dionysius states at the beginning of his *Mystica Theologia*:

> But you . . . whenever you strive for mystical contemplation, leave behind you all the senses and all the workings of the mind, and all the things of sensation and the intellect and all things not existing and existing; and, as far as possible rise up and seek unknowing, the union which is above all substance and understanding. So, transcending beyond your self, free from everything retaining you, you and your entire being will be borne aloft, away from this worldly existence, to the sovereign-substantial ray of Divine Darkness.[64]

This 'non-cognitive union' with God, which the soul may receive as an act of grace, when it ascends to Him 'unknowing', is ultimately motivated by love of God as 'knowledge that is beyond all knowing', and so is not based on any divinity of the soul itself, but on a fundamental annihilation of the soul's own being.[65] In this respect Dionysius was able to exert an authentic Christian influence on the Middle Ages.

Two points in Dionysius' understanding of mysticism seem to be important for all of later Christian mysticism. First, he prepared the literary vessel, the treatise *De mystica theologia*, in which mystical experience not only found

[63] von Balthasar [note 51], p. 209. On Neoplatonic antecedents cp. P. Crome, *Symbol und Unzulänglichkeit der Sprache: Jamblichos, Plotin, Porphyrios, Proklos*, Munich 1970.

[64] *Von der mystischen Theologie* 1 (ed. by Ivanka [note 55], p. 91).

[65] Cp. Ivanka [note 52], pp. 281-83.

narrative expression, but also received its coherent logical and theoretical structure. Secondly, this formal structuring of mystical experience on the plane of the *ratio* provides from the very outset both a linguistic and a philosophical framework of mystical theology. It is true that Augustine's reflections on mystical experience a century before had offered a model analysis of the psychological side of mystical theology by proposing a theory of mystical vision,[66] but in Dionysius' mystical theory the accent is shifted from the isolated, psychologically comprehensible spiritual event to the fundamental question as to how the Christian soul may achieve union with God at all (a constant eschatological demand). The discussion on mysticism in subsequent history developed up to the sixteenth, seventeenth and eighteenth centuries, when the *Theologia mystica* had its heyday and became established as a (rather short-lived) scholarly discipline,[67] and when a conflict occurred between two not always reconcilable approaches. On the one hand, there was the view that normal Christian religious experience culminated in mystical union, on the other,

---

[66]Cp. B. Kälin, *Die Erkenntnislehre des Hl. Augustinus*, Diss. Fribourg/Switzerland, Sarnen 1920; E. Hendrikx, *Augustins Verhältnis zur Mystik, Eine patristische Untersuchung*, Würzburg 1936; H.U. von Balthasar/M.E. Korger, *Aurelius Augustinus, Psychologie und Mystik, De Genesi ad Litteram* 12, Einsiedeln 1960; M.E. Korge, 'Grundprobleme der augustinischen Erkenntnislehre erläutert am Beispiel von 'De genesi ad litteram XII', Recherches Augustiniennes 2 (1962), pp. 33-57; L. Wittmann, *Ascensus, Der Aufstieg zur Transzendenz in der Metaphysik Augustins*, Munich 1980; see also relevant essays in "*Augustinus Magister*", 3 vols, Paris n.d.; K. Rahner, *Visionen und Prophezeiungen*, Basle 3rd edn. 1958.

[67]M.de Certeau, 'Mystique au XVIIe siècle; le problème du langage mystique", in: *L'homme devant Dieu, Mélanges offerts au père H. de Lubac, Du moyen âge au siècle des lumières*, Paris 1964, pp. 267-91; M. de Certeau, *L'absence de l' histoire*, Paris 1973; M. de Certeau, *Politica e mistica, Questioni di storia religiosa*, Milan 1975; M. de Certeau, *La fable mystique*, XVIe-XVIIe siècle, Paris 1982; R. Spaemann, *Reflexion und Spontaneität, Studien über Fénelon*, Stuttgart 1963.

the attitude that, in a more precise sense, it was the paranormal and charismatic phenomena that elevated a normal Christian life to the level of mystical experience.[68] This is where the controversy arises as to whether Augustine was a mystic or not, or the question stemming from Spanish mysticism as to the nature of actively 'acquired' and passively 'infused' contemplation.[69]

In terms of Christian doctrine, these issues will have to be qualified by referring to the duties of obedience and preparedness that must be fulfilled by believing Christians. Experience in an isolated sense of the word must be accorded less significance in view of the basic obligations, although the Bible grants the faithful the freedom that "*they should seek the Lord, if haply they might feel after him, and find him.*" (*Acts* 17, 27)[70]

II

In the introduction I have referred to the strong interest displayed in mysticism by different branches of the humanities and sciences. I ask myself the question as to whether these affinities do not conceal a hitherto unrecognized potential as regards how to approach an understanding of religious experience. So in the following I would like at least to outline the

---

[68] On the discussion of this issue among scholars in mysticism see F.D. Maaß, it Mystik im Gespräch, Materialien zur Mystik-Diskussion in der kath. und evangelischen Theologie Deutschlands nach dem ersten Weltkrieg, Würzburg 1972, pp. 83ff.; E. Salmann, *Gnadenerfahrung im Gebet, Zur Theorie der Mystik bei A. Stolz und A. Mager*, Diss. Münster/W. 1979; von Balthasar [note 30], pp. 313-20.

[69] Maximilian Sandaei, it Theologia Mystica Clavis, Cologne 1640, p. 156; R. Dalbiez, 'La controverse de la Contemplation acquise,' in: *Technique et contemplation, Etudes Carmélitaines*, Paris 1949, pp. 81-145; von Balthasar, 'Christliche "Mystik" heute', in: J.Kotschner (ed.), *Der Weg zum Quell, Teresa von Avila* 1582-1982, Düsseldorf 1982, pp. 11-52, esp. p. 25.

[70] Cp. von Balthasar [note 30], p. 319f.

possibilities philosophy and poetry have at their disposal to render mystical experience intelligible.

1. The history of philosophy blatantly shows that philosophy has both a hard and easy task with mysticism. All too facile an approach has been taken by that kind of philosophy, which, without availing itself of the possiblities of accurate definition germane to it, lumps in sheer monotony all of mysticism together in the umbrella term 'Mystizismus', and disparages it as 'weird', 'obscure', 'confused', 'subjective', 'anti-rational', 'mysterious', 'backward', 'idiosyncratic', 'morbid', 'degenerate' and 'decadent'.[71] The eighteenth and ninteenth centuries in particular outdid themselves in this kind of aversion. Let me mention only Kant, Schopenhauer, Feuerbach, Marx, Dühring, and Nietzsche. Nonetheless, there is a large number of eminent modern philosophers who view mysticism in a much more differentiated manner. Amongst many others, reference should be made to E. von Hartmann, R. Eucken, F. Mauthner, G. Landauer, E. Cassirer, H. Leisegang, E. Troeltsch, M. Scheler, K. Jaspers, M. Heidegger, E. Bloch, L. Wittgenstein, Baumgardt, H. Bergson and a whole series of Catholic thinkers and religious philosophers.

One fact must be established. All philosophy deriving from Platonism and Neoplatonism, and medieval Christian philosophy in particular, has always discussed the question of the possibility and authenticity of man's union with God in infinitely varied manners. Mystical experience — in its

[71] Cp. *Historisches Wörterbuch der Philosophie* 6, Stuttgart 1984, cols. 273ff. On the relationship between philosophy and mysticism see note 18 above. See also G. Krüger, *Religiöse und profane Welterfahrung,* Frankfurt a.M. 1973; Th.H. Hughes, *The Philosophic Basis of Mysticism,* Edinburgh 1937; W. Allen, *The Timeless Moment,* London n.d.; W.T. Stace, *Mysticism and Philosophy,* London 1961; L. Kolakowski, *Falls es keinen Gott gibt,* Munich 1982, pp. 89-138; I. Trethowan, *The Absolute Atonement,* London 1971, pp. 227-86.

classic definition *cognitio Dei experimentalis*[72] — strives for nothing less than this union. The problem is that philosophy and mysticism are viewed separately for the reason that mystical experience is often improperly equated with personal spiritual phenomena. As we have seen, we encounter mystical experience, if we encounter it at all, in the form of language, i.e. mystology. In language such a private experience can be conveyed — and this is frequently the case. However, an isolated experience in the mystical text is often explored beyond its setting — the grace-given union between man and God as removed from any psychological or narrative dimension. This process results in mystical theology proper, which by no means eschews philosophical argument; on the contrary, it develops it up to the utmost borderline, as it focuses on the meta-rational or trans-intellectual union between man and God as the solution to this paradox. A concept of mysticism such as proposed by Rudolf Otto[73] is, of course, inadequate for such purposes. Speaking of the 'irrational' in the context of the most illuminating experiences man can have, is obscurantist and prohibitory.

What is meant can be shown most clearly in the example

[72]Thomas Aquinas, *Summa theol.* II-II, q.97, a.2; see F.D. Joret, *Die mystische Beschauung nach dem hl. Thomas von Aquin*, Dülmen/W. 1931, p. 146; on the formula and its reception see A.M. Haas, 'Die Problematik von Sprache und Erfahrung in der deutschen Mystik', in: *Grundfragen der Mystik*, Einsiedeln 1974, pp. 73-104, esp. p. 75, note 1 and p. 93, note 45.

[73]R. Otto, *Das Heilige, Über das Irrationale in der Idee des Göttlichen und sein Verhältnis zum Rationalen*, Munich 26th to 28th edns. 1947; R. Otto, *Aufsätze das Numinose betreffend*, I/II, Gotha 4th edn. 1929; R. Otto, *Westöstliche Mystik, Vergleich und Unterscheidung zur Wesensdeutung*, Munich 3rd edn 1971. This critical comment in no way detracts from Otto's achievements in establishing a typology of mysticism. H.Bremond, *L'inquiétude religieuse, I: Aubes et lendemains de Conversion*, Paris 6th edn. 1919, p. 129ff. already vehemently criticized the concept of 'the irrational' as a category to denote the ' Mystical'.

of Meister Eckhart. It is once again he who is at the forefront of discussion, after recent years have underlined his historical impact on Dominican theology in the fourteenth century. The philosopher in Meister Eckhart comes to the fore, when, with rigorous philosophical arguments, he endeavours to expound the self-constitution of human consciousness in the light of the divine *Logos*, i.e. the Birth of God.[74] To begin with, it must be conceded that Eckhart scholars of all people have erroneously, and sometimes distortingly, employed the word 'mysticism' in interpreting Eckhart. Eckhart was one of the most consistent opponents of all-too-rampant visionary mysticism.[75] That is not to say that the word 'mysticism' is completely inapplicable to him. Quite the opposite, I am convinced that it is indispensable to an understanding of the master. But the mistake must not be made of wanting to find Meister Eckhart's philosophy and mysticism neatly stacked beside each other. The opposite is the case: "At the core of the intellectual problem he [Eckhart] places a mystical exigency."[76] Even for an advocate of the strictly philosoph-

[74]K. Flasch, 'Die Intention Meister Eckharts', in Röttges/B. Scheer/J.Simon (eds), *Sprache und Begriff. Festschrift für B. Liebrucks*, Meisenheim a. Glan 1974, pp. 292-318, quotation p. 317. See also by the same, 'Kennt die mittelalterliche Philosophie die konstitutive Funktion des menschlichen Denkens? Eine Untersuchung zu Dietrich von Freiberg', Kant Studien 63 (1972) 182-206, esp. p. 206. Whether Eckhart was a mystic or not is still a controversial issue, as is clearly shown by the articles and discussions in Alois M. Haas, *Gottleiden, Gottlieben*, see footnote 1.

[75]Eckhart, *Lateinische Werke* II, 109, 10-15. Cp. A.M. Haas, 'Traum und Traumvision in der deutschen Mystik', in: *Gottleiden, Gottlieben*, pp. 109-26; O. Langer, 'Enteignete Existenz und mystische Erfahrung, Zu Meister Eckharts Auseinandersetzung mit der Frauenmystik seiner Zeit', in: K.O. Seidel (ed.), *So predigent eteliche, Beiträge zur deutschen und niederländischen Predigt im Mittelalter*, Göppingen 1982, pp. 49-96, esp. p. 70ff.

[76]"on peut dire que ..., les oppositions qui apparaissent entre le thomisme et les formulations métaphysiques de maître Eckhart sont

ical approach it is true that the much-worn name of mysticism points to something that is fundamentally correct. In his philosophical understanding of Christianity, in his critical amendment of the Neoplatonic metaphysics of the One and the *Nous*, Eckhart does not shrink from drawing the conclusion that whoever thinks the infinite oneness cannot be thought of outside it.[77] Moreover, for Eckhart this oneness is by no means purely speculative, but can be experienced. This is something he expresses, partly polemically, partly in missionary zeal, in his German sermons, albeit in a context completely alien to that of the history of philosophy. Hence the influence of the mysticism of the Beguines and the German converts on him, and its relevance for practical life, must not be underrated, nor should his *cura monialium*, which is well attested in history. If Eckhart can be called a philosopher, then primarily in the old monastic sense of the word, in which the quest for a felicitous life was not divorced from the *vita activa*. But then the question must be asked whether his primary concern was with a philosophical establishment of "the self-constitution of human consciousness",[78] or rather with tracing human consciousness back to its divine origin. Preaching in Paris on the feast of St. Augustine, Eckhart at any rate testifies to a profound knowledge of the significance of the powers of cognition and of the intellect. Endowed with the gift of Grace, they are able to become *sapida scientia, sapientia*, so that man gains "a foretaste of divine sweetness"

presque toujours dues ā l'insertion, au coeur même du problème intellectuel, d'une exigence mystique qui est d'un autre ordre." M. de Gandillac, *Maître Eckhart, Traités et sermons*, Paris 1942, p. 14; see also E. zum Brunn/A. de Libera, *Maître Eckhart, Métaphysique du verbe et théologie négative*, Paris 1984, p. 26ff.

[77]Flasch, *Die Intention* [note 74], p. 301; B. Mojsisch, *Meister Eckhart, Analogie, Univozität und Einheit*, Hamburg 1983.

[78]Cp. the theses put forward by Flasch [note 74].

in extasi mentis.[79] The entire ascetic burden of abstraction including '*abegescheidenheit*' [detachment] is laid on cognition, so that the philosophical process itself becomes the instrument of union with God.

Viewed historically, the relationship between philosophy and mysticism has often been a series of misunderstandings once the dissociation of theory and practice had become an established fact, and it had become wishful thinking to change it. All the same, there are a few bright spots where the original unity of both approaches can be glimpsed; I am thinking of Plato's *Seventh Epistle*, of the Neoplatonists Plotinus,[80] Proclus,[81] and Prophyry. I would like to quote a philosopher who elsewhere expressed no approval of mysticism, although he owed much to it: Friedrich Nietzsche. According to him, philosophy is informed by an experience epitomized in the assertion: 'All is one'. This sentence "has its origins in a mystical intuition, [a sentence] we find with all the philosophers together with recurrent attempts to express it better and better".[82]

2. Whereas philosophy can be integrated in mysticism in terms of its endeavour for an absolute discourse, focussing on the *principia* and *prima philosophia* of everything, poetic language can be incorporated even more easily, as the mystical discourse aims at mystagogy, a process of communication

---

[79]Eckhart, *Lateinische Werke* V, 94, 11mF., n. 6. Cp. zum Brunn/de Libera [note 76], p. 28.

[80]J. Trouillard, *La purification plotinienne*, Paris 1955; J. Trouillard, *La procession plotinienne*, Paris 1955; M. de Gandillac, *La sagesse de Plotin*, Paris 1966; P. Hodot, *Plotin ou simplicité du regard*, Paris 1973.

[81]W. Beierwaltes, *Proklos, Grundzüge seiner Metaphysik*, Frankfurt a. M. 2nd edn. 1979; J. Trouillard, *L'Un et l'âme selon Proclos*, Paris 1972; J. Trouillard, *La mystagogie de Proclos*, Paris 1982.

[82]Schlechta, Werke III, p. 361. On the tradition see W. Beierwaltes, *Denken des Einen, Studien zur neuplatonischen Philosophie und ihrer Wirkungsgeschichte*, Frankfurt a.M. 1984.

diametrically opposed to the commandment of silence underlying the original meaning of the word 'mysticism'. But this is only one aspect enabling comparison between the poetic and the mystical experience.[83] Just as poetry in its purest locutions evinces a tendency to efface its communicative signatures and withdraw to the liminal position of a 'poésie pure', mystological utterances also manifest and articulate a downward progress towards the ultimately ineffable; a progress determined by the acute awareness of their incommensurability with what is to be said. It is not necessary to exaggerate the affinity of both modes of speech into a hierarchical subordination of poetry to mysticism, as attempted by Henri Bremond in his well-known discussion of the 'Poésie pure' in 1926. For him, it is an established fact "that poetic activity is a natural and profane replica of mystical activity ...it is a diffuse and ponderous replica, full of gaps and blanks, so that the poet is ultimately only the shadow of a mystic, only a foundered mystic".[84] The ontological status of both modes of experience is surely different.[85] And yet, at the culmination of his revelations, the mystic knows no other linguistic means than poetic expression, particularly when the *Mihi adhaerere Deo bonum est*[86] is uttered in the form of eulogy or ecstatic *jubilus*.[87] Mechthild of Magdeburg provides many examples of a unique command of the most fervent mystical language and incorporates all the poetic structures imaginable.

---

[83]On the following discussion see my reflections in: A.M. Haas, *Sermo mysticus, Studien zu Theologie und Sprache der deutschen Mystik*, Freiburg i. Ue. 1979, pp. 19ff, 76ff.

[84]H. Bremond, *Mystik und Poesie*, Freiburg i.Br. 1929, p. 213.

[85]H. Halbfas, 'Die Vermittlung mystischer Erfahrung', in: H. Cancik [note 5], pp. 132-45, esp. p. 135ff.

[86]Psalm 72 (73), 28. Cp. S.D. Sfriso, *Adhaerere Deo. L'unione con Dio, Filologia e storia di una locuzione biblica*, Brescia 1980; J. et Maritain, *Situation de la poésie*, Paris 2nd edn. 1964, p. 35.

[87]H. Grundmann, 'Jubel', in: H. Grundmann, *Ausgewählte Aufsätze*, Teil 3: Bildung und Sprache, Stuttgart 1978, pp. 130-62.

An explanation will have to be found for why Christian mysticism employs both linguistic modes of the unspeakable and means of effusive expression. With other religions Christianity shares the notion of God's 'ineffability', as well as that of union with Him. This ineffability is the product of religious reflexion on the Absolute. On the other hand, in Christian doctrine the ineffable God is Himself *Logos*, the One who, to use Eckhart's words, has Himself become the word ("*selber gewortet*").[88] Apart from the apophatic forms of expression and the themes of deprivation and desire accompanying it, we also encounter in Christianity the main current of cataphatic and symbolical, rhetorical and allegorical modes of speech.[89] Let mention be made only of the erotic imagery of union that has shocked many prude readers. The accounts of human experience, such as presented in scripture in their mystical-allegorical meanings are not mysteries inaccessible to the mystic, but models encouraging him to speak untrammelled, because these accounts testify to the 'omnipotence of God', whose word always antecedes man's.[90]

As regards the distinction made by Irene Behn[91] and Walter Haug[92] between the 'mystical text' (=mysticism, i.e. a

---

[88] Eckhart, *Deutsche Werke* I, 66, 3.

[89] E. Biser, *Theologische Sprachtheorie und Hermeneutik*, Munich 1970; E. Biser, *Religiöse Sprachbarrieren, Aufbau einer Logaporetik*, Munich 1980.

[90] For a profound vindication of 'bridal mysticism' as a phenomenon of incarnation see von Balthasar [note 69], p. 46ff.

[91] I. Behn, *Spanische Mystik*, Düsseldorf 1957, p. 8, distinguishes "between mysticism, i.e. the experience itself, and mystology (or mystography), i.e. the reflection on, and speaking or writing about mystical experience within the framework of specific categories (which may, but need not necessarily, be based on actual experience) . . . In addition, Behn discerns the concept of mystagogy, defined as the theoretical and practical guidance towards mystical experience, conducted by those who have been gratified with it." (von Balthasar [note 30], p. 307).

[92] See Haug's essay in: K. Ruh, *Abendländische Mystik im Mittelalter*, Stuttgart 1986, p. 494ff. An extensive philosophical basis for Haug's

verbal structure in which no differentiation seems possible between the experience itself and concurrent speech voicing it), and 'texts on mysticism' (mystology, mystical theology), I consider such a division necessary and meaningful as a method, but would ultimately like to qualify it, as I suspect that a highly gifted poet might well manage to construct a mystical text so that it would be indistinguishable from genuine mystical ones. On the other hand, Spanish mystics have a preference for couching their lyrical verse, often indiscernible from profane love poetry, in a language rich in scholastic connotations. In this context the question will have to be asked as to where, within the linguistic framework, the authentic mystical experience can be found. The answer is presumably in a combination of both forms of literary expression [i.e. mysticism as defined above, and mystology/mystical theology]. Even so, I gladly concede that the endless output of mystical theologies, particularly by the Carmelites in the sixteenth and seventeenth centuries,[93] is a source of sheer frustration. But I must qualify this sentiment by saying that Teresa of Avila did not tire of having her mystical experiences examined and confirmed by mediocre mystical theologies.[94]

Irrespective of how systematic thinking may define the relationship between poetic and mystical speech, either as an analogous one, according to which poetical speech is on a level with mystical language in creating linguistic patterns for human emotions and sensibilities, or as a hierarchical re-

---

analysis may be seen in D. Licciardo, *De la analogia en el conocimiento de Dios por la experiencia mistica*, Zurich 1965.

[93] Jose de la Cruz, *Historia de la Literatura mistica en Espana*, Burgos 1961; 'De Contemplatione in schola teresiana', Ephemerides Carmeliticae 13 (1962); Melquiades Andres Martin, *Los Recogidos, Nueva vision de la mistica espanola* (1500-1700), Madrid 1976.

[94] F. de Ros, *Un maître de Sainte Thérèse: Le père François d'Osuna*, Paris 1936; F. de Ros, *Un inspirateur de Sainte Thérèse: Le frère Bernardin de Laredo*, Paris 1948.

lationship in which the mystical discourse should epitomize the ultimate fulfilment of poetic expression, because it incorporates poetry's most profound natural intentions, I think that in this context we would adhere to the mutual transfer of linguistic patterns between poetry and mysticism. These insights entail that philology — provided it remain intellectually flexible enough and avoid overly dogmatic philosophical or doctrinal concepts of mysticism — may with certain justification also regard mysticism as the legitimate subject of its scholarly attention. In my view, philology especially has the asset of being able to focus on the object of its research without major ideological bias, i.e. it can focus on its linguistic structure and concrete entity. Moreover, the philological approach to the study of mysticism seems to me to be the ideal one, not least for enabling a comparative analysis between mystical systems of different religious provenance. This is not because such a comparison should aim at syncretism, but quite the opposite, because, from a philological point of view, the differences between variegated mystical systems become particularly pronounced as long as the context of linguistic tradition is not neglected.

III

The question "*what is mysticism*" can surely be answered only after considering, first, mysticism's infinitely varied manifestations in the course of history and in different religions, and, secondly, the perhaps even more variegated interpretations with which these manifestations have been regarded from the most diverse angles.[95] In practical terms this means that the individual historical variants of mysticism should

[95] For this reason the aspect of religious history seems to me to be vital in the research of mystical experience. Cp. the early study by F. Heiler, *Die Bedeutung der Mystik für die Weltreligionen*, Munich 1919. The differences in mentality between East and West cannot be grasped with-

have priority in mystical scholarship and that the question as to the essence of mysticism should, on principle, be answered only in relation to the relevant mystical system. Nevertheless, it is possible to discern models of mystical phenomena, i.e. a kind of typology, whose innate disparities should not disguise the features they share. Within the Christian tradition I see this common denominator in the idea that mystical experience seeks its ultimate goal in the act of *unio*, the cognitive and loving union of man and God. Yet, the intensity of such an *unio mystica* does not provide a yardstick to measure the degree of perfection attained by the mystic. So the experience of union also necessitates alienation from God. Paradoxically, it involves experience of the Divine by experiencing Divine Absence.[96]

Let us endeavour to define mysticism from man's subjective perspective and propose the following thesis. Mystical experience is both a growth in knowledge and in love between man and God. Pivoting on the holy mysteries and

---

out taking the different basic attitudes to mysticism into account. Cp. the seminal study by J.A. Cuttat, *Asiatische Gottheit — Christlicher Gott, Die Spiritualität beider Hemisphären*, Einsiedeln n.d.; J.A. Cuttat, *Begegnung der Religionen*, Einsiedeln 1956; J. Sudbrack, *Herausgefordert zur Meditation, Christliche Erfahrung im Gespräch mit dem Osten*, Freiburg i.Br. 1977.

[96]This means that the apophasis relating to God — *si comprehendis, non est Deus* (Augustine!) — also has an impact on man, experienced as an immense increase in the agony of spiritual suffering. Mystical experiences of hell, the *resignatio ad infernum*, or the "*gotzvroemdunge*" of Mechthild of Magdeburg belong here. Cp. Sandaeus [note 69], pp. 311-19; J. Sudbrack, *Abwesenheit Gottes*, Zurich 1971. It is this point that provokes Protestant criticism of mysticism. The process of mystical annihilation is exposed (and thus seen relatively) as a 'human' device striving to possess God in a non-historical way. Cp. R. Bultmann, *Theologische Enzyklopädie*, ed. by E. Jüngel/K.W. Müller, Tübingen 1984, pp. 115-29. Although there is no doubt that some Promethean elements can be traced in mysticism, they are at the same time eliminated in mystical experience.

elusive to expression, it is ultimately inexpressible, encountered by man as a grace-given bestowed union with God and attained without any conscious effort (even though the element of distance to God, the *regio dissimilitudinis*,[97] is experienced as a corollary). But this would lead us right into the field of the different modes of experiencing union. They allow us to speak about the variant forms of mystical experience. The two basic tendencies discerned by Christian mysticism permit us to talk with Heraclitus of "ways ascending" and "ways descending"[98], or anabatic and katabatic mysticism. This differentiation seems fundamental since it reveals all the problems of a structured progress to perfection. Neoplatonic Christian mysticism follows both the schemes of ascent and descent, whereas perhaps even as early as Bernard of Clairvaux, or, at the very latest, from the Dominican mysticism of the fourteenth century onwards, an independent katabatic mystical tradition has developed, which chooses as metaphors the valley of humility, or, ultimately, the abyss of the soul, instead of the *mons contemplationis*. It is striking that women such as Mechthild of Magdeburg display a preference for the imagery of descent and falling. Here it is a moot point as to whether katabatic mysticism does not render God's coming into the world more appropriately than anabatic mysticism.[99]

In Christianity (e.g. the different religious attitudes of the Franciscans and Dominicans), a major role is played by the distinction between a more speculative and a more affective

---

[97] Cf. M. Schmidt, '*Regio dissimilitudinis*, Ein Grundbegriff mittelhochdeutscher Prosa im Lichte seiner lateinischen Bedeutungsgeschichte', Freiburger Zs. f. Phil. u. Theol. 15 (1968), pp. 63-108.

[98] See the still appealing and by no means outdated article by K. Goldammer, 'Wege aufwärts und Wege abwärts', Eine heilige Kirche 22 (1940), 25-57.

[99] Cp. H.U. von Balthasar's indefatigable plea [notes 30, 1, 69] for an incarnational concept of mysticism that does not avoid an incorporation in physical realities.

mysticism (cherubic and seraphic mysticism).[100] Whereas the speculative tradition is averse to visions and sensational spiritual phenomena, the affective tradition is more susceptible to such praeternatural occurrences (e.g. St. Francis' stigmata).[101] The two types can likewise be termed mysticism of the Divine Essence ('*Wesensmystik*'), and mysticism of Love. Another form of mystical experience surfacing, as it were, recurrently and independently in all Christian traditions is 'nuptial mysticism' ('*Brautmystik*'), in which man and God meet on the personal level, as bride and bridegroom. This erotic mysticism in the shape of the 'sacred marriage' is so precious because it vividly conveys the specifically personal dimension germane to the meeting between God and man.[102]

---

[100] Cp. Jo. Scheffler (Angelus Silesius), *Der cherubinische Wandersmann*, Critical edition, ed. by L. Gnädinger, Stuttgart 1984.

[101] O. Schmucki, *De sancti Francisci Assisiensis stigmatum susceptione*, Collectanea Franciscana 33 (1963), pp. 210-26, 392-422; 34 (1964), pp. 5-62; 241-338; W.Jacobi, *Die Stigmatisierten, Beiträge zur Psychologie der Mystik*, Munich 1923; J.M. Höchst, *Von Franziskus zu Pater Pio und Teresa Neumann, Eine Geschichte der Stigmatisierten*, Stein a. Rhein 3rd edn. 1974; H. Thurston, *Die körperlichen Begleiterscheinungen der Mystik*, Lucerne 1956; J. Lhermitte, *Echte und falsche Mystiker*, Lucerne 1953.

[102] '*Bridal mysticism*' is characterized not only by including the sphere of the body, but much more so, by emphasizing the personal dimension. This explains its unique dignity. Nuptial mysticism has both a social and an ecclesiastical dimension, not only by virtue of its origin — the mystical experience corresponding to that of the *Song of Songs* — but also in essence. So an important criterion of the authenticity of Christian mysticism is not only its external, but also its internal ecclesiastical attitude: "The individual Christian can only be the 'bride of Christ' as an *anima ecclesiastica*, as a soul desiring to be nothing but the church, the community of all Christians." (von Balthasar [note 69], p. 50)

SOURCE OF ALL BLISS

Mysticism of Śaiva Siddhānta and an Insight into its Saṃnyāsa Tradition

Swami Nityananda Giri

Introduction

This presentation is offered invoking the grace of a great sage of recent times, Sadguru Gnanananda, the guru of Swami Abhishiktananda. Gnanananda lived at the peak of mystic experience, where all schools of thought are reconciled and transcended. He seemed to represent to every seeker his own faith. He was a master of both Śaiva Siddhānta and Vedānta lore and quoted profusely from the texts of both traditions. He emphasized the importance of eschewing philosophical disputation and going beyond discursive thinking.

Swami Abhishiktananda asks him:

> "What is Swamiji's position concerning Reality? Is it *dvaita* or *advaita*? When all is said and done, does any difference remain between God and creatures? For instance, is it possible for man to enjoy God and eternally partake of the joy? Or, is there finally, beyond everything, only being non-dual (*advaita*) and indivisible in unlimited fullness?"
>
> "What is the use of such a question?" replied Sri Gnanananda quickly. "The answer is within you. Seek it in the depths of your being. Devote yourself to *dhyāna*, meditation beyond all forms, and the solution will be given to you".[1]

---

[1]Swami Abhishiktananda, *Guru and Disciple*, SPCK London, 1974, pp. 24–25.

It is an experience which cannot be labelled. "Then why are you so determined at all costs to find a name for that which is by very definition stripped of every possibility of being named?" Gnanananda exclaims elsewhere.[2]

Like Sadguru Gnanananda, Bhagavan Sri Ramana also did not see much difference between Siddhānta and Vedānta. According to him, Siddhānta is a philosophy of devotion and grace and at the end of acts of devotion and meditation, one attains *parā-bhakti* when, having completely overcome the attachment as 'mine' to all things except God, he revels in the Bliss of Supreme Love and service of the Lord (*irai-pani-nitral*). Vedānta with its path of knowledge as self-enquiry leads one "to know the truth that the 'I' is not different from the Lord (*Īśvara*) and to be free from the feeling of being the doer (*kartṛtva ahaṃkāra*). Whatever the means, the destruction of the sense of 'I' and 'mine' is the goal and as these are interdependent, the destruction of either of them causes the destruction of the other, and the state of silence beyond thought and word is achieved. The end of the paths of devotion and knowledge is one and the same."[3]

In India, the various schools of philosophy are derived not from speculation but from the direct experience of men of God. The mystic experiences Reality in different ways. Moving in his own unlimited spiritual freedom, the liberated sage spontaneously records the glimpses of his experience without caring for consistency. Thus we have various insights into Reality depending upon different moods of the mystic. They are reduced to the philosophical concepts of various schools of philosophy which suit the different aptitudes of the seekers. Such concepts in turn together with the psalms and songs of

---

[2]Swami Abhishiktananda, *Guru and Disciple*, SPCK London, 1974, p. 89.

[3]*Bhagavan Ramana Maharshi, The Collected Works of*, Ed. by Arthur Osborne, Sri Ramanasramam, 1979, pp. 51–52.

the Saints, which are spontaneous outpourings bearing the indelible stamp of their mystic experience and constitute the source as also the reference, take us back to their ineffable experience which defies categorization.

All these spiritual exercises consisting of study of scriptures of the various traditions and of reflection are at best to cultivate our minds. The Divine chooses to reveal Itself in Its own way at Its own time to the person chosen by It, when he is therefore drawn to It in rapturous love.[4]

With these words of introduction, it is proposed to make a few reflections on some concepts of Śaiva Siddhānta, particularly with reference to the self's transcendent experience still retaining the trace of its individuality. Dr Ranade refers to this as asymptotic approximation to Reality. The hyperbole never meets the asymptote but goes on approaching it continually and meets it at Infinity. So too the mystic's experience is a continuous, ever-growing, intuitive and super-sensuous one, almost but not total merging in God.[5]

Attention is also drawn to the place of *saṃnyāsa* in this tradition and how it is the result of the most powerful descent of grace. Such *saṃnyāsa* as in the case of Saint Tayumanavar, leads one beyond all concepts to the transcendental experience of silence.

Śaivaite philosophy covers the entire spectrum of Hindu thought. While in all its forms, it deals with three *padārthas* (categories) viz. *pati* (God), *paśu* (self or soul) and *pāśa* (bonds that fetter the soul), in the reality attributed to thirty six *tattvas* (principles) and in the independence assigned to souls and matter, it varies from the idealistic monism of Kashmir Śaivism at one end to the pluralistic (in the sense of non-absolutistic) realism of Śaiva Siddhānta at the other, thus

---

[4] *Kaṭha Upaniṣad* II.23.

[5] R.D. Ranade, *The Bhagavad Gītā as a Philosophy of God-realisation*, Bharatiya Vidya Bhavan, 1982, pp. 63–64.

providing a wide range of philosophical perspectives. In all the forms of Śaivism we find the insistence on knowledge as essential to salvation and as the prime cause thereof, a typical characteristic of the best Hindu thought.[6]

Śaiva Siddhānta conceives Reality in three ultimate irreducible modes — *pati*, *paśu* and *pāśa*. Though all the three are equally ultimate and eternal, *paśu* and *pāśa* are dependent or finite existences and *pati* is an independent Infinite Being. Their otherness is only affirmed in an existential sense, as also is their essential relatedness. *Pati* (God) is the Infinite and unlimited, the very Source and Ground of Being. As the transcendent Reality, *pati* is called Śiva.[7]

God is the Supreme Reality, at once the Absolute of Philosophy and the Supreme Personality, embodying every perfection, which compels adoration. He is the Supreme Spirit of Intelligence, Lord Śiva. There is none to equal or excel him. Eight are the attributes of Śiva: Self-existence, purity, self-knowledge, omniscience, freedom from *mala* (defilement), boundless benevolence, omnipotence and Bliss. 'Śiva' means the Auspicious, the Source of all Bliss.

"Although *pati* is the transcendent Spirit, He is at the same time immanent in the conditions of finite life and existence, constitutive of man's bondage. As immanent in them, *pati* is the Redeemer of man from the limiting conditions of bondage."[8] "The name '*Hara*' indicates the redemptive nature of God. He removes all the impurities of the soul and redeems it from *saṃsāra* (transmigration)."[9]

---

[6]Cp. S.S. Suryanarayana Sastri, "The Philosophy of Śaivism", *The Cultural Heritage of India*, Vol. II. Sri Ramakrishna Mission Institute of Culture, Calcutta, 1969, p. 387.

[7]K. Sivaraman, *Śaivism in Philosophical Perspective*, Delhi, Motilal Banarsidass, 1973, pp. 8–9.

[8]Ibid., pp. 22–23.

[9]T.M.P. Mahadevan, "*The Idea of God in Śaiva Siddhānta*", Sri-la-Sri Arulanandi Sivacharya Swamigal Sivajnana Siddhiyar Endowment

He is *nirguṇa*, beyond *prakṛti*, free from its three *guṇas* of *sattva*, *rajas* and *tamas* which are finite. He is called *turīya* (the fourth), because He is beyond the states of waking, dream and sleep which are conditions respectively of the three *guṇas* of *prakṛti*.[10] He is at once immanent in the universe and transcendent to it. He is *viśvamaya* (of the form of the universe). But the universe does not exhaust His nature. He is also *viśvādhika* (more than the universe). He exceeds the universe, while being its Ground. Hence He cannot be perceived and comprehended by thought. He has no name and form. There are no identifying marks setting limits to Him.[11]

Existing is His own right, He is *Sat*, Being, He is *Cit*, the Supreme Intelligence, Self-luminous and knows all directly. It is God's intelligence that enlightens the soul, enables it to gather knowledge of the world through senses and other accessories of itself and of the Lord. He is *Ānanda* Himself, infinitely blissful. The Lord bestows bliss on all.[12]

His functions are *sṛṣṭi* (creation), *sthiti* (preservation), *saṃhāra* (destruction), *tirodhāna* (concealment) and *anugraha* (bestowal of grace). Of these, the first four have as their end the last one. The ultimate aim of the grand Divine plan of the universe is the liberation of the soul through a shower of grace. Śiva hides the truth from the soul, projects the world as the field of its experience in which it evolves spiritually, and finally He emancipates the soul through His grace. The world process is Śiva's *līlā*.[13]

Lecture 1953, Annamalai University, 1955, pp. 3–5.

[10]Cp. T.M.P. Mahadevan, *Invitation to Indian Philosophy*, Arnold Heinemann, 1982, pp. 311–13.

[11]T.M.P. Mahadevan, "*The Idea of God in Śaiva Siddhānta*", art. cit., pp. 3–5.

[12]R. Ramanujachari, *Śaiva Siddhānta*, Tiruppanandal Endowment Lectures, 1984, Annamalai University, pp. 10-12.

[13]T.M.P. Mahadevan, "*The Idea of God in Śaiva Siddhānta*", art. cit., pp. 3–5.

The transcendent nature of Śiva is emphasized by regarding Him as the efficient cause of the world. The threefold change of origination, sustentation and destruction of the world has its source in Him. But God Himself does not undergo any change. He is the unchanging Ground of all the changes.[14]

The instrumental cause is Śiva's Śakti and the material cause is *māyā*. *Māyā* is so called, because as the universe is revolved (*mā*) into it and is evolved (*yā*) from it.[15] It is from *māyā* that souls are provided with locations (*bhuvana*, worlds), instruments (*tanu*, bodies and *karaṇas*) and objects of experience (*bhogya*). *Māyā* is inert and requires the intelligent direction and guidance which comes from Śiva through His *cit-śakti* (power of Consciousness).[16]

Śiva has no forms. God is with form and is formless as well. He is usually spoken of as in eightfold form (*aṣṭa-mūrti*). Manikkavacagar, for example, sings[17]:

> Earth, water, air, fire, sky, the sun and moon,
> the sentient man, these eight forms He pervades.
>
> *Tiruvacakam* 319
> *Tiruttonnokkam* 5
> Trans. by J. H. Nallaswami Pillai

> There is no form for Him whose glory is everywhere.
>
> *Śvetāśvatara Upaniṣad* IV.19

> That day when I became Thy slave, I saw not Thy divine form. Even today, I fail to perceive Thy blessed form. To those who ask: "What is the form of Thy Lord?" What shall I say? What

[14] K. Sivaraman, op. cit. pp. 22–23.

[15] Sivagnana Yogin's *Mapadiyam*, pp. 149–50.

[16] T.M.P. Mahadevan, *Invitation to Indian Philosophy*, op. cit., pp. 311–13.

[17] Ibid.

may be Thy form? Hast thou any?
Karikkal Ammaiyar,
Adbhuta Tiruvantadi, v.61

He is formless and yet has form. To the wise, He has the form of awareness. He has form.
Umāpati Śivācārya, *Tiruvarutpayan*, v.5

He assumes several forms so that the devotees may adore Him in them. "If it be said 'Thou art formless', You have a form; if it be said 'Thou hast a form', you are formless. Thou art neither the formed or the formless".[18]

Praise be to thee who hast forms and art formless!
Praise be to Thee who hast a thousand names!
Manikkavacagar,
Potri Tiruvagal, lines 193, 200

Śiva comes as the preceptor (*guru*) in order to instruct, teach and give the souls liberating knowledge. Out of his boundless love, He becomes tangible to terrestrials. *Anugraha* is His nature. Love is His being. Tirumular declares that there is no difference between God and Love.[19]

Paśu is the self or soul. It is distinct from the body, indestructible, pervasive, varied, endowed with *malas* (impurity), non-inert, enjoyer of the fruits of its own actions, agent, possessor of limited knowledge and having an over-lord. Its destiny is to realise *pati* by conquering *pāśa*.

Paśus are naturally infinite, pervasive and omniscient. Yet they experience themselves as finite, limited and little knowing due to *pāśa* or the three bonds — *āṇava, kārma* and *māyā*.

---

[18] R. Ramanujachari, *Śaiva Siddhānta*, Tiruppanandal Endowment Lectures, 1984, Annamalai University, pp. 10–12.

[19] T.M.P. Mahadevan, "*The Idea of God in Śaiva Siddhānta*", art. cit., pp. 3–5.

The Stages of Sādhana

Āṇava is a connate impurity. It is "a primordial and positive conditioning impurity, beginninglessly present in the souls like verdigris in copper, beginninglessly 'clouding' the soul and thereby occasioning the phenomenal life of man."[20] The concept of *āṇava* in Siddhānta corresponds to that of the beginningless ignorance or *avidyā* in Vedānta. As it is the original cause of bondage, it is called *mūlāmala* and compared to darkness (*irul*). Being non-intelligent, it is operated upon by the Lord through His power of obscuration (*tirodhāna śakti*).[21] It is due to *āṇava mala* that the pervasive (*vibhu*) soul cognises itself as finite, as if it were atomic (*aṇu*). Conditioned by the consequent limitation of cognitive and conative powers, the soul is prompted by appetition and aversion to engage in action. Action brings merit or demerit which it enjoys in a series of births. This is the second impurity of *karma* — the bond forged by deeds.[22] It is "the realm of moral causation involving the sequence between action and its result, which sustains the phenomenal existence through a succession of rebirths."[23] *Māyā mala* is the third impurity which is the material cause of the universe. It provides for the soul means, objects and field of enjoyment, to work out the result of *karma*. This is the *aśuddha* or impure *māyā* which provides "the phenomenal realm of existence, inclusive of subjective and objective spheres – the 'impure' matter subject to the law of time."[24] *Śuddha* or pure *māyā* helps the onward spiritual progress of the soul endowing it with "a super-phenomenal realm of existence – 'pure' matter, above the scope of '*aśuddha*' *māyā* and *karma* – which

---

[20] K. Sivaraman, op. cit. pp. 22–23.

[21] T.M.P. Mahadevan, *Invitation to Indian Philosophy*, op. cit, pp. 315–16.

[22] Ibid.

[23] K. Sivaraman, op. cit., pp. 22–23.

[24] K. Sivaraman, op. cit., pp. 22–23.

while partaking of the nature of phenomena serves to mediate between the infinite *pati* and the finite *paśu*."[25] But the knowledge and illumination due to the *'śuddha' māyā* are limited. *Pati* (God), *paśu* (self or soul), *pāśa* (bond) namely *āṇava mala, kārma, māyā – śuddha* and *aśuddha* – are the three 'eternals' of the Śaivaite philosophy.

"The various schools of Śaivism accept the three categories but there are differences in the conceptions of the nature of the relation between (a) *paśu* and *pāśa* and (b) *paśu* and *pati*. The spectrum is from radical dualism through qualified dualism to non-dualism. The relation between self and God in the state of liberation is the deciding point."[26]

In Śaiva Siddhānta the gulf between the transcendent and infinite nature of *pati* (Śiva) and the relative and finite realm of the phenomena which constitute the *pāśa* (bond) is overcome by the principle of *paśu* (self) whose nature as *sat-asat* (real–nonreal) permits participation in both the realms. The nature of the self is to be properly understood as it is relevant to the importance given to grace and to the realisation of the self's oneness with Śiva as an experience. The self cognises the phenomena through the accessories of *pāśa* such as senses and by completely identifying itself with the object to be known. Such cognition is *pāśa jñāna*, a demonstrative knowledge of knowing perspectively as subject of knowledge confronting the object.[27]

Pati (Śiva) is impartite and pure consciousness and hence cannot be knower (*pramātṛ*) like *paśu* which alone can have demonstrative knowledge. *Pāśa* which is only an object (*prameya*) cannot also be a knower (*pramātṛ*). Śiva and self are alike in intelligence. But the former is pure consciousness which is revelatory. The latter, the self, is "the subject that

[25] K. Sivaraman, op. cit., pp. 22–23.
[26] Ibid.
[27] Ibid., pp. 375–79.

receives the revelation, because it can know Śiva only as and when 'shown' (*upadeśin*)." Self can "know only by identifying itself with the thing to be known by 'being' or 'becoming' the thing known (*tadbhāva-bhāvita*)." Thus self is only gross consciousness (*sthūla cit*); Śiva, on the other hand is subtle consciousness (*sūkṣma cit*), "who knows by Himself and knows all without experiencing, for this reason that is, without identification." "It is therefore that Śiva is revelatory (*upadeṣṭṛ*) to the recipient self (*upadeśin*). It is like what light is – external light or light of the soul in relation to sight."[28] Self attains to *pati jñāna* or knowledge of Śiva at the self-disclosure of *pati*, Śiva, the Lord. Thus, the self has the paradoxical nature of being neither *sat* nor *asat* but being in a sense both, *sat-asat*. This notion of self as *sat-asat* "rescues the appearances and saves phenomena on one hand and also makes the spiritual realisation of union with Śiva possible as an experience."[29] It is because self is a knower (*pramātṛ*), that its attainment to liberating knowledge, *pati-jñāna* is a possibility. The imparting of *upadeśa* may vary according to the spiritual maturity of the soul, which has to be 'shown' so that it may know that it is true. This is the descent of grace or *śaktinipāta* when Śiva appears in the guise of a preceptor (*sadguru*) who vouchsafes to the self this true vision of Himself. "The last feature of the self's becoming what it experiences, explains why even after disassociation from *pāśa*, *paśutva* still lingers in the form of 'me' and 'mine' against which the only available means of *sādhana* again consists of conscious meditation upon identification with *pati* by '*Śivo'ham*' *bhāvanā* and *nididhyāsana* culminating in the recovery of self by integration with Śiva (*śiva-yoga*) and transcendent Enjoyment of Śiva (*śiva-bhoga*)."[30]

---

[28] K. Sivaraman, op. cit., pp. 375–79.

[29] Ibid.

[30] Ibid.

As pointed out earlier, Śaiva Siddhānta is in accord with the Upanishadic dictum "Through knowledge only is release." The phases of *jñāna* contain the stages of hearing (*śravaṇa*), reflection (*manana*) and contemplation (*nididhyāsana*). This is in respect of *paśu, pāśa* and *pati*. Emancipating knowledge or *pati-jñāna* is integral intuition of the truth of existence at its source, which entails freedom of the self from the finitude, from the thraldom of bondage which is preoccupation with the phenomenal existence — body, senses, world and worldly goods. *Paśu-jñāna* encompasses the divide of subject and object. Its intuition of itself as ever in inseparable union with Śiva follows Śiva's revelation of Himself, when the light of the Divine rends the veil of obscurity. Thus *pati-jñāna* (that effects dissipation of *pāśa* (*pāśa-kṣaya*) is non-empirical and intuitive and grows into the ineffable *śivānubhava*.[31] But there can be no knowledge of the Lord (*pati*) without the knowledge of and insight into the other two, viz. *paśu* and *pāśa*. The three interact to result in the final transcendent experience of Śiva. In the knowledge of each of the three, there are three progressive stages of:

(a) *Rūpa* — which is *prima facie* definition (*lakṣaṇa*) of things whose purpose is to differentiate and designate;

(b) *Darśana* — the metaphysical reason and insight, self-critical with discrimination between the real and the appearance, yet, not integral knowledge;

(c) *Śuddhi* — Consummatory knowledge, direct, immediate and intuitive, undistorted by impediments of impurity — an awareness above knowledge.[32]

These three stages of knowledge of the three ultimates, of

---

[31] K. Sivaraman, op. cit., pp. 380-81.

[32] Ibid., pp. 371–75.

pati, *paśu* and *pāśa*, together with their culmination in the recovery of self in the transcendent enjoyment of Śiva, constitute what are known as *daśa kāryāṇi* or ten actions or functions of spiritual life: *tattvarūpa, tattvadarśana, tattvaśuddhi*; *ātmarūpa, ātmadarśana* and *ātmaśuddhi*; *śiva-rūpa* and *śiva-darśana, śiva-yoga* and *śiva-bhoga*. They are stages of knowledge covering the entire spiritual journey from self's unquestioned 'oneness' with *tattvas* (*tattvarūpa*) to the all-embracing experience of the Plenum (*śiva-bhoga*). The first eight of *daśakāryāṇi* constitute the means (*sādhana*) and the last two the fruit or result (*phala*).[33] Whilst *darśana* is illuminative insight, *śuddhi* is freedom.[34] Obviously, there could be no *śiva-śuddhi*, but only *śiva-yoga*, which is integral union with Śiva.

Tattva-rūpa and *tattva-darśana* go with *ātma-rūpa*.[35] From the prima facie understanding of *tattvas* (*tattva-rūpa*), self graduates to the discriminative philosophical wisdom (*tattva-darśana*) when it realises their character as objective and mutable (*asat*) and non-intelligent (*acit*).[36] This follows in the wake of *ātma-rūpa*, the perception that self is neither *sat* nor *asat* but what comprehends both as such.

There is a coincidence between the next three of *daśa kāryāṇi*, namely *śiva-rūpa, ātma-darśana* and *tattva-śuddhi*.[37] *Ātma-darśana* follows in the wake of *śiva-rūpa* perception of Śiva in the guise of the preceptor (*sadguru*), who vouchsafes the true vision. Also as a corollary to this *Śiva-rūpa-ātma-darśana*, there follows *tattvaśuddhi* which means real freedom from *tattvas* i.e., freedom from unquestioned identification with *tattvas* with the sense of 'I' and 'mine'. This *śuddhi* or freedom is the consequence of a felt disil-

---

[33] K. Sivaraman, op. cit., pp. 371–75.

[34] Ibid., pp. 380-81.

[35] Ibid.

[36] Ibid., pp. 375–79.

[37] Ibid., pp. 396–99.

lusionment of their 'reality' through the inculcation of the preceptor.[38]

"With the advent of the preceptor-given knowledge, the gross manifestation of *pāśa* in the form of *tattvas* ceases to obtrude."[39] But the complete dissipation of *pāśa* (*pāśakṣaya*) is yet to be attained. "Even after *tattva-śuddhi*, the root *mala* still remains as is evident from the dogging illusion of 'I' or selfhood which now after dissociation from the not-self assumes prominence. Through *tattva-śuddhi*, one is led beyond *tattvas* to self (*ātma-darśana*), which now appears to be foundational. There is no freedom from *paśutva* till one intuits the truly foundational *jñeya* Reality. Self emptying (*ātma-śuddhi*) should supervene on gaining insight into self's reality."[40] The three-fold *sādhana* for *ātma-śuddhi* which goes together with *śiva-darśana*, comprises of '*Śivo'ham*' *bhāvanā*, recital of *śrī pañcākṣara* and *antaryāga pūjā*. In the last of the three, Śiva is contemplated as 'dancing' in the sanctuary of one's being in the heart lotus in a form made of the five letters of *pañcākṣara*. Thus *bhāvanā* — meditation, *mantra* — recitation and *kriyā* — action, harnessing mind, feeling and will, as thought, speech and action towards the same goal, namely *ātma-śuddhi*, prepare it for *śiva-yoga* — *śiva-bhoga*.[41]

'*Śivo'ham*' *bhāvanā* is contemplation of self on its true identity with *pati*. It helps it to stand integrated in union with God, as 'one' with His Being. The contemplation of the absoluteness of Śiva-Śakti and of self's inconsequential reality, which is implied in *śrī pañcākṣara* recital brings about total surrender, giving up one's own will. Thus in *śiva-yoga* (integral union with Śiva), through a union of being, freedom from lingering effects of *mala* potent with seeds of duality is

---

[38] K. Sivaraman, op. cit., pp. 380–81.
[39] Ibid., pp. 405–11.
[40] Ibid.
[41] Ibid., pp. 399–404.

achieved, whilst through union of will, freedom from residual effects of *māyīya* and *kārma* is attained.[42]

It is however to be noted that both in *ātma-darśana*, self's insight about its reality in contrast with not-self, and in '*Śivo'ham*' *bhāvanā* (Śiva is 'I'), *paśutva* still endures although imperceptibly with seeds of duality.[43] The self recovers its ultimate reality by totally surrendering its egoity through its encounter with God.[44]

In *śiva-rūpa*, Śiva by the application of His *kriyā-śakti* sets at naught the sum total of stored up *karma* of the past (*sañcita*), together with its material locus of the form of *adhvan*, which 'house' the *karma*, namely *māyīya*. This is done symbolically in the act of *nirvāṇa-dīkṣā* by the *guru*, the main feature of which is *adhva-śuddhi*. The self freed from the weight of *kārma* and *māyīya* is qualified for the dawn of *jñāna*.[45]

"In *śiva-darśana* by the application of His *jñāna-śakti*, Śiva dispels the prime evil of *mala* which has been limiting the self's potentialities from eternity and reduces to naught in advance the fresh influx of *karma* due to self's present earthly life, *āgāmin*."[46] That part of *karma* which has already begun to bear fruit and has caused the present embodiment, *prārabdha*, is destroyed only by experience."[47]

"In *śiva-rūpa* there is freedom from not self (*tattva-śuddhi*). In *śiva-darśana* is achieved freedom from assertion of self-being (*ātma-śuddhi*). In *śiva-yoga* is attained freedom from the root source of 'me' and 'mine', which outlasts all efforts of relinquishing self-assertion and persists by the very

[42] K. Sivaraman, op. cit., pp. 405–11.
[43] Ibid.
[44] Ibid.
[45] Ibid., pp. 382–88.
[46] Ibid., pp. 405–11.
[47] Ibid.

act of discriminating self from not-self, This leads to the freedom of *śiva-bhoga.*"[48]

It further grows into the Bliss of unitive life, *śivatva* or *śiva-bhoga.* In *śiva-yoga* there is only a foretaste of Bliss (*sukhaprabhā*), a negative consequence of the dissolution of *paśutva.* In *śiva-bhoga* is the positive experience of Supreme Bliss (*parama-sukha*) of the self-being flooded with *śiva-ānanda.*[49] *Śiva-yoga* is the twilight. *Śiva-bhoga* is the dawn. *Śiva-yoga* marks the fourth or *turīya* with reference to the three other states of *sakala, kevala* and *śuddha.* The *śiva-bhoga* is *turīyātīta*, 'beyond the beyond' i.e., transcendental.[50] The former is a stage of Advaitic relation with *Śakti* whereas the latter (*śiva-bhoga*) is the ensuing Advaitic experience of *śivatva* when *śakti* sinks into Śiva.[51] Saint Pattinattar expounds it clearly in his definition of *niṣṭhā* as :

The beauteous Kacchi Ekampan affirmed:

> One should do away with and run away from
> Delusive friends and woman — the deathless
> *mala.*
> Then should one accompany the Mother who is
> true Grace,
> And then be oned with the Father — now totally
> oblivious even
> Of the Mother who led unto Him. This indeed is
> *niṣṭhā.*
>
> Saint Pattinathar, v.10
> *Thiruvekambamalai*[52]

This is *śiva-bhoga* which is the transcendent experience. In it the self has an unbroken and immediate inward self-intuitive

[48] K. Sivaraman, op. cit., pp. 405–11.
[49] Ibid., pp. 412–18.
[50] Ibid.
[51] Ibid., pp. 399–404.

awareness of unity of being with Śiva as *jñāna*; perpetual dedication towards Śiva, the transcendent 'I' in the self, as *kriyā*; and ecstatic love for the Indwelling Person within its own personal being, growing from fullness to fullness as *icchā*. Thus *śiva-bhoga* is a mystical, 'face to face' experience of reality in terms of an encounter ever-renewed and eternally new.[53]

The attainment of *śivatva* is understood as complete mergence of being in Śiva, in the idealist school of Śaivism known as Kashmir Śaivism. But, in Śaiva Siddhānta, it is a realization of an identity of an essence in spite of difference in existence. When the scriptures teach non-duality (*advaita*), they do not mean to deny the existence of the two, but the duality of the two. They say 'they are not two' — and not 'there are not two.'[54] *Advaita* does not mean non-difference but only non-separatedness from God. The soul after release still continues to exist as soul without merging into Śiva. The soul now enjoys its nature which is *śivatva* or *śiva-bhoga*. The released soul enjoying the nature of God as its own, delights in being a devoted servant of God. The soul has this transcendent experience of the Bliss of Śiva, when the obscuring powers of the *mala* are neutralized and rendered impotent. *Mala* continues to exist but without the sting of its veiling power. The nature of *mala* in the *pāśa* and that of *paśu* as *sat-asat* make for self's transcendent experience in *śiva-bhoga* in which Śiva 'experiences' Himself so that the self may experience Him. This is the feature of the 'existential' root of Śaiva Siddhānta doctrine of the 'eternity of the three in *mukti* too.'[55]

A mere righteous life of *dharma*, of desire-prompted action and enjoyment with its implication of attachment and

---

[53]K. Sivaraman, op. cit., pp. 412–18.
[54]S.S. Suryanarayana Sastri, op. cit., pp. 295–96.
[55]Ibid., pp. 412–18.

passions and of the egocentrism implicit in them does not bring about by its own momentum the development of the spiritual qualities essential for *jñāna*, such as equanimity of mind and surrender to God. Performance of daily, special and optional duties make for a high level in the life of action, but it still comes within *paśu-puṇya*, or merit which is also a bondage, though with golden fetters. On the other hand, action consecrated totally to Śiva is *śiva-puṇya*. "Even worldly deeds can be in this manner transmuted into *śiva-puṇya*. Thus even in the very midst of the flux of kārmic life, of action and reward, is to be found the clue for eventually transcending the natural law of deed and consequence." The *tirodhāna śakti* of the Lord not only provides for the soul a life of action with ego-drive which makes for bondage, but also leads to its release through a spiritual life of *śiva-puṇya*. Above the vocation of duty comes that of doing service to Śiva and the fourfold scheme of *śiva-dharma* of *caryā, kriyā, yoga* and *jñāna* is the *sādhana* for the progressive un-doing of the sense of egoism by conscious surrender of all actions to the Lord.[56]

Caryā is the first stage of external worship of images and rituals and service such as cleaning the temple and gathering of flowers etc. God here assumes a grossly visible form (*sakala*). The action resembles those of a devoted servant to the master. It is *dāsa-mārga* leading to *sālokya*, residence in the realm of God. The next stage is *kriyā* where the modes of worship are inward as well as outward as in recitals of prayers, meditation and fire rites. God is in visible-cum-non-visible form (*sakala-niṣkala*) and the devotion here is akin to that of a son to his father. The son serves the father overtly and spontaneously and with inward allegiance. This is *satputra-mārga* and the objective is *sāmīpya* or nearness to God. The third discipline is *yoga* which means union and here signifies

[56]S.S. Suryanarayana Sastri, op. cit., pp. 389–94.

contemplation and inner worship. In this stage God is non-visible (*niṣkala*) and the path is *sakhā-mārga* in which the *sādhaka* is the 'friend' of God. It leads to *sārūpya*, gaining the form of God.[57]

These three stages of *sādhana* imply progressive revelation of God (*tirodhāna śakti*) by a steady undoing of the veiling powers of *mala* which hides self's vision of the Real. The self is now led to the final stage of *jñāna*. It is the *sanmārga* (the Right Path) because it takes the soul straight to *sat* which is God. Devotion in this stage is typified in the self-surrendering love between a lover and his beloved. The fruit is the ultimate human good, *sāyujya* or union with God.[58] The path of *jñāna* with hearing (*śravaṇa*), reflection (*manana*) and contemplation (*nididhyāsana*) and the culminating experience (*niṣṭhā* or *samādhi*) has been detailed earlier, with its further classification into *deśakāryas* culminating in *śiva-yoga* and *śiva-bhoga.*

By long experience of the cycle of birth and death, the soul learns "to equate empirical good and evil, realizing the one as fleeting and intrinsically worthless as the other and becomes indifferent to the acquisition of good *karma* as well as bad."[59] It thus attains a tranquil frame of mind disinclined alike towards so-called merit and demerit. This is *karma sāmya.* The stage is now set for the release of the soul. Such a person is now inimical to the active operation of the veiling power of *mala.* The hold of *mala* reflected in the soul's inveterate impulse for exteriorisation and entanglement in the phenomena has now been slackened.[60] With the soul's disillusionment about world experience, "the *mala* that so long obscured and hindered is now ripe and fit for the Divine surgeon's knife."[61]

---

[57] S.S. Suryanarayana Sastri, op. cit., pp. 389–94.
[58] Ibid.
[59] Ibid., pp. 295–96.
[60] Ibid.
[61] Ibid.

The grace that was operating by veiling, as it were, with the veil of *mala* till now (namely *tirodhāna śakti*) has now become transfigured into the grace that reveals (*anugraha śakti*). The soul now seeks the omniscience which is its own nature and birth-right. This is the on-set of Divine grace, *śaktinipāta*.[62] It is quick or slow depending upon the capacities and the *sādhana* of the soul. When the grace has fully set in, the Lord reveals Himself and instructs the soul. To the *vijñānākalas* (with *āṇava mala* only), He reveals Himself as their own Inner Light; to the *pralayākalas* (with *āṇava* and *māyā malas*) in a divine supernatural form; and to the *sakalas* (with all the three *malas* of *āṇava, karma* and *māyā*) as a preceptor apparently like one among themselves and gives them the *dīkṣā* or initiation.[63]

Dīkṣā — Initiation

Dīkṣā is the divine act of initiation. The word implies a gift (*dāna*) and a loss (*kṣaya*) — gift of knowledge and loss of bond of *mala*. "It secures the destruction of *pāśa* and attainment of *mukti* which is union with Śiva." It is a manifestation of *Śakti*, the power of Śiva (*śivasya vyāpakātmaka śaktiḥ*). It enables the *sādhaka* with the least powerful descent of grace to discharge his daily, special and optional duties enjoined in the Āgama and hear the revealed Word. To the aspirant with most powerful descent of grace, it is the immediate means of *mokṣa* qualifying him for directly receiving *jñāna*.[64]

Of the three well-known initiations, *samaya dīkṣā* confers fitness to enter a life of ritual (*śaivācāra* or *caryā*); and *viśeṣa dīkṣā* to practise *kriyā* and *yoga*. The third initiation, *nirvāṇa dīkṣā*, qualifies one for directly receiving *jñāna* and is therefore considered the immediate means of *mokṣa*.[65]

[62] S.S. Suryanarayana Sastri, op. cit., pp. 395–96.
[63] Ibid.
[64] Ibid., pp. 382–88.
[65] Ibid.

The various commentators on the concerned scriptural texts differ in their classification of types of *dīkṣās*. *Dīkṣā* when it involves *homa* or fire rites is called *hautrī* or *aṅgī* (with parts). When *homa* is done actually it is known as *kriyā hautrī*. The other in which the *homa* is performed mentally by *bhāvanā* it is *jñāna hautrī*. In it the preceptor mentally enters the body of the disciple, considers his *nābhi-sthāna* (navel) as the *kuṇḍa* (pit for fireplace) containing *śivāgni* and performs by *bhāvanā* the *homa* to purify the six *adhvas*.

Hautrī dīkṣā is unique and includes other *dīkṣās* as its parts. Such ancillary *dīkṣās* are of six kinds: *nayana* (look); *sparśa* (touch); *vācaka* (words, i.e. initiation into the *pañcākṣara*); *mānasika* (mental); *śāstra* (scriptural study of Śaivāgamas and Śaiva Siddhānta); and *yoga* (practice of *nirādhāra śiva-yoga*). These subsidiary initiations only without the fire rites of *hautrī* will constitute partial initiation or *aṅga dīkṣā*.

Nayana dīkṣā is of three kinds:

> (i) *Śṛṅgāra* — in which the preceptor is like one who had achieved identity with *Garuḍa* by yogic powers, as a result of chanting the *mantra*, and treats a person bitten by snake by looking at him and drawing off the poison, bathing him in *amṛtakalā* by identification with the moon, to remove the fatigue.
>
> (ii) *Nigraha-avalokana* — in which the *guru* destroys the disciple's identification with *pāśa* by his gaze through which his own consciousness is merged with that of the disciple.
>
> (iii) *Anugraha-avalokana* — in which the preceptor's look is that of grace for the spiritual well-being of the recipient soul.[66]

[66] V.A. Devasenapathi, *Śaiva Siddhānta*, University of Madras, 1974, pp. 238–41.

In *sparśa dīkṣā*, the preceptor performs certain rites by touch to remove the pupil's bondage and to make him like Śiva, just as base metals are transmuted into gold by the proverbial touch of the philosopher's stone.

In *mānasa dīkṣā*, the *guru*, starting from his own outgoing breath (*recaka*) and through the incoming breath (*pūraka*) of the disciple and his *suṣumṇā nāḍī*, reaches his heart centre and raises his awareness to the *jñānāgni* (fire of knowledge) in his *dvādaśānta* (twelfth abode) in the head. The preceptor contemplates in his own heart on the disciple's consciousness being pervaded by that of Śiva, like salt being dissolved in water, and reinstates it in the *kuṇḍali-sthāna* of his body.[67]

Those who are eligible and are able to perform *nitya, naimittika* and *kāmya karma* daily, special and optional rites, are initiated to them by *sādhikāra dīkṣā*. Others are given *nirādhikāra dīkṣā*.

When the *mantra* includes a *bījākṣara*, it is *sabīja dīkṣā*; otherwise it is *nirbīja*.

Samaya and *viśeṣa dīkṣās* are both *nirādhikāra* and *nirbīja*.

In *dīkṣā*, a spiritual purification is achieved, issuing in the dawn of knowledge. The main feature of *nirvāṇa dīkṣā* is *adhva-śuddhi*. In it, the *adhvan* representing the *mantra, pada, varṇa, bhuvana, tattva* and *kalā* are purified by the progressive merging of the gross into the next less gross by *kriyā-śakti*. Then the stored up or *sañcita karma* together with its material locus (*māyīya*) is set at naught and the soul is freed from their burden. Then he is initiated into *mukti pañcākṣara* and *jñāna pada* of Śaiva Āgamas.

When the *nirvāṇa dīkṣā* results in immediate release, it is called *sadyo-nirvāṇa*. In the *asadyo nirvāṇa dīkṣā*, the release comes after death.

When *sabīja nirvāṇa dīkṣā* is given to householders, it

---

[67] Sivagnana Yogin's *Mapadiyam*, Sirappuppayiram, pp. 18–27.

is called *lokadharmiṇī* or *bhautika*. The same when given to those who are leading a life of celibacy and renunciation is called *śivadharmiṇī* or *naiṣṭhika* when the tuft of hair is removed (the head is tonsured). This is an immediate prelude to *saṃnyāsa dīkṣā*.

Saṃnyāsa

Śaiva Siddhānta, like Advaita Vedānta, holds that the path of knowledge is *sādhana par excellence* and is the true path (*sanmārga*) and *karma, dīkṣā, bhakti* etc., which are indeed well recognized spiritual disciplines are the other *sādhanas* in the secondary sense which lead to *jñāna*.[68] Yet in Śaiva Siddhānta we do not find the same affirmation as in Śaṅkara Advaita that *karma* is totally incompatible with knowledge and there should be total renunciation or *saṃnyāsa* of all *karma* as a prelude to *jñāna-niṣṭhā*. We do not find here the insistence that one should take to *śravaṇa* or hearing only after being initiated into *saṃnyāsa*. This can be well understood, as Śaiva Siddhānta is a theistic school where worship of God finds an important place till the end of *sādhana* and the liberated soul also continues to be a devoted servant of God. Hence *upāsanā* with *bhāvanā* of '*Śivo'ham*' and recitation of *mukti pañcākṣara* are prescribed in the life of a *saṃnyāsin* also. This worship is however internal. This *pūjā* is *jñāna pūjā* and *antaryāga pūjā* (internal worship). Although God is the 'wholly other', He is yet one with the soul at the same time and we can worship Him in the sanctum of the heart.[69]

Yet, we find the phenomenon of *saṃnyāsa* well pronounced in the Śaiva Siddhānta tradition also, as it is itself the fundamental characteristic of the Hindu approach to the Divine Reality. As the means to the ultimate value to be cherished in human life or *parama puruṣārtha*, which is

---

[68] Sivajnana Yogin's *Mapadiyam*, Sirappuppayiram, pp. 380–81.
[69] Ibid., pp. 399–404.

mokṣa, saṃnyāsa finds the most respected place in the fourfold scheme of life or *āśrama.* It is called fourth in relation to the earlier three *āśramas* (stations of life) of student, householder and forest-dweller. Although *saṃnyāsa* may seem to be the culmination of the first three, it is still a total break from them and complete transformation, as a ball turned inside out — indeed a rebirth in spirit, as the initiation itself implies when the *sādhaka* takes the *dīkṣā* clad in space as though born anew and assumes a new name which indicates total absorption in the Divine. It takes him beyond all *dharmas*, ethical and religious duties. He has now conquered the natural impulse of externalization and entanglement in phenomena. He has declared the fundamental necessity of leaving the world and all the creatures in embarking on a total interior life. He has realized the transitoriness of all things finite and for him even the celestial worlds are included among the relative phenomena which are fleeting in nature. He has also understood in the depth of his heart, the truth of the Upaniṣadic dictum "By renunciation, thou shalt enjoy!"[70] We can enjoy true liberty only in respect of all such things as we neither possess nor desire. It is the ascent of Mount Carmel:[71]

> That thou mayest have pleasure in everything,
> seek pleasure in nothing.
> That thou mayest know everything, seek to know
> nothing.
> That thou mayest possess all things, seek to possess nothing.

"In detachment, he finds quiet and repose. He covets nothing. Nothing wearies him by elation and nothing oppresses him

[70] *Īśāvāsya Upaniṣad*, Mantra 1.
[71] John of the Cross.

by dejection because he stands in the centre of his own humility."[72]

The poverty of a monk is true self-stripping and casting off of all wealth, material and immaterial. It is a complete detachment from all finite things. Chastity is "the extreme and limpid purity of the soul, cleansed from all personal desire and virgin to all but God." Obedience is the abnegation of self-hood and mortification of the will which result in a complete self-abandonment, a "holy indifference to the accidents of life".[73] These are *karma sāmya* and *malaparipāka* (ripening of the *mala*) which bring with them the descent of grace, *śaktinipāta*. *Saṃnyāsa* is a departure from the worldly round, to delight in solitude, steeped in the thought of God and living in the Eternal Now, dead to the past, indifferent to the present and least of all worried about the future. The irresistable inner urge, the inner awakening frees the *saṃnyāsī* from all duties. *Saṃnyāsa* overtakes him and it is immaterial whether he has been given the formal external *dīkṣā* or not, or whether he carries the insignia or not. We find in the lives of saints such a sudden and total transformation on the descent of grace.

Besides such spiritual geniuses, Śaiva Siddhānta provides for initiation into *saṃnyāsa* for qualified aspirants. It is the commencement of preparation for a mystic life which is also the result of descent of grace although of lesser intensity. The *guru* puts the disciple through a very tough period of trial and probation and after finding him fit for *saṃnyāsa* confers it on him at an appropriate time chosen intuitively with the guidance of the Divine grace. In Hinduism, such conferment of *saṃnyāsa* is done with great care as it is the path of no return and it is only when there is a break of *karma*, that one

---

[72] Evelyn Underhill, *Mysticism*, E.P. Dutton & Co., Paperback edn. 1961, pp. 205–206.

[73] Ibid.

receives such *saṃnyāsa dīkṣā.*

The initiation into *saṃnyāsa* follows *nirvāṇa dīkṣā* which is *jñāna dīkṣā.* Its aim is attainment of *paramokṣa* which is beyond the other lower levels of *mukti* such as *sālokya, sāmīpya* and *sārūpya* which are attained through *caryā, kriyā* and *yoga* respectively. The discrimination between these lower levels of *mukti* and the higher *paramukti* and hankering after the latter are themselves indicative of a very highly spiritually advanced nature in the aspirant receiving *saṃnyāsa dīkṣā.*

The Āgamas speak of three types of *saṃnyāsins: tapasvī, vividiṣu* and *vidvān*[74].

Tapasvī is devoted to his own *tapas* or contemplation of Śiva. He has nothing to study, no scriptures to hear and resolve to fulfil. He does not let other people know his depth of knowledge. Nor does he gather disciples. He may not even carry *daṇḍa* or *kamaṇḍalu* or for that matter any other insignia and may not even reveal his knowledge of languages. Seeking solitude and avoiding the company of men, he may be stayIng in a forest or spending his time underneath a tree.[75]

Vividiṣu is one who 'wants to know' and has been initiated into *saṃnyāsa.* His fourfold activities are study, teaching, hearing of scriptures and contemplation of Śiva.[76]

Vidvān is one who has been specially anointed as *ācārya* and is qualified to initiate others. He is well qualified with knowledge and experience for that purpose.[77]

Śivāgra Yogin, a famous saintly commentator, in his book *Śaiva Saṃnyāsa Paddhati* especially clarifies that apart from the first three castes, those belonging to the fourth are also eligible for initiation into *Saṃnyāsa.* The initiation of the former is the same as in *Vaidika* tradition with the prelim-

[74]Śivāgra Yogin's *Śaiva Saṃnyāsa Paddhati.*

[75]Ibid.

[76]Ibid.

[77]Ibid.

inaries of *jīva śrāddha*, tonsure etc. and the pronouncement or *uccāraṇa* of *praiṣa mantra* which is renunciation of all the three worlds of *bhūḥ, bhuvaḥ* and *suvaḥ*. In the case of the fourth caste, instead of *praiṣa mantra*, the initiate repeats five times in increasingly louder voice the *śloka* in which he declares his renunciation of all, father, mother, son, wife and everything, except Śiva alone. Śivāgra Yogin's manual on *saṃnyāsa* gives complete details of the rituals connected with initiation, *bhikṣā, śravaṇa* etc. After giving a detailed account of *samaya, viśeṣa* and *nirvāṇa dīkṣās, saṃnyāsa dīkṣā* is described as given to those leading a celibate life and already initiated into *nirvāṇa dīkṣā* as a means of attaining *paramokṣa*.

The famous sage Tirumular's *Tirumandiram*, which is the tenth book in Śaivaite canonical literature, devotes a section to renunciation. He says that *saṃnyāsa* is the result of *śaktinipāta* on the soul's attainment of *karma sāmya* and *mala-paripāka*. To such a *saṃnyāsin*, Śiva reveals Himself, and the Lord is his sole friend and refuge. Tirumular stresses the necessity for the *saṃnyāsin* to strictly abide by the monastic code and be eternally vigilant and extremely persevering, in accordance with the instructions of his *guru*. The reference seems to be both to the enlightened ones and also to those on the path amongst *saṃnyāsins*. Only those who have completely conquered *vāsanā mala* and the challenge of phenomena and have overcome ignorance and transcended time, attain to union with Śiva. *Saṃnyāsa* is the total conquest of senses and channelizing of all the energies Godward. He concludes the section with a reference to the awakening of *kuṇḍalinī* and rising to *sahasrāra* and the beatific vision of *paraśiva*.

Saint Tiruvalluvar in his *Tirukkural* praises the greatness of renunciates in ten couplets. To the minds of Śaivites, Saint Pattinathar symbolizes the highest watermark of *vairāgya*.

His Psalms on the transitory nature of all human relationships and worldly goods are most popular and inspiring.

> Neither place nor kin will last;
> Neither wives nor hard-earned name will last;
> Neither children nor honours will last;
> So too, wealth will not;
> None in this world will last; Your feet alone
> Are everlasting, Oh Kacchi Ekampa!
>
> St. Pattinathar, v.13,
> *Tiruvekampamalai*[78]

His definition of *saṃnyāsa* is one of the most exacting descriptions to which every *mumukṣu* should aspire to live up to:

> The renouncer of domestic life is a million times
> Greater than he who is poised in household *dharma*;
> Than even he, is the one who is a renunciate at heart
> Ten million times greater.
> How can I articulate, O Kacchi Ekampa, the glory
> Of him who by his study and knowledge had quelled all *adharma*
> And lives dead to the world, rid of twofold *karma* and *vāsanās*?
>
> St. Pattinathar, v.1,
> *Tiruvekampamalai*[79]

He equates the true *saṃnyāsin* to a *jñānī* and describes him in the following words:

---

[78] St. Pattinathar, Eng. trans. by T.N. Ramachandran, International Institute of Śaiva Siddhānta Research, 1990, pp. 17–21, 58–59.

[79] Ibid.

> They roam (in forbidden places) like a ghoul,
> Lie like a carcass, like a dog eat alms when given
> And wander like a fox anywhere.
> They deem good women as mother and speak
> to all,
> As they would to their kin, with humility
> And are like babes.
> Behold them, the true and clarified *jñānis*!
>
> St. Pattinathar, v.35,
> *Podhu* (General)[80]

His description of the freedom in which the *saṃnyāsin* moves about is equally inspiring. One is reminded of the Buddhistic texts in which the monk is compared to the rhinoceros.

An extremely interesting and famous *sādhana* manual is *Ozhivil Odukkam* by Sirkazhi Kannudaiya Vallal. The theme of the book is obvious from the title itself, which means 'quietitude in retirement'. One full chapter is devoted to *vairāgya* and another to *saṃnyāsa*. He says that pure *saṃnyāsa* is a stage of *ātma-śuddhi* attained through *ātma-darśana* and *ātma-rūpa*. *Saṃnyāsa* is the result of *śaktinipāta*. He particularly emphasizes the need for external *saṃnyāsa*. He also holds that the external and internal aspects of *sannyāsa* mutually supplement each other.

Silence: Beyond Duality and Non-duality

Saint Tayumanavar lived in Tamil Nadu about two hundred years ago. His Psalms have a rare metrical beauty and melody and bear the unmistakable stamp of his direct experience of God. The mystic poet's spiritual experience hinges on the 'One Word' spoken to him in secret by his *guru* whom he calls '*mauna guru*' or 'the silent teacher' or, 'the teacher of

[80] St. Pattinathar, op cit, pp. 17–21, 58–59.

Silence'. It is the injunction '*Be still*'. Thus he "bade him to be still in a state of selflessness", Tayumanavar says: "He with one word with grace prevenient, made me his own and made me live by love". By perseverence in this way of Silence and with total surrender to God and *guru* implied in the one Word, he attained to the bliss of union with God.

There is an apparent difference between Vedānta and Śaiva Siddhānta. In the former, the soul, being non-different from God in its essential nature, merges with Him. In the latter, the soul is distinct, eternal in its nature with a *mala* or impurity of *āṇava.* Hence after union with God, the soul still retains its individuality with the veiling power of *āṇava* neutralized. Thus, the soul has an experience of its union with God Śiva and His transcendental Bliss. Tayumanavar in his Psalms refers to '*Vedānta Siddhānta Samarasa*', an eclectic harmonizing of the two. He speaks of 'the godly *samarasa* which consists in an affirmation of neither oneness or twoness' in the great silence. These words remind us of a line in a minor work (*Prakaraṇa Grantha*) of Śaṅkara, *Prauḍhānubhūti* (the Great Experience): 'In the *samarasa* devoid of duality and non-duality, silence is best accepted.'[81] '*Samarasa*' means reconciliation or harmony. By *sama* is also meant *Brahman* and by *rasa* the Impartite Awareness. It is to be clearly understood that this *Vedānta Siddhānta Samarasa* is not yet another doctrine of philosophy. Neither is it a mere academic acquiescence or syncretism. Tayumanavar calls it '*Mauna samarasa* which is above all creeds'. It is the highest experience of mystic Silence, which is beyond all mentation. It is the final leap at the culmination of incessant *sādhana* or spiritual endeavour and total renunciation (*saṃnyāsa*), in a tradition which leads beyond itself in the experience of the transcendence.[82]

---

[81] *Dvaita-advaita-vivarjite samarase maunaṃ paraṃ sammatam.*

[82] T. Isaac Tambyah, *Psalms of a Śaiva Saint*, Asian Educational Ser-

Elsewhere Tayumanavar identifies *Vedānta Siddhānta Samarasa* as total and complete surrender. He says: "Always, my deeds are Your deeds. I am non-different from you, as my being as 'I' cannot be apart or without you. The nature (*svabhāva*) of *Vedānta Siddhānta Samarasa* is just this."[83]

I may conclude with a few readings from psalms of Tayumanavar rendered as free translations into English:
On the impermanence of worldly goods and relationships:

> Father, mother, wife, child, kinsmen, all these are but people gathered at a fair — of this there is no doubt. Palaces, armies of cavalry, infantry, elephants and chariots, all this pomp and splendour, are just a juggler's show. This body, full of filth, is further afflicted by the parasites of deceit, envy and miserliness by devastating the mind. Why then is it that I have not cultivated desirelessness and a conviction that everyday that passes is equal, but continue to be caught up in the swirling vortex of the turbulent mind, unmindful of the veritable flood of your grace that is waiting to cleanse and devour me?
>
> Oh Lord, who art enthroned in my heart as pure consciousness (which knows no dawn or setting) and as plenum of existence (*sat*), hard to seek and intuit! Oh Glory of Light and Bliss!
>
> *Tejomayanandam* 3

He hails God as Turīya, the Great Silence:

> Countless are the lands of my birth, countless my names assumed, countless the kinsmen, countless the bodies I have borne as the fruits of my

vices, 1985, pp. 107–13.

[83] T. Isaac Tambyah, op. cit., pp. 107–13.

deeds, countless the actions performed, countless the thoughts, countless the fame and prosperity enjoyed, countless too the heaven and hell I have passed through, countless are the good gods, countless the differing religious creeds — wherefore, realizing by the *jñāna cit śakti* (energy of consciousness of awareness), I bow in obeisance to God, who like the myriad clouds together, pours the rain of ineffable Bliss, filling the eyes of the beloved ones and the skies. To the form of *turīya*, the Great Silence, the treasure *par excellence*, called by the Vedas by countless names and described by them in countless ways, to this great Being, which is *jñāna*, the Awareness and *ānanda*, the unsurpassed and Infinite Bliss — I offer my obeisance!

Para Śiva Vanakkam 2

That which is the limitless expanse; the source of the five elements; where prevails the Great Silence that speaks not; that which is the Transcendent Bliss beyond the reach of the mind; that which is revealed by the Grace of the *jñāna guru*; which draws to Itself and 'swallows' the devoted; and, that, when it blends with all things (and bears names and forms), which is difficult to discern — on That we meditate!

Porul Vanakkam 3

Away with impure desire! Seek mokṣa!

When all thoughts subside in the great stillness, it is called '*aham*'. This state of mindlessness is grace (*arul*). In that interiority of *niṣṭhā*, abides grace. As the finitude of the self is transcended, the state of grace emerges of itself. That is oneness with Bliss. (The soul in that state becomes one with *Śiva*, *Tat.*) There is nothing beyond. They alone who have attained to this beatific state obtain the final release from rebirth. All other desires, as for wife, children and kinsmen, constitute the impure *vāsanās* (latent mental impressions). — Therefore stamp out desires with the help of (*guru*'s *upadeśa* of) the 'one Word'.

Ninaivu Onru 1

Silence, the samarasa (harmony) of Vedānta and Siddhānta:

It was the fullness of Thy grace that drew me to abide in that state of mind which is the Witness, accepting all that happened to me and all that did not befall me; that gave me the intuition to grasp clearly the tradition of *samarasa* (harmony) of Vedānta and Siddhānta; that led me on the path of knowledge which shows the falseness of the body which is not lasting; and to the realization that attainment of Eternal Bliss is the final Liberation; and endowed me with an inner love that runs in profusion like pellucid water.

If you deign to save me who have none else to protect me, I pray that you graciously grant me an unceasing love of the Transcendental Silence, beyond the ken of all the worlds!

O My Lord! Wherever I turn and look, I only see an all-embracing unbroken, full and all-pervading Bliss that is your form!

Paripūrṇāndam 8

The *Vedas, Āgamas, Purāṇas, Itihāsas* and all else mainly proclaim in detail the paths of *advaita* (non-duality) and *dvaita* (duality). The valuable and commendable *dvaita* (dual) is verily the fountainhead of the *advaita* (non-dual) Awareness. This is also in accordance with reason (inference), experience and scriptures and is acceptable to the protagonists of both the systems. Therefore, I have no need any more of the fourfold *sādhana* of *caryā* and the rest. I become that which I meditate on. Therefore, if I meditate on you as my own Self, I shall intuit the non-dual Reality. When you are the Gracious Father who comes to each aspirant in the manner of his seeking, what then is my want?

O My Lord who art the Life of all lives, the *summum bonum* both here and beyond and the all-pervading Reality!

Engum Nirainda Porul 3

The Vedas declare that God and the soul are in essence the same both being in the nature of Consciousness. Phenomenally, they appear as dual entities. In the state of *niṣṭhā* or *samādhi*, which the *Śaivāgamas* speak about, they are non-dual.

Udal Poyyuravu 16

Oh! The final repository of Siddhānta! O Dakṣiṇāmūrti of Siragiri! The Silent one, that taught me that beyond union and separation, beyond the pairs of opposites, beyond evolution and involution, beyond the *guṇas* of *prakṛti*, beyond death and birth, beyond the fixed symbol, beyond impurity, beyond seeking, beyond the spatial directions of above, below, middle or beside; beyond *bindu*, beyond *nāda* and beyond the five-fold differentiation of elements; beyond the empirical knowledge of the knower; beyond sorrow; beyond one (non-duality) and two (duality); beyond the word and beyond the mind — immersed in the Ocean of Infinite Bliss is that effortless transcendental Awareness, beyond one's seeking! You graciously blest me with the subtlest grace and the love of a mother and place both your feet on my head!

You taught me that the objectless Awareness (or *nirvikalpa samādhi*) is the Eternal Tradition; without mentation or chant of *mantra*, without saying that in the state of Liberation there is one or two, without imagining it as light or space or form or *nāda* that is sound, seeing without seeing is the spiritual culture, which yields the greatest Experience, beyond any *sādhanā*. Oh Blessed One! Grant that I may intuit That which you have imparted to me and let me be in the holy company of your illumined devotees!

Chinmayānanda Guru 8, 9

In the Hindu tradition, as also in the Christian tradition, the yearning soul is likened to a bride who rejoices in the Lord, her beloved. In the ballad of spiritual experience called by him as 'A Revel In Bliss' (*Ānanda Kalippu*), Saint Tayumanavar in verses of exquisite beauty and sublimest feeling of love, narrates his own mystic union with God. A few verses are rendered in free English translation:

He who is the Uncreated and Eternal,
Light in me luminous, Awareness and Bliss,
He shone as the silent Teacher, sister,
spoke the unspoken Word in Chinmudrā.
Śaṅkara Śaṅkara Śambhu...

"Sever all attachments within" bade He
"Cling but to me" And Oh! Sister!

I gazed unswerving
At the Source within. How shall I describe
that Experience?
Knowledge unmediated, imparted He to me.
Śaṅkara Śaṅkara Śambhu...

"Manifest and Unmanifest, hitherto cognized
That your mind perceived, all of them, negate"
Said my Lord, sister. Marvel at
His felicity in making me His Self.
Śaṅkara Śaṅkara Śambhu...

Love onto those who love Him, the true One,
My silent Lord, all Bliss and grace incarnate,
Placed His holy feet on my head. Lo! Sister
The mind was dead, I had vision of the Self.
Śaṅkara Śaṅkara Śambhu...

"See God in all with the eyes of grace", said He
Understanding it not, I saw many with senses and
mind,
And darkness was all I beheld. Why was it so,
sister?
The Seer in me I had failed to see.
Śaṅkara Śaṅkara Śambhu...

Lest I deem Him from me separate
'Without duality, be with a still mind'
Blest was I with this only instruction, sister,
Oh! How can words express the Bliss it led me to?
Śaṅkara Śaṅkara Śambhu...

Realizing the state of Bliss of Śiva,
Seeking the Infinite Expanse of Being, casting off
The darkness of Ignorance, sister, I saw nothing
But the Lord's *Cidākāśa*, full of splendour.
Śaṅkara Śaṅkara Śambhu...

There is the birth and beginning of thought;

In Him it dies to be reborn but purer;
Where all the states exist, yea, there I am,
The Seer not seeing a second, there I stand.
Śaṅkara Śaṅkara Śambhu...

Is there any 'here' and 'there'? — When one sees
That Effulgence of Impartite *Sat Cit Ānanda*
Filling and pervading all, the Transcendent Real,
Can we postulate of Him 'One' or 'Two'?
Śaṅkara Śaṅkara Śambhu...

'Yea' and 'Nay' contrasts — do they exist
Oh! Thou seeker of Bliss! stand still and see
The way of knowing the One — not the awarer
but Awareness be.
The goal of the Vedas, sister, He teacheth me!
Śaṅkara Śaṅkara Śambhu...

Saint Tayumanavar, *Ānanda Kalippu*,
vs. 1, 3, 8, 10, 13–15, 20, 21, 30.[84]

---

[84] Based on the English translation of Isaac Tambayah, *Psalms of a Śaiva Saint*, Asian Educational Services, 1985, pp. 107–13.

THE MYSTICISM OF JESUS THE CHRIST

Raimon Panikkar

rabbi . . .
poû meneis,
erchesthe kai opsesthe
Rabbi . . .
ubi manes? . . .
Venite et videbitis
Master . . .
Where do you stay? . . .
Come and see.
Jn I.38–39

I. THE APPROACH

That which was since the Beginning,
which has been heard by us,
which has been seen with our eyes,
which has been looked upon
and touched by our hands:
The Word of Life.
And Life has been manifested,
and we have seen her
and bear witness to her
and announce her to you:
Eternal Life,
which was with the Father
and has been manifested.
I. Jn I.1–2

1. The Occasion

In the preparation for this seminar on Śaiva and Christian mysticism I noticed with astonishment that among the many topics on Christian mysticism the most central paper was lacking: the mysticism of Jesus Christ. Two reasons appeared to me to explain this absence. The one, rather positive; the other somewhat negative.

The positive reason was the parallelism and regime of equality we wanted to maintain. Christianity and Śaivism are two powerful and ancient traditions. We should treat them on an exactly equal footing, avoiding any kind of bias in favour of either tradition. It would be awkward, to say the least, to include a paper on the mysticism of Lord Śiva — in person, as it were. We were directing our attention to the experiences of his disciples.

Similarly, we were focussing our attention also on the mysticism of the disciples of Lord Jesus Christ. But whereas the attempt to speak of the self-consciousness of Śiva makes little sense, the attempt to describe the self-consciousness of Jesus, difficult as it may be, is not altogether out of the question.

We perceive here immediately the need to establish comparisons on a double basis. All too often comparisons have been carried on from one single perspective. The historical aspect of Śiva is irrelevant; not so that of Jesus. Śiva is neither an *avatāra*, nor an incarnation. We are able to speak of a Śaiva mysticism without imposing on Lord Śiva our ideas about mysticism. Śaiva mysticism is the mystical vision that Śaiva believers have had about reality in and through what they believe is Śiva's grace or illumination. Christian mysticism could be said to be something similar. And, in fact, most studies on Christian mysticism take this path. But there can be no doubt that Christian mysticism is directly or indirectly embedded in the personal experience of Christ, both as an objective and a subjective genitive. The homeomorphic equivalent of Christ here is not Śiva but his Śakti.

The negative reason for the absence of such studies may lie in the mostly unconscious Christian 'prejudice' that Jesus Christ is above all others and beyond any comparison, so we do better to leave him out of 'Comparative Mysticism'. We shall know the Master in and through his followers. This is fair enough within the Christian tradition, but our seminar was not a specifically Christian one and we could not *a priori* avoid treating Jesus as, say, Abhinavaguptācārya, for both are certainly historical figures. Jesus should not be a tabu for Christians. They may consider him as God, and one does not make any anthropological, let alone psychological, analysis of the Godhead. It would be absurd to speak of God's mysticism. But he was also a Man, and one ought not avoid trying to study him as one would study any other individual. It has been rightly remarked that "Jesus the preacher of the message became Jesus the preached message."[1] In point of fact, most christologies deal with the message and are based on the impact of Jesus on the first communities.[2]

But can we understand the message without understanding the messenger? We 'hear' what he said. We know how the others understood him. And this may be the reason why in Christian theology, with the exception of the mystics, so little emphasis is put on personal experience. Are we at all allowed, at least in some degree, to re-enact his experience, in order that our understanding will be not just a whimsical subjective perception, but a re-enactment of the original experience? Thus, the rather high sounding title of this study which expands on the paper given at the seminar.

---

[1]McGinn (1991) 63. The same point is made by Swidler (1988): "The teaching Jeshua, not the taught Christ" (p. 10–19).
For bibliographic references see *Bibliography R. Panikkar* in *Appendix* (author's names followed by year of publication).

[2]Cp. Thompson (1985) which honours its subtitle and yet it is centred in 'the Jesus event'.

We have just indicated that the 'Sitz im Leben' of this meditation is not the usual Christian milieu. Traditional Christian theology deals either with the complexities of the Christian religion seeking to understand and formulate its own basic tenets, or it deals with the effort to present Christian beliefs in a manner comprehensible to the secularized post-Christian people of the western or westernized world. A dialogue in depth from within the basic insights of Christianity and Śaivism has hardly taken place up to our times. The Śaiva religions can be called at most a-Christian, but they are neither anti-Christian or post-Christian as the word non-Christian generally suggests.

Being partners in dialogue at this symposium as either Christian or Śaiva believers, and aspiring to understand Christ in this context, the background of the following reflexions should not be that of inner-Christian controversies or that of the usual Christian apologetics. The background is not what I would call the Abrahamic phylum of humanity, but rather the general horizon of the Indic mentality, mainly of Vedāntic spirituality. The first condition for teaching Sanskrit to Gopal is to know Gopal, says an Indic saying. The first condition to make oneself understood is to know your partner. This implies, obviously, to know the context into which the partner is going to insert what one is about to say — in order to understand it. History, past and present, tells us too much of far-reaching misunderstandings caused by not following this elementary rule.[3]

By doing this I do not pretend to indulge in comparative studies. I aim only at being intelligible within a context which is not the Judeo-Christian-Muslim-Marxist-scientist one. And in order to be more concrete, I have given a certain preference to the Upaniṣadic mentality, without affirm-

[3]We begin to have some attempts in this direction. Besides Akhilananda (1949) cf. Ravindra (1990) and Sugirtharajah (1993).

ing that it represents a pan-Indic horizon.

I attempt therefore a christian discourse in silent dialogue with a Śaiva mind — and heart. A christian text purporting to make sense in a Śaiva context. I insist on this point — although writing in a western language I should also take into account western-christian sensitivity. And in fact the critique of some theologians has made me aware that I should not neglect the modern exegetical perspective which, I take for known. Our discourse has been going on for twenty centuries and we need to pay our respects to our ancestors — and contemporaries.

I repeat; we cannot neglect tradition, but we have no right to freeze it either. And in fact, an increasing number of westerners, especially younger generations, feel more and more estranged by the venerable exegetical and theological approaches.

An example and, I am tempted to add, a paradigm, may be helpful. Latin American Christology as reflected and practiced by the so-called Theology of Liberation. "We cannot help but formulate certain suspicions," writes one of its best exponents: "For some reason it has been possible for Christians, in the name of Christ, to ignore or even contradict fundamental principles and values that were preached and acted upon by Jesus of Nazareth."[4]

The Indic background of this study is and is not similar to that of Latin America. It is similar, inasmuch as the present-day social structures and historical situation are perhaps even worse than those of Latin America. The word *dalit* epitomizes what we want to say. It is neither a christian word nor an exclusively christian concern, but it cannot be ignored by any christan reflection.[5] Any christology in India, worth the

[4]Sobrino (1978) in the Preface to the English edn., p. xv.

[5]Cp. the telling title of Alegre (1995), and specially the contribution of Gonzalez Faus (1995).

name, should be mainly *dalit*-christology.[6]

The Indic situation is but also dissimilar on two main accounts. On the one hand, although colonial christianity may have its part of responsibility for the present situation, the 2% of the christian population cannot be compared with the over 80 and perhaps 90% of the christians of the Latin-American continent. On the other hand, the Indic psyche as well as the religious traditions of Indic peoples (which are much larger than the boundaries of the Indian nation) have another experience of and approach to reality than the mainly historical awareness of the abrahamic traditions.

I had to insert this remark for the sake of clarification but I should equally emphasize that this study is not a christology, but a mystical meditation on the Man of Nazareth against the backdrop of Indic cultures — and for this reason I do not shun the word 'mystical', ambivalent as it sounds in many circles. But my intention is not christian apologetics.

Some readers may find it awkward that I insist in giving Greek and Latin quotes, and even, although sparingly, introduce some Sanskrit words. This is done on purpose. The more we dare to go forward, the more we need to be rooted in tradition. Most of the christian reflection is not based on King's James' version, most of our present insights have been, since long ago, patrimony of humanity, although in different contexts. Those 'foreign' words are like immigrants in our countries. They enrich our awareness that we are not alone, and prevent us from becoming provincial. Even the 'English' *koinê* today cannot be limited to the idioms and sensibilities of the inhabitants of the British isles.

I should finally remark that the literary genre of this study is neither exegesis nor apologetics, neither christian hermeneutics nor religious psychology, neither confessional theology nor mere rational philosophy. The word with which

[6] Cp. Pieris (1988) and Wilfred (1992) as examples.

I would be less unsympathetic would be intercultural philosophy — without defining it further.

* * *

2. The Notions and the Problem

In this context I would describe mysticism as the set of more or less coherently formulated doctrines about the ultimate experience(s) of reality. This ultimate experience of reality is the locus of the mystical experience. *Mysticism* is the narrative of the mystical experience.

By *doctrines* I mean intelligible propositions formulated in a particular language, this latter understood as a human universe, the human way of being in and experiencing the world.

The word *reality* as used here stands for the largest word embracing all that is, is thinkable, or in any way enters in our consciousness, even if as unthinkable, ineffable, non-being or the like. The word derives from *res* and suggests thing and word.

By *ultimate* I understand intellectual irreducibility. Something is *ultimate* when it cannot be reduced any further, when the sequence of thoughts stops, when the idea cannot be deduced from another that is more general or certain, or when the intuition does not go further. I imagine Plato would call it 'the principle without (further) foundation" (*archê anypothetos* (Rep. 510b). By saying this I am not affirming that what is ultimate for some individual or group needs to be ultimate for everybody else (against Plato in 511b who calls here the *anypothetos* the "principle of all": *toũ pantos archê*). One of the most intriguing discoveries in the praxis of dialogue is the fact that what for me is non-negotiable or evident, i.e. ultimate, for the partner may be disputable or not at all ultimate! What I take for granted does not need to tally with my partner's myth.

By experience I understand conscious immediacy, i.e., an awareness of something immediately present. There is no intermediary, no mediation. The field of experience is human consciousness. Experience could be said to be rooted in the *turīya* (*Māṇḍūkya Upaniṣad*) from which, as a raw material, proceed all states of consciousness. Experience lies at the root of any cognitive phenomenon, be it of the senses, the intellect or any other organ by which we come into contact with reality — without specifying to what extent, if at all, reality accepts degrees.

In this sense, any experience is ultimate. *Qua* experience it cannot be derived from anything else or deduced from another instance. But the experience I may have touching a stick (which my eyes see as crooked when half plunged obliquely in water) does not represent an ultimate for my mind, since my mind may interpret the whole phenomenon in many different ways and ascribe to it various degrees of truth, reality or appearance: Is the snake I see with my imagination a real snake, or is it perhaps a rope which I discover with my mind? Or is the rope, as I think it to be, perhaps after all a divine manifestation or no rope at all?

An *ultimate reality* is thus a reality which I cannot deduce from anything else nor reduce to something else.

The *mystical experience* would then mean that experience which discloses to the subject the ultimate reality, as we have described it.

This is only a formal description. It cannot be otherwise, because we claim the validity of this description beyond the many actual interpretations of it. We leave open what this ultimate reality may actually be.

It is customary to speak of "union with the divine" (be it by love or knowledge), of 'touching' the sacred, etc. While agreeing with most of those descriptions within their respective contexts we neither restrict mystical experience within theistic or deistic worldviews, nor to a 'religious' phenomenon — 'religious' here understood in a very restrictive sense, as if atheism could not also be religious. At any rate, the field of mysticism has little to do with para-normal or para-psychological phenomena.

A first problem is whether we can compare such experiences at all. And the problem is compounded because the very contexts are different. It belongs to what I have called *diatopical hermeneutics.*

It has been asked, for instance in christian milieux in India, at least since Brahmabandhav Upādhyāya and more recently in the case of Abhishiktānanda, what is the relation between the christian religious experience and the advaitic experience.[7] Our comment here is purely methodological.[8]. We should first describe both experiences within their respective contexts: personal/non-personal, historical/non-historical, biblical/Upaniṣdic, somewhat dualistic/somewhat monistic. We should not shun either the approach from within (qualifying the christian experience as unique, and the upaniṣadic one as supreme) or the approach from without (describing the christian experience as dualistic or social, and the upaniṣadic as monistic or solitary). 'Del enemigo el consejo' says a spanish proverb.

The comparison cannot be performed on an equal basis. Indeed, there is no possible comparison between two ultimate experiences.[9] There is no meta-ultimate and thus neutral point of reference. We know by now that any question involves the questioner, and that the answer, therefore, is an

---

[7] "Mais quel rapport y-a-t-il entre la conscience religieuse du chrétien et l'expérience de l'advaita?" Dupuis (1989) 87.

[8] Cp. the enlightening chapters in Gort (1992) studying in general, and in particular cases whether we can share religious experience — although the case of Christ is not mentioned.

[9] Cp. Smith's (1992) controversy with Steven Katz and the corresponding bibliographical references.

answer not only to the question but also to the questioner.

Should we then give up any attempt at a cross-cultural understanding? Not necessarily, provided we remain aware of the intrinsic limits of the entire endeavour. The bearers of the respective experiences should engage in a dialogical dialogue, well aware that the first item in the agenda, after the very willingness to dialogue, is to agree in the rules of the selfsame dialogue.

In each so-called experience we have an unbreakable 'cord of four strands'. We may distinguish but not separate them. We see the one through the other, and at the same time we are able to identify those four strings, although unable to isolate them.

In each experience we have the *pure experience*, that spontaneous, untemporal and unreflexive act by which we enter into immediate contact with reality. This experience is the source from which all the further activities of our spirit emerge.

We have, secondly, the *memory* of that experience which allows us to make it an object of description, analysis and what not. The memory makes present the pure experience to our mind, and, in a certain way, enriches it, since it combines with it our past experiences, and focuses our consciousness of it.

Thirdly, there is the *reflexion*, the thinking, the conscious awareness of the experience mediated by the memory of it. This reflexion allows us to interpret the experience according to the categories we have at our disposal. It is clear that the moment we speak and reflect we are indebted to our entire upbringing, idiosyncracy and culture. We often tend to consider our interpretation of the experience to be almost as valuable and universal as the experience itself.

There is, fourthly, the fact that our own reflexion is not exclusively our own as sociology of knowledge makes it clear:

we are not alone, we are integrated in a complex context of an entire culture. We are intrinsically dependent on the space and time where and when we happen to live. Our interpretations not only draw upon the memory of our experience; they also draw upon the whole treasure of our past experiences and upon parallel and similar ideas we have inherited from our own personal and collective past which act as a sort of feed-back. The interpretations of others influence willy-nilly the understanding of our own interpretation. We could call it the *reception* of our experience into the complex body of knowledge in which we ourselves are included.

In a word: E=e.m.i.r.

The complete experience is a compound of experience, its memory, our interpretation, and its reception in the cultural body of our time and place.

What then do we ask, for example, when we put the question of "the christian experience and the advaitic experience"?

We have enough documents in our hands about m, i, and r. But still we cannot say much about E if we do not know e, the first and most important variable. We have heard many times since Lucretius that if horses were to describe their Godhead they would picture it as a great, wonderful and almighty Horse — philosophical subtleties notwithstanding (for the human mind can overcome a certain anthropomorphism). We know that faced with the same empirical (sensuous) experience our descriptions may vary considerably — even though we belong to the same culture.

A possible approach to a reliable description of the two experiences would be if we could find one and the same person as the subject of the two experiences. And even then the ultimate hiatus would not be overcome, as the other three elements of the experience are already mutually influenced by the parallel ones — unless we were dealing with a totally schizophrenic person, in which case the testimony would not be valid.

However, our task is not to compare experiences in general, but to study the alleged or possible mystical experience of Jesus the Christ. In order to know the experience of somebody we need to share in that experience. But how can we know it? We may know the different cultural backgrounds, we may also detect that we have similar interpretations, and even surmise that our memories show a certain correspondence, but can we proceed further? Should we not stop here? Nobody can have an experience by proxy. It would not be experience. The experience is personal and intransferable.[10]

But could it be that faith is precisely this sharing in the ultimate experience? Or that person is more community than individuality? Or that Godhead is more shared infinite (eternal) Life than an individual Supreme Being?

If we are to attempt to describe the experience of Christ we cannot avoid such truly formidable problems.

* * *

To explore the mysticism of Jesus Christ is a daunty task indeed.[11]

We are attempting to enter the holiest enclosure of somebody else, that we purport to reach the understanding of a being whose nature is precisely to possess self-understanding. Unlike all other objects of our knowledge, we cannot understand a human being if we do not understand its self-consciousness. Man is a self-conscious animal. And Jesus Christ was also a Man. A Man, however, who seemed to have taken seriously for himself and for others ("ye are Gods", Jn

[10]Cp. my chapter "The Supreme Experience" in Panikkar (1983) XXVII pp. 291–317.

[11]Cp. Renwart (1993) where he analyses some fifteen contemporary books of Christology. None of them touches our point. A very important book, but of 'narrative theology', is Kuschel (1990).

X.34) that we "may share divine nature" (II Petr. I.4). And in fact this has been the inmost natural aspiration of every christian — even of every Man, since the urge to become infinite ("like God", in a particular set of languages) seems to be constitutively human. In spite of differences, Jesus was not the only one to reveal to us the abyss of the *aham-brahmāsmi* ("I am Brahman"). This in no way means that Jesus is an *avatāra* among many.[12] I have made it clear time and again that the docetic figure of an *avatāra* is morphologically different from the christian belief in the incarnation.[13] The divine can descend many times in the form of an *avatāra* which is simply a visible form of God; whereas plurality of incarnations in the christian context is as contradictory as a plurality of Gods in a monotheistic worldview. They all would coalesce.

How can we proceed? Is there any appropriate, or even legitimate method? Should we not be the other person if we want to know how the person understands herself? *Individuum ineffabile*, said the ancients. The necessary knowledge of the context in order to understand a text here becomes paramount. Within the individualistic worldview represented and to some extent introduced by the cartesian *cogito* the difficulties are insuperable. But we know that every text is also a pretext to say something, and that we need to reach the texture of a text in order to discover the pretext above and beyond the context.

This, parenthetically, is an important ingredient for diatopical hermeneutics, the interpretations of contexts being governed by principles different from that of texts. We also need to understand the pretexts: an existential affair which

---

[12] Harnack betrayed his bias clearly: "were I to hold it (the doctrine of the pre-existence of Christ), I would have to assume that revelations of God had also taken place in pagan peoples" — apud Kuschel (1992), p. 38.

[13] Cp. my two responses Panikkar (1989/3) and (1994/48).

transcends the merely conceptual understanding of a text.

Our query skyrockets, because here we are not primarily dealing with a text, but with a person — whom we come to know, nevertheless, through a series of texts. Or can we also have access to the mystery of the person by other means? One thing we may advance however. The texts may not be all that is needed in order to understand and know a living issue ("the letter killeth" II Cor. III, 6), but we cannot bypass the texts (cp. II Tim. III.16; II Petr. I.20; etc.). We cannot deal here with the entire problematic, but we should mention it so that we may overcome the modern and nominalistic temptation of solving truly human problems by isolating abstract parameters.

* * *

Let us restate our query. There was a Man, almost 2000 years ago. In comparison with other figures of world history, he was not exceedingly extraordinary. He was a straight-forward and just Man who did not allow himself to be trapped in any extreme position, whether political or religious: a Man who died young because he irritated the powers that be with his unflinching attitude against hypocrisy. He was put to death.

For the past two millennia his death, or rather as many would prefer to say, his resurrection has inspired millions, has been the central point of reference and has mightily influenced, unlike anyone else, the course of history. He did not write a single line; he spoke and acted. A handful of simple folks gathered in his memory and commemorated his death and life.

What did this Man think of himself? Is it not sheer blasphemy to dare to enter into the inner sanctuary of a person? But if for so long a time he has been the central symbol for so many people from every walk of life, we may be allowed to ask why and attempt to unveil the mystery of this Man.[14]

But we should proceed step by step.

The Text

The traces of Jesus are sufficiently clear. There are thousands of studies retracing and scrutinizing his footsteps in the minutest detail. Fortunately enough the traces are not so innumerable: Some thirty years of quiet existence (and I would underscore the importance of this silent period); some three years, or perhaps only one, of intense activity. We possess the four gospels plus a limited number of canonical and non-canonical documents, and some vestiges in later literature.[15] We know, further, his impact for twenty centuries, eliciting exalted apologetics, vicious attacks, and a gamut of interpretations between these extremes, as well as novels and films about the Man of Nazareth. All this also belongs to the picture of Jesus. We will limit ourselves, however, to his immediate historical past.

We know some of his words, many utterances attributed to him, a good number of his deeds, and we may reasonably surmise his main intentions.

The rough picture that emerges from all this may be reduced to the following:

Jesus was a young Galilean who lived in a troubled area of a small part of the world, a marginal area by the political standards of the time. He belonged to a people who were

---

[14] No wonder that a theologian, so shunned by many, could write "that the important thing is not to evoke in oneself the same feelings as Christ, but to grasp Christ himself", Adolf von Harnack apud Kuschel (1992) p. 40.

[15] For canonical sources cp. the *New Testament* and for non-canonical cp. the *Apocrypha* and also ORBE (1975) and following volumes of the same collection. For a useful "Inventory of the Jesus Tradition by Chronological Stratification and Independent Attestation" cp. Crossan (1991) pp. 427–50 with 522 items.

proud of their millennial history and felt that an imminent catastrophe was coming as a result of internal crisis, and especially of external dominance by a foreign and powerful empire. Whether he was a full jew or only on his mother's side,[16] Jesus did not join the conservative sadducees, the extremist zealots, nor take the middle path of the pharisees or the more esoteric essenes. He stood alone and felt an immense compassion for the *'am ha-arez*, the uneducated simple folks, and for a time aroused their enthusiasm, although he was only followed, without much understanding, by a handful of men and women of different social strata, mainly of humble origin. This happened almost two thousand years ago. He was crucified by the romans, at the instigation of his own people. During that period thousands of people had been crucified for not complying with the political *status quo*. Today almost everything is forgotten except the life of that intriguing and singular figure of Joshua, the son of Mary.

As for his acts, they took the form of doing good to the simple people by healing them in body and spirit, and preaching the forgiveness of sins. Occasionally he engaged in dispute with the learned; more often he preached in the open to the humble. His best remembered sayings, the Beatitudes, which were supposed to have been delivered on a mountain side or on a plain in the countryside sounded beautiful but a little naive. To his more immediate friends (as he called them) he may have delivered a more intimate message, emphasizing unity and intimacy with him. He seemed to follow the ritual of his own tradition, although apparently with a certain freedom, even to the extent of introducing a rather disconcerting meaning into the jewish idea of sacrifice.

Most of his doctrines were within the frame of his own jewish tradition, stressing love of God and neighbour, peace for all, and freedom from fear. We can find those lofty doc-

[16] Cp. Rosenberg (1986), pp. 27 sq. et passim.

trines in many prophets and saints (to utilize these two words of jewish tradition) of most of the human traditions. Some have also interpreted him as a coward, a liar and a Man who aroused expectations and promised spiritual rewards, though well aware that he could not deliver them. In sum, the son of Mary aroused hatred and love in both ancient and modern times.

The Context

All those traces were not left in the air, but were imprinted on jewish soil, in roman times and in the context of semitic ways of thinking and experiencing the world. His audience was not of Africa, Greece, India, China, or Europe; his background was not even of Iran, Egypt, Babylonia, Sumeria.[17] He knew how to read and probably also write, but he did not show any knowledge of the wide world or of other cultures, than his own — in spite of occasional echoes we may hear of other traditions, if we come from other backgrounds. They may simply be human factors common to the human race. We may speculate about his journeys abroad while young, but apart from having no proof of this whatever, we find hardly any trace of other cultures either in his words or in his behaviour.[18]

---

[17] "Jesus shows no sign of Hellenistic influence" Maisch/Vogtle (1969) p. 176. The different entries of the *Sacramentum Mundi* (1969) III, 174–209 (with abundant bibliography) are worth reading. The descriptions by Crossan (1990) are also enlightening.

[18] Cp. four very different and yet related descriptions of the Man Jesus: Ben-Chorin (1967) (who incidentally does not quote any of the Jesus' texts we are going to comment upon) describing "Der Nazarener in jüdischer Sicht"; L. Swidler (1988) making of the jew Yeshua "the measure of what it means to be Christian" (p. 1) — of course, a Yeshua who is "feminist and a very radical one" (p. 95) and androgynous; A. Rosenberg (1986) who liberates Jesus from his Old Testament ancestry and presents him as literally *bar nascha* (Son of Man); Augstein (1972) showing the incongruencies of all the theologies and churches building upon the shaky foundations of a concocted Jesus of Nazareth.

In a word, we cannot understand Jesus without situating him in his immediate jewish popular context. I say 'popular' because we do not detect in his life any traces of a scholar. He was not a Gamaliel, a Paul of Tarsus, an Akiba or any other of the intellectual giants of his tradition. Whatever 'the Quest for the historical Jesus' in the christian theology of the last two centuries may mean and whatever tensions we may find between the latter and the 'Christ of faith', the personality of Jesus the Christ is impossible to understand if we erase or minimize the concrete traits of a jewish individual who lived and died not more than sixty generations ago.

Our Texture

These sixty generations have contributed heavily towards both clarifying and blurring the understanding of Jesus. He has been regarded as anything from the Son of God to an impostor, or a small insignificant figure who was made a scapegoat by several groups of people for their own particular purposes, religious, political, gnostic, fanatical, or lofty. Probably no other figure in history has been pictured in more variegated forms.[19] I refer not only to the so-called 'Lives of Jesus', but also to all the Jesuologies underpinning all kinds of theologies, christologies, ecclesiologies, and what not. Can we pass through that jungle?[20] It has been remarked by an exegete that the proliferation of exegetical studies reminds him of the argument of the Epistle to the Hebrews questioning "the efficacy of the Temple sacrifices on the grounds that

[19] Cp. Pelikan (1987) for a fascinating description of western history through the positive impact of Jesus upon the world. ... "as respect for the organized church has declined, reverence for Jesus has grown" (p. 232).

[20] Cp. the ironical and sad remark by a brilliant Indian exegete (who died of an accident in 1995 riding his bicycle!) "How many of the more than 1500 books and articles published on the Gospels each year really touch upon problems which matter to people?" Soares-Prabhu (1981) 320.

they have to be offered 'for ever, year after year' (for why, unless they were ineffectual had they to go on and on?)".[21]

We could build three huts, one for religious people, a second for politicians, and a third for sceptics and the indifferent; but we cannot elaborate a picture of Christ that would elicit some kind of consensus. This very impossibility, which poses a great challenge for what I have called a christophany for our times,[22] serves our purpose very well because it offers a description of some traits of the 'personality profile' (to speak irreverently) of Jesus of Nazareth. An example may explain this point.

We may assert that an alleged Jesus said "I and the Father are One". I am not hereby affirming that the son of Mary actually did say it, nor that this proves his divinity, or that he was actually mad when he said it, or was a genuine rogue in putting forward such a claim. I merely say that the traces of the historical or mystical Jesus, as they have come down to us, bear witness to such an affirmation.

We may perhaps also say that he was the lover of Mary Magdalene, the secret father of John the alleged evangelist, a refined hypocrite, and a cunning coward who had a secret political plan to overthrow both romans and jews in order to establish his fundamentalistic messianic reign; or we may say that he was only a fanatic illegitimate jew whose plans went sour because Judas, the Sanhedrin, or whoever, checkmated his moves. Perhaps we now know him better through the fruits his followers have left behind. We cannot discard *a priori* any possible interpretation, although we should defend

---

[21] He goes on saying: "may not we similarly wonder about the effectiveness of a method which continues to pour out an endless succession of studies on the same narrow compass of subjects . . ." Soares-Prabhu (1981) 317. I am reminded, of course, of the fundamental methodological question of the *Bṛhadāraṇyaka Upaniṣad* that it is not analyzing objects how we shall know a subject (BU III, 4 sq.).

[22] Cp. Panikkar (1992/34).

our stance *a posteriori*, presenting a convincing picture of his personality in a way that is somewhat independent of our particular judgements.

I am saying that our particular spectacles indeed shape the form we see of Jesus, but that the fact of being aware of having lenses and also having an idea of how they form or deform the image allows us to qualify our description with the necessary factors of uncertainty or variability in order to make possible a concrete picture which may be credible to a fair number of those for whom the name of Jesus is not a matter of indifference.

I am not going to argue whether my interpretation is the correct one. I present it as a plausible one.

Our query was whether we can penetrate into the inner chamber of another individual, or do we have to be content with reconstruing a past event like a detective story? The basic issue is whether christian faith is exclusively based on trust in theological or ecclesiastical detectives who retrace the footprints of the historical 'founder' of christianity, or whether it also has another source. Does christian faith rely on a historical book or on a personal experience? Is it something like grace or simply the intelligent conclusion of a syllogism? A fundamental question indeed!

I should not be misunderstood by western christians who abide by the myth of history. It makes no sense denying that Jesus was a jew, a historical individual of a couple of millennia ago. But there is no point in ignoring that in many parts of the world, and for the coming third christian millennium, the figure of Christ could or actually does make sense if seen under another light. In traditional christian language I would affirm, that if Jesus was a jew, the risen Jesus, i.e. Christ is neither gentile, greek, or jew . . . But there is no point now in indulging in theological controversies. Our aim simply is to understand the figure of Christ within a wider context than the Semitic and historical one — which is, incidentally, the texture of over half of humankind. Does one need the circumcision of the mind in order to understand the Man from Galilee when his closest associates already dismissed the circumcision of the body?[23]

I would like to reassure christians that nothing is lost of the depths of christian tradition by relinquishing a certain monopoly on Christ, and that our interpretation fits into orthodoxy — if we do not identify orthodoxy with microdoxy. And I would reassure those who are not within the christian belief that nothing is lost of the depths of their respective traditions by understanding the figure of Christ as the christian name for a homeomorphic equivalent of 'what' other religions express and understand differently. The great difficulty, to put it philosophically, comes with the substantialization of that 'what'.

It may be retorted that the proper context of Jesus was the jewish world and that we are not allowed to extrapolate. Yet the first generations of christians, perhaps beginning with John and culminating in Ephesus and Chalcedon, already made the transplant into the hellenistic world. It should, therefore, not be forbidden to proceed to a further intercultural transplant. I may be reminded that we are not now in the same situation as in those foundig times. I would simply reply: "Jesus Christ is the same yesterday, today and into the ages" (Hebr. XIII.8). In other words, because I do not deny history or indulge in a 'gnostic' interpretation of Christ, I take history seriously and I do not reduce it to times past.[24]

[23]Cp. Panikkar (1992/47).

[24]I found Dupuis (1994) only after the last redaction of this study. This book comes very close to our problem, presenting a christology centered in the person of Christ and open to the other religions of the world. He criticises dogmatic and genetic methods as deductive and finds a hermeneutical triangle "in the mutual interaction among text, context and inerpreter" (9). This allows him to "call for many diversified the-

Let us return to the Man Jesus, and 'come and see'.

3. Three Anthropologies

We have the main question still pending. To be sure we cannot do without the text. But the text is not enough. We remember after all that the devil can quote Scripture for his purpose (cp. Matth. IV.6). We cannot bypass the text, but how can we pass through it without getting entangled in barren subtleties or pernicious views — as the buddhist would say?[25]

The answer is clear: Tradition is, along with Scripture, a necessary hermeneutical tool. But tradition, like Scripture itself, is polysemic as well as fluid, changing and alive.

All too often tradition is understood as a set of doctrines crystallised in dogmatic formulations interpreting scriptural texts. We then have a sort of doctrinal christianity, almost an ideology erected on the basis of some historical facts as interpreted by succeeding generations. The result is a body of doctrines, a belief-system, like the constitution of a state or a charter of an institution, which allows for cohesion, discipline and efficiency. But is religion simply an organisation? Is faith only the correct interpretation of doctrine?

---

ologies and Christologies" (10), to the point of paving "the way for a Christology of religions". Perhaps these pages may be, if not an approach to such a 'Christology', yet a stepping stone in that direction since I do not intend any christology but only a meditation on a realistic not docetic christophany.

[25] Our study is not concerned with a critique of 'Biblical Criticism'. We may pay heed, however, to it: "For it is precisely this use of a *historical* method to interpret a *religious text* which explains the failure of critical exegesis to disclose the real meaning of the Gospels, while supplying masses of information about them . . . A method fashioned to obtain exact *information* is being used to interpret a text which aims at the personal transformation . . . The method is thus incommensurate with the intention of the text . . . It may be incommensurate with the nature of the text too". Soares-Prabhu (1981) 318.

We have often forgotten that tradition means much more than this. The 'handing down' (*tradere*) of tradition is not reduced to producing a corrected, well-edited, and up-to-date version of Scripture. What tradition transmits is life, faith, a sense of belonging and community, an orientation in life, a sharing in a common destiny. Christian tradition is not just doctrine. It is also *ecclesia* in the deepest sense of the word. It has to do, not only with what Jesus said or did, but with who he was — and who we are.

We are saying that Tradition is more than authoritative or normative hermeneutics. What tradition hands over is more than a text or an interpretation. It transmits a living and thus spoken word. The intention and even the nature of our texts, transcend what a critico-historical method is capable of extracting from them. But how do we know this? For some centuries a certain apologetics has tried to convince us that the texts themselves witness to their intention and nature. But if the same text validates itself, we are falling into a vicious circle, and it is an invalid witness. The criterion has to lie outside the text itself. And we cannot be satisfied with the general recognition of the hermeneutical circle that we require a particular pre-understanding because we know of other equally valuable pre-understandings which contest our interpretations. In a word, we need something outside of and prior to all texts and scriptures. Here, incidentally, vedic exegesis could offer some help. We may simplify our problem by stating that Word is not Scripture, that Word is irreducible to Writing and even to interpretation. 'Apostolic succession', to use a traditional notion, is more than orthodox transmission of doctrines.[26]

If Jesus Christ means something to christian tradition it is because in one way or another christians *hear* (cp. Rom.

[26]. . . "die Schrift [ist] nicht das Wort, sondern das Zeugnis des Geistes vom Wort" . . . Balthasar (1961) I.28.

X.17) 'words of eternal life', and not mere correct statements about the state of the world. We need to know the Man: *Ecce homo*! This is our concern.

"Whom do the crowds say me to be?" Jesus asked. Notice that the I is grammatically avoided, if we translate the greek literally (Lk IX.18 cp. Mk VIII.27. Mt XVI.15). This 'me' was obviously Jesus the Man who stood before his disciples.

Before the predicates of the famous petrine answer (Messiah, Son of God) there stands the very subject: *su*, *You* (you are . . .). We should open our ears and eyes to the mystery of the *thou*. He asks about his 'I' and the response says 'You'. This *thou* can be understood in terms of a threefold anthropological paradigm at least: Man as an individual, as a person, or as image of the divine — although this threefold division is neither the only possible nor an exclusive one. In fact, we shall build on all three aspects.

We shall first describe Jesus within the predominant modern framework of western individualism. Secondly, we shall offer some reflections within a larger western framework, and, thirdly, make a brief reference to the Indic reception of the problematic.

(a) Individualistic

That Jesus is or rather was an individual is something undeniable — even if Scripture and Tradition refer to Christ as a generic Man, a second Adam in whom all human nature is assumed.[27] What is an individual: an isolated substance? The prevalent human consciousness today, mainly of western origin, is that Man is an indiviualistic entity.

Within this framework, we have only one door into the holy of holies, the mystery of individuality: we cannot cross the threshold, but we can observe the traces left by the person

[27] Cp. vgr. Panikkar (1981/X) p. 74.

concerned. These traces are detected through an unavoidable triple mediation: *what* the traces in themselves manifest of the individual concerned, *how* the traces appear over against the ground on which they stand, and *what* form they take when seen through our personal eye-glasses. This is to say:

(i) the words and deeds of the individual as the individual's signs;
(ii) (these) words spoken and deeds done within a very concrete context (which gives them meaning and value); and
(iii) our interpretation of all this through our own particular vision, which in its turn is coloured by the set of presuppositions without which we cannot approach the investigation of the traces.

Three formidable dragons defend the intimate castle of private individuality — one is tempted to say, of the sacredness of Man.

But this is not all. If we succeed in lifting the drawbridge that would introduce us into the interior castle of the other's *individuality*, we will be overwhelmed and overpowered by it unless we show the symbol of authenticity, the credentials that give credibility to our witness. This can happen only if the centre of that castle is not a private property of that individual, i.e., if that centre somewhat belongs also to our own centre. Only in ourselves, we may encounter or perhaps understand the mystery of the identity of another being.[28]. I can meet the identity of someone else only by sharing in the very identity of the other.[29] Everything else is mere bureaucratic identification, not real identity.

[28]Cp. two important works, which we cannot comment here: Chatterjee (1963) affirming that without the prior condition of intersubjectivity, "there can be neither the concept of 'my' self nor that of the 'other' self." (217), and Ricoeur (1990) distinguishing between 'identité-idem' (*same, gleich*) and 'identité-ipse' (*self, Selbst*) (13 and *passim*).

[29]Cp. Panikkar (1977/3).

Identification consists in situating the other within a coordinate's system so as to avoid confusion with any other being. Each being is univocally determined. In our case we could identify Jesus of Nazareth as that jew, son of Mary, born most probably in Bethlehem around the year 4 *small BC*, who after some years of activity in his own country died on a roman cross in Jerusalem under Pontius Pilate. Such identification does not leave any doubt about *what* we are talking about.

But have we really reached the core of that individual? Have we really come to know him, have we penetrated into his personal intimacy, his self-consciousness, into what he sincerely thought of himself?[30] Identification is not identity. In order to come near to his identity we need another type of approach, above and beyond the first. We need loving knowledge. Otherwise we reach only the *what*, not the *who* of the person.[31]

Phenomenologically speaking, love is a non-dualistic experience.[32] This is why love is so reluctant to enter into any Husserlian *noêma*. Love is neither sameness nor alterity, neither one nor two. Love requires differentiation without separation; it is a 'going out' towards the other that rebounds in a genuine 'going in' into oneself, a discovery of the other through the total acceptance of the other in the bosom of my self.

Without love we may be able to have a certain acquain-

[30] For a description of the theological discussion about the 'faith of Christ' (Hebr., XII.2) whether it is an objective or a subjective genitive, i.e. whether we can say that Jesus Christ could have no faith, because he had vision, or whether he had also faith, cp. Collins/Kendall (1992). Cp. also the chapter "Jesus' Faith" in Schoonenberg (1971) p. 146: "Believing is a deed or attitude of the whole person: it is not merely a recognition of truths.

[31] Cp. Panikkar (1972/6) and (1972/14).

[32] Cp. Panikkar (1983) XXVII, "Advaita and Bhakti" pp. 277–89.

tance with an object, locate that object, describe its features, and predict its behaviour. This is generally called 'scientific knowledge'. But our case is not the cognition of an object, but the knowledge of a 'thou', itself a knowing subject. In order to do this I have to know myself in such a way that there is room for the other within myself, so that the 'other' is not just an 'outer', but the other *of* my-self, another self — perhaps of the Self. At any rate, in order to know the other truly, the movement has to be reciprocal: an encounter has to occur, I have to be loved by the other so that I may see the other in the mirror into which my own self has been converted by the love of the other. Christian scripture says: "if one loves God, one is known by him" ["si quis autem diligit Deum, hic cognitus est ab eo"] (I Cor VIII.3); "Then I shall know as I am known" ["tunc autem cognoscam, sicut et cognitus sum"] (I Cor XIII.12).

Practically all human traditions have emphasized purity of heart as the most essential requisite for knowledge and for authentic life.[33] Only a *sahṛdaya* ('Man-with-a-heart') is capable of grasping the full power of a sentence, says Indic poetics.[34] Only the pure of heart will be able to truly see the other, the others, the Other, God: "Blessed are the pure in heart, for they shall see God" (Mt V.8). It is also what John says: "In this we know that we have known him, if we keep his commands" (I Jn II.3). If our praxis is correct, our theory will be true. Or even more boldly: "I wrote to you, children, because you have known the Father" (I Jn II.13; cp. also 14). We can know him (cp. Jn VIII.28).

Can we really cross this drawbridge? Can we open up the chamber of our self so as to make room for another 'self'? Can

[33]Suffice to mention the Upaniṣadic requirements for studying sacred lore; cp. as a single instance Śaṅkara, *Vivekacūḍāmaṇi*, 16–37.

[34]Cp. Gispert-Sauch (1974), 139, in a short and important study on biblical exegesis from an Indic perspective.

the 'fusion of horizons' required for an authentic understanding reach a fusion of selves without confusion? Or should we sit respectfully at the threshold of the other self-consciousness and simply gaze like the friends of Job? Christian mystics spoke of becoming 'alter Christus'. We are purporting here to experiencing 'ipse Christus', perhaps encouraged by St. Paul's outburst: "I live, no more (my) ego, but lives in me Christ" (Gal. II.20. Cp. Col. III.4).

To sum up, if Man is just an individual, there is not much scope in pretending to penetrate into the ego of another one. Man *has* individuality, but *is* more than an individualistic entity.

We have until now presented the problem assuming the modern western dogma of human individualism. However, the modern notion of human individuality does not need to be interpreted to mean that each of us is a monad without windows. We could be still monads, but with relationships to other individuals. Yet this assumption, this myth actually, does not represent a universal conviction, and even present-day western philosophical reflection is beginning to take notice of serious criticisms of such an interpretation. Today's predominant culture, western in origin, seems to have exhausted the advantages of individualism, and people within that very culture are discovering that such a stance leads to philosophical solipsism, sociological atomism, and political quantification of the human being, resulting isolation, consumerism, and undeclared wars of all against all.

It is in this climate that modern reflection on the *humanum* is situated. One of its most positive features is the new emphasis on the person over against the individual.

(b) Personalistic

We have already said that there are other ways of approaching the question of who was Jesus.

I describe the person as a knot in a net of relationships. Individuality would be the abstract knot, i.e., the knot abstracted, severed from all the threads which precisely make the knot. The knots without the threads are nothing, the threads without the knots could not subsist. The knots have a very practical use; they allow efficient ways of treating the individual, from identification cards to the human rights of the individual. But a knot is a knot because it is made of threads tied together with other knots through a network of threads. The knots are not unreal, nor the threads, for that matter. They belong constitutively together. But this is too spatial and objective a simile. It shows how an individual knot is impossible, and how all the knots imply each other and hang together. Reality is the net, reality is relational. But the simile does not stress sufficiently that other human intuition, which is both eastern and western, that in each being all other beings are somewhat reflected, included, represented. The *en panti panta* ("everything in everything" or "all in all") of Anaxagoras, the *sarvam-sarvātmakam* of śaivism, microcosm/macrocosm corelation of Aristotle and the Upaniṣads, the *pratītyasamutpāda* of buddhism, the *speculation* of neoplatonism, the *perichoresis* of christianity (and Anaxagoras) and the specular nature of the universe (from *speculum*, mirror) along with the universality of the *intellectus agens* of the medieval scholastics up to modern scientific morphogenetic and magnetic fields, seem to suggest a less individualistic worldview in which the castle of our story may not need such formidable dragons for its defence.

Our purpose is to share in the self-awareness of Jesus of Nazareth. But, first, we should tackle the general problem of the possible 'interpenetration of consciousnesses'.

Are we so sure that each individual consciousness is a closed fortress? Is not the real *cogito* a *cogitamus*, and the *sum* a *sumus*? Even more: is it so certain that Being is a dead thing, or that the idea of reality as a Mystical Body or a *dharma-kāya* is simply a figure of speech. Are we so convinced that consciousness is only an individual epiphenomenon, even private property?

Our doubt is whether the very problem how to know *another* self has been correctly stated. We are touching on one of the main philosophical issues of our times, one which emerges in a number of fundamental philosophical reflections. We could adduce the example of the object/subject split both on the epistemological and on the ontological level. The problem of the *anima mundi*, with all its political and ecological consequences refers also to the same question. It is the problem of personalism, and that of an animistic worl-dview.[35]

I understand by worldview a conscious reception of the world, or rather the impact that the *kosmos*, understood as the entire reality, makes on our conscious being. An animistic worldview would regard the nature of reality as alive, and, in a sense, personal. 'Being is personal', could be a short formula — which of course needs explanation. Person would then be the primal level of Being — and not as in most vitalistic movements, just a late epiphenomenon of reality, a sort of accident of Being. All too often ontology speculates on Being as if dealing with lifeless entities. I am defending the personal character of reality. I understand person as *anthrôpos*, as that irreducible dimension of reality under which we experience it. The person is the *sat-puruṣa*, the true Man, the whole reality, we may say, relying on the *puruṣa-sūkta* of the *Ṛg Veda* (X.90,

[35]The reader may hear echoes in what I am going to say of a good number of contemporary philosophers. I mention some of them in the bibliography, but the list is not exhaustive: Bergson, Berdiaef, Blondel, Boulgakov, Buber, Bultmann, Cullmann, Ebner, Gasset, Gilson, Guardini, Heidegger, Marcel, Maritain, Mounier, Nédoncelle, Ortega y Gasset, Rahner, Scheler, Schweitzer, Zubiri, without citing living thinkers or those of older times. I do not mention here Indic thinkers since the problematic is somewhat different.

though this expression is here not used).

For a scientific-evolutionistic pattern of thinking, to know the temporal genesis of something is equivalent to its intelligibility. This has led many to imagine that Being, considered as the most general idea at the basis of everything, is an amorphous reality, the *ens communissimum* of the scholastics. Everything is supposed to have evolved from an inert primal matter (at the big bang or not) either by its own dynamism or by dint of a Supreme Engineer (to console the naïve believers). Perhaps in contrast to an "ontologie personnaliste"[36] this dead ontology is the source of a certain discredit alien of metaphysical speculations. One should add that the christian terror of pantheism led the scholastics to make a radical separation between *ens realissimum* (God) and *ens commune* (ultimately an abstraction).[37] We may recall the old discussions on 'ontologism'.

Our problem is the knowledge of the 'other'. Can my ego encounter, and ultimately know, another ego? It is obvious that if 'person' means to be the private proprietor of one's own being, 'Selbstgehörigkeit',[38] and, ultimately, if Being is impersonal, there is no possibility of trespassing on individual boundaries. We have to respect and eventually tolerate each other, and this is all. Privacy has an ultimate status. This has led to the deleterous notion of God as an Other that

[36] Nédoncelle (1970) 41–47. The entire first part is entitled 'Être et personne', although he does not elaborate on the problem sketched here.

[37] That was the fear of Garrigou-Lagrange (1953), the dominican who for decades dominated Roman Theology, a great expert in mysticism, and who could not deny that the Incarnation seemed to tarnish the absoluteness of God: 'L'acte pur est irreçu et irreceptif', *irreceptus et irreceptivus*. "S'il était reçu dans une puissance, il serait participé et limité, s'il recevait une perfection nouvelle, il serait en puissance par rapport à elle, et ne serait plus Acte pur", p. 345. He is right; ontological monotheism does not leave room for the christian Incarnation — in spite of all the 'distinguos' of Thomas Aquinas.

[38] Guardini (1950) 99.

scrutinizes our intimacy and interferes with our identity, as an alienating Stranger who de-humanizes us.[39]

If, on the wake of German idealism we divide reality into I and Non-I (which simply retranslates the Cartesian dichotomy between *res cogitans* and *res extensa*), if we begin with the great divide between spirit and matter, we shall end with an atomistic view not only of matter, but also of spirit. Leibniz draws the philosophical consequence, and modern individualism its sociological follow-up. It is clear that the Non-I cannot merge with the I without destroying the I or destroying itself. The principle of non-contradiction cannot be dethroned from any 'diction'. But reality is not composed of I and Non-I. Reality is not dialectical; reason is. The Thou belongs also to reality and the Thou is neither contradictory nor foreign to the I. The Thou is neither I nor Non-I. The relationship is advaitic.

The I-Thou relationship is not dualistic like the relation of two substances. I and Thou are not two 'things'. They are constitutively related. There is no I without a Thou — and vice-versa. Nor is it a monistic relationship. They are constitutively related. There is no I without a Thou — and vice-versa. Nor is it a monistic relationship. They are not identical. I-Thou is irreducible to I (alone) or to Thou (alone), or to a superior It (of a higher unity). To discover myself as Thou is to discover my deepest identity, neither in the face of 'another', nor within a narcissistic mirror. It amounts to discovering my dynamic *ipse*, to being my-self: *tat tvam asi!* The *tvam* belongs inseparably to the *tat*. 'That art Thou'. How can I know another person? How can I even dare penetrate

[39]This is one of the main concerns of Schoonenberg's theology (against the atheism of Sartre, Camus, and others). God "does not dehumanize us, but makes us fully human, ultimately through his Word become man...our divinization is our humanization", Schoonenberg (1971) 7. Already Guardini had addressed this problem half a century ago.

into the holy of holies of the personal intimacy of another human being?

This is, I repeat, a wrong question. Wrong in itself, because if we mistake a person for an individual, there is an internal contradiction between being one individual (*divisum a se ab aliis vero distinctum*) and being another individual. I would cease to be the individual that I am if I were to really know another individual *qua* individual — and vice-versa. The knowing or intruding individual would destroy the individuality of the known individual, who would cease to be the individual that it is. This knowledge of the other (which is obviously a 'knowledge' without love) destroys the other; it alienates. We speak of a real knowledge of another person and not of our capacity to predict behaviours and control events. We refer to that knowledge which reaches a certain identity with the thing known. And whatever be the case for so-called inanimate entities, our case refers to the knowledge of persons.

A person is neither an individual nor an impersonal *Dasein.* By virtue of being ultimate, person defies any definition. Person is relationship because Being is relationship. Being is a verb, a communitarian, i.e. personalistic action: *esse est coesse* — and *coesse est actus essendi.*

If this is the case, a person is not only communicable, it is itself communication. An isolated individual person is a contradiction in terms. The very nature of knowledge, and not mere calculus, is already personal, has a personal character. To know is to share personhood. And personhood is relationship. A person is not only communicability; it is communion. I am person inasmuch as I am communion. Communion does not mean possession: it does not mean that other beings (objects or other people) belong to me; it is not a property of objects. Communion means belonging together as subjects (and not as mere objects of a higher subject). Communion does not mean that an I possesses a thou (or a thou an I), but that both belong together, that there is not the one without the other, and vice-versa. The I is not prior to the thou nor does the thou make the I. They are strictly reciprocal, their being is a *coesse*, a *Mitsein. Ser es estar juntos.*

This implies that I cannot know another individual if I treat that individual as an object. In this latter case, I may identify an it, but I cannot discover its identity. "Nobody can say Jesus is Lord except in the Holy Spirit" (I Cor. XII.3). This statement would sound rather absurd if saying meant uttering terms and not knowing, that is becoming, what one knows.

It is enlightening to remember that scholastic philosophy since at least St. Ambrose,[40] and probably St. Justin[41] believed that any truth, regardless of who said it, comes from the Holy Spirit,[42].

The *aliud* may be hell for the individual (Sartre), but the *alius* is part and parcel of the person. Alienation does not come from meeting the *alius*, but from being swallowed by the *aliud*. It is lack of love which transforms the *alius*, in the last analysis the thou, into an *aliud*, a thing, an object (which, the moment it has power, becomes threatening and instils dread).

While the question of the personal awareness of Christ was not a great problem once the tenets of the Council of Chalcedon were accepted (the Christ person is the divine person acting in two natures as his 'organs'[43]), in the first part

[40]Cp. *Glossa Lombardi* (PL 191, 1651 A) and also *Glossa ordinaria* (PL 17, 245 and 258 B), as well as the Ambrosiaster. In I Cor. XII.3 (PL 17, 245 and 258 B).

[41]Cp. Mourroux (1952) 222 for further commentaries.

[42]Thomas Aquinas liked to repeat this phrase: "Omne verum a quocumque dicatur, a Spiritu Sancto est", cp. *Sum. theol.* I–II, q. 109, a. 1 in 1; *In Joan.* VIII, lect. 6; etc.

[43]Cp. John of Damascus, *De fide orthodoxa*, III.15 (P.G. 94, 1060) with

of the twentieth century there was a furious controversy on the so-called 'I of Christ'.[44] Tellingly, this was already a question at the dawn of 'christian humanism' in the beginning of the twelfth century.[45] To endow Jesus with a human personality seemed to deprive him of his divinity. The problem, as is often the case, lies with the unexamined premises. In order to ascertain the unity of Jesus Christ, the first christian councils concurred in declaring that in Christ there was one single person (which could only be the divine second person of the Trinity) and two natures (the human and the divine), which obviously require two wills so as to preserve human freedom. But the moment that the humanness of Christ was stressed and its autonomy recognized (otherwise we could not consider him a Man), the problems were compounded. If the I of Christ is the divine person and at the same time Jesus had a full human consciousness, how could a divine omniscient consciousness coexist with his human consciousness? The subleties of such a theology are fascinating and amusing. We are not entering into the controversy.

It is instructive to learn when the question of the human consciousness of Christ became a problem. Within an a-personalistic ontology the issue could not arise. With the birth of individualism and the philosophies inaugurated by Descartes and Kant, the issue became philosophically insoluble. If Christ was a human individual, he could not be, at the same time, a divine individual. The *sola fide* was the only answer. But the intellectual apartheid of such a *fides* could not last long and the issue became a burning one. Who is this Christ? The theology of the post-enlightenment throws the question back to Jesus. It is not, who the people say that the

---

whom Thomas Aquinas agrees. Cp. his *De veritate* q. 27, a. 4: "Humana natura in Christo erat velut quoddam organum divinitatis".

[44] Cp. Xiberta (1954); Galtier (1939), (1947), (1954); Parente (1951).

[45] Cp. Santiago-Otero (1970).

Son of Man is? (Mt XVI.13), but 'who do yourself say you are?'

To sum it up. If Man is a person (and not an individual), sharing in the self-understanding of the other is not impossible, but has its limits. The I understands the other all the more the more this other is a Thou; and this other becomes all the more a Thou, the more it is known and loved by the I. The ancient *disciplina arcani* that only the initiated could understand (and thus participate in the ritual) is related to what we are saying. For a similar reason, christian faith was traditionally required of the person beginning the study of theology.

For those for whom Jesus Christ has become a Thou there can be a certain participation in what christian scripture calls the Spirit of Christ (Jn XIV.26; XVI.13), and thus they can have a certain knowledge of Jesus Christ (Cp. I Cor. II.16 and even I Jn V.20).

But this knowledge has its dangers which should not be ignored: hallucinations and pathological imaginations of all sorts. It also has limits: the Thou shares consciousness with the I, but both are distinct and cannot be reduced to one. This is *advaita*, non-dualistic. The history of mysticism shows many examples of false and unsound confusions. The I and the Thou are not just interdependent, but *interindependent*, as in the Trinity.

We will never penetrate fully into another individual consciousness precisely because each of us shares that very consciousness in a unique way.

This is our question. But we have still to present a third perspective.

(c) Ādhyātmik[46]

We wish to know Jesus. We said that there was only one door into the intimacy of a being: to investigate the traces left by words and deeds. If we open that door and penetrate the individual's *sanctum sanctorum*, are we not violating sacred boundaries and projecting our own awareness into somebody else's sacred property? Under two conditions such a method is legitimate: that we are conscious of what we are doing, and ask permission for such an incursion. This was the approach of our first type of anthropology — which is suspiciously similar to scientific experiment. (Experimental psychology).

We said also that we do not need to force the door because personal consciousness is not an enclosure but a common ground where human beings find their communion being together and interacting. What we then need is to share the same ideals, ultimately to love, which will enable us to commune because we already participate in the same personal structure of reality. This was our second approach — which is significantly similar to (deep) psychological *observation.*

But there is also a third approach, that of sharing not just ideas and ideals, but Being. Does not christian Scripture and Tradition insist that we have to have the same sentiments as Christ, be one with him, and be transformed into him? This is the way of *experience* — the mystical method.

Needless to say, we understand the word mystical as related to the immediate vision of the 'third eye' of the twelfth century scholastics. It goes also without saying that mystical experience cannot displace the reason or the senses. The *oculi*

---

[46] We use on purpose this and other words of an until now foreign culture to the judeo-christian tradition. Not only cultures stifle when closed; also religions. We use the word *ādhyātmik* in the sense not of Sāṃkhya (as a third type of sorrows — the internal ones) but of Vedānta as 'relating to the Self (*ātman*)', as concerning an integral anthropology in which real Man is considered in all its dimensions, as *sat-puruṣa.*

fidei, mentis et sensus belong together. Indeed, this integration is the task of contemporary philosophy. An intercultural approach is here crucial. Our study is an effort in this direction.

We started by asking, how can we get to know Jesus? We then asked, how can we know another individual or another person. Our implicit assumption was that knowledge is our private act by which we come to know others. What if knowledge were not primarily our individual property or activity, but something in which we participate? Reflection would then be not consciousness that my ego knows, but awareness that I share in knowledge, that knowledge is bestowed upon me.

Commenting on Scripture Richard of Saint Victor, expressing a belief of more than one tradition, wrote that love is the source of awareness, that once we are aware of something, contemplation emerges, and from this contemplation knowledge originates.[47]

Millennia earlier, this insight had been the epitome of many a civilisation. Know 'yourself', greek wisdom said, echoed by the christian mystical tradition.[48] Know your 'Self' reemphasizes the Indic tradition: the Self which is your true Self and not precisely 'your' self, not 'yours', and only when it ceases to be yours it will emerge as the Self — which is, to

[47] Jn XIV.21. This sentence, paradoxically enough, seems to give pre-eminence to praxis and from there to love: "He who has (received, accepted) my precepts and follows them, he is who loves me; and he who loves me will be loved by my Father, and I will love him and manifest myself to him" (He, the Man, male or female). "Ex dilectione itaque manifestatio et ex manifestatione contemplatio et ex contemplatione cognitio". Richard of St. Victor, *De trinitate*, Prolog. (PL 196, 888c). The knowledge is certainly a 'cognitio ad vitam aeternam' according to Jn XVII.3. The text adds: "Sed sicut in fide totius boni inchoatio, sic in cognitione totius boni consummatio atque perfectio" ("Whereas in faith there is the beginning of every good thing, we find in knowledge the fullness and perfection of it") *id.* (889 A/B).

[48] Cp. Haas (1971) for a detailed description of this tradition.

be sure, your Self (cp. Mt XVI.24; Lk IX.23).

This means that true knowledge is not of any object. Hence, if we convert Jesus into the object of our knowledge, we may gain a fragile objective knowledge of an individual called Jesus, but we shall have deformed the self-knowledge of Jesus, who did not know himself as an object, and we shall not participate in his self-knowledge. And if Man is characterized by self-knowledge, as long as we do not share in the self-knowledge of that Man we shall not have known that Man. "You cannot know the knower of knowing" says one Upaniṣad (BU III.4.2). "Whereby should one know the knower?" asks further (BU II.4.14). "He, the *ātman*, is not so, and not so...But whereby should one know the knower?" says the same Upaniṣad a little later (BU IV.5.15).

The Upaniṣads teach that if we start by the hunting of an object, there will be no end to it: more and more objects will appear in our horizon, and specialization will go on and on without end. Besides, they warn us, this objective knowledge is not 'that (knowledge knowing) which everything is known'; and this is the question: "whereby can one know it?" (BU II.4.14). The answer cannot be found by following Descartes' 'Regulae', for even assuming that we could succeed in knowing the knower, by this very fact the knower would cease to be the knower and would become the known — known to us and for us. We would have reified the subject, converted it into an object. And our question was about the subject.

There is however a way to know the knower. An accepted English word is realization. The upaniṣadic answer is to become the knower to realize it. We are not far from what apparently Jesus is telling his disciples: Overcome any fear and become what I am, be what I am, eat me, remain in me, . . .

Tat tvam asi is the ultimate upaniṣadic injunction: "that, you are"; discover yourself as a thou, as the thou which says *ahambrahmāsmi*: I am *brahman*. This can only be truly *said* once one has realized that *ātman* (is) *brahman.* The three personal pronouns are here at play. All three are required for the complete realization.[49] A Spanish expression says it poetically: 'el camino más corto pasa por las estrellas', 'the shortest way (between two persons, two hearts) passes through the stars', which is how I would understand a cryptic upaniṣadic text: "He revealed himself threefold": *sa tredhā ātmānam vyakuruta* (BU I.2.3).

The knowledge of the other is not presented here as knowledge of the 'another'. It is simply knowledge, the knowledge that dawns when one becomes what one knows, what one should know: "That is the *ātman* in you, which resides in everything" (BU III.4.2). There is no question here of invading intimacy or objectifying the supposedly 'other'. The other has become your Self. Is it not written: 'Love your neighbour as your Self'?

This is what in one form or another practically all mystical schools have stressed. There is only full knowledge by participation, by reaching identity with the known, and this is more than just an epistemic activity. To come to know Jesus is not just to gain information about the son of Mary, not even about what it means to be the 'Son of God' (Harnack in this sense was right). To come to know Jesus is a mystical act — the highest performance of the human spirit.

To sum up. If we share a human nature and this nature has an intellectual facet, self-knowledge is not only knowledge of our respective egos, but sharing in knowledge (in the knowledge of the self — as subjective genitive). A monistic worldview will say that this knowledge is not possible as long as we are not just pure knowledge. A monotheistic worldview will maintain the privilege of a Supreme Being and grant us only an asymptotic and analogous knowing process. A trinitarian vision will grant both identity and difference. We may

[49] Cp. Panikkar (1977/XXV), pp. 696 sq.

know and become the other in as much as we share in the same reality, but reality being irreducible to unqualified oneness we shall never lose our uniqueness — and mystery. To be sure, the other in this experience is not an *aliud.* It is the *thou* in polar relation with the I. "No one knows the Son except the Father, and no one knows the Father except the Son and any one to whom the Son wishes to reveal (him)" (Mt XI.27).

It should be clear by now that our enterprise is not a problem to be solved, but a life to be lived.

* * *

Let us recapitulate.

We want to know the self-experience of the Man Jesus, we dare to speak about the mysticism of Jesus the Christ.

If he is just another historical individual who lived in Palestine two millennia ago, we shall have to follow the current exegetical method. It will be very useful in situating the context of that individual and is a necessary corrective against projecting our own assumptions onto a non-existent background. But we would remain respectfully at the prescribed geographical and historical distance: Jesus, a fascinating and intriguing Stranger, an *it.* We may — or may not — find that "It is the Way". A doctrine.

If in our consciousness we discover ourselves as persons, i.e. as I-Thou polarities, the reality of the thou will disclose itself (thouself) to us more and more in the measure that our intimacy is illumined by the loving intellect: Jesus; a living and mysterious companion, a *Thou.* We may find — or not — that "Thou art the Truth" A personal encounter.

If in our process of knowing ourselves we touch an innermost Self into which our ego has been transformed, i.e. if we become or realize that Self, we will discover in it that very figure which triggered our search: Christ, a symbol of that

Self which, without it, we would not dare to identify ourselves with, the *I*. We may find — or not — that 'I am the Life' A mystical experience.

The three disclaimers after the three dashes of our last paragraphs are not an anti-climax or expression of a personal fear. They perform a threefold function.

First, our considerations do not elicit an apodictic conclusion. They are not syllogisms. There is place for freedom.

Second, our reading is not the only possible one. There is room for other interpretations.

Third, our meditation may have gone astray in spite of my convictions and good will. There is a welcome for corrections.

* * *

This long introduction paves the way, and at the same time tells us that the three methods are not only legitimate, but that they are relative to their respective world views. Since we are aware of this pluralism we will try to complement one method by the other.

II. THE UTTERANCES

meinate en emoi,
kagô en hymîn

"Manete in me,
et ego in vobis"

"Dwell in me,
as I in you"
Jn XV.3

In a topic like this the questioner is not partially, but totally involved — although not committed to defend any 'party line'. My only commitment is to what I experience as true — to put it briefly, for this very statement is not an uncritical one: "It is by experience that Men come to science and art".[50] But my experience is not infallible when it comes to its expressions, which need to be open to critique and dialogue.

My involvement has to be total since the question is an existential one. It asks critically what is the ultimate sense of life.[51] This question about the ultimate meaning of life is the homeomorphic equivalent to the question about the identity of Jesus Christ. When we ask who is Jesus Christ we expect an answer that will disclose to us much more than the biographical data of just an individual. Who was Akbar or Moctezuma are important questions, but we do not relate them directly with the ultimate meaning of life, as we would do with the thrust behind the question about Jesus Christ. The answer may be disappointing or different from what one expects, but the question is charged with that expectation. Expectation does not amount to presumption, since our question is a critical one and we should be prepared for any answer. As to the question why asking about Akbar or Moctezuma could not have the same momentous weight, the answer is that it could, but that in fact it has not had it. Christian imperialism? It could be, if we were to forget (as it has been often the case) three qualifications to our issue:

(a) The question about anybody triggers the search for the mystery of Man and of reality and in this respect the question about Jesus is just one example of the question about the mystery of any person. And, in fact, from Homer to Glenon, in the western world, there have been many such icons. Jesus

---

[50] *apobainei d'epistêmê kai téchnê dià tês empeirias toĩs anthrópois* (*Hominibus autem scientia et ars per experientiam evenit*) *Arist., Met.* I.1 (981 a).

[51] "...le 'Christ' paraît échapper à tout essai de neutralité et donc d'objectivité. (...) Le Christ, ici, est en quelque sort la *somme jamais totalisée de toutes les interprétations* ou perceptions du Christ qui peuvent se dire en l'humanité". Bellet (1990) p. 23. The entire book could be read as a "Cinquième évangile, qui s'appuie sur les textes, mais d'un appui sans appui, puisque la parole est livrée à sa liberté nécessaire" (p. 60).

is just one of them — central for some, irrelevant for others.

(b) The fact is that the historical relevance in time, space and events (for good and for ill) shown by Christ's impact on human life makes him, if not the only one, certainly, a rather important case. Furthermore, in the general climate of western culture, christian or not, history counts. The centrality of history is probably pre-christian and owes a great deal to the Semitic mind, but christians have been the main heirs of the Abrahamic traditions even to the extent of elaborating a complete *Heilsgeschichte* which claims that history culminates in a 'history of salvation'.[52] At any rate history, including the western way of reckoning time itself, has become the criterion of reality largely on account of that very Jesus Christ as he has been interpreted.[53] In this sense the question about Jesus Christ is different from the question about Ashoka, to cite another name.

(c) The very question about the importance of Ashoka, or about anyone for that matter, is already a question conditioned by the importance given to history by the western reflection on the relevance of Jesus of Nazareth. However, the importance of the historical Jesus, dependent as it is from the centrality of history, is not synonymous with the relevance of Christ for the peoples of the world. But we should not pursue this thought further.

We should be clear about our assumption that the question about Jesus is important to our lives. We cannot dismiss our prejudices altogether, but we should be aware of them and ready to eliminate them should they prove to be an obstacle

---

[52]Cp. my criticism in Panikkar (1975) 1.

[53]I have stated elsewhere that the new fad of saying or writing CE meaning Common Era makes things much worse, since 'Before' or 'After Christ' is a much more neutral point of reference than qualifying this era as the common one when it is not for chinese, jews, tamils, muslims and most of the peoples of the world. If christian imperialism is bad, western colonialism is worse.

to the finding of truth. *Amicus mihi Plato . . .* But it is undeniable that the interest of many a reader, and certainly mine, about the mystical experience of the Man of Galilee is not because of sheer curiosity about a certain individual (respectable and unique as every person is), but because that Man intrigues us (and others) in a special way, and we surmise or believe that his existence is of capital importance for our lives. It is not an indifferent topic.

* * *

We said that involvement does not amount to commitment. We may become disappointed and go away because that Man may not have words of eternal life for me, or because the very words 'eternal life' have become meaningless or even a lie. But the question about the identity of Jesus Christ claims to be an ultimate question. And, I repeat that the answer may be negative. We ask who was that somebody because that somebody has carried significant weight in the history of human life on earth, and has a central meaning still for me and many others. We ought to examine critically if those expectations are justified; but to ignore these expectations would not do justice to the very question which is charged with twenty centuries of history. A context of twenty centuries is the minimum, since for many the very question is pregnant with four millennia (since Abraham), and for others it spans the entire context of human history since the beginning of the universe. The question about Jesus Christ is not an innocent question indeed.[54]

This awareness makes impossible to bypass methodologically a reference to the one who asks the question. Although

---

[54] I have often said, somewhat polemically and within a certain context, that I refuse to owe my allegiance to a sect which has existed only for 2000 years in a restricted part of the world. I do not deny the scandal of historical concreteness, but it is in the concrete that I find the universal.

I do not want to be autobiographical, I cannot deny my convictions nor should I repress them. This implies that my approach may be a combination of the three methods inasmuch as I am convinced of their validity. I do not dispense with form-criticism, historical criticism, knowledge of canonical and apocryphal texts, orthodox and heterodox interpretations, and the like. At the same time I do not accept the hunter epistemology of researchers who imagine themselves without any presupposition, and shoot at anything that moves. Nor do I proceed pietistically, or from a sentimental vision of Jesus — and a one-sided evaluation of history. Christian history is not a model of righteousness.

Our question is not pure speculation, nor a mere theologumenon. For me to be a christian means to have encountered Christ personally; and to be a philosopher (or theologian if one so prefers) means thinking critically about this experience (in this case). The authentic christian is not so much the follower of an ideology or the believer in the belief of others, but the one who has encountered the reality of Christ.[55] Without this encounter it all remains a superstructure (*adhyāsa*). The meaning of any christian sacrament, according to orthodox formulation, is an encounter with Christ. Let us not forget that the grace of Christ is Christ himself, and that the *opus operatum* of catholic theology is not 'magic' but the *opus operantis Christi*.

Now, this encounter is all pure imagination or a mere meeting of ideas or perhaps ideals if it is not a meeting of persons, a personal encounter, i.e., a meeting in the deepest core of our existence, an encounter which embraces all of our being — many mystics say a falling in love. But all this would remain an illusion if this encounter were not possible, if the

[55] I have corrected my spontaneous phrase 'person of Christ' to make the statement as neutral as possible. Cp. Frei (1975) for an important analysis of this Presence of Christ.

true Christ were only a figure of the past or a construction of our fantasy, or at best a remembrance of something gone by. The encounter is not with the 'Messiah' or 'Son of the living God' recalling the petrine confession (Mt XVI.15), but with the 'You' ('thou art') of Christ.

In brief, this encounter is feasible if communication and communion is possible in that deepest core of our being: the person. Here we have another example of what I call the *circulus vitalis* against the *circulus vitiosus,* the vital breakthrough against the vicious begging of the question. It could well be that we have such an idea of person because we have gone through this experience of a personal encounter. At any rate, we say that this encounter is personal, because person is precisely this type of relationship. An isolated individual (if it were to exist) would not be a person. Yet person is our most intimate reality, the most mysterious. It is incommunicable, because it is (already) communion.

Here is where I should apply to myself the theory of the *pisteuma.* It is easier to speak of it in the third person. I cannot describe the meaning of Durgā for a believer in Durgā if I do not reach the *pisteuma* of the believer, which may be different from the *noema* of the onlooker. Similarly, I will not give a proper description of Jesus Christ if I put in *epochê* my belief in that symbol. In confessing my belief I shall automatically avoid any possible absolutization such as believers in reason are often prone to make when they speak of pure reason. I will constantly remember that it is my belief.

* * *

All this needed to be clarified at the outset because it both justifies and relativizes the choice of texts.[56]

---

[56]Tellingly enough, the excellent chapter by Dodd (1970) on the 'Personal traits' of Jesus (49–64) describes some of Jesus' observations regarding things and people but not the utterances concerning himself. Cp.

The choice of the three texts or groups of sayings shows already a certain preference. I could defend the choice by saying that christian tradition has considered them to be central. But here again this understanding of tradition depends already on an option — even if it follows the historical routine of what scholars call the Great Church. I am sufficiently aware of the dark historical facets and manoeuvres of that Church so as to be able to overcome such a routine. The texts are certainly not the only ones one could chose, but they yield a certain picture of the mystical experience that the Man Jesus Christ may have had according to tradition — notwithstanding value judgements of any type on exegetical remarks situating and grading the texts.

My comments claim to be valid even if the historical Jesus did not utter those words or was not the second person of the Trinity. I takehim to be at any rate a *prototypos* of the human condition. It should be clear by now, that if I speak of experience and of encounter with Christ this cannot be a meeting with a Jesus of the past. It would then be merely remembrance or hallucination.

By saying this I am in no way ignoring the immense work of exegetical analysis, nor am I contesting traditional orthodoxies. I am not even attempting to situate Jesus Christ in an Asian context, saying for instance that he is the *sadguru*, the (or a) *jīvanmukta*, the supreme *satyāgrahī*, *advaitin* or *yogi*, the incarnate Prajāpati, *cit*, highest *avatāra, ādi-puruṣa*, divine *śakti*, tempiternal *auṃ* or the like.[57] Nor am I comparing Christ with key-figures in other religions.[58] Having delved

---

also Kahlefeld (1984). ("Christentum ist eine Beziehung auf die konkrete Gestalt Jesu Christi"). Cp. also the somewhat dated and yet valuable books by Felder (1953) and Graham (1947) both of which have a chapter on 'The Personality of Jesus' and Felder even a subchapter on 'The Interior Life of Jesus'.

[57] Cp. Sugirtharajah (1993).

[58] Cp. as mere examples Robinson, J.A.T (1979), Fries (1981), Venkate-

into most of those subjects elsewhere I am trying here a much humbler, although riskier enterprise: a personal exercise in what the ancients said *fides quaerens intellectum*, convinced as I am that faith is the life of Man (Habac II, 4; Rom. I, 17; Gal. III, 11; Hebr X, 38) or that faith is the way to liberation (*Upadeśasāhasrī*, I, 1).[59] 'If you do not believe you will not survive (or understand' says another traditional interpretation of a probably more down-to-earth original Hebrew text (Is VII.9).

Having said this much, I discover immediately that I am not alone either in the experience, or in the interpretation of it.[60] In fact most of the genuinely mystical interpretations of Christ point in the same direction. There is also a revealing similarity with the affirmations of scores of philosophers and sages from other traditions — without affirming now that they all say 'the same' (as of a Kantian 'thing in itself').

Be this as it may, it is further worth pointing out that, although christianity claims to be based on the person of Jesus, except for some ontological and cosmological interpretations of Jesus Christ, during the first centuries (the councils of Nicea, Chalcedon and Constantinople being the most representative), most christian self-understanding is based on the historical narratives of the words and actions of Jesus, as interpreted by tradition, rather than on one's own personal consciousness. We should recall once again the almost unanimous tradition of most religions that faith or initiation is required for the authentic study of 'sacred doctrines'. However, in the modern christian tradition there is a strong wind

sananda (1983), Koyama (1984), Knitter (1985), Thomas M.M. (1987), Ishanand (1988), Dupuis (1989), Keenan (1989), Moran (1992), Lefebure (1993).

[59] Cp. the important statements on *śraddhā* (faith) by the *Bhagavad Gītā*: III, 31; VI, 37, 47; VII, 21–22; IX, 23; XVII, 1–17; etc.

[60] Cp. the emerging non-western christologies in recent times, some of them mentioned in the bibliography. Cp. also Amaladass (1981).

of objectivity which has dispelled the mystical awareness and blown it to the outskirts of christian life. The christic faith, which began as a *religiousness of the Word,* evolved more and more, sociologically speaking, into a *religion of the Book. Intelligenti pauca.*

Whoever that young rabbi might have been or whatever self-consciousness he might have had, the important and decisive thing was supposed to be the belief in what had been written down about him, not only in the first (canonical) documents, but also in the subsequent (conciliar — and for some even, papal) writings. And, to be sure, in spite of many divergent ideas, there is a certain consensus in acknowledging what he did and said. All the problems seemed to have been solved for a time by saying that he was the Son of God, or at any rate an extraordinary prophet, an instrument of the divinity for a cosmic and historical role. In a word, his function, his doctrine, his example, seemed to be what really matters. Christian faith became almost synonymous with acknowledging a set of facts and doctrines. The living figure of Jesus Christ was wrapped around and protected by a heavy doctrinal garb, like those traditional south-European Madonnas almost buried under heavy vestments, jewels and flowers. The recent Roman Catholic Catechism seems to be a case in point. I am contesting neither the legitimacy nor the truth-contents of those belief-systems. I am only undertaking another pilgrimage, or rather trying to be a fellow-traveller on the human path who this time has unloaded his rucksack.

To put it differently. It is customary today to speak about a christology 'from above' in contrast to a christology 'from bellow'. I shun labels, but if at all I would call this study a christology 'from within' — well knowing that the 'reign of the heavens' is *entos*: neither 'among' nor 'inside' but 'between' us. For this reason I am submitting my experience to the dialogue and critique of the 'us', the 'you' of the community.

One did not need to be overcurious over the Man Jesus since he was considered to be ultimately a divine being. This attitude was understandable as long as the christian emphasis was on theocentrism. Jesus remained simply an instrument of God: he raised him from the dead, he inspired him regarding what to say and what to do, he was behind him when performing miracles. After all, Jesus said that he came to do the will of the Father and that he spoke only what the Father wanted him to say. Listening to him the christian obeys the will of God. What else do we need? Is it not unhealthy curiosity to scrutinize what the Man Jesus felt and experienced apart from what he plainly said and did?

We should not forget this warning. We may feel the need of psychoanalysing Jesus. We cannot forbid to do this; and it is legitimate. Yet, we should then not speak of his mystical awareness, but of his psychological make-up. This is all the more an important caution because the increased interest in psychology, the weakening of a certain image of God, and the growing fascination with the Christ figure outside ecclesiastical precincts seem to justify this desire to know about the Man Jesus and what impelled him to say and do what he said and did.[61] What did he think he was?

We may let him stretch on the couch, but we may also walk with him and ask him *where* he lives (Jn I.38), i.e. from where does he speak. We follow this second path as a via media between experimental psychology and deductive theology. Yet, we know that he was rather elusive.[62] If lives of

---

[61] A reference here to Drewermann (1984/1985), (1987/1988) seems unavoidable. In no way should we minimize the importance of the theological controversy around his ideas. Cp. Benedikt-Sobel (1992).

[62] "I do indeed think that we can now know almost nothing concerning the life and personality of Jesus". Bultmann (1985) 8. "This much misunderstood quotation should not be taken to mean that Bultmann

Jesus continue to multiply uncontrollably today, is it all curiosity or a mere literary device? Or is it because his figure is still inspiring both for good and for ill? Jesus remains an intriguing figure.[63]

The western christian and post-christian traditions might perhaps be interested in such approaches — as the many modern novels about Jesus show. But we happen to approach the figure of Christ, not with psychological curiosity, or apologetic aims, or even theological intentions (to resurrect Arius' ideas, for instance) but we try to approach him from the Indic perspective, which almost unconsciously asks what sort of 'divinely-intoxicated' person or what type of religious hero was that historical figure, who has triggered one of the most prominent movements in the last two millennia.[64] Let us not forget our context. What he did, we roughly know, what he might have said we have also heard, what has come out of all this lies in front of us. Is it not a legitimate question to ask simply once again who he was? We know what christians have said concerning who he was.[65] What did he himself think

denies all knowledge of the historical Jesus. What cannot be known is the inner life, the heroic struggle, which so fascinated the earlier interpreters". Baird (1977) 39.

[63]We have already alluded to the interest of Christ in a wider context. Cp. Stöckli (1991) for a Steiner-approach, Schiwy (1990) for a New-Age thoughtful presentation and Massa (1995) for short contributions on a mystical understanding of Christ.

[64]The 32 pages article on Jesus Christ by Geiselmann (1962) ends with the following: "Was wir hier vor uns haben — darüber sollten wir uns nicht täuschen — , ist nur das spezifisch abendländische Verständnis von Jesus Christus. Vielleicht werden uns andere Seiten an Christus aufgehen und neue, den Abendländern nicht zugängliche Tiefen erschlossen, wenn einmal östliches, asiatisches Empfinden und Denken das Mysterium Christus ergründen". p. 770. This quotation may be supplemented by the so often cited sentence of Keshub Chunder Sen in the middle of last century in India: "It seems that the Christ that has come to us is an Englishman . . . ".

[65]Artists have often a deeper intuition: "Whoever he was or was not,

that he was? How did he bear his human consciousness?[66] He asked about who people said that the Son of Man was. We throw back the question and ask: What do you say of yourself? Who do you say you *are*? Or should we be satisfied by his elusive answer to John the Baptist? (Mt XI.2–6).[67] We should here underscore the importance of the newly emerging 'feminist christologies'. They offer not only a badly needed corrective to patriarchal (and 'kyriocentric') interpretations, but also an essential complement to christological studies.[68]

Is it perhaps a blasphemy to dare enter into the personal intimacy of that Christ?

* * *

When all is said and done, we have still to make a final leap. It is not a merely theoretical exercise, nor an act of the will. It is an experiential and existential plunge into the depths of reality, into what Paul calls the depths, the abyss of the Godhead (Rom 8.39; Eph 3.18; I Cor 2.9.10). We could call it the christian mystical experience.

---

whoever he thought he was, ...he was a man once, whatever else he may have been. And he had man's face, a human face." Buechner (1974) begins his pictorial book with splendid photographs throughout ages and cultures.

[66] "Sed primum quod tunc (ad primum usum rationis) homini cogitandum occurit, est *deliberare de seipso* . . . " D. Thom. *Sum. theol.* I–II, q. 89, a. 6. And again: "primum quod occurit homini discretionem habenti est quod *de se ipso cogitet*, ad quem alia ordinet sicut ad finem" (ib. ad 3). My emphasis "the first thing which happens to Man (when he reaches the first use of reason) is that he ponders about himself . . . ". And again: "the first thing that happens to a Man coming of age is to think about himself so that he organizes all the other things (as means) to his end". Could Jesus be an exception to this?

[67] I should acknowledge the excellent Christologies of Kasper (1974), Sobrino (1976), Rovira Belloso (1984), González Faus (1984), which nevertheless do not consider the fact that christology could be relevant to other cultures and religions as well — as nowadays Dupuis (1994) does.

[68] Cp. as a single example, Schüssler Fiorenza (1990) with abundant bibliography.

Christ's experience was his personal experience. If I relate it to my own personal experience it is because I have been told about his words, so that the verbalization of my experience takes the form, and uses the language that I have learned from his impact upon me. It remains nevertheless my personal experience. I do not sit silent behind his couch. Nor does he stretch himself there behind me. I go to visit him in his dwelling place and we converse. I have a personal experience about my own identity. When I try to expresss it, I might have been influenced by what I learned, and I may use christian or even Christ's vocabulary — and perhaps by this very fact give the impression that I pretend to re-enact his experience. It is simply how I actually interpret my own experience. On the one hand, having meditated on Christ's words and deeds, they may have shaped my experience or given me the frame wherein to express it. On the other hand, the personal experience of my own identity may have found in Christ's example an image and even a model of my own personal experience. I am assuming here neither that it is his grace which made me participant in his experience (as christian scripture suggests) nor that I have had it totally independently on my 'own'. *Hypothesis non fingo.*

Having acknowledged this inextricable relationship, and disregarding now the question whether I am also capable of expressing my own personal experience in other languages, or whether other traditions have also shaped at least the interpretation of my experience, I shall describe my own personal identity as a hermeneutical clue to understand Christ's experience from whatever sources we deem appropriate. We should not put aside critical awareness.

When awakening to reality, when simply awakening to self-consciousness, I find myself piercing through all the layers of being which I discover as veils. These veils reveal to me the shape of what I appear to be, but conceal at the same time what I am. In this conscious pilgrimage towards the core of what I am, I do not find any ground, any resting place on anything, either in me or present to my own consciousness. I cannot identify myself with my body or with my soul or with what I am today, was yesterday, or shall be tomorrow. I discover myself above, beyond, outside, or simply different from anything I can be conscious of. My 'own' ground is an abyss, an 'Abgrund' (or even *Ungrund*). Quite simply I do not discover or find myself. I may or not share the conviction that because I do not come from myself, I must have come from somewhere else. This may be a legitimate logical conclusion, but it is not an experience. The experience of contingency is tangential (as the word says), not transcendent. What it touches (from *tangere*) 'touching us together' (*cum tangere*), cannot be, by definition, the untouchable (transcendence). It is rather the experience that what 'I am' is not the 'creation' of somebody else nor has it an external origin, but that it shares in, is part of that same flow which we call reality.[69] Nobody can experience transcendence. 'Nobody can see God'. What I truly am cannot be something that I am not. All that *I have*, I have received — from my parents, ancestors, culture, earth, and so on, from an evolutionistic past, or *karma*, or God. But what *I am* is surely not identical with what *I have*. The *me*, I have (it), and all the rest along with it. The I, I am (it) — although I may not know what (it) 'is'. This latter is not even the same question.[70]

I may have to confess that it might not have occurred to me to ask who I am, if others had not prompted me to ask it, thus inciting me to search for an answer. I don't know.

[69] "Dicitur autem creatura fluvius (says the traditional Thomas Aquinas), quia fluit semper de esse ad non esse per corruptionem, et de non-esse ad esse per generationem". *Sermones festivi*, 61 ("The created being is called a river, because it always flows from being to non-being by disintegration, and from non-being to being by coming to life").

[70] Cp. Panikkar (1986/10).

Self-alienation is rampant in our days.

Since my youth I was given the answer that it was God who created 'me', but since that time, although I was not able to formulate it until later on, I had the experience that this very 'me' was not really I. I have a 'me', but I am not identical with that 'me'. 'My' I seems to stand beyond that 'me'. But of that I, which is in some way inseparable from my 'me', nothing could be said. I felt responsible for all that the 'me' did, but not completely accountable for what this 'me' was (or is). All has been given to 'me' — my ideas, my ways of reaching intelligibility, besides, of course, my time, space, birth, inclinations, and what not. No scientific answer is here sufficient. It all may be the fruit of the total evolution of the human species that has come to be 'me', but all this does not yet reach or uncover the I. The I is not the 'me', although the 'me' uses, sometimes abuses, and other moments usurps the I.

I have long meditated upon a passage from the *Ṛg Veda* (I.164.37):

> What I am I do not know.
> I wonder secluded, burdened by my mind.
> When the Firstborn of Truth has come to me
> I receive a share in that selfsame Word.

But a commentary here is out of question.

A paradox appears. The more my 'me' acts, the less the I is active, the more the I acts, the less the 'me' intervenes. The explanation seems obvious: I cannot say, nor know *what* I am because the possible predicates can never be, *qua* predicates, identified with the subject. My self-consciousness can never be totally objectified. The I is prior or superior to the knowing what or who I am. Making a long story truly short, I came to experience *me* as the *thou* of the I. The I moves me as a thou, the thou is the *agora*, the *kṣetra*, the field of the I.

My task was more to listen than to speak. I could also sense that my so-called prayer was more an allowing to be led than asking for help, more a reaction to a quandary put to me than a query presented to somebody else. To call God the Thou seemed to me, with all due respect, unconvincing — and egocentric. God, if at all, is the I and me the thou.

Yet in moments of difficulty, of suffering, and of trial in my life I spontaneously began to say You, God, Father, Divinity — and, of course, most often: Christ, my *iṣṭa-devatā*.

On a second round, as it were, the roles inverted: the *intimior intimo meo* of Augustin, Ibn'Arabi, Thomas, Eckhart, Calvin and so many others, began to become real. My little *me* was not relevant, not ultimate. I discovered an echo in a cryptic sentence of Paul: It is not my *me* that counts. (Act XX.24). The I was elusive, but a more real self appeared which was neither my ego nor a divine I. My true self could be neither a simple rational animal nor a divine being. A *mesitês* (I Tim II.5) was dawning within, a mediator (not an intermediary) between the infinite (whose traditional name is God, Transcendence, the absolute I . . .) and my ego, my me. To my mind, and heart, of course, came all the texts which describe the indwelling of Christ in the deepest core of my being, and similar statements by great spiritual masters of other traditions. I could also personally re-enact the four adverbs of the Council of Chalcedon,[71] the theanthropy of Boulgakov and the *theosis* of so many Fathers of the Church. Should I say that it is the experience of divine immanence? One could call it also the Advaitic experience. The alluded mediator is *anthrôpos* Jesus Christ — as Second Adam in whom the entire human nature is represented (Cp. I Cor XV.22 and Denz 629). I experienced the inner 'energy', 'grace', 'power' that

[71] I experience the human relation with the divine to be, not in hypostatic union, of course, 'inconfuse, immutabiliter, indivise, inseparabiliter' (without confusion, immovable, indivisible, inseparable).

was my inmost self, and that made me do things which are otherwise inexplicable (although psychology can always interfere) offering explanations in two dimensions only. But I am speaking of 'memory' and giving already too much of an 'interpretation'.

I am aware that these 'confessions' make it easy for critics to say that I am reading into the Gospel instead of 'decoding' them objectively. Besides unearthing the fallacy of 'pure objectivity' I would retort that the 'argument' turns in my favour, since the fact that a simple Man like me (and so many others) could have such experiences, makes more believable that the 'Man Jesus Christ' could have had them albeit in a far more eminent way. "Omnis cognitio est per aliquam similitudinem" (Thomas, *Sum. theol.* I, q. 14.a 11, ad 3), as is also said by Aristotle and Kant.

* * *

Before we turn to the alleged insights of Jesus the Christ, let us exemplify our method by analysing a sentence which we may suppose has been uttered by a being like me: 'I am an elephant who flies in the skies'.

At first sight I cannot understand such a proposition. I cannot re-enact the statement 'that I am a flying elephant' — that a human being is an elephant that flies. I have to acknowledge that the sentence is unintelligible to me. True understanding of a sentence amounts to discovering the intelligiblity of the sentence, i.e. to being convinced of the truth of what one understands.[72] I am then bound to limit myself to affirming that a certain human individual, apparently in his senses, makes such a (for me preposterous) affirmation. I project my confidence on another person and trust that for her the sentence has a certain meaning hidden to me.

[72]Cp. Panikkar (1975/3) for the philosophical underpinnings of the following paragraphs.

If I still try to decipher what that person may possibly mean when making such a statement, I may come to the following conclusions:

Although I have to confess that I have not myself acquired such a state of consciousness; nevertheless, having studied totemism, shamanism and other related phenomena I can more or less figure out that a human individual may well identify herself with an elephant — and those who have experienced the feelings and intelligence of those pachyderms may agree with me and may be able to get a kind of elephantine consciousness, and truly affirm that she is (also) an elephant. Stretching my empathy to the utmost I may reenact the sentence 'I am an elephant', although with caution, provisos and trepidation, because I have not abandoned my human consciousness as well.

I will have to confess, however, that the proposition is not totally intelligible to me, and that I can make only some partial sense of it through empathy with somebody whom I trust and who says 'I am an elephant'. In short, I may 'believe' that the sentence 'I am an elephant' may have certain meaning for a very special human being, although I do not fully reach that 'level' or that stage of consciousness.

But the second part of the proposition is unacceptable to me: 'flying in the skies'. Here I will have to say that my fellow-being is either dreaming or suffering an hallucination. No real elephant, I will argue, ever flies in the skies. My hero is certainly wrong in venturing such an affirmation. It is simply senseless, and with my best will and desire to believe I will have to conclude that the Man is either deceiving him/herself or deceiving all of us. He/she may be a (very special) human being with supernatural flying powers; she may identify herself with an elephant, but not with a 'flying elephant', for an elephant does not fly.

Furthermore, connecting the two parts of the sentence I

will come to the comforting suspicion that the first part is probably also an illusion. If my *noêma* rejects both parts, my *pisteuma* may stretch up to the first section of the sentence, but both *noêma* and *pisteuma* oblige me to reject the second part of the statement. We cannot believe what we believe is unbelievable even though based on the authority that Christ is God, the Church has a divine 'hot-line' or the *magisterium* a superior type of knowledge or the like. If a thousand scriptures assure me that the fire does not burn, I will not believe them, said the Mīmāṃsakas more than a thousand years ago.

We should distinguish between rational knowledge and other possible kinds of knowledge, as most religious traditions assert. But we cannot contradict ourselves. Belief has to be reasonable and reason believable. I may believe what I cannot understand, but I cannot believe the (for me) unbelievable. I may believe anything provided I believe it believable. Tertullian may say 'credo quia absurdum' because he believes that the 'absurdum' may be believable — thus upsetting the rational (natural) order. But we should stop here.

In sum, there is no point in formulating statements if we are not able to make sense of those formulations. There is no point in saying 'I and the Father are one', if the sentence is for us apriori meaningless. And it is meaningless if we are closed to non-sensual and non-deductible propositions. And we shall be closed to the meaning of those propositions if our life moves only on the sensual and purely rational levels, i.e., if we are insensitive to the third dimension of reality, blind to mystical awareness.

No more need be said. At the risk of seeming to project this experience on Jesus Christ, or rather believing that this experience may be a shadow of Christ's experience, I approach what I consider the three *mahāvākyāni* of Jesus the Christ.[73]

---

[73] *Mahā* (great) *vākya* (sentence). The Vedāntic tradition has con-

1. Abba, Pater!

The Text

It is almost a moot question to ask which of the texts we shall introduce is more relevant, since everything is connected. But most probably this first group of texts could be said to be central to the entire christian understanding.[74]

(i) Abba, Father,
all things are possible to thee;
take this cup away from me.
Yet not what I will,
but what thou will

Mk XIV.36
(cp. also Mt XXV.39,
Lk XXII.42; [Jn XII.27]).

Quite a revealing duplication! *Abba* means father and *patêr* means father.[75] If Jesus spoke in aramaic he may not have reduplicated the word, but I imagine that Mark (and his source(s)) was impelled to do this in order to render the ambivalence of the word: on the one hand, daddy, biological father, lovable head of the family, and on the other, the more common name for the closer and less terrifying aspect of the Deity in many religions, including judaism, of course —

densed the teaching of the *Upaniṣads* in five 'great sentences' called *mahāvākyāni*.

[74]We give the greek only where we find it important. We sometimes draw on more than one translation in order to show different shades of meaning. When nothing is stated, the translation is our own, leaning of course on the many existing versions.

[75]"Even without our willingness to venture on the hopeless enterprise of dissecting the psychology of Jesus (...)" begins Schillebeckx (1985) 146 in one of his considerations on Abba. Elsewhere he concludes that Christ's "*Abba* experience is the source of his message and praxis" (125).

patriarchalism not withstanding.[76] After reading many documents of the ancient religions, one might wonder whether calling God Father and Mother is an anthropomorphism, or whether, on the contrary, calling the parents father and mother, is a theomorphism. Human fellowship with the Gods seems sometimes closer to primordial Man than merely family relationships.

The word *abba* was probably kept in the first christian liturgies to stress the special relationship with the Divinity which the word meant on the lips of Jesus.[77] He might, as the Gospels report, have constantly pronounced it, but it appears only once verbatim. On other occasions *patêr* alone appears.[78] In John we have 35 times *ho patêr mou*: 'my father'. It is important to remark that the only time in which the Aramaic word is reported on the lips of Jesus is in his almost desperate prayer at Gethsemane: pleading to be spared that 'time' but adding that the Father's will be done.[79]

Jesus is undoubtedly convinced that God is his Father. He speaks of God as my Father[80] in a provocative way (Kittel says "disrespectful")[81] for his own jewish tradition.[82] He

[76] Cp. a good summary in Schrenk (1967) especially pp. 945–59, and Quell (1967) for the AT (pp. 959–82). Cp. also Heisler (1961), pp. 464–666; Van Der Leeuw (1956) 20 (pp. 195–201) for a few references.

[77] "The cry Abba is here regarded as an experience of fundamental signifiance" Schrenk (1967) 1006.

[78] "*Abba es*, sin duda, la palabra teológicamente más densa de todo el Nuevo Testamento" writes González de Cardenal (1975) 99 in his chapter "La invocación 'Abba' y su valencia cristológica" (97–104), with many bibliographical references. The whole work is a valuable contribution to the "Comprensión de Cristo a la luz de la categoria del *encuentro*" (XIII).

[79] Cp. Schrenk, p. 985, for the other references. The New Testament uses the word 'Father' 415 times, most often in reference to God.

[80] We refrain from quoting the overwhelming number of studies on this subject. Cp. the bibliography contained in the few works we cite.

[81] Kittel (1964) I.6.

[82] Cp. a summary with pre-Semitic and other sources in the very first

refers to him as Father in the intimacy of his prayer: in jubilation (Mt XI.25; Lk X.21), on the Cross (Lk XXIII.34, in exalted prayer when facing death by being stoned (Jn XII.27, 28), in direct prayer to his Father (Jn XVII.1.5), calling him holy or righteous Father (Jn XVII.11,25), etc.

The two other times in which the Aramaic word appears are in the Epistles of St Paul. The context is our human calling upon the father (*Abba* is a vocative). We are capable of doing it by the power of the Spirit in the relationship of true filiation.

> (ii) For all who are guided by the Spirit of God are children of God. The Spirit you have received is not a spirit of serfdom leading you back into fear but a Spirit that makes us children, enabling us to cry 'Abba! Father'! The same Spirit joins with our spirit in testifying that we are God's children; and if children, then heirs: God's heirs and Christ's fellow-heirs, since we suffer with him so that we may be glorified [also] with him.
>
> (Rom 8, 14–16)

When Paul sets on our lips this cry of 'Abba Pater', he affirms that it is our being children of God that entitles us to utter such a cry, and adds immediately that both the divine Spirit and our spirit bear witness that God is our Father, i.e., that we are his children. It is this witnessing of our own spirit that emboldens us to speak about Jesus' Spirit.[83]

The same experience is described in the third text:

---

article of Botterweck-Ringgren (1973), 1–19. Although Jahweh is called Father of the people of Israel Ringgren affirms: "Sonst wird Jhwh sehr selten im AT als Vater bezeichnet" (17) adding that "God as father does not have any central position in the faith of Israel" (19). For the notion of Son in Israel cp. also *ib.* I.668–82.

[83] The astounding sentences of I Cor II.10–16 are worth meditating for our purpose.

(iii) And because you are children, God has sent into our hearts the Spirit of his Son, crying, 'Abba, Father!' So you are no longer a servant but a child, and if a child also an heir through God.

(Gal IV.6–7)

Here is again a 'vital circle', a sort of *perichorêsis*. It is because we are children that God sends his Spirit, and because God sends his Spirit we are his children. Christian theology has seen in Christ the 'cause' of our filiation.

The Interpretation

Two fundamental ideas emerge from those texts: Jesus calls God his Father and empowers his disciples to do the same by virtue of the inner working of the indwelling divine Spirit.

What does it mean?

First of all, it means what it says within the jewish tradition of that time which echoes the entire Semitic world of the two previous millennia. 'God is Father' — and Father means begetter, educator, protector, ruler, lover. This belongs undoubtedly to a patriarchal culture which we may and should criticize. But precisely because of this patriarchalism the word has an 'inclusive meaning' as giver of life. Purified from its anthropomorphic underpinnings, it can be interpreted as denoting source, origin, foundation — as later tradition will understand the word father when using it in the trinitarian doctrine. It has little to do with gender or sex.[84]

But secondly, and strikingly, since the very beginning, as his contemporaries noticed, Jesus stresses that God *is his* Father, his 'Daddy' in such an intimate manner that christian tradition affirms that Jesus of Nazareth had no other Father. Whether we can reconcile our sentence with the existence of

[84] It may be for this reason that Lee (1993) writes: "It appears strange that Israel seems almost intentionally and for a long time to have avoided calling God its 'Father'." (p. 49)

another purely human father, not in competition with the divine Father, is not our concern. We are only trying to understand Jesus' experience. To be sure, Jesus seems to have had a very special experience of his divine sonship.

The numerous texts in which Christ refers to his Father are so well attested and have been so thoroughly investigated that we do not need to elaborate further on this: Jesus calls God his Father.

Only one remark seems pertinent at this point. The Father-Son relation is so intimate that we slide either into an anthropomorphic idea of God (God is the Father of Man) or a theomorphic image of Man (Man is the Son of God). Classical theologies underscore the former. God is a transcendent Father. More contemporary christologies, the latter. Man is an immanent Son.[85]

The two other texts are also relevant although they have sometimes been marginalized in comparison with the first. We do not wish to argue now whether *teknon* (child) and *hyios* (son) mean the same or whether the *hyiothesia* of Rom VIII.15 means adoption as a legal form (*fictio iuris*) or may have another less legalistic meaning. At any rate, the texts explicitly tell us that we may also share in Christ's filiation to the Father. The texts make plain that Christ is the 'cause', the 'head of the Body', the reason why we also share divine nature (II Petr. I.4).[86]

These two latter texts are not reported as Jesus' words;

[85]González Faus (1984) could be adduced here as a beautiful example. Commenting on John (and his Prologue), he remarks against some theologians "que Juan no ve más divinidad en Jesús que la de ser hombre" (331) and quotes several times (221, 238, 333) L. Boff's sentence, refering, of course, to Jesus: "así de [tan] humano sólo puede serlo el mismo Dios" ("only God can be human to such an extent").

[86]Gregory of Nyssa defines christianity as *tês theias physeôs mimêsis* ("imitatio divinae naturae") "an imitation of divine nature", *De professione christiana* (PG 46.244).

but they show the central message of Christ as understood by a qualified disciple of Jesus: If Jesus truly calls God his Father, those who have received his Spirit have the same power of calling God their Father: they have been adopted as children with the same rights. This can only be the case if Jesus is understood to be our brother. Brothers are those who have the same father.

Needless to remember that calling does not mean naming in a merely nominalistic sense. Every call, active or passive, amounts to an empowering (cp. Rom IX.12, Hebr V.4; I Cor I.9; etc.). The power of the name (and of naming), of course, has weakened in modern consciousness.

In a word, if Christ calls God his Father we too can re-enact this experience by the gift of the Spirit (cp. Rom VIII.9). If we both (Christ and us) call God our Father, we may then try to understand what Jesus said.

The Experience

I venture the following desciption *salva reverentia*:

> You, divine mystery, whom my own people call Father, you are truly the direct origin, the begetter of what I am, you are the source from which I proceed. I sense that your life passes through me, that my life does not proceed from me, but from a source which gives me not only life in general but also words, ideas, inspiration, and all what I am. What I speak is always somewhat 'heard'. If I were born in an *apauruṣeya* tradition I could as well have said that I experience the very language of things and situations, that I can hear what they say. But as I belong to a monotheistic people, I express that experience by saying that through them (things and events) I discover your voice and your will. Peter surmised it, and that's

why I blessed him: He told me '*Thou Art*' (You are) — and then he felt the need of adding some attributes belonging to the culture of his people: 'Son of the living God' 'Anointed', etc. This was too exclusively linked with jewish culture, and I told him not to proclaim it. In the language of later centuries I could say that I experienced the *creatio continua*, or rather the constant *generatio*. I am being constantly begotten, created, sustained, given life, inspired . . . by that invisible Mystery which people call God and picture in the most diverse ways. 'Today you have been begotten' was what I heard at the Jordan and on Mount Tabor — and the word *Son* still reverberates in my ears.

In saying this I am stressing an intimate and constitutive relation, but nevertheless a hierarchical one. You are the Father, I am the Son; you are the Source, I am the river of living waters gushing forth from You. Without you, nothing. I have learned obedience, the hard way, as Paul rightly suspected (or whoever wrote Hebr VIII.7–9). There is difference between us. Only you are good, it is not my will that counts. I do not even know your 'plans'. I have the clear consciousness that my task is a historical one, as I will have to go away and back to you. Although I was unwilling to be called a prophet, I feel that the common sense of the people was not mistaken when they ascribed to me a historical role to perform or, put in less theistic language, that my personal calling was that of doing something for my fellow-beings and for the universe at large. I had a unique task to perform, and at the end of my short life I could

> cry that I had done it. As for the rest, into your hands I entrusted my spirit.

Does all this make sense to us? Yes, it does. If, in one way or another, we could not re-enact what those words convey, the entire talk about Jesus would be a futile exercise in barren speculation, except perhaps for a conscious or unconscious desire to manipulate Jesus' figure in order to create or maintain a power structure based on that lofty figure. But we have to confess, and we are not alone in this confession — that we find those words pregnant with 'eternal life', because we can truly have a similar experience.[87] Perhaps influenced by his own polemic words in response to the jews ("ye are Gods") (Jn X.34 quoting Ps LXXXII.6) the christian tradition has often told us: 'Ye are Christs', '*alter Christus*', or as I would dare say, '*ipse Christus*', following the doctrine of Paul. "Have the same sentiment among you which was in Christ Jesus" (Phil II.5) says Paul in an untranslatable phrase: *toûto phroneîte* (*hoc sentite*, renders the Vulgate, 'mind' [AV, RV], 'attitude' [NAB] 'bearings' [NEB]): share in the same intellectual experience, in the same intelligence or insights than Jesus the Christ. This is the experience we are invited to perform.

It makes sense to me, and I am able to re-enact that experience, or rather to formulate my own experience using that language (although I may be also capable of speaking other languages):

> *Abba, Pater*! I am not the source of my own being, I am pure gift, I have received all that I am, including what I call 'my' I. Everything is grace. I surely experience contingency (to use a philo-

[87] I have found only in Fridolin Stiers the wonderful translation of 'eternal life' (*zôê aiônios*) with 'unendliches Leben', 'infinite Life' — cp. Jn XII.50; XVII.3; Rom VI.23; etc.

sophical concept). I do not find in me my own foundation, the 'reason' of my life.

There is still more. Not only do I discover experientially my own contingency, I equally experience that it all comes from 'you', a mysterious Source which many have substantialised 'it' as a 'Supreme Being'. To call you 'Father' certainly means a filial relation. It means the experience of being begotten, of emerging, as it were, from a Source and sharing its nature. It is the water of the Source which flows down the river, it is not a different water. Yet it does not necessarily mean that 'there is' a Substance which *is*, and besides being, also functions as father. The very name father is a function, not a substance: the father fathers. My Father is not a Being which besides his many activities also gives birth to me. He has no other 'activity' than this one. It is *my* Father who fathers me. It is about this experience of being 'fathered', begotten, produced, given birth that I am speaking and not about somebody else. I am neither substantializing nor projecting into the past something that is an experience, and thus can only be of the present. Nor am I 'personifying'. I rather experience 'it' as the '*fons et origo totius divinitatis*' to quote the Councils of Toledo, as the *theotês* to echo St. Paul (*hapax legomenon* [Col II.9]), as the 'Silence' (*sigê*) out of which the word came, to follow St. Iraeneus.[88] I also know other expressions, although I would not use them (*causa sui, das ganz Andere, ens a se,* etc.). Undoubtedly if I were born in another time and

[88] "Et nous aussi, nous avons conscience de note moi, incrée et créé" says such a traditional theologian as Boulgakov (1982) 193.

> culture I would have called you Mother, and the metaphor would have been probably more powerful and certainly more immediate.
>
> I also feel that this is not my exclusive privilege. Every human being has you as Father; every being is fathered by you, the fountainhead of everything. Truly we are not orphans. We exist because we 'ek-sist', proceed from such an infinite source which is not pinned down by any name, or as one mystic said: You are 'sunder Namen' (nameless), 'über alle Namen' (above all names), '*innominabilis*' (unnameable), and '*omninominabilis*' (named by everything).

Having stated the relativity of the formulation, I may still dedicate a paragraph to the appropriateness of the 'Abba, Pater'.

First of all, it is a vocative, and the three passages where it occurs all tell us of extreme situations, of a cry, a shout, a prayer accompanied even by the shedding of blood. It is a spontaneous outburst of joy, of suffering, or of hope. It is not the literary style of the third person, of the narrative about others or past situations. Nothing short of a personification will satisfy human nature when in extreme situations, it experiences the bottomless life of the creature. We need to personify. An *iṣṭa-devatā* is the most human way to deal with that dimension of the human experience — to find the adequate divine icon for us. We need a divine person.

This is not all. 'Father' stands not only for Source, Power and Person. It stands also for Protection and specially for Love. In the deepest recesses of my human awareness I discover not just love in myself, but that I am capable of loving precisely because I am loved. Human love is a response. Love has been bestowed on me. I am capable of loving because I have been loved. I am not always identifying the Source and the Love, but I experience love as my attraction towards a source, and I experience, at the same time, that the love with which I am loved has also been received. I am not making arguments with love, as people are prone to make with reason, but I can well experience that the Source of everything is also the origin of Love. I experience once again, although often on a minor scale the cited *perichorêsis.* Sometimes I do not respond to the same person with the same love with which I am loved, but I pass it on, as it were, to a third person. I may not have responded adequately to the love of my parents, spouse or friend, but I lavish that love on my children . . . to put an example. The 'dance' goes on. A current of love circulates through the three worlds.

Thirdly, the Father combines in a unique way Power and Love, two ultimate 'ingredients' of the universe. The Father is immensely superior to the son; he is the protector. And as already said, the symbol Father stands equally for Mother, giver of Life, existence, nurture, and Love. This symbol stands at the same time for equality, sharing, participating in the same venture. The son is equal to the father, and this equality is felt even more if the 'father' is mother. And again son here is our patriarchal language, for it indicates simply the offspring, the daughter as much as the boy. *Abba, Pater*, means both Superiority and Equality.

In short, I can certainly re-enact the 'Abba, Pater!' Man is not an orphan, the Earth is her Mother, the Heaven is her Father — as many ancient and primordial traditions assert.

I can read the story of the Man of Galilee in a way in which I discover in what an eminent way he realized this experience, to what extent he felt the nearness and, at the same time, the distance between Father and Son.

If mysticism tells us about the experience of the ultimate reality, the mysticism of Jesus the Christ is the experience of that equality and difference with the Giver of Life, the Source of the universe. *Abba, Patêr!* Every Man is a child. And we may now understand his saying about the children and the kingdom of Heaven. Those who really undergo the father-experience are not precisely the parents. And most theologies commenting on this passage betray — as I have until now — an adult experience. It is not the father who says 'father'. It is the child who shouts and sings and cries 'Father!' — and here the capital case is proper. It is not just a sentiment of dependence or of love. It is rather a primordial feeling of belonging. For this reason we may as well or even better say Mother — what the historical Jesus could certainly not say. To make this experience we do not need to be scribes or Pharisees, learned or religious; we need simply to have been children. Not everyone is a father or mother, but everybody has been a child.

There is but one point in which my experience, if it does not differ, surely qualifies the old and venerable expression. And saying this I voice the feeling of many of my contemporaries, including christians. I am encouraged by Christ's example of not freezing tradition and impelling us to continue and deepen his task (cp. our third group of texts). Creation is not a finished product. And yet I am saying it hesitatingly:

> I can pray and believe in *Abba Patêr!* but with a similar suffering and pain with which, it is reported, you prayed it at Gethsemane. The word 'father' is blurred in our present-day lives. Patriarchalism is bad, but the destruction of the family without any substitution is worse. And we are also all-too aware of the difficulties involved in a pious discourse regarding a loving and almighty father who allows the immense tragedies of all times and those of our technocratic period in an increased way.
>
> I am quite relieved when I discover that the

old formula 'Credo in unum Patrem omnipotentem' does not correspond to your experience. You experienced almost the opposite in the Garden and excruciatingly on the Cross (Mt XXVII.46; Mk XV.34). I experience your Fatherhood, but not your almighty Power, your All-Might,[89]. How could your almighty power allow all this? And all the efforts at an answer seem similar to the response that "God reveals the Trinity just to humble our intelligence". I cannot believe all these *theologumena. Abba, Pater!* is an excruciating prayer, indeed, but not a dehumanizing one.

But there is more. Here perhaps other cultures have shaped my experience. I can understand our need for personification, but not the anthromorphism of the personalistic interpretation of the divine Father-figure. *Abba, Patêr*! represents for me neither the belief in an Other (Substantial Being), nor, and much less, the belief in my embellished Self. Neither dualism (You over there and we

[89] Let us recall the pertinence of the Italian saying 'traduttore traditore' in reference to the christian creed on the 'all-powerful' God, origin of so many theological quandaries. Although the world '*omnipotens*' is found in some early confessions of faith, they translate the Greek *pantokratôr* whose meaning is rather *omnia potens*, i.e. the one who has dominion over all. The *Epistola Apostolorum* (cira 160) in its first article says: "in Patrem dominatorem universi" (Denz 1). We find also: "Credo in unum Patrem omnium dominatorem" (Denz 5) besides the majority of texts referring to *pantokratôr* (*pantokratora*) like Denz 41, 42, 44, 46, 50, 51, 60, 61, 64, 71, etc. The *Vetus Latina* has still *omnia potens*. It was St. Jerome who consecrated the *omnipotens* in the Vulgate. Rebolle (1995) 147 remarks also that *pantokrator* was also the translation of the divine title of *Yahweh seb'âôt*, 'God of the armies' which was also translated as *Kyrios tôn dynameôn* ('Lord of the powers'). Michaelis explains in Kittel (1964) III.915 that *Pantokratôr* refers to God's "supremacy" and not to "power over all things".

> down here), nor monism (an all-swallowing God or an alone-standing self-sufficient Man). Here is where your expression 'my Father' becomes full of life. The Father belongs to the 'I am' that I also am. In this awareness I overcome the naïve belief that my Father is all-powerful — besides other philosophical aporias of the same notion.
>
> And this is not yet all. The designs of 'my Father' are inscrutable, because there is not a super-divine intellect which has planned beforehand the destiny of the universe. My Father is my Father being my Father, and being the Father of all, not being an independent Engineer who has calculated (or miscalculated, according to some) the destiny of the universe. Neither mathematics nor logic are above the divine mystery which you called the Father.

This first experience, however it might be qualified and modified with the following text which stresses equality and the same nature with the Father, is irretrievable and definitive as much as the second one. Human consciousness may reach a supreme stage, as some mystics may claim, but even then when that consciousness reverberates on human shores (we, humans are those who speak of 'infinite consciousness') it shows an infinite difference from the Source. This is precisely the experience of the Trinity. The self-identity of each 'person' is so perfect and absolute that there is no neutral place where diversity could appear. Hence difference is also infinite. Pantheism is not the answer.[90]

[90] We may apply the famous difference between creator and creature (Denz. 806) also to the Trinity. Nothing is finite in the Trinity.

2. I and the Father are One

The Text

Just as the first utterance was not a unique sentence but the expression of a repetedly expressed conviction, this second statement also pervades the entire message of Jesus: his equality with the Father — along with the many qualifications the Gospel writers or he himself may have introduced.

We should mention here the interest of a certain tradition, as well as of modern exegetes, in severing the Synoptics from John's Gospel.[91] Our concern is not with the *ipsissima verba*, but with the complex figure of Christ as understood not only by the first generations but by the christians up to our present times, i.e. by the Church.[92]

I insist. Either the christian believers have projected on the figure of Jesus Christ their desires, anxieties, and expectations, either they are victims of a hallucination, mild as it may be, because the Man Jesus was not what they imagine him to be, or that Man offers a real ground for christian belief.[93]

To repeat, either these sentences make sense for us today, or they are said by an 'elephant flying in the skies'. It should be acceptable if it were a question of God uttering incomprehensible sentences, but then Christ would be just a divine *avatāra* and not a real Man.

Among the many quotations, we adduce only three:

(i) *egô kai ho patêr en esmen*
Ego et Pater unum sumus (Vg.)

[91] Once again stressed by Massa (1995) 2.

[92] Dupuis (1994) 52 writes that if we are not certain of the *ipsissima verba* the *ipsissima intentio* 'can be safely ascertained'.

[93] Suffice to mention Arthur Drews' name (*The Christ Myth* of 1909) with all the 'religionswissenschaftliche' discussions which are still relevant today.

"I and my Father are one" (AV)[94]

Jn X.30

The immediate context of this *mahāvākya* is enlightening. It depicts a heated dispute, even if it may have been reported and re-arranged later. After he had pronounced that statement the jews wanted to stone Jesus, and stoning was unto death. The issue is of life and death.

We will not describe the context of the entire passage. One comment only: Jesus does not dilute the issue. On the contrary, he does not minimize the answer, he maximizes it by daring a 'blasphemous' exegesis of a Hebrew psalm (LXXXII, 6): "You are Gods".[95] It is all epitomized in the finale of the dispute, when he declares that his works should serve as a manifestation of the truthfulness of his words. We are challenged to accept the witness of the works and recognize that

in me est Pater, et ego in Patre (New Vulgate)
Pater in me est, et ego in Patre (Vg.)
The Father is in me, and I in the Father (NEB)

Jn X.38

In another germane text this unity is extended to all those who shall believe in him:

---

[94] We may compare with other translations:
"I and the Father are one" (RV).
"My Father and I are one" (NEB).
"Le Père et moi, nous sommes un" (BJ)
"Ich und der Vater sind eins" (Neue Jerusalemer Bibel, also Rösch and Stier).
"Jo i el Pare som una sola cosa" (Montserat).
"Jo i el Pare som u" (Mateos/Rius Camps).
"Yo y el Padre somos una sola cosa" (Nacar/Colunga).
"Io e il Padre siamo una sola cosa" (Barbaglio).

[95] Cp. Botterweck-Ringgen (1973) in a multitude of places (vgr. I, 681) and Strack-Billerbeck II, 542 sq. and III 223 sq. of the jewish context.

> May they all be one: as thou, Father, art in me, and I in thee, so also may they be in us . . . that they may be one, as we are one; I in them and thou in me, may they be perfectly one. (NEB)
>
> Jn XVII.21–23

This is already an introduction to our second text.

(ii) *ho heôrakôs eme eôraken ton patera*
Qui videt me, videt [et[96]] Patrem (Vg.)
Whoever has seen me, has seen the Father (NRSV; NAB)[97]

Jn XIV.9

If the first context is full of danger and dialectics, this one is full of sorrow and melancholy. It belongs to the so-called last sayings of Jesus, his testament, and farewell discourse. After so much talk about the Father Philip dares to ask to be shown the Father. The answer also has a sad tone:

> So long a time I am with you, Philip, and you have not known me?

He does not say: I have been already a long time with you speaking about the Father, how is it that you still do not know *him*? He does not say him but me!

---

[96]Some Greek texts have *kai* which is given in the Vulgate. On the other hand the New Vulgate says: "Qui vidit me, vidit Patrem".

[97]We give other translations:
"He that hath seen me hath seen the Father" (AV and RV).
"He who sees me sees also the Father" (Confraternity/Challoner-Rheims).
"Qui m'a vu a vu le Père" (BJ).
"Wer mich gesehen hat, hat den Vater gesehen" (Neuer Jerusalemer Bibel).
"Qui m'ha vist a mi, ha vist el Pare" (Montserat).
"Qui em veu a mi present està veient el Pare" (Mateos/Rius Camps).
"El que me ha visto a mi ha visto al Padre (Martin Nieto).
"Chi ha visto me ha visto il Padre" (Barbaglio).

"Anyone who has seen me has seen the Father" (NEB).

Therefore, you have not seen me. The text explains it further:

> Don't you believe that I (am) in the Father and the Father (is) in me?
>
> Jn XIV.10

Our point is that these affirmations made sense for Jesus or for those who since the very beginning put them on the lips of Jesus — and for countless generations thereafter.

(iii) *kathos, aposteilen me ho zôn patêr kagô zô dia ton patera, kai ho trôgôn me kakeinos zêsei di'eme*
Sicut misit me vivens Pater, et ego vivo propter Patrem, (:) et qui manducat me, et ipse vivet propter me (Vg./New Vg.)
As the living Father sent me, and I live because of the Father, so he who eats me shall live because of me. (NEB)[98]

Jn VI.57

The context here is the eucharistic dispute. The unity between Jesus and his Father is extended to all who will participate eucharistically with him.

---

[98] "As the living Father hath sent me, and I live by the Father: so he that eateth me, even he shall live by me." (AV).
"As the living Father sent me, and I live because of the Father; so he that eateth me, he also shall live because of me" (RV).
"De même qu'envoyé par le Père, qui est vivant, moi, je vis par le Père, de même celui qui me mange vivra, lui aussi, par moi" (BJ).
"Wie mich der lebendige Vater gesandt hat und wie ich durch den Vater lebe, so wird jeder, der mich isst, durch mich leben" (Neue Jerusalemer Bibel).
"Així com jo, enviat pel Pare que viu, visc pel Pare, així gui em menja a mi viurá a causa de mi" (Montserat).
"A mi m'ha enviat el Pare, que viu, i jo visc gràcies al Pare; així, també qui em menja a mi viurà gràcies a mi" (Mateos/Rius Camps).

We leave aside one of the most famous utterances of the johannine Jesus: *egô eimi*, "ego sum", "I am" (Jn VIII.58) which echoes the traditional self-description of Yahweh in Ex III, 14 ("I am who I am"). Another polemical "I am" comes at the climax of Jesus' trial (Lk XXII.70), and the 'I' sentences of Jesus have been closely scrutinized. We also pass over that other elusive sentence which Jesus gave when directly asked who he was (Jn VIII.25), and which is difficult to translate. Important as the *egô eimi* statements are, we prefer to leave them out in order not to indulge in theological discussions.[99]

The Interpretation

A more animistic and less individualistic interpretation of these texts might be very helpful, but we want to limit ourselves to our attempt at being able to re-enact the experience behind those words.

What appears clearly in those words is the traditional *perichorêsis* which here is not reduced to the intra-trinitarian realm, but extended to all creation. Is there anything 'outside' the Trinity? The text seems to say that there is a 'current', a Life one is prone to read, which transits from the Father to Christ and to all who commune with him.[100]

From a monotheistic pespective, the radical separation between the human and the divine seemed threatened by those blasphemous confessions. This was Christ's challenge. The first christian thinkers understood it well. "God becomes Man in order that Man become God".[101]. There is a bridge

[99] Cp. Stauffer in Kittel (1964), and in general Lamarche (1965) 1–18, and Liebaert (1965) as well as the other fascicles of vol. III, all of them with abundant bibliography.

[100] 'Quaecumque sunt a Deo ordinem habent ad invicem et ad ipsum Deum' ('Whatever is from God is related to each other and to the same God') was a common christian belief. D. Thom. *Sum. Theol.* I, q. 47, a. 3.

[101] Cp. Clement Alex. *Protept* I, 9 who seems to be the first to have ex-

and the bridge can be crossed over.[102] This Man seems to say that the abyss between the human and the divine does not exist. Probably because of this he eliminated fear and preached love. We have already cited the phrase of *Psalm* LXXXII, 6 "You are Gods".

Besides the 'politeness' of some modern translations of the first text which invert the order of the sentence and the inclusion of the possessive because of the context, we may remark the use of the plural in the verb. The text does not say: 'I am one with the Father'.

The sentence does not say 'I *am* equal with the Father' (or equal to) but 'I and the Father *are* equal'; 'We *are* one'. There is an irreducible 'We', an ultimate 'I and Father'. There is Father and Son; they are different, i.e., Father and Son. The Father is Father, the Son is Son. To be sure, the Father is Father, or rather is the Son's Father, because *he* fathers; and the Son is such because he is the Father's Son.

In a word, there is identity and difference. The difference is Father and Son. The identity is that One, *hen*, *unum*. We should make a simple but momentous remark. Properly speaking, we should not have used the current language which says 'difference'. Father and Son are certainly not identical,

---

plicitly spoken of our divinisation (giving a new meaning to *theopoieîn*). Cp. also Ireneus, *Adv. haer.* III, 19 (P. G., 7. 939 B). St. Gregory the Theologian puts it even more concisely: *hina genômai tosoûton theos, oson ekeînos anthrôpos* (So that I become God in the measure that he [became] Man) (*Oratio theologica* III, 19 [PG 36, 100 A]). For these latter and other quotations, cp. Hausherr (1955) 306–7. Overspanning almost twenty centuries we may quote perhaps the last great scholastic philosopher, underscoring the experiential dimension of christianity: "El hombre es una proyección formal de la propia realidad divina; es una manera finita de ser Dios . . . dios es trascendente 'en' la persona humana, siendo ésta deiformemente Dios . . . El cristianismo es religión de deiformidad. De ahí que el carácter experiencial del cristianismo sea la suprema experiencia teologal" . . . Zubiri (1975) 62.

[102] Eckhart says it with even greater precision: 'filius dei fit homo et filius hominis fit filius dei', In Jn III (LW III.118).

but they are not different either. They could be different only over against a common ground which allows for the difference from each other. But this is only the case if we substantialize both, make of both two substances which obviously would then be different. If we take the Abba-experience in its depth, the Father is Father and nothing else, and so the Son is nothing but Son. Neither Father nor Son are substances.[103]

Father and Son are not different; they are correlates. The one implies the other and there is not the one without the other.

Here the expression 'my Father' acquires its most profound meaning. He had received the retort: 'our father is Abraham' (Jn VIII.39). He answered: "If God were your Father, you would love me" (Jn VIII.42), you would understand that the power comes from the Father (Jn V.19). The expression *my* Father coresponds to the controversial *monogenês, unigenitus*, (Jn I.14; 18; III.16; 18; I Jn IV.9)[104] and

---

[103]The oblivion of tradition is sometimes intriguing not to say suspect. Cp. one single example: *oute ousias onoma ho Patêr . . . oute energeias, scheseôs de kai toû pôs echei pros ton Hyion ho Patêr, e ho Hyios pros ton Patêra . . .* " Nec essentiae nomen est Pater, o viri acutissimi, nec actionis; sed relationem eam indicat, quam Pater erga Filium habet, vel Filius erga Patrem.

[And the example is enlighening] Ut enim apud nos haec nomina germanam quamdam coniunctionem et necessitudinem declarant, ad eumdem modum illic quoque genitorem ac genitum eamdem naturam habere significant". Gregorius Nazianzenus, *Oratio theologica*, III, 16 (PG 36, 96). The name 'Father' is not a substance [not an essence, not a thing]. Nor it is an action [an energy, a power]. O most learned of people! (*ho sophôtatoi*). It is a relation from the Father to the Son and from the Son to the Father. . . meaning that begetter and begotten have the same nature (*homophyian*).

It is the same saint who said: "Do you want some time to become a theologian? . . . Keep the commandments!" giving also the reason: "the praxis is the way to contemplation". *ibid.* XX, 12 (PG 35, 1080 B). This is why I expressed not only intrigue, but suspicion.

[104]The NEB translates as "Father's only Son". This does not render the idea which still is dimly conserved in "only begotten of (from) the

should be related to the controversy about the *prôtotokos*, *primogenitus*.[105] Of course, neither expression is used by Jesus. We may interpret it not as an exclusive, but as an exhaustive sonship. Jesus is not an only son as offspring of a father who could have had many children, but as the ever being born, *semper nascens* as Eckhart would say, from the Father.[106] In this sense the Son can only be one, because the Father is constantly begetting him. Many a controversy and misunderstanding would have been avoided if this interpretation had been taken into consideration.

What concerns us here is the immediate awareness of corelations without which we may easily misunderstand this and other texts.

There is a Source, a source of my being and even a mysterious Source of Being. But this Origin is only such because it originates. The Father is father because (it) fathers; the Son is son because (it) is begotten. There are two poles of one reality. Yet that 'reality' is nothing but the relation (between the 'two').

The Experience

I experience that I live because of that link. It is the link of life.[107] I experience that this life has not been bestowed upon me, it has made me, so that it is me, and I can say 'my

---

Father" (AV & ṚV).

[105] The NEB also evades the literal translation: "his is the primacy over all created things" [in note: "born before"]. "The first born of every creature (of all creation)" (AV & ṚV respectively). Cp. Col I.15; Rom VIII.29.

[106] Commenting on Jn I.1–2 Eckhart writes: "et si semper in principio, semper nascitur, semper generatur" (LW III.9).

[107] "Prius vita quam doctrina" wrote Thomas Aquinas, adding: "vita enim ducit ad cognitionem veritatis" because, as he himself said "vita viventibus est esse".

Life' as Christ said 'my Father'.[108] "As the Father has life in himself, so also he has granted (*edôken*) to the Son to have life in himself" (Jn V.26). We share Life as the source and the river share water. We are water, and as long as the water flows I am not the source but the water of the source.[109]

This experience is far from pantheism, which would be a merely conceptual interpretation of that experience. I am water, but my water is not your water. 'Water' is a mere concept, and 'all is water' a mere abstraction. Each water is unique. And the 'higher' the water we could say stretching the simile, the more different from the common denominator 'water'. Not all thinking is an algebra of concepts.

Let me try my own words: I and the Father are one in the measure that my ego disappears; and my ego disappears to the degree that it allows itself to be shared by anyone who comes to me, 'eats' me, or seeing me does not see me, but what I say or rather what I am. This happens when I have that transparency which is all the more pure the more I am rid of my little self.[110] When my ego is obtrusive, people

---

[108] Cp. St Augustin, *In Ioannis Evangelium Tractatus* XXVI, 19, commenting that if Jesus can say "I live because of the Father" ("vivo proter Patrem" Jn VI.57) while the Father is greater than he (Jn XIV.28) we can also 'live because of Christ' who nevertheless is greater than us.

[109] St Augustine expresses it in a traditional manner: "Quae est ergo doctrina Patris, nisi verbum Patris? Ipse ergo Christus doctrina Patris. Sed, quia Verbum non potest esse nullius sed alicuius, et suam doctrinam dixit seipsum et non suam, quia Patris est Verbum. Quid enim tam tuum est quam tu? et quid tam non tuum quam tu, alicuius es quod es?" *August, Tract. in Ioan.*, XXIX (PL, 35.1629). ("Which is the Father's doctrine if not the Father's Word? Christ himself is the Father's doctrine, if he is the Father's Word. As it is impossible that the Word be of nobody, but it has to be of somebody, he declared that he himself is his doctrine and not his doctrine, because he is the Father's Word. What is more yours than yourself? But what is less yours than yourself, if what you are is somebody's?"). Augustin is commenting upon "my doctrine is not mine, but his who sent me" (Jn VII.16).

[110] We may now complete the quotation of Gregory of Nazianz: "Vis

clash with me, and often meet only their own projections, what they already expect to be and imagine they are. My ego is like a wall against which they rebound.

When I am transparent, I am fearless and truly myself, my Self. Transparency allows for a spontaneity that flows from me only when I am pure. I experience the poverty in spirit precisely in this way. The reign of the heavens is mine when I possess nothing for myself. Blessed are the poor in spirit (Mt V.3) is not a statement about economics. It is the invitation to discover that the entire universe is mine, or rather me, when there is no 'me', no ego to disturb this belonging.[111]

That the pure of heart shall see God expresses the same experience (Mt 5.8). The beatitudes are neither doctrines, nor moral advice, nor injunctions: they are the celebration of the most intimate awareness that, if I do not want anything for my selfish ego, I have everything and am everything. I am one with the source when I, too, act like a source, allowing all that I receive to flow out — like Jesus.

Certainly the person who listens to me hears my voice, sees my face, reads my thoughts, and suffers all my limitations. But it sometimes happens that someone hears through my voice, sees through my face, perceives beyond my thoughts, and gets an insight behind my clumsiness. He who really sees, I would dare say, sees already the Father, the Mystery, Reality.[112]

This is only possible if this intimate union is not selfish,

---

theologus aliquando fieri ac divinitate dignus?" (*tês theotêtos axios*) *Loc. cit.* To be worthy of the Godhead is the requisite for doing authentic *theo-logy,* to utter worthy words about the ultimate mystery.

[111] Cp. the daring statement of Juan de la Cruz saying that all is his: "The heavens are mine, the earth is mine, and the peoples . . . God himself is mine, because Christ is mine and all for me" *Màximas y sentencias*, 25.

[112] I see a homeomorphic equivalent to this experience in the Mahāyānic insight of equating *nirvāṇa* and *saṃsāra*. Who truely experiences *saṃsāra* discovers *nirvāṇa*. Nāgārjuna, *Mādhyamikakārikā*, XXV.19–20.

not egoistically preserved, but shared in communion, service, and love. Are not those experiences more frequent than it might appear?

Christ did come not so much to 'teach' doctrines, but to communicate life, experience (Jn X.10), ultimately, to communicate himself: his 'own' life — that of the Father. I do not deny that he had those experiences in such a degree that my own insights fade away as pale imitations. But we do not need to play the humble-minded and the sinner, in order that he may appear the saint and the divine. I even sense that Jesus does not like those attitudes. "*Ego dixi, dii estis*" as already quoted (Ps 82.6, Jn 10.34). Why, then, should we not feel entitled to speak like a God? Personal dignity implies that we are not just one of the many rings in a lifeless chain of entities (even of Being), but that each one of us is unique, irreplaceable, because of infinite value, divine.

I insist that none of those experiences are foreign or inaccessible to us. We truly understand what he was talking about. And now, what we said at the beginning may become more plausible, that even if we cannot be sure that our Man of Galilee had uttered such words, we have heard them in our hearts; that message pervades our life and reveals the ultimate experience of the human being. Should I quote not a sentimental mystical writer but Thomas Aquinas: "If Christ would have entrusted his doctrine to writing, people would imagine that there is nothing else in his doctrine than what Scripture contains."[113] All this is not at all demeaning for a symbol which claims to have reached the supreme *kenosis*.[114]

[113] "Si autem Christus scripto suam doctrinam mandaret, nihil alius de eius doctrina homines existimarent quam quod scriptura contineret", Sum. Theol. III, q. 42, a. 4. He reminds us of texts (Jn XXI.25 and II Cor III.3, and cites Pythagoras and Socrates as 'excellentissimi doctores' who did the same. We could add Buddha, Mahāvīra and others.

[114] I spare the reader of my indignation when consulting most of the modern tanslations of Phil. II, 7, a fundamental text for a true encounter

This is not 'deification' in a mythological manner. It is rather the sober and serene awareness that the indwelling of the divine mystery is not imagination, that I am participating in this cosmotheandric adventure of reality. And again this does not at all deny that this supreme human experience (that of being a vessel of infinitude) can be expressed differently by other traditions. Are we not saying, after all, that Jesus Christ is the revelation of the infinite Mystery hidden in the cosmos since times eternal (Rom XVI.25–26)?

Even if I am far away from being eucharist, bread of life for others, and very slow to realise that whoever comes in contact with me enters into communication with the very source of life which veritably gives Life to me and all others, or still so opaque that not everyone who sees me sees the Father, I cannot deny that all those experiences are my experiences and within the reach of any human being. Might not precisely this be the truly 'Good News'?

'I and the Father are one.' How else could it be? The Father is not a Supreme Being who accidentally lets his sperm beget some children so that they may also exist. The Father is nothing but Father, i.e., fathering. If 'he' would disappear I also would be annihilated — as so many christian thinkers said.

We have already dispelled the fear of pantheism, recognizing that our differences are infinite — as in the Trinity. Our oneness with God, our divine character, as christian tradition was fond of saying, does not constitute an undiscriminated fusion. And yet, it does not allow for separation either. The Source is not me, but it is not separated nor separable from me.

We made a passing reference to the scholastic *creatio continua* — which liberates us from living in a fixed and unfree

with many religions of Asia, specially buddhism, as thinkers of such cultures begin to discover.

universe. We may also mention another experience which is difficult to communicate, because both words and thoughts recoil, as an Upaniṣad affirms.[115] It could be expressed within the atmosphere of Meister Eckhart as *incarnatio continua*.[116] But perhaps silence is most fitting at this juncture.

* * *

When I react against being called *a* human being or when I am critical of evolutionistic thinking and claim to be Man, just Man, it is not that I do not include women in Man or do not recognize the merits of the Darwinistic hypothesis. It is that I react against the epidemic of modern superficiality which tends to obscure one of the most central human experiences: that of being unique, divine, centre of reality, constitutively linked with the source of all, a microcosm reflecting the entire macrocosm; in a word, one with the Father, infinite, incomparable, not interchangeable. The I is not the me. I am not just the product of evolution, a speck of dust or mind in the middle of an immense universe. In sum, I am not a member of a classification; I am the classifier. And this is also the case, obviously, for everyone and everything. The dignity of Man consists precisely in being aware of it: I and the Father *are* one. And that is what the Mediator, *anthrôpos Christos Iêsous* (I Tim II.5) dared to say.

3. I should go

The Text

(i) *all'egô tên alêtheian legô hymîn, sympherei hymîn hina egô apelthô. eàn gàr mê apelthô, ho paraklêtos ou mê*

[115] "When words recoil, together with the mind, unable to reach it — whose knows that bliss of *Brahman* has no fear" *Taittirīya U.* II.9.

[116] Cp. Wilke (1995), 237–62 specially her sub-chapter '*creatio continua ist incarnatio continua.*'

> *elthê pros hymās ean de poreuthô, pempsô autòn pros hymâs*
>
> Sed ego veritatem dico vobis: expedit vobis ut ego vadam. Si ego non abiero Paraclitus non veniet ad vos; si autem abiero, mittam eum ad vos. (Vg.)
>
> Nevertheless I tell you the truth: it is for your good that I am leaving you. If I do not go, your Advocate will not come, whereas if I go, I will send him to you (NEB).[117]

We do not need to linger on the scene, even though it is very moving and might have been constructed afterwards. It is, nevertheless, a human, an all-too-human situation: The future does not look bright, his followers will be persecuted, and the pervading mood among his disciples is that he is leaving rather abruptly without having achieved anything, almost abandoning them. One could understand Judas' frustration and despair: Jesus' mission is ending as a total fiasco. He has not provided for anything durable, or left any institution. He neither baptised nor ordained, nor, much less, founded anything (although he might have stated his intention of doing so). He sent them away like sheep among wolves and even at the end refuses to change his tactics. The wolves are having

[117] "It is expedient for you that I go away: for if I go not away, the Comforter will not come unto you" (AV and RV).

"It is expedient for you that I depart. For if I do not go, the Advocate will not come to you" (Confraternity/Challoner/Rheims).

"Il vaut mieux pour vous que je parte; car si je ne pars pas, le Paraclet ne viendra pas à vous ..." (B.J.).

"Es ist gut für euch, dass ich fortgehe. Denn wenn ich nicht fortgehe, wird der Beistand nicht zu euch kommen" (Neue Jerusalemer Bibel).

"Es gereicht euch zum Guten, daß ich weggehe. Denn: Wenn ich nicht weggehe, kommt der Mutbringer nicht zu euch" (Stier).

"Us convé que me'n vagi; perquè si no me'n vaig, no vindrà el vostre valedor a vosaltres, ..." (Mateos/Rius Camps).

"è bene per voi che io me ne vada, perché, se non me ne vado, non verrà a voi il Consolatore ..." (Barbaglio).

it. Only one thing he promises: the Spirit.

We need not delve into the meaning of that polysemic verb *symphérô*, which literally means to bring together, gather, collect, and in this particular case has the meaning of being profitable, advantageous, expedient, and fits with the entire situation.

His life is coming to an end. Yes, he is going to the Father (Jn 14.12; 16.17; 28; 20.17; etc.). Still he is going away. He consoles them saying that he is not leaving them orphans (Jn 14.18); but he clearly states that they will no longer see him. And the ghost of his oncoming death is present all the time.

He promises them consolation, comfort, an intercessor, a mediator, a helper, a Paraclete. In other texts this advocate is described as the Spirit and is often called the 'Spirit of truth' (Jn 14.17; 26; 15.26; 16.13; etc.) perhaps recalling the language of the Qumran Community.[118]

(ii) *hotan de elthê ekeînos to pneûma tês alêtheias,*
hodêgêsei hymâs eis tên alêtheian pâsan
Cum autem venerit ille,
Spiritus veritatis deducet vos
in omnem veritatem

However, when he comes who is
the Spirit of truth, he will guide you
into all the truth. (NEB)

Jn XVI.13

The text cannot be more explicit. Once he goes the Spirit of truth will come and introduce us into the entire truth. Is this naive trust in Man or blind confidence in the Spirit? Jesus is supposed to have also said that it is the Spirit who gives

---

[118]The *Manual of Discipline* of the Qumran Community confers on the 'spirit of truth' the function of "enlightening the heart of Man, putting straight the path of righteousness, ...giving understanding and intelligence, ...spirit of discernment" etc...1 QS IV, 2–6.

life: "Spiritus est, qui vivificat" (Jn VI.63) — although some exegetes may prefer to contextualize this saying within the eucharistic discussions.

(iii) *ho pisteuôn eis eme ta ergo ha egô*
kakeînos poiêsei, kai meizona toutôn poiêsei,
hoti egô pros ton patera poreuomai
Qui credit in me, opera, quae
ego facio, et ipse faciet, et maiora
horum faciet, quia ego ad Patrem vado

Whoever believes in me
will perform even greater works,
because I am going to the Father (NJB)[119]
Jn XIV.12

We recall the theological distinctions traditionally employed in order not to allow the disciple to surpass the master, although this text seems to affirm that this is the case.

Nevertheless, the statement suggests that we are only at the beginning of a new dispensation, and that our task is to set it forth in a creative and even more wondrous way. But we return to the sentiments of Jesus when he said those words or gave occasion to his first disciples to put those sentences in his mouth.

The Interpretation

The traditional interpretation of the entire 'last discourse' of Jesus is wellknown. Jesus seems to be conscious of his mission and responsibility. The 'Farewell talk' gives hints of the

---

[119] Cp. other translations:
"he who has faith in me will do what I am doing; and he will do greater things still because I am going to the Father" (NEB).
"anche chi crede in me, compirà le opere che io compio e ne farà di più grandi, perché io vado al padre (Barbaglio)."
'Wer an mich glaubt, der wird die Werke, die ich tue, aber selber tun. Ja, grössere als die wird er tun, weil ich zum Vater gehe.' (Stier)

Trinity and the Church, and contains an undeniable example of the climate of the first christian generations. Christians would be hardly understandable without those chapters.

Modern scholarship has done wonders in filtering layers of redaction and scrutinizing the possible historical happening(s) that gave rise to this text. But there is no denying that in one way or another, the promise of the Spirit seems to belong to the kerygma of Jesus.[120]

But our concern is different. We are interested in understanding the Man capable of making those utterances, and we are trying to do this by examining whether we may be able to re-enact the experience behind those words. It may be true that the first christian generations believed that the Son of God, wanting to establish his Church and conscious of fulfilling a role given by his divine Father, made that wonderful speech that the Gospels narrate. It could be interpreted as the climax of his teaching. But even if this were the case we also realize that the attitude reflected in this text is typical of the Man of Galilee. He preached by his example. Hence, instead of visualizing a triumphalistic 'mise en scène' by the later christian communities in which Jesus seems to be overly confident about his Church, we may understand those words as the narrative of a realistic situation that shatters all idealistic expectations.

Jesus seems to have failed and missed every opportunity to establish his Church. The enthusiastic crowds wanted to make him king. He went away. The apostles wanted to keep him on the mountain. He scolded them and descended to the plains. Satan wanted to offer him all the kingdoms of the world. He refused. He did not even want to listen to Scripture and convert the stones into his own food, but preferred that the stones remain stones. He was certainly not a diplomat

[120] Cp. the expression of Gonzalez Faus (1995) 124 'extra Spiritum nulla salus'.

able to endear himself to the authorities. This time he did not go away. He was caught and got rid of. He died, abandoned.

We are not, therefore, commenting on a single statement and spinning out a special exegesis. We are trying to understand his experience and asking whether eventually our experience agrees with the fundamental attitude we detect in his words and deeds.

He was constant with that message. He lived up to it and he preached it: *mê merimnate*! (Mt VI.25–34; Lk XII.11, 22): Do not be anxious about the future, be carefree, do not think before hand what you are to say . . . (Mt X.19).

In this connection, it seems appropriate to report a moving scene which reveals the humanity of Jesus. It is not the question of an omniscient being just to elicit repentance for Peter's betrayal — whoever may have written the passage and whatever may be its historical degree of reality. We refer, of course to the question 'after breakfast': "Simon son of John, do you love me more than all else?" (NEB) or ["more than these'] (Jn XXI.15 sq.). He has to go anyway, even if he is risen, and he just begs for love, for human love. He can leave if he is reassured about being loved. He does not ask: 'Simon of John, have you understood my message? have you realised who I was?' Even the reference to not being able to go where he would like to go and do what he had dreamt of doing has an autobiographical (and prophetic) tone: "I leave it all to love — and not to my will or to programmes of any sort. I have to go, I simply go, and leave you with a question: Have I elicited your love? Those who, like Peter, are not sure of yourselves, because of the many betrayals, but still love me — to you I entrust my message." He behaved truly as a servant — and not as a *pantokratôr*.

We are not exposing christian doctrine, but trying to understand a human experience. We can only do this, if we do not divorce the alleged author of those words from his life, and his sharing in the human condition along with us.

The Experience

The question we are asking is whether we can understand that utterance without minimizing or diluting it, but also without making it and similar statements supernatural declarations of a super-human consciousness. I ask myself, a normal person, how can I understand what goes on in a human heart uttering those words? Do we not call him our Brother? — and Friend, as he told us?

I am not in the same situation, and few feel called to perform such a guru role, although in any family and loving atmosphere such a situation is thinkable and possible. But I may try to articulate that experience.

> 'I should go, otherwise the Spirit will not come': I should not care about perpetuating my life, since unless I go, Life will not continue and be passed on to others. Otherwise, all that I have been, felt, experienced, loved, and seen, will remain barren and descend with me into the tomb. I am not the private proprietor of my life — that Life which has been bestowed upon me. If I cling to it, Life will not flow, not live.
>
> I should not hanker after immortalizing myself or be worried that my projects, ideas, ideals be strictly followed and observed according to my desires. There is dynamism in Life, there is the Spirit of Truth which I myself may be able to set free from me. This Spirit will pervade others by herself and on her own initiative without my having to pre-plan it. This is freedom. "Where the Spirit is, there is freedom" (II Cor. III.17).

This lived experience, we said, represents a truly liberated soul, a more difficult experience to attain than that of being called to partake in the divine nature (II Petr. I.4). It implies having reached a total transparency and having transcended both the burden of the past and the fear of the future.

I leave many of my projects undone, many of my aspirations unfulfilled. I may die young, and even if blessed with years of life, the more I live the more I discover what I could have done and still could do. At any rate, the tasks in and of the world are not yet finished. Did I dream to finish them? have I not learnt that Lao tse, Socrates, Shankara, Kant, Gandhi, my mother (to put disparate examples), all departed but not their spirit? To be a Man is to be unique for the time being — and leave the 'work' to others. I know that I shall go, but it takes time to learn that I should go. Eternity is not a long or indefinite time. Eternal life is not go on living into the future.

The first *mahāvākya* looks somehow at the past: The Father is 'before' me, more powerful than myself, the Source. The second statement concerns somewhat the present: We are of the same nature, we are one, our link is life-giving, it is my own existence. This third utterance is directed towards the future and the overcoming of its grip on us: I should go, I certainly shall go away, and I do not regret it, I do not hanker after a desired 'immortality', after a prolongation of my existence, not even of *my* ideals, thoughts, plans, projects. If one loves "unto the end" (Jn XIII.1), one trusts the loved ones. I do not want to freeze the flow of Life which comes from the Father and will go on. I share in that Life, I participate in this adventure, I do not need heavy luggage: '*Consummatum est!*' The Spirit will come, even if I do not send her, even if I do not have power over her and it is not me who sends her. She will come. "The Spirit and the nymph say. Come!" (Apoc XXII.17).[121] And we who hear, respond: Come!

---

[121] It is significant and moving to read this text of Revelation as the motto of Serge Boulgakov's Christology, *Agnets Bojii* of 1933, a 'book

To be sure, I may not be able to live up to that intuition always, but I cannot deny that I truly *know* it (in an experiential sense) if I live a truly authentic life without any ego. There is then an egoless force, power (*exousia*), within me which 'sends' the Spirit into the world. It is the Spirit which I succeed in identifying with when my heart is pure.

There is still more: "If I do not go away, the Paraclete will not come". We leave unexamined who or what this 'One called alongside', this 'Comforter', 'Consoler', 'Advocate', 'Intercessor', 'Called upon', 'Invoked', is. I sum it all up with the traditional word of Spirit.

If I cling to my life, my *ego*, my mission, my task, my ideal, or obviously worse, my possessions, my family, people, world; if I do not let it all go, if I do not renounce any desire of prolonging my life (even if I call it immortality) and insist on building monuments to my creations and yearn to set in order what has cost me so much effort to produce so that it may not all be lost, Life will be stifled. I am transient, or rather, I share in the *perichorêsis*, in the dance of the entire universe, in the constant rhythm of all, in the trinitarian or cosmotheandric display of reality.

This is perhaps the most striking experience of Jesus: to be carefree, not to be anxious about the future, to learn from the flowers that today they bloom, and tomorrow will have faded away, to renounce dreaming about the future and living a life always projected into the future — thus missing the tempiternal moments of our human existence.

I can well understand the Man of Nazareth feeling sadness but not concern, pain but not despair and a deep serenity not without joy, feeling that it is good that he goes away, that he has lived, and lived life to the full, and that others will

---

on the theanthrophy of Christ and ours', which begins by stating that "the salvation, wrought by Christ, takes place in the soul of Man, more precious than the world", Boulgakov (1982) IX.

perform even better works than he himself, if they can trust the Spirit in every one of us.

Yeshua ha nôzeri, Jesus of Nazareth is leaving, we all are leaving. He does not found anything, nor start any religion. He does not perform the role of a master, a title he did not like. His time has come and there he goes having fulfilled his mission, which did not appear to be precisely a grand success. His only testament is his Spirit.

The assumption of my human condition, the realization that my time is over and that I should go away, the conviction that the Spirit should not be stifled nor controlled or directed: this is the supreme experience which is at the same time the most common human experience. The Son of Man does not want exceptions or privileges.

This is the ultimate test. I shall go, I have to go. The ego will die making room for the Spirit. This is Life, and Resurrection.

III. CHRIST'S MYSTICISM

> Jesus said to his disciples: make me a comparison; tell me what I am like. Simon Peter said to him: You are like a righteous angel. Matthew said to him: You are like a man who is a wise philosopher. Thomas said to him: Master, my mouth will not at all be capable of saying what you are like. Jesus said: I am not your master, because you drank (and) became drunken from the bubbling spring which I have measured out. And he took him (and) went aside (and) spoke three words to him. Now when Thomas came (back) to his companions, they asked him: What did Jesus say to you? Thomas said to them, If I tell you one of the words that he said to me, you will take up stones (and) cast (them) at me, and a fire will come forth

from the stones (and) will burn you up.
The (coptic) Gospel of Thomas, 13
(B.M. Metzger's translation)

1. Eva me suttam

'Thus have I heard', that there was a Man who came into the world and realized that he was one with the Origin of the Universe, although he was not the Origin, that he had come from that Source and to the Source he was to return, that meanwhile, in the intervening time allotted to him, he passed his life doing good, although without performing anything pre-planned or truly extraordinary, even if all he did was intense, achieved, authentic. A just Man who walked around and did not join any extremist group, seemed to be condoning everything except hypocrisy, and although he did not make discriminations he seemed to take the side of the oppressed and downtrodden, and as such he finished his life. He saw the Origin originating everything and suffered the impact of the forces of evil, but had an unlimited confidence in the blowing of that wind which he called Spirit, pervading everything, so that this was his only legacy.

He saw himself as a Man. Son of Man, *barnasha*, he called himself, and for this very reason discovered for himself and for others that his humanity was nothing else than the other side of divinity, inseparable though distinct; so distinct that he was painfully aware of the existence of sin. Yet inside himself, as inside every human being, he saw not evil but the kingdom of heaven. That he preached and lived.

His birth was obscure. Most of his life he passed in the penumbra, and his death was still more obscure. Yet he did not feel frustration of any kind, and when tempted by power he despised it; and when he failed he dared to promise his real presence not only through the Spirit, but also through ordinary food and drink. He left a force, power, love, words, which he said were not his own. He did not elaborate any doctrinal system; he spoke the language of his time.

'I have heard' something else. I have heard twenty centuries of meditations on that Man and scores of doctrinal systems of all types. I cannot ignore them. And, on the other hand, I cannot study all of them. Great minds have given us stupendous syntheses. I have learnt from many of them. But then I have heard also from other extraordinary human figures of the past, and even the present. Sanctity (to use this word) may be a rare plant, but it grows in all climates and times.

I have heard also painful competitions and biased comparisons, mostly by followers and epigones. I have been almost forced sometimes to take sides and make personal decisions. A heard word has come to my rescue: "who is not against you is for you" (Lk IX.50; Mk IX.40), although contrary statements (Mt XII.30; Lk VIII.3) have saved me from literal readings and interpretations out of context. The 'you' of the community is not the 'me' of the risen one.

I heard also that we cannot do without the power of discernment, and this has led me to discover the primacy of the personal experience in order to reach what another tradition knows as *nitya-anitya-vastu-viveka* (discernment between things temporal and eternal — which may re-echoed in a famous work by a now almost forgotten P. Nüremberg). Having to rely on myself I had to work towards the purification of my whole being, and this ever-unfinished task has liberated me from any sort of absolutization of my convictions.

I have heard so many things that I had to listen more atentively to the Spirit.

2. Itipaśyāmi

'Thus do I see', that Jesus' inner life discloses a universal experience. History shows it. But even I, intensity and purity apart, am capable of understanding and re-enacting that experience. In fact, every Man is able to do this, although the language, and indeed the doctrines, may be very different, even mutually irreconcilable.

I am not adopting a dialectical posture, affirming that I do not hesitate to say 'I am God', because God said: 'I am Man'. This would be wrong. I am describing my experience in a more intimate and personal way. I simply feel that the Divine is in me and I in that Divine reality; that I experience that oneness which makes my life truly real. Yet, I equally realise how far I still am from that fulfillment. In a paradoxical way, the closer I believe to be to that ideal, the farther away I feel from it. And when I look around and into human history I understand the anguished question: 'How many are those who reach salvation, fullness, realization?' Perhaps the door opens at the last minute. I do not know. Is it all 'annihilation', 'emptiness'?

The *kenosis* of the 'Son of Man' is not his privilege. It was not because he was humble; it was because he was Man. It is perhaps one of the most pregnant manifestations of the human condition. We are all kenotic, emptied of the divinity which indwells in each one of us; we are all divested, as it were, of our most authentic garb; we all, having divine origin and being temples of the divinity, appear, not only to others, but also to ourselves as mere slaves, subject to suffering and death, failure and ignorance. He did not hide it. Only a divine person can reveal such humanity.

And yet, I see much more than this. I behold, although I am clumsy at manifesting it, that not just his life, but also my life has an infinite value, precisely because it is finite in its shape and name. It is unique, and thus, incomparable; it cannot be compared, put on any equal footing with anything. It is in my finitude, in my concreteness, the consciousness of my contingence that I touch (*cum-tangere*) the infinite, the divinity.

I see that the Man of Galilee lived that human condition of mine, because he shared it. It is this sense of uniqueness which makes my dignity. Nothing and nobody can replace me, because my place in the entire universe is irreplaceable. This is the mystery of Man.

The Son of Man shows to me that I have to realize myself also as son of Man, just as Man. Many people tend to identify themselves with the role they perform: citizen, politician, worker, medical doctor, peasant, parent, spouse. More subtle still are the religious identifications: christian, buddhist, monk, priest; or spiritual roles like those of a saint, guru, *saṃnyāsin* and the like. We should by all means be good individuals and perform our duties. But all these performances do not exhaust my being, they do not touch the core of what I ultimately am: a microcosm of the entire reality, an offspring of the *sat-puruṣa*, an image, a complete image of the Divinity. I know the All, the Father, *Brahman*, God and (at the same time) I am a spark, the Son, *ātman*, creature: the Thou of the I by virtue of the Spirit. The Man Jesus, as I see him, realized this union, *henôsis*, as Origen called it (or *anakrasis*) distinguishing it from the hypostatic communion at the Incarnation which he called *koinônia* (*Contra Celsum*, III, 41). Completely human and fully divine, as the first Councils formulated it. And this is the divine facet of the human condition common to all of us — including Jesus the Christ, of course.

Indeed, we do not need to denigrate ourselves because we want to exalt him. Without him we would not know it; we would not even realize it. He is the Son, the Head, the Cause, the Saviour . . . But again here, He, like the Kingdom that comes and is already here, does not appear with ostentation and fanfare. Even more, He, the mystery which christians cannot but call Christ has a Supername which may be re-enacted by so many names which we do not know, nor need to know. 'Lord, when did we see you . . . ?'

3. Sat-puruṣa

The mysticism of Jesus Christ is simply human mysticism. What else could it be? It is the ultimate experience of Man precisely as Man. This word stands not for an individual or a specimen of a human species, but for the fullness of what we all *are*. We speak of divinization, but this could be an alienation if one ceases to be Man. We may believe in annihilation, but this may become an evasion if one abandons what one truly is. We may accept our humanness, but this may be also synonymous with passive acceptance of our defeat if we demean what we truly are, or fall into a flat 'homocentrism' closed to any self-transcendence.

His experience, I dare say, was the pure human experience transcending all particularities without denying them. Only by being concrete we can be universal. His experience was not that of being a male, a jew, let alone a christian, a member of a class, caste, party or religion, but just a Man, Son of Man. This was his *kenosis*, and thus the possibility to speak to us all from the bottom of our true humanness, or in whatever name we want to express the authentic core of what we truly are. And paradoxically enough, the more we divest ourselves of all attributes and roles, the more we are ourselves and discover us to be completely human and more and more divine.

Since we are human we, as individuals, have to go. All have gone, including Jesus. Since we are divine, at our going the Spirit will come. We do not leave reality orphan of our presence. We have been — for ever.

All this may be incompatible with a rigid monotheism. We are not God; only God is God. But Christ is the Son of God one with the Father, because the divine Mystery is sheer

Gift, Donation. Or, in traditional words, the Son is begotten and the Spirit proceeds from the Source. The entire universe is involved in the process. The entire reality, in christian language, I discovered half a century ago, is Father, Christ and Holy Spirit — which later on I called the cosmotheandric experience.

From this experiential level if a śaivite or any other person should tell me that one does not need Jesus or even the name of Christ, I would unhesitantly reply: but of course not; let him go, do not cling to him (Jn XX.17), to that name or that symbol, otherwise the Spirit will not come 'to teach us all truth' which unveils to us that nobody has the monopoly of the personal realization. It is fitting that 'he' goes both for christians and the others alike. "Why do you call me good?" (Jn XVIII.19) "The Father is greater than me." (Jn XIV.28) or, as Marius Victorinus said after converting from neoplatonism to christianity around 360: "The Father is to the Son as Nothingness to Being" (as *ho mê ôn* to *ho ôn*). In the *kenosis* of our ego rises precisely what we truly are.

Any word we use is charged with unavoidable connotations, but if I try to describe the mysticism of Jesus the Christ I will not be able to put it without words. "The *puruṣa* is all", says one Vedic rik (ṚV 10, 90, 2). It all depends on how we interpret it: Cosmic Man, divine Man, perfect humanity, etc. *Ecce homo*! said Pilate (Jn XIX.5). *Puruṣottama*, 'Highest Man' (cp. BG VIII.1; X.15; 15; XV.18–19) is the supreme divine form (*paramaṃ rūpam aiśvaram*), says the *Gītā* (XI.3.9).

If I were to say that Jesus Christ is the one who fully realized his human condition this would be just a phrase if not spelt out by saying that this is also our destiny; and it would be a very limiting statement if explained outside its proper context: the *paramaṃ puruṣam divyam*, 'divine highest Man' says again the *Gītā* (VIII.8.10). We are touching ineffability.

We cannot understand mysticism in the third person. We

cannot do it in the second person either. But the first person has to have a partner to speak to, if it has to break the silence. This partner cannot be an imaginary reader. It has to be a Thou, an *iṣṭa-devatā*, who then turns the tables on me and converts me unto a thou. Silence is then the final experience which reveals that the word comes out of Silence by the power of Love.

EPILOGUE

Is this the seed of a new christology?

It would be no wonder that to a new epoch in world history should not correspond a new understanding of Jesus the Christ. Understanding which is not brought about by mere rehearsal of traditional doctrines (a necessary condition, however) but by a 'new life in Christ', by that *fides oculata* which keeps not 'looking up to heaven' like the Men of Galilee, but re-enacts the *incarnatio continua* of which also the ancients (Eckhart) spoke. The healthy reaction of a 'christology from below' represented by the Liberation Theology needs the complement of a *christology from within*, which at the same time acts as a bridge with the 'christology from above'. The three are needed. Without spousing an adoptionist christology (God adopts Jesus as his Son) nor a pneumatic one (a spiritual divine being took flesh in a point of history. In the Beginning (of time) was not Jesus, but *en archê*, at the (tempiternal) Origin was the *alpha* and *ômega*, which christians call Christ.

Were I to go on putting labels I would speak of a *christophany from the centre*, which should be distinguished from the so-called christocentrism. I would remind christians that 'lex orandi, lex credendi', and the others that those liturgical hymns were not just poetical licenses but theocosmological insights. [Bellarmino, after all, was right when defending against Galilei, that we cannot have 'pure science' without an underlying cosmology — defective as the cosmology of his time was]:

> Iesu, Redemptor omnium,
> Quem lucis ante originem
> Parem Paternae gloriae
> Pater supremus edidit.
> Tu lumen et splendor Patris
> Tu spes perennis omnium, . . .
>
> Latin Liturgy of Christmas (Vespers)
>
> Jesus, Redeemer of All,
> whom, before light's origin
> equal to the Father's glory
> the supreme Father gave birth
> You, light and splendour of the Father
> You, everlasting hope of all.

In spite that the same hymn sings of the day "currens per anni circulum", and that in the Laudes hymn Christ is again called "Beatus auctor saeculi" ("originator of [who gives increase to] the temporal age[s]) the western modern reception has been, by and large, to read those texts within a linear conception of time. We could understand them also, more in tune with the great christological texts of Scripture, within a different temporal scheme: Since the very Beginning, at the Origin (*en archê, in principio*) reality was (is) Father, Christ, Spirit (to use christian names) and when 'the fulness of times' came, what we call Incarnation took place (and also time), so that the manifestation (*phanerôsis*) of Jesus is a revelation of reality — of what we are. Let us remember that if we do not make of God an anthropomorphic and composite Being, the revelation of God can only be God himself (and not just an 'outburst of his mind'). The Logos of God is God says the trinitarian insight. The mystery of time is the unfolding, the distention (Augustin would say) of the Trinity 'ad extra'.

But 'outside' God there is nothing. The entire reality, and not only an exclusively transcendent God, is trinity.

I began by describing the 'Sitz im Leben' of this study which triggered these reflections. I should end by referring to another wider 'Sitz', the field of our overall human situation in the socio-politico-economico-spiritual predicament of three quarters of those whom we still call our human fellow-beings. What has a christology to say to all those who will not 'make' it? 'Venceremos' ('we shall win') is a powerful psychological shot, but to the thousands, nay, millions of victims who perish on the way to an each time more problematic 'Promised land' is either wishful thinking or an alienating drug. We have to go deeper and owe an answer to the *amharez*, the *dalit*, down-trodden — and not only economically or politically, but also spiritually and humanly.

The socio-political implications of this vision should be clear. That Man Jesus Christ shatters all our dualisms. *Qui fecit utraque unum*, sings the Liturgy. And yet this *unum* is neither philosophical monism nor theological monotheism. The *dykaiosynê* of the Gospels is not 'righteousness' (for heaven) on one side and 'justice' (on earth) on the other. 'On earth as it is in heaven' says the most popular christian prayer. The Son of Man is Son of God. There is no God here, Man there, and the Earth below; the spiritual and the celestial at the one side, and the material and political at the other, time now and eternity later, the individual isolated or the collectivity undifferentiated. He was neither a political liberator, nor a world-denying ascetic, and much less a member of the clergy, but just a Being (we have no other word) living the fulness of humanness which includes the sharing of the Divine — revealing thus what we are called upon to become.

Once again: Christ as a mere God, even if exclusive Son of God, does not convince. He did not step down from the

Cross. Christ is not the God of history. A mere 'Man for others', a historical hero and wonderful model does not help either. If once in a while David is lucky, innumerable more times is Goliath the victor. Where do all revolutions lead us to? The struggle for Justice is not 'justified' by a prospective victory (once again linear time) but because it is our human vocation — for the *lokasaṁgraha* (upholding of the universe) would I dare say jumping on to another tradition (BG III, 20 and 25).

In other words. If the mystery of Christ is not our own mystery, if our christology is not more than archaeology (of the past) or eschatology (of the future) we better leave it as a museum piece.

The cry for a new spirituality is a cry of the Spirit. And it is this Spirit which is the very Spirit of Christ according to tradition. The christology of the third millennium cannot be sectarian, nor a mere consolation for 'believers'. The Son of Man died outside the Holy City.

The 'within' we are timidly suggesting is the inmost depth of all of us, the abyss where in everyone of us the infinite and the finite meet, the material and the intellectual, the cosmic and the divine. The christianness of the third millennium is called upon to undergo this experience.

DIVINE RECOGNITION: PRATYABHIJÑĀ

H.N. Chakravarty

It is known to everybody that the Divine remains abiding in everything — sentient and insentient, but on account of some veil we are unable to conceive it in the beginning. But when we hear about its glory and greatness, its nobleness and graceful nature from the mouth of a reliable and competent person who has some definite knowledge regarding its sublime nature we become eager to approach him knowing definitely that the Divine is the most lovable, is dear of all dears — the *summum bonum* of all aims. The supreme aim of human life is first to realize, later to relish the love of the Divine in multifarious ways.

Recognition is the sure path to realize one's identification with the Divine. The common people do not have sufficient knowledge regarding the concept of *pratyabhijñā*, the central concept of the philosophy also called Kashmir Śaivism, originally propagated by Utpaladeva.[1] Therefore it is relevant to throw some light on it. The idea is mostly illustrated by presenting an example of how recognition occurred in the life of a lost prince. The prince was taken away by some robbers when he was a small baby. He was reared up by some, looked after by some others. After a few years when he grew up to be a young man he was identified by some ministers as the lost prince. He was brought before the king and without disclosing to him his real identity he had been entrusted with some responsible duties to perform with the purpose of

[1]See Bibliography in Appendix.

getting him well-trained in performing the duties of the king perfectly. When he became excellently ripe the real identity is revealed to him in the beginning in a general way, that he belongs to a noble family but later it is disclosed to him that he was the son of a king. Then it was furthermore brought to his knowledge that he was the son of the particular king in whose presence he was just standing. Thus he was brought face to face to the noble Lord of the domain. In this way he recognized himself as the prince. This is a simple case of recognition which begins with recognition in a general way, but later all the specific attributes belonging to him as his essential nature follow one after the other in a sequence, only to fill the bowl which as it were remained empty so long on account of separation from the Lord.

In the spiritual literature the aspirant's way to the Divine is described as a journey. The course the aspirant follows has a number of voids, therefore he has to encounter these voids which are comparatively extensive than the one left behind. The aspirant feels within that they are nothing but chasms, gaps between the Lord and him. The aspirant desires to cross the void, a gap between the lover, the devotee himself and the beloved, the Divine itself. As the journey continues, the gap seems to the devotee as if bridged. As this process continues the devotee experiences satisfaction to some extent. This is known as *madhurapāka*, gradual fulfilment of the inner being.[2] But it is to be noted here that direct realization or Recognition does not occur all at once to all, irrespective of comparative acquirement of competency. Because the nature of seekers varies, some are well-advanced in spirit with purity of innate essence. Because of the purity of the innate nature some are bestowed grace by the Lord immediately, but for others the path of intuitive judgement is to be followed. It is a wide path along which one can proceed. This

[2]Cp. *Tantrāloka* III.260—61.

is the path of knowledge with the characteristic of right form of reasoning, *sattarka*. It is known to scholars that *tarka*, the path of argument, fails to lead a person to achieve a solid ground. The Sūtra in Vedānta: '*tarkāpratiṣṭhānāt. . .*'[3] says that argument is unstable because it is refuted by counter arguments and so on, for this reason *tarka* is to be discarded. But we also know that *tarka* is an efficient method which makes unification between two things possible, between one and the other. It is a sure link — a bridge which connects two entities. *Mālinīvijaya Tantra* defines Yoga thus:

> *yogamekatvamicchanti vastuno'nyena vastunā,*
> MVT IV.4ab
>
> (Wise people) like to define yoga as a unity of one entity with the other.

Not only that, it serves as a staircase by which one leaves that which is to be rejected and embraces the one which is to be accepted. Therefore in the Upaniṣad *tarka* has been praised as a sure means for *anusandhāna*, a method of unification.

It has further been stated in Śaivism, that *tarka* is the best limb of Yoga.[4] By the right application of the right form of reasoning one is able to discern the right from the wrong.[5]

We live in the world of isolation separate from one another by creating walls of distinctions of fame and riches, of position and status, and we live in the island of the ego, *ahaṃkāra*. But when by the grace of *guru* we are able to see the light — the light which unifies all, brings all in the embrace of the Divine, we realize oneness, the singleness of Light within.

In order to see the Light we do not require to go further. It is near, it is everywhere. But first of all we should realize the Light recognizing it to be the very essence of ME

---

[3] *Brahmasūtra* II.1.11.
[4] *Tarka yogāṅgam uttamam.*
[5] *Tantrāloka* IV.15.

as I. Then it occurs to the aspirant that everything is made of that Light. It has emerged from it, is made of it. To realize that everything that is known as *idam*, the object, is really *Brahman*, but differentiation, the variousness, the divisions, the *nānātva* is unreal. The reality is one singleness but multifariousness is also real which shows itself by the dynamic pulsation of the Divine, dancing in the rhythmic play of delight. The Divine is nothing but *camatkāraikarasa*, the one harmonious uniflavouredness of the experience of joy. So the delight of the Divine does not reject anything but unifies, brings all together, if there is really anything separate from it. The real nature of the Divine is not at all static but dynamic, by the energy of which He embraces all in one integral cognition (*akhaṇḍāmarśa*). But it expands itself and contracts. Expansion (*prasara*) is the nature of immanence of the Divine and contraction (*saṃkoca*) is transcendence. Both are true. When we are able to recognize his transcendent nature we only traverse as if half of the journey. Unless we are capable of seeing or realizing with the light of recognition that everything is composed of the Light we fail to achieve the highest goal. The highest goal only becomes complete when the two halves meet in unison, in full equilibrium in the union of Śiva and Śakti, the unity of the dynamic with the static.

We know of Umā's penance for obtaining Śiva as her beloved husband. Śiva appeared before her in the disguise of a *brahmacārin*, a celibate, to bless her with boons. She was unable to recognize him as Śiva himself and rejected all the boons bestowed on her. But as soon as the real recognition as to the reality of Śiva dawned forth in her she was beyond all delights.[6]

[6] Cp. *Kālidāsa, Kumārasambhava* v.85: "On seeing him, the daughter of the Mountain-lord, all atrembling and her body covered with perspiration, and having one foot raised to walk away, was uncertain whether to go or to stay, like a river hampered by the impediment of a mountain in the path." (Tr. M.R. Kale)

When real recognition as to the divine nature of the devotee occurs, one feels within a state of unsteadiness indicating movement and cessation of movement. It cannot be indicated by the term movement nor the absence of movement. It is beyond movement and yet movement infinite. Movement in the core of rest while in rest it is on move infinitely.

The Śaiva doctrine looks into the Reality as having three aspects. It is composed of three principles known as *nara, śakti* and Śiva, the object, the dynamic instrument and the Supreme. The object in general is known as *nara*. The gross object, the instrument of knowledge and the limited subject come under *nara*. The *śakti* is a link between *nara*, the object, and Śiva, the supreme subject. Therefore it is essential that the limited subject for the purpose of unification with the Supreme should take recourse to *śakti* which alone is capable of leading the limited self to attain Śiva nature. As in Christian spirituality the Trinity is the basic principle, so is Trika in Kashmir Śaivism. It is stated that God the Father, God the Son and the Holy Spirit are the three units of the single body of the One. Every being is in essence made of the love of Christ, the Son. The indwelling Spirit, consciousness in essence, leads the being to approach the Lord, for without the help of the awakened *śakti* real recognition is impossible. Therefore, realizing this truth, Utpala, the saint, assuming the role of the *guru* states in the beginning of the *Pratyabhijñā Kārikās:*

> By means of revealing the dynamic power this doctrine of Recognition is presented.[7]
>
> ĪPK I.3

The Supreme Divine is eternally abiding in every atom of existence in the form of action, knowledge and bliss as an integral unity embracing all in one and is still beyond them.

[7] *śaktyāviṣkaraṇeneyaṃ pratyabhijñopadarśyate.*

Though permeating all beings, the hidden (*gūḍhātmā*) one does not reveal itself.[8] The question that suffers the soul of the seeker is: why the One who is the soul of everything does not reveal itself to him. Putting this question the devoted seeker gives the answer himself:

> There is, within me,
> The tiniest dark spot
> That keeps you hidden.
> Completely wiping away even that,
> Reveal, O Lord, your spotless form.
>
> *Śivastotrāvalī* XIII.2[9]

The great Lord composed of imperishable body embracing the whole world consisting of the bliss of nectar of eternal consciousness (*citsudhārasamaya*) remains unattainable so long as the grace of the Lord does not touch the inner self. Only when the grace touches the ardent soul then the road opens to the view of the seeker which leads him from the illusory to empirical and from empirical to the eternal existence of infinite bliss of one's own.

According to *Pratyabhijñā* doctrine every being is in essence perfectly free (*paripūrṇa svatantra*) and blissful. It is the perfect equilibrium of knowledge and activity, but on account of the veiling and delusive power of *māyā*, the pure light, the real nature of the Lord, remains out of reach. Only those on whom the grace of the Divine has dawned, can realize what their real nature is (*āyatadṛḍha śaktipātasya*).

The principal requisite for bestowing good to others is the recognition of one's own nature that it is none else than divinity, the most auspicious Śiva. When one is able to recognize Śiva to be one's own self, one attains the state of the

---

[8] *eṣa sarveṣu bhūteṣu gūḍho'tmā na prakāśate*, *Kaṭha Up*. III.12.

[9] Trans. by C. Rhodes Bailly, *Shaiva Devotional Songs of Kashmir*, SUNY Press, 1987.

Supreme Godhead. This supreme Self is unlimited light possessing all-transcending power which leads the seeker to attain the highest of human goals.

The doctrine as presented in the *Pratyabhijñā Kārikās* by Utpaladeva and a detailed exposition of it as has been given by Śrī Abhinavaguptācārya in two of his commentaries, the one long and the other a little shorter, is the source of the present paper.

Pratyabhijñā is ordinarily translated in English as 'recognition', a kind of direct perception of the one which was once directly known but on account of the play of deluding power called *māyā* is forgotten but it is cognised again as if face to face (*sāmmukhyena*).

The term *pratyabhijñā* has been analytically defined by Śrī Abhinavagupta in the commentary called *Vimarśinī* in the following way:

> Recognition is a knowledge of the Light as facing the self reversely.[10]
>
> ĪPV p. 19

The above definition contains three components viz. *prati, abhi* and *jñā* which mean *prati* — towards, *abhi* — face to face and *jñā* means knowledge. The whole sentence then means direct knowledge of one's own self face to face.

Manifestation of one's own self is not a new experience which was not experienced before, for the Light, the real essence of the self is an unbroken Light (*sakṛt vibhāto'yamātmā*). It shines once and remains shining eternally but the power which is inseparably united with it, creates in the unbroken flow of light an illusion of cleavage, a break as it were which shows itself in the form of *vikalpa*, determinate knowledge. Because of this the notion of *vikalpa* makes its appearance in the form that 'this is of this character, not

[10] *pratīpam ātmābhimukhyena jñānaṃ prakāśaḥ pratyabhijñā.*

of this': *idam ittham nānittham.* But when real *pratyabhijñā* shines forth, it is the unification of experiences of what appeared before (*bhāta bhāsamānarūpānusandhānātmikā*). This unification of experiences is the very life of *pratyabhijñā* or *pratyabhijñā* itself.[11]

In the spiritual tradition of India three stages regarding the journey of the seeker for truth are generally accepted. The first is *prabodhana*, real awakening. It is followed by *sāmmukhya*, coming face to face with the Lord. Then the stage of *sambodhana*, addressing the Lord as one's own dear. The soul remains overpowered in deep slumber which in the language of Āgama is the state of *paśu* or *jīva* with limited knowledge and activity. During the period of slumber the *jīva* has little knowledge regarding its real nature. It has no leanings for knowing the truth both of the ultimate and the essence of his own nature. But when the slumber begins to break the question what his real nature is, arises in his inner soul. Then he feels an urge for knowing the purpose of his existence and the real goal. It is known to all that grace of the Lord does not occur in a person by supplication and prayer (*upāyaiḥ na śivo bhāti*), but shines only spontaneously. It is a well-accepted view that grace is one of the Lord's five functions. Therefore we are unable to show any reason when He will show grace to anybody. As veiling (*tirodhāna*) of His own nature is the play of His, in the same way *anugraha* is also another aspect of His functions, therefore individual initiative is of no value regarding when it will touch the soul. As soon as the fall of grace (*anugrahaśaktinipāta*) occurs it not only purifies the soul of the seeker but rouses him up from the deep slumber in which he was lying deadly asleep. The awakening of the soul opens to the view of the seeker a new vista along which he will have to approach the beloved.

---

[11] *Svātmāvabhāso hi na ananubhūtapūrvo'vicchinnaprakāśatvāt tasya*, IPV, p. 20.

The *Mālinīvijaya Tantra*[12] has described three means for absorption in Śiva. By adopting one of these means the individual is able to attain the ultimate end of life. They are named as *śāmbhava, śākta* and *āṇava*. They are denoted by the terms will, knowledge and activity, respectively. Without taking recourse to any one of them which are directly linked with Śiva (*śaivīmukham*), it is impossible to have realization of one's true nature. The means called *śāmbhava* is of the nature of *icchā* (will) which implies *pratyabhijñā* in which everything whatever it may be, shines as a reflection in a mirror by the will of the Divine.[13] This Divine is the support or the bearer of the reflection which assumes the form of the universe. This implies the immanence of the Lord in creation. This universe is the domain that brings consciousness in manifestation (*caitanyasya vyaktisthānam*) by means of cognition (*āmarśana*). In the language of Abhinavagupta it is speech (*vāk*) or reflected consciousness, or in another word it is called *paranāda*, the supreme sound. It eternally pulsates in the transcendental cognition as its essential nature, *aham*, in the form of I.

But those whose understanding is not so refined and whom the grace of the Divine has not touched so keenly conceive them as bound in the morass of existence. On account of *vikalpa*, thought constructs, the beings think themselves bound. Because of the presence of these *vikalpas* one cannot cross the world of bondage and remains bound by false views regarding the world and the self. Thought constructs are the play of *mātṛkās* (syllabic sounds) which go on creating thoughts or concepts. They are ever engaged in veiling the real nature of beings. It is stated in the *Spanda Kārikā* thus:

> The powers are ever in readiness to conceal his

---

[12]MVT II.21-23.

[13]Cp. the article by B.N. Pandit in this Volume.

> own nature,
> for without the association of words, ideas cannot arise.[14]
>
> Sp Kā III.15

It seems relevant to say that thought constructs are of two types, the one is impure which is the source of bondage, but the other is pure which really is the dynamic energy of the Supreme. When it is known rightly by the seeker it leads one to attain the highest end of one's life.

Therefore one must get rid of impure *vikalpas* by sowing the seeds of pure *vikalpas*. One should approach a teacher (*sadguru*). It is from him that he is able to know about the truth. Then he further confirms his right understanding by studying the texts. The order that he follows is the teacher, then the scriptures and finally one's own intuition: *gurutaḥ*, from *guru, śāstrataḥ*, from texts, *svataḥ*, from one's own intuitive knowledge. It is only by his intuitive judgement (*sattarka*) that one can ascertain the real nature of the things and is able to discern what is to be rejected and which should be accepted. The impure *vikalpas* are the forces standing in opposition to those of pure *vikalpas*, but the latter are able to uproot those *vikalpas* which put the soul enticed with the worldly existence.

The path the awakened soul treads on along the journey to his goal has certain stages of spiritual development. In the beginning it starts when the seeker receives the grace of the teacher (*gurukṛpā*). Then follows the disciple's competency in consulting the Āgamic texts which contain material that is really helpful for understanding the truth. It is quite relevant to say that real conviction regarding the Truth does not arise or shine forth until it spontaneously manifests in one's own nature (*svataḥ*). The text shows to him the vision of

[14] *svarūpāvaraṇe cāsya śaktayaḥ satatotthitāḥ*
yataḥ śabdānuvedhena na vinā pratyayodbhavaḥ

recognition indirectly and guides his understanding to grasp the truth following the five-formed syllogism. The text beginning with '*kathaṃcidāsādya*' and so on is a statement about recognition. It is a summary of the subject-matter, '*uddeśa*'. The mid-portion of the work states the reasons (*hetvādi*) and the last verse '*iti prakaṭito mayā'*, thus 'I have shown' etc. is the conclusion. Thus, the work, that is, a text like the *Īśvarapratyabhijñā Kārikā* which presents the subject-matter in a syllogistic form including five terms, serves as a means of recognition to instruct others, and that is its object.[15]

The doctrine named *Pratyabhijñā* is a unique spiritual tradition. It is a path that leads everyone to realize the Divine within one's own being. It is not only a means (*upāya*) but at the same time it is the ultimate end (*upeya*). Everybody can embrace it whether one has earned competency (*adhikāra*) or not. Utpaladeva, the author of the doctrine, being so graceful to the mortal world plunged in the sea of troubles, utters in the same strain of the Vedic seers for delivering good to the people:

> Let all the sons of immortality listen
> These celestial abodes were
> Well-established in You.[16]

After realizing recognition, Utpaladeva, the divine teacher in order to shower grace to the world says:

> Having somehow realized my identity with the Supreme and wishing to render service to humanity, I am establishing self-recognition which is a

---

[15] *evaṃ pratyabhijñātavya samasta vastu saṃgrahaṇena idaṃ vākyamuddeśarūpaṃ pratijñāpiṇḍātmakaṃ ca, madhyagranthastu hetvādinirūpakaḥ iti prakaṭito mayā' iti ca antyaśloko nigamanagranthaḥ, — ityevaṃ pañcāvayavātmakamidaṃ śāstraṃ paravyutpattiphalam.* ĪPV under verse 1.

[16] *śṛṇvantu viśve amṛtasya putrāḥ, ā ye dhāmāni divyāni tasthuḥ*, *Ṛgveda* X.13.Ic.

means of attaining all that is of value.[17]

ĪPK I.1

This opening verse of *Pratyabhijñā Kārikā* contains some very meaningful words: *janasyāpyupakāramicchan*, after realizing his identity with the divine the author feels an urge within to deliver it to the world. He takes up the method of bestowing it by means of *prakhyā* and then *upākhyā*. First realizing the light of the divine in himself, he wants to bestow it to others by means of reflected consciousness, by placing those who pass from one existence to the other (*jana*) near (*samīpam*) the Lord in order that they may attain the nearness of all the good belonging to the Lord (*parameśvara dharmasamīpatākaraṇam*). That is, they are given the pure nectar or essence in such a way that they may realize oneness with the divine essence, knowledge and activity abiding inseparably with the Lord.[18]

According to the doctrine, whatever shines is the Divine in essence. The objects that appear as jar externally and that shine as pleasure or pain internally, when seen in their essence they are nothing but light. But it is quite relevant to mention here that this light is not simply a light that floods everything and then obliterates, but it is such a light that not only makes the body of all appear as one's own body, but it pulsates as the very life of everything. Everything shines as composed of the light. Everything that is manifest is simply his glory *sarvo mamāyaṃ vibhavaḥ*. It is an all-pervasive light encompassing all, which unifies all with the divine by demolishing the barrier of separation. Abhinavagupta states the fundamental insight in his commentary, which we may summarize

---

[17] *kathañcidāsādya maheśvarasya*
dāsyaṃ janasyāpyupakāramicchan,
samastasampatsamavāptihetuṃ
tatpratyabhijñāmupapādayāmi.

[18] *dharma* = *dṛk* and *kriyā*.

thus:

The inner self, which is called *paśu* and is referred to as 'I', is not different from the Supreme Self, who is essentially the light of consciousness, grasping both the subject and the object: on the contrary, I am the transcendental being, and He is I. There is no difference between the two.[19] For the real seeker of the truth *anusandhāna*, unification of everything as one and viewing all as an integral unity of the light of consciousness, is a process which certainly leads one to attain the greatness of Śiva. He gives in his commentary in a nutshell how the process of unification occurs.

> The category of earth cannot exist without the category of water, for it is in the medium of firm-support (*dhṛti*) only that solidity is found....All these realities are simply nothing without Bhairava who is absolutely autonomous and the very quintessence of perfect Light.[20]
>
> P.T.V., Tr. Jaideva Singh, p. 117

In other words the recognition of Supreme Consciousness is an easy approach for the attainment of the true self. It is stated with emphasis that only by means of inquiry (*anveṣaṇa*) into the source of *pramā*, the light of consciousness which lends its light to the distinctly manifest objects like blue and pleasure, one is able to attain the Supreme Consciousness. Therefore, Śrī Abhinavagupta writes:

> The attainment of the true self is possible only through close unification of right knowledge re-

---

[19] ĪPV IV.1.12.

[20] *na bhavanti ca dharādīni uttarottaratattvānı jalādipūrvapūrvaṃ vinā . . . sarvameva cedaṃ prathamānaṃ svatantraparipūrṇaprathāsārabhairavaṃ vinā.* P.T.V, pp. 47–48.

> garding well-manifest objects like blue and pleasure and so on.[21]
>
> ĪPV I.1

The limited form of knowledge shines as separated from the all-inclusive light of the Lord. Thus the limited one gets its fulfilment even though it rests in the source, the very light. But for the limited soul the act of swinging from 'this' (*idam*) to 'I' (*aham*) always continues resting in the object and later in the subject touching the two ends first in the objective level and next in the level of the subject. The rest (*viśrānti*) at the level of the object is relative, while the rest that occurs at the level of the subject is relative-cum-absolute. With the attainment of the light absolute (*pāramārthika*) which is an unbroken continuum, everything then shines as composed of light. But on account of the will of the Lord a cleavage shows itself within that single one, with the result that this first appears very indistinctly, then it shines distinctly as if completely separate from the light, the main-spring of everything. But *aham*, that is I, remains all the time linked with the object. This truth remains veiled to the view of the limited consciousness but as soon as the truth is realized even for a moment, or in other words, when the glimpse of recognition dawns in a soul, he feels all at once that the object he sees, the delicacy he feels, the sweet sound he hears is nothing but the manifestation of the light of consciousness and he himself is shining within that (*nijāntaragatam*). It is also stated in the text:

> All the appearances (*ābhāsas*) are essentially of the nature of consciousness, so they always exist internally.[22]
>
> ĪPK I.8.7

---

[21] *sphuṭatarabhāsamānanīlasukhādipramānveṣaṇadvāreṇaiva pāramārthika pramātṛlābhaḥ*. KSTS Vol. I, p. 18.

[22] *cinmayatve'vabhāsānāmantareva sthitiḥ sadā.*

> The manifestations have their existence in the light of consciousness of the universal Subject. Whether they be in the state of internality or externality, they are essentially of the nature of consciousness.[23]
>
> ĪPV I.8.7

In the language of the devotee we may say that though the Supreme Lord is abiding very near, we are unable to realize him until we attain the true insight. The devotee knows rightly what He really is, so he states with conviction:

> O Lord of the Gods!
> You are an object of incessant worship
> By the great ones,
> But are yourself a worshipper.
> Here in this world
> You are an object of vision
> From both within and without,
> But are yourself a seer.
>
> *Śivastotrāvalī* IV.25[24]

Though Utpaladeva was a staunch non-dualist, he was also a true *bhakta*, devotee, who always tread along the path of delightful devotion (*bhakti*) *par excellence.* It is such a state which is an equilibrium of both devotion and knowledge. Devotion is nothing but enjoyment of the highest bliss of absorption in multifarious ways which dissolves all obstacles on one hand and on the other makes the devotee worthy to realize the great Brahman everywhere and in every situation.

> Therefore with the consciousness
> Of the true essence of things

---

[23] *iha avabhāsānāṃ sadaiva bāhyatābhāsatadabhāvayoḥ*
api antareva pramātṛprakāśa eva sthitiḥ, yata ete cinmayāḥ

[24] Trans. by C. Rhodes Bailly, as also the following quotations.

That emanates from the removal of
The obstacles to the nectar of your non-duality
Make me worthy, O Lord of the Gods,
Of the worship of your feet.

Śivastotrāvalī XII.5

Śrī Abhinavagupta defines *bhakti* as absorption in the highest bliss (*paramānandāveśa*), by the force of which the devotee realizes *brahmasattā*, the presence of *Brahman* in every state (*sarvāsvavasthāsu*).[25]

Absorption (*samāveśa*) in the Supreme is really devotion which does not at all tarnish non-duality but adds brightness to it.[26] Regarding the three stages referred to above that the aspirant has to pass through, these are: *prabodhana*, awakening of the soul. It occurs only through descent of grace followed by the offering of initiation by the spiritual teacher (*sadguru*). It is then followed by *sāmmukhya* of the aspirant which means that the aspirant realizes face to face the glory of the Lord. This is not all. When the aspirant experiences the delightful union with the Lord he feels an anguish for quenching his thirst for nectar over and over again. It is termed as a great festivity (*pūjana mahotsava*) where meditation goes on spontaneously. The Truth is meditated upon without the aid of verbal media. It continues in the core of the heart as reflection of Light in a clear mirror. This meditation has been given a very clear exposition in the *Tantrāloka*:

> The light is self-manifest and is perfectly free. It is in essence pure consciousness and abides steadily in the heart. Though every category is composed of it yet his meditation is to be performed in the recess of the heart. The knower of the Truth

[25] Cp. ĪPVVim Vol. I, p. 29.; cp. also *Gītārthasaṃgraha* XII.2: *māheśvaryaviṣayo yeṣāṃ samāveśaḥ — akṛtrimastanmayībhāvaḥ.*

[26] Cp. *Gītārtha Saṃgraha* XII.

> perceives the Lord in the inner sanctum of the heart.[27]
>
> *Tantrāloka* V.20-21

The author clarifies the view with the simile of the flower of the plantain tree. As the outer covers of the flower when peeled off one after the other the flower inside makes its appearance, in the same way the seeker of the Truth should delve deep after removing the outer coverings which are nothing but all the principles, some gross and some subtle; then he is able to stand face to face or directly realize the effulgent light of the Lord.

If we are allowed to follow the *krama*, the sequence may be as follows:

> Let there be that great festival of worship
> Where the Supreme Lord himself
> Is meditated upon, seen and touched.
> Be always mine through your grace.[28]
>
> *Śivastotrāvalī* XIII.6

The order that is seen in the journey of the aspirant is *dhyāna*, meditation in the beginning. At the ripeness of meditation the vision of the Divine Beloved makes its appearance. This vision is real, not a creation of the mind. The eager look of the devotee sees at a distance a glimpse of the Divine and he is keen to have his vision in the core of the heart. This vision of the beloved makes the aspirant assured that the day is not far away when he will be able to embrace bim. The eyes of the beloved speak of this by his compassionate look. At this stage he goes on looking constantly at Him. By the words *dṛśyate svayam* the Supreme Lord gives his own vision without any

---

[27] *yaḥ prakāśaḥ svatantro'yaṃ, citsvabhāvo hṛdi sthitaḥ, sarvatattvamayaḥ .. īkṣate hṛdayāntasthaṃ tatpuṣpamiva tattvavit.*

[28] *dhyāyate tadanu dṛśyate tataḥ, spṛśyate ca parameśvaraḥ svayam, yatra pūjana mahotsavaḥ sa me sarvadāstu bhavato'nubhāvataḥ.*

external aids. Then occurs the ultimate contact. This is indicated by the word *spṛśyate*, 'touched'. All these steps occur by the grace of the Lord not outside but in the void of consciousness (*cidākāśa*). Then the stage that becomes manifest to the devotee now is that of the relation of Thou and I. The devotee is then able to address his beloved as 'Thou', that is in the second person. Though there is the absence of duality at this stage yet separateness remains manifest so long as a total merging does not come about. The devotee always likes to maintain his separateness, a sort of distance from the Lord in order to relish bliss with its numerous facets until the bowl of emptiness becomes completely full.

According to the Śaiva doctrine of Kashmir devotion has not been given so much importance as we find it in the Vaiṣṇava tradition. The Vaiṣṇavas are regarded by the Advaita Śaivas as established in the lower level of spiritual development, for to them *bhakti* is only an attachment (*rāga*), and as such it leads them to attain a certain stage, not the ultimate. But to Utpaladeva *bhakti* is a great treasure.[29] Those who are richly endowed with the blessing of devotion do not require anything for their need. It is known as *parābhakti*, the sublime form of devotion. It flourishes in the aspirant. When he attains steadiness in devotion that is when proper maturity in the realization of the non-dual nature of the Lord occurs he feels himself the real recipient of everything that the Master showers on him (*dīyate asmai sarvam*).

Śrī Abhinavagupta also does not lag behind when he speaks of devotion with high spiritual fervour thus:

> Now I, who am your devotee, having become transformed into you, am as if composed of your essence. On seeing you or realizing you as my own

---

[29] Cp. *bhaktilakṣmīsamṛddhānāṃ kimanyadupayācitam*, ĪPV I.1.

> self, I pay obeisance to you and me over and over again.[30]
>
> *Mahopadeśa Viṃśatikā* V.4

These quotes definitely stand as a sound proof that thinkers like Utpaladeva and Śrī Abhinavagupta did not hold any disparaging views regarding *bhakti*, rather it adds brightness and beauty to the tenet of non-duality.

Following the text of *Pratyabhijñā*, I shall now proceed to explain how divine recognition is transmitted to others. It is well-known to the people in general that the spiritual teacher guides the disciple by giving him initiation so that he may proceed along the noble path leading to liberation. Knowledge of the highest kind is transmitted to the disciple, by whose power the latent impression lying in him is destroyed. And after the fall of the body he attains Śivahood.

This in short is the description of the formal type of initiation. But as the nature or the innate characteristic of every human being differs, initiation and spiritual practice which follows it also differ. Therefore for some *sattarka*, the right form of judgment, is the means which paves the way for the person of ripe intuition and acumen of intelligence to realize the noble Truth by himself (*svataḥ*). But it should be remembered here that before proceeding along the path it is essential that he should first of all receive a glimpse of the Divine by the kindness of the teacher.

It is quite relevant here to state how direct knowledge of the divine recognition arises in the disciple. Śrī Abhinavagupta says that the teacher, who has already attained identity with the Divine, is endowed with all the glories of the Lord. He is the embodied form of Śiva himself. He is said to be the *bimba*, the source or original image, while the domain of the heart of the disciple which has become perfectly

[30] *bhavad bhaktasya saṃjātabhavadrūpasya me'dhunā,*
tvāmātmarūpaṃ saṃprekṣya tubhyaṃ mahyaṃ namonamaḥ.

pure like the mirror, is capable of receiving the light as reflection (*pratibimba*). The analogy that is used in this context is called *bimba-pratibimba nyāya*, the analogy of the source and the reflection. The source (*bimba*) is one but the reflections may be many. Therefore the teacher representing *bimba* is able to bestow good to many.

The doctrine of *Pratyabhijñā* is a means (*upāya*) to attain liberation or revelation of one's own Śiva nature.[31] It is a means by which recognition comes about. It is the way leading to the ultimate goal which is also known as recognition. "Recognition as such may be called the penultimate goal which terminates in the manifestation of Lordship with all His glory as a single light"[32] in one's own being. Ordinary people who do not have any knowledge regarding its nature and about the goal to which it leads, if they hear by chance that a person who has realized his identity with the Supreme, the most desirable of all desires, and established His Recognition, is desirous of doing good to all troubled with birth and death and bestow grace to them, the final release becomes assured to them. They receive recognition as reflection reflected from the original source. The sure knowledge of the fact makes them aware of the truth in the first stage, but as soon as they become intent on taking the course of recognition, they reach the second stage. In this stage they imagine themselves free from the limitations of time. The third stage manifests itself when they realize the steady recognition of perfection in their own nature. This process has been indicated by the grammatical terms third and first persons.

> The meaning denoted by the term third person terminates in the meaning denoted by the first person.[33] ĪPV v.I, p.27

[31] *pratyabhijñāyate anayā.*
[32] *samastasampatlakṣaṇa paramaiśvaryaikarūpaprathanam.*
[33] *prathamapuruṣārthaḥ uttamapuruṣārthe paryavasyati.*

In the above way we have tried to give a summary view of the doctrine of recognition. It is relevant to say something regarding the nature of *sattarka*, the right type of judgement. The system known as *Pratyabhijñā* is not a text of logic though it involves some arguments and counter arguments only to help the seeker of the Truth to stand steadily on the stable ground of conviction free from doubts and misconception.

The author presents the doctrine of Recognition by bringing to view, that is in the sphere of perception, the power of *dṛk* and *kriyā*, knowledge and action which are inseparably united with the Lord, so that taking recourse to them one is able to recognize one's own self.

When finally the devotee realizes recognition he feels that everything shines in the light of the divine as one with it.

> Being self-luminous
> You cause everything to shine;
> Delighting in your form
> You fill the universe with delight;
> Rocking with your own bliss
> You make the whole world dance with joy.
>
> *Śivastotrāvalī* XIII.15

ON LETTING GOD BE GOD

Meister Eckhart and the Lure of the Desert

Sr. Brigitte

Meister Eckhart himself says, all his sermons have one theme only, namely *the Birth of God in the Soul.*[1] This is worked out in detail in Sermons 1 and 2, and is mentioned in the majority of the sermons. There are, however, lesser themes of which I have chosen a few.

Let God Be God

According to his earthly existence man is a contingent being, owing its existence to another. Eckhart uses the example of branch and tree or a face in a mirror. The branch is the 'work' of the tree and has no existence apart from the tree, and yet the tree is incomplete without it. The image in the mirror is the exact replica of the person represented, yet is totally dependent on that person. The end and purpose of the spiritual life is not to become aware of the indwelling presence of God; rather man must come to understand himself just as he is as the expression of the divine reality. Man *is* divine life. 'God and I are One', Eckhart does not tire to assure his readers or listeners. God manifests himself in man. For as long as man is not aware of this he remains the prisoner of his ego, but once he discovers the illusory and transient nature of the ego, duality is transcended. He can see through things into their reality. Then he can let God be God. Let us hear Eckhart himself:

[1] For an introduction to Meister Eckhart's life and times, see the appendix which will provide the necessary background.

> At the point where the image enters, God departs with all his divinity, but where the image departs, there God enters. Well, my friend, what harm does it do you to let God be God in you? Go entirely out of yourself for God's sake, and God will go entirely out of himself for your sake. When these both depart, what remains is a simple *One.* In this One the Father gives birth to his Son in the innermost source.[2]

This ego, which prevents man from letting God be God in him, is not evil. It is an essential part of man, and its function is to express the self. However, like the faculties and the intellect, it is mortal and will pass away with the body. This the ego can't accept, since it considers itself to be the true person. Eckhart of course does not use the term 'ego' but 'self-seeking' or 'mit Eigenschaft' in the Middle-high-German of his time, which meant 'with attachment to self'. In his sermons, specially sermon 6, he applies it to the attitude of religious people towards their piety and good works. Thus he talks of people who perform works like fasting, vigils, prayers, in order to obtain something from God in return. These he calls 'merchants', for they trade with the Lord, and he throws them out of the temple. The sellers of doves are not thrown out, but they are scolded for they are too attached to the performance of their good works, though they do not try to trade with God.

Eckhart uncovers the self-deception of the human heart in so much that passes for religion: the covert glance for recognition and reward, the longing for praise. To give one example:

> Many people imagine themselves to be holy and perfect; they use big words, and yet they desire so much and long to possess so much, have such

[2] Vol. 1, p.118.

> a high opinion of themselves, and imagine themselves very recollected, and yet they cannot accept *one* word (of rebuke) without justifying themselves. You can be sure that they are far from God.[3]

Like other mystical writers Eckhart speaks of an uncreated something in the soul or of the little spark of the soul, deeply buried under layers of self-seeking. If man succeeds in dying to his ego-love by a mystical death from this imprisonment in time and space and the beguiling variety of creatures, then the birth of the Son takes place in the soul.

Eckhart advises his listeners to throw out of their souls the saints and our Lady and even their thoughts about God, e.g. that he is good, just, wise. He tells his startled audience:

> If I say 'God is good' — it is not true. *I* am good, God is not good! I would even say: I am *better* than God. For what is good can become better. But now God is not good and therefore cannot become better. ...The most perfect thing a man can say of God, out of the wealth of his inner wisdom is to keep silence. So be silent and don't prattle about God.[4]
>
> And don't dress him up in the clothes of his attributes or his names of Father, Son and Holy Spirit, but "take him in his dressing room where he is an undifferentiated One."

A Master says, "if I had a God whom I could know, I would never regard him as God: Whatever you know about him, he is not that. ...So know nothing about the God who cannot be pronounced in the word 'God'!"

---

[3] Vol. 2, p. 6.

[4] Vol. 2, p. 332.

What should I do then?

"You must die entirely to yourself and flow into His self, and your 'Your' in his 'His' shall become one My, so perfectly one that with him you will realise his uncreated being and his unnamable nothingness."[5]

To let God be God demands the extreme of spiritual poverty:

"Who seeks nothing and desires nothing save God alone, to him God gives and discovers all that lies hidden in his divine heart."

> "That is why I am going to lure her and lead her out into the wilderness and speak to her heart." (Hosea 2:16)

Prayer

Given Eckhart's understanding of the relationship of God and man, it is not surprising that he should question our understanding of prayer: "People often say to me, 'Pray for me!' Then I say to myself, why do you go out of yourself? Why not remain within and use the wealth that is yours? You have the fullness of truth in yourself."[6] "All creatures are a nothing. He who seeks a nothing cannot complain if he finds nothing. He only found what he was looking for."[7]

Prayer and praise are effective in proportion as the soul is like God, for: "What is like God in the soul praises God, in the same way as a painting praises its master, who has imprinted his art on it. The prayer that can be expressed with the mouth is unworthy of God."[8]

In reality we need ask God for nothing, for he is always more ready to give than we to ask. Indeed, "God can no more

[5] Vol. 2, p. 333.
[6] Vol. 1, p. 119.
[7] Vol. 1, p. 284.
[8] Vol. 1, p. 259.

do without us than we can do without him. Even if it were true that we can turn away from God, God can never turn away from us. I will not ask God to give me anything, nor will I praise him for giving it to me. Rather I will ask him to make me worthy of receiving, and praise him that it is his nature that he *must* give."[9]

> If a man thinks he will get more of God by meditation, by devotions, by ecstasies or by a special infusion of grace, than by the kitchen stove or in the stable – that is nothing but taking God, wrapping a cloak around his head and shoving him under a bench. For whoever seeks God in a special way gets the way and misses God, who lies hidden in it. But whoever seeks God without any special way gets him as he is in himself, and that man lives with the Son and is life itself.[10]

The same teaching is found out at length in the sermon on Martha and Mary, where in contrast to the obvious meaning of the gospel passage and all commentators on it, Eckhart insists that it is Martha who is praised by the Lord, for Mary is attached to him by her emotions, while Martha serves him while going about her work. As Mary matures spiritually she will also become a Martha.

Eckhart advises us never to ask for perishable things. If we must pray let us pray for God's will and for nothing else:

> We deafen God day and night and shout, 'your will be done!' and when God's will is done we are angry. That is not right. When our will becomes God's will, that is good; but when God's will becomes our will, that is far better. If your

[9] Vol. 1, p. 101.
[10] Vol. 1, p. 116.

> will becomes God's will, if you fall ill, you would not wish to be well contrary to God's will, though you might wish that it be God's will that you should be well. And if you are still ill, — in God's name! If your friend dies — in God's name![11]

In another sermon we read:

> The just man does not need God, for what I have I do not need. He serves God for no reward; he has God so he needs no reward. In all his doings a man should turn to God and look to God alone. Let him go forward confidently, not considering whether what he does is right or wrong. One should follow the first intuition, then one reaches the state where one should be.[12]

However, Eckhart remains human! In a delightful passage he says: "Sometimes in times of prayer I say these words: 'Lord, what we ask of you is so small! If anyone were to ask me for it, I'd do it for him. And it is a hundred times easier for you, and you will do it more willingly. The greater the request, the more willingly you give."[13]

And, "God is ready to give great things if we are ready to leave all things to his goodness."

The Birth of the Son of God in the Heart of Man

Under this imagery Eckhart develops his mystical teaching. He deals with the subject fully in two sermons, but, as he says, it is the theme of all his teaching. Eckhart may not have known St. Athanasius' saying, 'God became man that man might become God', but he quotes St. Augustine: "What

[11] Vol. 1, p. 92.
[12] Vol. 2, p. 78.
[13] Vol. 1, p. 119.

does it avail me that this birth is always happening, if it does not happen in me? That it should happen in me is what matters." In the same sermon he quotes John 1:11,12 "...as many as received it (the light) became in authority sons of God; to them was given power to become sons of God."[14]

"We shall therefore speak of this birth, of how it may take place in us, and be consummated in the virtuous soul." Eckhart warns here and elsewhere that only those who are serious about prayer and are absolutely pure and live in noble fashion, and are collected and turned inward, are capable of this experience. "Not running out through the five senses into the multiplicity of creatures, but all inturned and collected and in the purest part (of the soul). He (God) disdains anything less."

The birth takes place in the 'ground' of the soul, also known as the 'little spark' or the 'castle', or the desert of the Godhead, which is so pure that no image ever enters.

> In the soul's essence there is no activity. Here is nothing but rest and celebration for this birth, this act, that God the Father may speak his Word there, for this part is receptive of nothing but the divine essence without mediation. Here God enters the soul with his all.

An imaginary question: "How does God the Father give birth to the Son in the soul?" Eckhart answers that the Father unites himself with the soul, and in that real union lies the soul's whole beatitude.

> Therefore you have to be and dwell in the essence and in the ground, and *there* God will touch you with his simple essence without the intervention of any image. And *therefore* there must be a silence and a stillness, and the Father must speak

[14]This and the following quotations are from Vol. 1, Sermon 1.

> in that, and give birth to his Son and perform his work free from all images.

A second question: "Is it better to do something towards this, to imagine and think about God? Or should he keep still and silent in peace and quiet and let God speak and work in him, merely waiting for God to act?"

Eckhart repeats that his works are meant for good and perfected people only. These must know "that the very best attainment in this life is to be silent and let God speak and work within." The more completely you are able to draw in all your powers to a unity and to forget all the things and images which you have absorbed, the nearer you are to this. And so, if God is to speak his Word in your soul, she must be at rest and in peace.

This is very strange language for anyone accustomed to a Jesus mysticism. It has to be seen in the context of Eckhart's understanding of creation pre-existing 'ideally' in the Godhead before becoming actual, existing as the thought and archetype of creation. In the beginning Godhead IS, before any differentiation into 'Persons'. This state Eckhart refers to as 'What I was before I was.'

> When I was in the Ground, the Stream, the Source of the Godhead, no one asked me where I was going or what I wanted or what I was doing; *there* was no one who might have asked me.[15]

Creation is a flowing, multiplicity flowing out of unity. Only now can God be known or named.

> When I flowed out all creatures spoke about 'God'. Why do they not speak about Godhead? All that is in the Godhead is *One* and one cannot speak of it. 'God' and Godhead are totally different. They have nothing in common.

[15]This and the following quotations are from Vol. 2, Sermon 56.

But 'flowing out' must necessarily culminate in a return, a return that is far nobler than the flowing out. The spearhead of this return is man's birth as God's Son in the bosom of the Godhead.

> When I come into the Ground, the Depth, the Stream and the Source of the Godhead, no one asks me where I have been or whence I have come. No one there missed me, for there 'God' ceases to exist.
>
> You shall love God as a non-God, a non-Spirit, a non-Person, nay more, as a pure, mere, bright One, distinct from all duality. And in this One we shall sink away eternally, from Something to Nothing.[16]

Our difficulty with Eckhart is our incapacity to escape from time. The 'flowing out' and the 'return' are not processes in time. In a sense we always are, always have been and always will be in our Source, in the Godhead. Time and space, for all their apparent reality, are illusory. The 'breakthrough' is precisely our birth in the Godhead.

The Way of Emptiness

Western mysticism has been deeply marked by suffering, whether in the form of 'dark nights', of intense physical pain or a sense of desolation, or a sharing in the passion of Christ. On the surface there is surprisingly little about suffering in Eckhart's sermons. The cross is only mentioned twice, both times in quotations from the Bible. Where suffering does figure, it is often to say that it is transitory, that like darkness, it has to yield when light comes. In one longer passage he states that whatever God sends is always best. It may not

[16] Vol. 2, p. 335 (cp. p. 333).

seem to be best of the time, but it is God's chosen way for our advancement. In a treatise called "The Book of Divine Consolation" Eckhart deals in detail with pain and suffering. It was written for the young Queen of Hungary after the assassination of her father. It is a difficult work and speaks much for her intelligence and spiritual maturity.

In the principal part Eckhart cites some thirty examples, "each single one of which might readily console a rational man in his sorrow." To give just one: "Consider that there is no harm that does not bring with it some consolation. If a man is in great bodily pain but has a house to be ill in, people to care for him, a doctor to treat him: let him consider poor people, sick or sicker than he, to whom no one gives as much as a glass of water."[17]

He considers also suffering as retribution: "All suffering comes from love and holding dear. Therefore if I love and hold dear perishable things, God still does not have the love of my whole heart." "A good man should be ashamed before God and himself when he notices that God is not in him, that created things are still at work in him." And "A good man should never complain: he should only complain of his own complaints."[18]

Eckhart suggests that all suffering lies in ego-love. Rightly accepted, suffering can rid us of egoism and so help us to grow in spiritual maturity.

He then turns to a more mystical explanation: "Empty yourself that you may be filled. ...To be naked, poor, to have nothing, transforms nature: emptiness makes water flow upward." He gives a vivid and characteristic example of the effect of suffering: "When material fire kindles wood, a spark receives the nature of fire. ... At once it forgets father and mother down upon earth, and hastens to the true Father

[17] Vol. 3, p. 67.
[18] Vol. 3, p. 68.

which is in heaven ...". In a passage too long to quote in full he writes:

> As it has already been said about emptiness or nakedness, as the soul becomes more bare and poor and possesses less of created things that are not God, it receives God more purely and is totally in him, and it truly becomes one with God, and it looks into God and God into it, face to face, as it were two images transformed into one. ... We have a plain example and proof even in the natural order: When fire works and kindles wood and sets it on fire, the fire diminishes the wood and makes it unlike itself, taking away its coarseness, coldness, heaviness and dampness, and turns the wood into itself, into fire, more and more like to it. But neither the fire nor the wood is satisfied with any warmth or heat or likeness until the fire gives birth to itself in the wood, and gives to the wood its own nature, and also its own being, so that they both become one and the same unseparated fire, neither less nor more. And therefore, before this may be achieved there is always smoke, contention, crackling, effort and violence between fire and wood. But when all the unlikeness has been taken away, then the fire is stilled and the wood is quiet.[19]

In this passage the link between suffering and the birth of the Son of God in the heart of man is clearly made, whether in relation to the passion of Christ or the sufferings of men.

Eckhart devotes one sermon to this paradox on the text "Blessed are the poor in spirit for their is the Kingdom of Heaven." He dismisses the customary interpretations — they

---

[19] Vol. 3, p. 116f.

are all right as far as they go, but not relevant to his theme. He defines the poor man as the one who *wants* nothing, *knows* nothing, *has* nothing.[20]

Of the man who wants nothing he says: "For as long as it is man's will to do the dearest will of God, he is not yet poor. For this man has still a will, and that is not yet poverty."

Of the man who knows nothing he says: "Man must not even know that God lives in him. He must be as free of knowledge as he was before he was. He must be empty of all knowledge, knowing neither about God, creation or himself."

The man who has nothing: "*this* poverty is the extreme form of poverty." To paraphrase a lengthy passage: The great masters say, and Eckhart has himself said it, that man should be free of exterior and interior possessions, so that God can be God and act in him. He now says it differently: he asks God to let him be rid of 'God'. For in his essential being he is above God, insofar as we understand 'God' as the beginning of creation. Only with this spiritual poverty man returns to his true nature which he has ever been and which he will ever remain. If he succeeds in this return out of the state of bondage to his 'I' and to creatures and is not caught up in bondage to his (idea of) God, but breaks through this as well, into the eternal and one divine consciousness in which the highest angels, the souls of men and the mosquitoes are one, then this breakthrough and return is nobler than man's entrance into creation. For he leaves behind the small, limited 'I'; here Konrad and Henry die, to be buried in the desert of the Godhead.

> When I flowed out of God, all creation said: 'God Is'. But this is not my beatitude. But in my return (to God) when I am free of my own will and the will of God and all his works and of God himself, then I am above Creation and am neither

[20]This and the following quotations are from Vol. 3, pp. 269–76.

> God nor creature. I am rather what I was and what I will be, now and ever. Then I experience a movement that raises me above all angels. In this movement I receive such wealth that God and everything to do with God cannot suffice me, nor all his divine works, for in this movement I discover that I and God are one. There I am what I was, there I neither increase nor decrease, but I am the immovable cause that moves all things. Here God finds no place in man, for with this poverty man becomes what he always was and will always remain. Here God is one with the Spirit and that is the purest poverty that can be found.

We will end this lecture with the words with which Eckhart ends his sermon: "Whoever does not understand this let him not be disturbed, for as long as man is not conformed to this truth, he will not be able to understand. For it is a hidden truth which comes straight from the heart of God."

Appendix

Meister Eckhart (ca.1260-1328/29)

Some Notes on his Life and Times

The seventy years spanned by Eckhart's life were a time of transition in Europe, marked by much violence and brutality, by a breakdown of law and order, by the passing away of old-established norms, by impatience with a fossilized Church and by the rise of charismatic movements which often began with reforming zeal but ended as heretical and fanatical sects. Politically it was marked by a disastrous interregnum lasting twenty years, when there was no emperor to keep the ambitions of warring princes under control; it was also marked by the first beginnings of nation-states. The papacy was at a very low ebb: under pressure from France the popes went into exile at Avignon (1309–77), while a rival pope ruled in Rome.

Heresies abounded; cities and whole countries were put under interdict and denied the sacraments, sometimes for years. At the same time there was religious zeal and fervour, particularly among educated women who entered convents leading to many new foundations being made, and many claimed mystical experiences. This state is reflected in Eckhart's sermons, since he was responsible for the spiritual guidance of these convents.

Little is known of Eckhart's life. He must have entered the Dominican Order very young; was educated in Paris and Cologne; he was evidently regarded as a very promising friar as he was given posts of responsibility when he was still very young. A further period of study in Paris gained him the coveted degree of Master of Theology, after which he is always known as Master Eckhart (Meister Eckhart). For all his responsibilities he found time for writing, mostly in Latin, though he never completed the major works he had planned. At this time he also wrote in German "The Book of Divine Comforts", which already contains most of the ideas he is famous for. After a period in Paris, lecturing and holding disputations, he was transferred to Strassburg (1314), and here he began his practice of preaching in German in convent chapels and parish churches. Probably these sermons were never written down by the Master. What we have is notes written from memory by sisters and others in the congregation. The sermons are characterized by bold paradox, by hyperbole, by speculation based on his deep knowledge of the Fathers as well as of Greek and Islamic scholars; by humour and a penetrating knowledge of human nature and its subterfuges.

About 1322 he was transferred to Cologne to occupy the Chair of Theological Studies, and continued his practice of preaching in German language. Here trouble began; the Archbishop was a Franciscan (at that time there was enmity and rivalry between Dominicans and Franciscans). The Archbishop was bitterly hostile to any kind of mysticism, which he associated with the 'enthusiasm' of the many semi-heretical sects. He instigated proceedings against Eckhart for allegedly spreading heretical ideas. Eckhart defended himself. The case was transferred to the papal court in Avignon. In 1329 a much shorter list of passages from those submitted by Cologne was declared erroneous, but before this judgement was passed Eckhart had died. Eckhart's teaching as a whole was never declared heretical. In any case Eckhart had publicly repudiated any of his teachings "insofar as they could generate in the minds of the faithful a heretical opinion" (note the careful wording!) or "anything erroneous or hostile to the true faith". Nevertheless, Eckhart's teaching was henceforth regarded with suspicion. It is therefore surprising that Eckhartian societies continued to flourish in North Germany and the Netherlands, the latest of which I know being in Leyden in Holland in the 17th Century, where an ecumenical group studied his teaching, one of whom popularised it in doggerel verse, which continues to be widely read and quoted.

References

Meister Eckhart: *Deutsche Predigten und Traktate*, edited and translated into modern German by Joseph Quint. Munich 1955. (Referred to as 'Qu.' in notes)

Meister Eckhart: *Sermons and Treatises*. In Three Volumes. Translated by M.O.C. Walshe. London: Element Books, 1979, 1981, 1985. (W. in notes)

Meister Eckhart. Translated by Edmund Cooledge. Contains

some commentaries, seven German Sermons and the Treatises. New York, Paulist Press (Classics of Western Sprituality), 1981.

Meister Eckhart by R.B. Blakney. New York: Harper & Row, 1941. Contains 28 sermons.

Matthew Fox: *Meditation with Meister Eckhart*, Santa Fe: Bear & Company, 1983. (Extracts from his writing for devotional use.)

Books about Meister Eckhart

Willigis Jaeger: *Kontemplation. Gottesbegegnung heute.* Salzburg: Otto Müller Verlag, 1982. (An English translation of this practical little book is available: *The Way to Contemplation: Encountering God Today.* New York/-Mahwah: Paulist Press, 1987.

Alois Haas: *Meister Eckhart als normative Gestalt geistlichen Lebens.* Einsiedeln: Johannes Verlag, 1979.

Heribert Fischer: *Meister Eckhart.* Freiburg and Munich: Karl Alber, 1974.

Cyprian Smith: *The Way of Paradox.* London: Darton, Longman & Todd, 1987.

Ursula Fleming: *Meister Eckhart, The Man From Whom God Hid Nothing.* London: Fount Paperbacks, 1988.

Matthew Fox: *Breakthrough: Meister Eckhart's Creation Spirituality in New Translations.* New York: Doubleday Image Books, 1980.

ŚĀMBHAVOPĀYA

The Divine Way in Kashmir Śaivism[1]

B. N. Pandit

The *Trika* system of the practical yoga of Kashmir Śaivism teaches such a Tantric path of practice which leads directly to the realization of the innermost aspect of the Self and yields, at the same time, liberation from age old bondages of ignorance, while an aspirant is yet living in a physical form. Yoga, known as *śāmbhavopāya*, or the Divine means, is the highest method of *Trika-yoga*. The stage of yoga known as *anupāya* is nothing but the position of the highest perfection in the practice of *śāmbhava* and not at all any other practice. As the name says, it is a "means without any means" or a "pathless path". The essential character of *śāmbhava* is sufficiently different from that of the two other methods of *Trika-yoga*, known as *āṇavopāya* (the individual means) and *śāktopāya* (the means of Energy).

The characteristic features of the *upāyas* or means of realization have been described in the *Mālinīvijaya Tantra*. The following verses describe the individual means (*āṇava*) and the means of Energy (*śākta*):

> *uccārakaraṇa-dhyāna-varṇa-sthānaprakalpanaiḥ,*
> *yo bhavet sa samāveśaḥ samyag āṇava ucyate.*
>
> MVT II.21

> The full *samāveśa* (absorption in the divine) occurs by means of *uccāra* (upgoing dynamic vital

[1] Edited by H.N. Chakravarty.

> energy), *karaṇa* (postures of the body indicative of certain inward states), *dhyāna* (meditation), *varṇa* (letters of alphabets permeated by the primal sound known as *nāda*), *sthāna kalpa* (concentration on stations of the vital energy, on different parts of the body and spots outside the body) is known as *āṇava*.

The same text defines *śāktopāya* in the following way:

> *uccārarahitaṃ vastu cetasaiva vicintayan,*
> *yaṃ samāveśamāpnoti śāktaḥ so'trābhidhīyate.*
>
> MVT II.22

> When an aspirant with one-pointedness of the mind apprehends that Reality which is not within the range of utterance (gross or subtle), he obtains absorption (in divine consciousness), then that *samāveśa* is known as *śākta*. (Tr. J. Singh)

All the varieties of *āṇavopāya* involve some regular practices in mental contemplation on the nature of different categories of objective phenomena of mental and material character. *Śāktopāya* is the name given to practice in subjective contemplation on one's own person and its real character, as discussed in the philosophy of Śaiva monism. A *yogin* has to contemplate regularly on his infinite, perfect and divinely potent pure I-consciousness, which is not to be confused with the limited ego. Such practice yields an intellectual realization of the true nature and character of the real Self, as taught in Kashmir Śaivism. Such realization of the Self is termed as *bauddha-jñāna*. Regular practice in such *jñāna* leads automatically to the position of *śāmbhava* when it becomes perfect.

The *śāmbhava upāya* has been described thus:

> *akiṃccintakasyaiva guruṇā pratibodhataḥ,*
> *jāyate yaḥ samāveśaḥ śāmbhavo'sāvudīritaḥ.*
>
> MVT II.23

> Absorption of the individual consciousness in the Divine results from an awakening imparted by the spiritual teacher who has freed his mind from all ideation, is called *śāmbhava.* (Tr. J. Singh)

The absorption that occurs by following the course either of *śākta* or *āṇava*, that course indeed leads to *śāmbhava*, for it is stated in the *Tantrāloka* that,

> *dvāvapyetau samāveśau nirvikalpārṇavaṃ prati,*
> *prayāta eva tadrūḍhiṃ vinā naiva hi kīṃcana.*
>
> TĀ I.226

> Both these absorptions (*āṇava* and *śākta*) proceed toward the sea of undifferentiated knowledge. Without being absorbed (in this undifferentiated sea of consciousness) nothing indeed exists.

They both get their rest in the absorption of *śāmbhava* which is characterised by the Supreme Light of the Divine.

The characteristic feature of the means known as *śāmbhava* is non-dual, while *śākta* is dual-non-dual and *āṇava* is dual (cp. TĀ I.230).

Some present-day teachers and thinkers may raise an objection by saying that such contemplative practice and its results come into the field of self-hypnotism. But in fact all of us are already moving within the deep rooted hypnotism worked out on us by *māyā*, the deluding power of the absolute reality, and are therefore taking wrongly the mental and physical forms as our real Self. *Śāktopāya* should therefore be taken as such a process of dehypnotization which relieves a *yogin* from the hypnotical finitude of his person and limitations in his powers to know and to do in accordance with his will, imposed on him by *māyā*, the most powerful hypnotizing force working in the whole universe.

Śāmbhavopāya transcends all practices in mental contemplation. It is a regular practice in direct realization of the true nature and character of one's real Self and by the self, not aided by any mental apparatus. *Āṇava* and *śākta* involve a sufficient amount of mental imagination, but *śāmbhava* transcends the mind and all mental activities. Mental ideation is the essential character of both *āṇava* and *śākta* types of yoga, while *śāmbhava* is perfectly free from all ideation. It is therefore known as *nirvikalpa-upāya*. Ideation and contemplation involve two psychic activities, namely, mental effort in forming ideas and the psychic manifestation of such ideas. The element of mental exertion plays a predominant part in *āṇava*, while manifestation becomes dominant in *śākta*. Exertion is action and manifestation is knowledge, as it is a psychic illumination. Therefore these two types of *Trika-yoga* are known respectively as *kriyā-yoga* and *jñāna-yoga*. A *śāmbhava yogin* pushes both such mental activities to the background and, with just the use of the power of the Energy of will (*icchā-śakti*), he enters into such a transcendental state in which the Self, consisting of self-aware pure consciousness, freed from the whole mental apparatus, shines by itself and keeps aware of itself as the infinite 'I', vibrating to and fro through its own divine essence. A regular practice in such yoga results in a state termed as *śiva-samāveśa*. It is such a state in which the finite I-consciousness becomes merged into the infinite, omniscient and omnipotent I-consciousness and the practitioner feels actually that he is not separate from Almighty God himself. A regular practice in such *samāveśa* results in the development of many divine capacities and such a *yogin* can excercise his divine grace on a being and such being gets liberation from his ignorance and all the resultant miseries. *Śāmbhavopāya*, being conducted through the exercise of such power of will, is known as *icchā-yoga*.

> *evaṃ parecchāśaktyaṃśasadupāyamimaṃ viduḥ,*
> *śāmbhavākhyaṃ samāveśaṃ sumatyantenivā-*
> *sinaḥ.* TA I.213

> This true means is known by the disciples of revered Sumati and others is a portion of the supreme Energy of Will and it is called the *śāmbhava* absorption (*samāveśa*).

Śāmbhava-yoga is of several varieties. The main element in all its varieties is the intuitive revelation of the real character of the Self. The Self realizes itself through the brilliant para-psychological lustre of its pure consciousness, without the least use of the whole mental apparatus. Two of the main varieties of *śāmbhava* have been discussed in detail by Abhinavagupta, respectively in his *Tantrāloka* and his *Vivaraṇa* commentary on *Parātrīśikā.*[2] Such varieties of *śāmbhava* are termed as *mātṛkā* and *mālinī.* Both such practices in *śāmbhava-yoga* are highly mystical in character and can be grasped correctly only through practice in *Trika yoga* and not through mere studies and discussions. Yet these have been described in such works of eminently high standard ever written on the advanced stages in mystic yoga.

The whole phenomenon is, in the philosophical view of Kashmir's monistic Śaivism, a manifestation of the outward reflections of the divine powers of Almighty God. He, while appearing in the form of the phenomenal existence, does not undergo any change or transformation, as maintained by Vaiṣṇavas in India and pantheists in the West. God is always the pure and absolute consciousness and does not undergo any change in his nature. He possesses wonderful divine powers. Being infinitely blissful in his nature, he is ever playful. On account of his divine playfulness, he plays the infinite game of cosmic creation, dissolution etc.[3] This is being done

---

[2]Wrongly called *Paratriṃśikā.* Cp. Abhinavagupta, *Parātrīśikā-Vivaraṇa. The Secret of Tantric Mysticism.* Trans. by Jaideva Singh, Sanskrit text ed. by Swami Lakshman jee, ed. by Bettina Bäumer, Delhi (Motilal Banarsidass), 1988.

[3]Cp. Bettina Bäumer, "The Play of the Three Worlds: The Trika

by him through outwardly reflecting his divine powers. All the phenomenal elements, called *tattvas*, are thus just the reflections of different divine powers of God. That is the truth about the phenomena, as maintained in Kashmir Śaivism. A Śiva-yogin has to transcend the whole physical and mental existence by uniting with the Divine will. He has to find out actually, through the power of his intuition, that he is none other than Almighty God. The whole phenomenal existence, consisting of all the created *tattvas*, is to be seen as shining within the lustre of his own consciousness as a multitude of the reflections of his own divine powers.

The following verses of *Tantrāloka* of Śrī Abhinavagupta explain briefly *śāmbhava samāveśa*:

> *saṃvidātmani viśvo'yaṃ bhāvavargaḥ prapañcavān, pratibimbatayā bhāti yasya viśveśvaro hi saḥ.*
> TĀ III.268
>
> He indeed is the Lord of the universe in whose consciousness this entire multitude of beings appears in infinite ways like reflections in a mirror.

The text further adds:

> *evamātmani yasyedṛgavikalpaḥ sadodayaḥ,*
> *parāmarśaḥ sa evāsau śāmbhavopāya mudritaḥ.*
> TĀ III.269
>
> Those who are 'marked' by the Divine way partake of a reflective awareness which arises once without setting in a non-differentiated consciousness (*avikalpa*) of the Self.

Abhinavagupta discusses *śāmbhava upāya* in his *Tantrāloka* (3rd *āhnika*) in the following way. The Divine Lord being

---

Concept of *līlā*", in: *The Gods at Play: Līlā in South Asia*, ed. by William Sax, New York (Oxford University Press), 1994.

transcendent (*upādhyatīta*) is beyond the reach of accidental attributes (*upādhis*), yet He shines in His innate glory where no *upādhi* has yet become manifest, and the other is going to merge in the sea of tranquillity (*praśamayogataḥ*). This *praśama* occurs in two distinct ways according to the comparative competence of the yogin. This competence is nothing but the keenness of the fall of grace (*śaktipāta*) by which the aspirant is touched. For the one who has been blessed by the graceful Lord, that is, by an intense impact of Śakti obtains immediate liberation. It is stated in the *Tantrāloka* (III.259 ff.) that the former teachers used to stress the point that the transcendent nature of the Divine on the one hand is beyond *upādhi*, that is, accidental attribute, but on the other even the aspirant who has received grace of the Lord in a lesser degree realizes the Lord. The Lord shines as if nothing has emerged yet (*prāgabhāva-rūpa*). The second is that negation which has been made existent by means of destruction or withdrawal. To clarify the above viewpoints it is stated that the autonomous Lord by His free will before manifesting the universe, when he becomes intent on creation and when all the attributes are as if about to flourish (*anullāsāt*) actually they have not yet flourished. This is known to be a state of *prāgabhāva*. Therefore the Lord's graceful nature is realized by the competent aspirant in two different ways. The one is by means of *śānti*, the way of tranquillity. His tasting of the sweetness of the Lord is preceded by the procedure of paying obeisance to the revered teacher and following the course of convention (*samaya*) and so on. This is termed as *madhurapāka*, 'cooking with sweetness', while the other is known as *haṭhapāka*, "cooked instantaneously." The aspirant realizes the Self as Consciousness shining like a blazing fire into which everything has already been consumed by the fire of Consciousness. The aspirant feels within that there is nothing more to be relished. He feels fully satisfied. Only the non-ending light remains ever ablaze without any break (cp. TĀ III.261).

> *sarvo mamāyaṃ vibhava ityevaṃ parijānataḥ,*
> *viśvātmano vikalpānāṃ prasare'pi maheśatā.*
> ĪPK Tattvasaṃgrahādhikāra IV.1.12
>
> He who knows that all this glory of manifestation is mine (i.e. belongs to the Spirit), who realizes that the entire cosmos is his Self, possesses Lordship even when the *vikalpas* (thought-constructs) have their play.

The method of a still superior variety of *śāmbhavopāya* is, at the outset, quite simple in its character and can be easily understood and practised. Such variety of *śāmbhava* is assisted, at the initial stage of practice, by *śāmbhavī mudrā*, a special type of psycho-physical posture. A *yogin* has just to sit firm in *padmāsana* posture and has to keep his body quite erect. His eyes are to be kept half open, with his sight falling loosely towards the tip of his nose. His hands are to be kept, right over the left, in his lap, with palms turned upwards. He should then stop slowly and steadily all his mental activities, without using any force. It happens by regular practice. Constant chains of successive ideation are to be brought to a stop. The mental apparatus is to be made so inactive and motionless that even the sound or movement of breathing is not noticed by the *yogin*. His mind has to give up its tendency towards moving outwards to catch hold of objects of thinking. It has to turn inwards and to come face to face with the inner I-consciousness (not the ego), shining through its natural divine lustre. At such juncture it shall be automatically lost in such highly brilliant lustre. The self of the *yogin* shall then see its own self through its own lustre and shall become directly aware of itself and its divine character. The *yogin* concerned shall actually realize that he is none other than pure and infinite Consciousness endowed with all divine powers of Godhead. That is *pratyabhijñā*, the recognition of the real aspect of the Self. That is the simplest means of the direct self-realization and the highest type of *śāmbhavopāya* as explained to the writer of this paper by his precepter, Ācārya Amṛtavāgbhava who had learnt it through the gracious kindness of sage Durvāsas.

Some ancient traces of the practice of such yoga can be found in the remains of Indus Valley Civilization. Its most ancient written description is found in detail in the sixth chapter of *Bhagavad-Gītā*.

Kālidāsa describes both the physical and mental aspects of such *mudrā* in a charming poetic style in his *Kumārasambhava* (KS III.45-50). It is the spontaneous posture of Umā in the moment of recognising Śiva:

> *taṃ vīkṣya vepathumatī sarasāṅgayaṣṭir*
> *nikṣepaṇāya padamuddhṛtamudvahantī,*
> *mārgācalavyatikarākuliteva sindhuḥ*
> *śailādhirājatanayā na yayau na tasthau.*
>
> KS V.85

> On seeing him, the daughter of the Mountain-lord, all atrembling and her body covered with perspiration, and having one foot raised to walk away, was uncertain whether to go or to stay, like a river hampered by the impediment of a mountain in the path. (Tr. M.R. Kale)

The mention of *śāmbhava* is found in *Avadhūta-Gītā*. Its elusive description is found in some sayings (*Vacanas*) of some Vīraśaiva saints, and in poems of the Hindi poet-mystic, Kabīradāsa. This type of *śāmbhava-yoga* has been described briefly but clearly by Ācārya Amṛtavāgbhava in his *Siddha-mahā-rahasya* (VI.21-23). In spite of all such clear descriptions of this superior type of *śāmbhava-yoga*, some aspects of its practice remain still unexplained and can be learnt only through the help of a master who has attained considerable success in its practice.

Practice in *śāmbhava-yoga* is frequently liable to two main types of lapses. Firstly, the practitioner may very easily enter into some delightful step in dreamless sleep, and finding it sufficiently sweet, may stick to it and may not at all aspire to reach the state of *turya*, that is, the state of intuitive revelation of the true character of the Self. Such sleeping state may provide with perfect rest, relaxation and tranquillity, but cannot lead to a true realization of the Self. It can, at the most, eradicate mental tension and remove physical fatigue and can charge energy to work.

Another probable lapse is the fact that a *yogin*, having still some desires and passions in his mind, may fall prey to misuse of some uncommon powers that do develop during the practice of *śāmbhava-yoga*. For instance, a *yogin* may develop telepathy or may attain capacity to know the past and future of people around him. Such a practitioner may, very often, become tempted to use his yogic capacities to earn respect, influence, name, fame, material prosperity, etc. Such misuse of yogic powers checks the spiritual progress of the *yogin* concerned and his unusual psychic capacities do also vanish after some time. Such things happen frequently to *yogins*. Their present life becomes useless and they have to mark time for the whole remaining portion of their life. Some of them repent very much on such account and some become mad on account of such intense repentence. Such half-mad monks can be found in India at many places. But a few among practitioners are very clever in such matters. They indulge in the misuse of yogic powers only to such an extent that does not deprive them of the whole mastery over such powers and continue to have influence on unwise common people. Some of such *yogins* do also exist at present in India, though they may be very few in number.

Śāmbhava-yoga of all the three paths mentioned above does actually develop supernatural psychic capacities in a *yogin.* But a *śāmbhava yogin*, having been initiated by a highly powerful preceptor, is saved of such lapses, through his gracious activity. Some powerful *mantra* (a mystic verbal formula), if practised regularly and correctly, can also save its practitioner from such lapses. The other and the most effective defence against such lapses is the intense devotion towards Lord Śiva. Such a devotee does neither stick to the sweet tranquillity of *suṣupti*, nor indulges in any misuse of yogic powers. He also develops super-human psychic capacities which help him in becoming perfectly sure about the authenticity of his yogic realization of being truly identical with Almighty God. Some signs of partial success do also appear occasionally in him while he is in the process of regular practice in such yoga, conducted with the help of *śāmbhavī mudrā.* Sometimes his physical form becomes lighter in weight than the atmosphere in his room and, as a result of such occasional development, his body starts an upward movement towards the ceiling of the room, with no change in the sitting posture of his form. At other times a sweet radiance, like that of the crescent moon, emanates out of his forehead. Sometimes a highly wonderful happening occurs when the subtle body of a *yogin* comes out of his gross body, leaving it lifeless for a while and re-entering it after moving about in the room. Deities, residing at various sacred places appear before such practical *yogin* when he roams about at such places. Most of such super-human experiences do occur just to divert a yogin from the path of self-realization. But sometimes some super-human beings appear before him just to help him in his upward spiritual ascent. All such things are controlled by the binding and liberating forces of Lord Śiva. The divine activities of the Lord are of multifarious character and consequently his play in spiritual ascent and descent does also appear in multifarious ways. That makes his divine cosmic play highly wonderful and interesting. It is the wonderful variety of the characters of a drama that makes it enjoyable to the public. How would Lord Śiva, the sole master of the universal drama, ignore this infinite play with respect to such individual variety?

Several other types of practice in *śāmbhavopāya* have been taught in some ancient important texts, but have not been elucidated by any authors of works on Śaivism. The key technique expressed in them is the same practice of remaining vigilant towards the pure brilliant and self-aware consciousness of the Self and not moving towards any ideation of any kind.[4]

---

[4] Some of such practices have been expressed in the works listed below.

(1) *Śivasūtra* I, *Sūtras* 5 and 6, ch. IV *Sat*-7, ch. III. *Sūt.* 20, 26, 27, 28, and 30.

(2) *Vijñānabhairava*, verse Nos. 49, 61, 75, 91, 101, 103, 108, 126 and 146.

(3) *Spandakārikā*, verse Nos. 6, 7, 11, 22. 41 and 43.

(4) *Śivadṛṣṭi*, Ch. VIII. Couplets. 17, 18.

(5) *Īśvarapratyabhijñā*, IV.16

(6) Abhinavagupta's *Anuttarāṣṭikā*, 2 and *Anubhavanivedanastotra*, 2, etc.

UNKNOWING AND PERSONALISM

In the Theological Tradition of the Christian East

Serge Descy

> Bearer of all names,
> how shall I name you?
> You alone the Unnameable!"
> St. Gregory Nazianzus
> *Hymn to God*, *PG* 37, 507

The following talk will attempt to present in a synthetic manner two aspects constitutive of the theological tradition of the Christian East — in this case Byzantine — which are closely linked : theological apophatism and the personal communication of God through his uncreated energies.

Why choose precisely these two aspects? Because, central within their own traditions, they allow one to establish common points or even direct parallelisms, in the comparative theology of religions, with other systems, and, notably, the Advaita-Vedānta and Śaivism.

No doubt this is because the Christian East has never made a clear distinction between mysticism and theology. The two dimensions are complementary and are indispensable to one another: there is no mysticism without theology for it is the symbolic expression which supports the human spirit in contemplation of the divine mystery and prevents possible aberrations. In fact, outside of a theological speech able to circumscribe truth as received and interpreted by the community of faith in its entirety — here, the church — personal experience would be completely deprived of all objectivity. But inversely, and above all, there is no theology without mysticism. Because a religion without mysticism would be nothing but pure ideology.

In short, theological dogma represents a limited and transitory knowledge which must lead beyond all knowledge to union with God. Practical in scope, it arises from history and is summoned to disappear in pure contemplative vision. "If you are a theologian, you have pure prayer, if you have pure prayer, you are a theologian" in the words of Evagrius Ponticus[1]. And it is in this same sense that the Cappadocian Fathers never ceased saying that there is no other way to know God than to live in Him.

Hence a purely mystical author, St. Simeon, is called 'the New Theologian' and two other mystical writers, St. John the Evangelist and St. Gregory of Nazianzus are both given the title of 'theologian' by the Eastern tradition. In fact, mysticism is considered to be the summit or perfection of all theology.

If mysticism and theology are closely linked in Eastern Christianity, it is obvious that the theological explanation of the experience of the ineffable — this being supposed to be an invariant in human history — can be most fruitfully compared with other theologico-mystical systems, such as the properly mystical philosophies of India. The latter might thus be capable of offering a wider epistemological framework for the interpretation of the Christian mystical experience. Moreover, the complementarity runs in both directions. But, it is certain — and this is what we would like to illustrate — that the mystical theology of the Christian East occupies a privileged, but not exclusive, position in this comparative task with which the faith is today confronted, faced with an irreducible religious pluralism.

[1] De orat., 60 (PG 79, 1180 B).

Another, no less important reason justifying the choice of this two-fold dimension of unknowing and personalism for our global approach to the mystical theology of the Christian East resides in the modernity of this dual intuition: in fact, in an altogether pertinent way it responds to the challenge posed to theology by contemporary philosophy and the human sciences. One can already cite here nihilism and the "death of God" current, the Heideggerian critique of onto-theology or the end of metaphysics, demythologization, hermeneutics and its definitive impact in theology, the problem of meaning, such as it is raised within the structural approach, the challenge of postmodern theology accompanied by the question on the irreducible meaning gap, and finally, analytical philosophies. We shall return to this briefly. The importance of this debate in contemporary society is evident. It is a question of the intelligibility of knowledge, which always necessarily expresses itself on the basis of the philosophical and socio-cultural categories of a given place and thus, one will always run up against an insurmountable limit linked to the very condition of language, that has to express through language what expresses itself in language.

The Meaning of Apophasis[2]

The theological unknowing which characterizes Eastern Christianity is usually designated by the word 'apophatism', from the Greek *apophasis* which signifies the negation of speech. Actually, this term refers to a mode of thought, an intention, an approach of the spirit, rather than to a theological current in the strict sense. We note that this question

[2]A general introduction to this subject is to be found in V. Lossky, *The Mystical Theology of the Eastern Church*, (trans. from the French), London, 1957; C. Yannaras, *De l'absence et de l'inconnaissance de Dieu*, (trans. from the Greek), Paris, 1971; C. Guerard, *La théologie négative dans l'apophatisme grec*, in Rev. *des Sc. phil. et théol.*, 68 (1984), pp.183–200.

about the value of human language in the naming of the Divine, which in the last analysis recognizes that the supreme form of knowledge is to know that one doesn't know, is rediscovered in many religions or wisdoms. In Greek thought, the apophatic approach, already germinally present in Plato, is systematized in the Platonic tradition and further radicalized by the neo-Platonists. Inasmuch as it is the heir of Platonism,[3] Christian theology is in its turn impregnated with the same approach, above all from the fourth century on. It is helpful to note briefly the significant stages of Christian *apophasis*, given the diversity of types that it includes.

As to the Platonic heritage and the period after the fourth century AD, it is preferable to speak of the 'aphairetical' method [from the Greek *aphairesis*, the act of taking away, abstraction] to designate negative theology insofar as it is an intellectual operation of abstraction.[4] In the tradition of the ancient Academy of Plato and for Aristotle, abstraction is a true mode of knowledge which consists in cutting away or in denying additions in order to climb towards the incorporeal and simple. One thus ascends from the complex to simple realities by cutting away what is not essential. This is why this 'aphairetical' method was able to be considered as a negative method. But the negations are here, in fact, affirmations because they are negations of negations, given that from the Platonic perspective, any addition to a simple reality, or rather any determination, is negation or a degradation in relation to a plenitude of being. This 'aphairetical' method presupposes the idea of an infinitude of being and permits surmounting the a priori impossibility of thinking it by a rational exercise of thought. In this sense, the traditional concept of negative theology, taken up and amplified

[3] Cp. E. von Ivanka, *Plato christianus*, Einsiedeln, 1964.

[4] P. Hadot, art. Théologie négative, in Encycl. Univ., t.17, Paris, 1985, pp. 1115 sq.

in Christian theology, is less pertinent inasmuch as it would apply to God propositions which deny any conceivable predicate. In so doing, it would logically deny the very divinity of its object and would thus contradict even its proper appellation of 'theology' or 'discourse on God'. The 'aphairetic' method issuing from Plato and the Platonic tradition ought not be understood as the recognition of an unknowable absolute. This approach, aiming rather at an intellectual intuition of the Unknowable, was assimilated by the Christian authors of the first centuries.

Yet, from Platinus onwards and for the neo-Platonists, the 'aphairetic' method no longer permits thinking the transcendent principle, nor having an intuition of it, because it is not an object and thus does not belong to the order of thought. The notion of '*aphairesis*' loses its meaning and is progressively replaced by that of '*apophasis*'. From the impossibility of thinking the transcendent one passes to the impossibility of speaking or telling about it: one can say nothing about this subject, but can only have a mystical experience and describe the state of our subjectivity.

It should be recognized that Christian theologians introduced the method and terminology of neo-Platonic apophatism into their own theology, thereby fitting themselves into what Paul Ricoeur calls the "*croyable disponible*" ["available believable"] of an epoch. But it must be acknowledged that this negative Christian theology — although essentially different from Platonic theology as to its basis — was to have an enormous influence as much in the East, especially from the fourth century onwards, as in the Latin Middle Ages.

The anonymous, Middle Eastern author of the end of the fifth century hiding behind the pseudonym of Dionysius the Areopagite[5] was not the inventor of the theoretical question

[5]Cp. V. Lossky, "La théologie négative dans la doctrine de Denys l'Areopagite", in Rev. *des Sc. phil. et theol.*, 28 (1939), pp. 204–21; M.

as to the distance between God and language, even though negative theology remains associated with his name. He is in fact preceded by a long tradition: the Desert Fathers, Evagrius, the Cappadocians, in particular, St. Gregory of Nyssa, and finally St. John Chrysostom. Nonetheless, throughout his writings, Dionysius poses the problem of knowledge of God in a radical manner. He distinguishes two possible ways in theology: one, imperfect, because it proceeds by affirmations [or positive theology], the other, perfect, proceeding by negations [negative or apophatic theology] which is the only one which is really suitable for the consideration of God. It is clear that there is an antinomy between the two ways, of which Dionysius will not perforce attempt to make a synthesis. On the contrary, the apophatic way is in his view the only way towards mystical union with God inasmuch as he remains absolutely unknowable for us. This way of ascending is compared to Moses' climbing Mount Sinai, when he freed himself from the grasp of all that is knowable, to penetrate into the mystical darkness of unknowing. Yet, God will always remain known at once by the mode of knowing and by the mode of unknowing, God remaining supereminent for both of them. The expressible and the inexpressible intermingle. Dionysius was to express the absolute unknowability and transcendence of God by attributes composed using *alpha privatum* or further, following the symmetrical attitude of unknowing due to deficiency, by using terms constructed with *hyper*, as for example, *hypertheos*, signifying "God beyond God".

To illustrate this, one could cite any number of passages from his various treatises. We shall refer to this very short one:

> God offers Himself to intelligence, to reason, to science . . . and yet neither intelligence, nor rea-

Corbin, "Négation et transcendance dans l'oeuvre de Denys", in Rev. *des Sc. phil. et theol.*, 69 (1985), pp. 41–76.

> son, nor any name can grasp Him. He is nothing like what is, and one cannot know Him in that which is. He is all in all. And He is nothing in nothing. He is knowing by all in all. And He is known by nothing in nothing...[6]

In his *Commentaries on the Divine Names*, Maximus the Confessor, following Dionysius, writes:

> God is called being and non-being. For He is nothing of what beings are. But He is raised in an unknown manner above all. God is nothing of what is known.[7]

Certainly, the Dionysian schema of negative theology establishes the supremacy of natural mysticism — which is the common good of all the great religions — over revealed theology. Yet, one must not conclude too quickly to the supratrinitarian bearing of this *apophasis*. As has been seen, Dionysius uses philosophical methods and categories like the Fathers of the Church. But he in no way becomes subject to them. Apophasis is not a preamble to Christian revelation, but is thought at the very interior of this Revelation. God is not the One, nor the Unity, in the sense of the Platonic tradition. God is in fact neither the one nor the multiple, indicating by this antinomy the ultimate bearing of the trinitarian mystery. We shall return to this.

Theological apophatism in the Christian East thus appears as a fundamental surpassing of the methodology of philosophical knowledge. In fact, for the whole Patristic tradition conceptual and dialectical reflection becomes incapable of thinking the infinite. True theological knowledge cannot be exhausted in analogical and causal definitions, nor in the

---

[6] *De divin. nom.*, 7 (*PG* 3, 872 A and B).

[7] *PG* 4, 189 A.

simultaneous synthesis of affirmations and negations but, at the same time, it contains them all and surpasses them. In other words, it does not suspend philosophical methodology but is aware that only renunciation of the logic of the created can prevent making a philosophical idol of God in the image of man.

Nietzschean nihilism and its hallowed formula "God is dead!"[8] receives a revealing illumination based upon the status of theological speech in *apophasis*. The God rejected by Nietzsche[9] is undeniably a moral God, an old Kantian inheritance. In subjugating men, Christianity has thus lost the really divine sense of the world, the sense of the infinite, beyond good and evil.

This preoccupation reappears in Heidegger's thought, which has exercised a considerable influence on 20th century philosophical research.[10] Still, this thought is not a disguised theology, but reminds theology of its status as hermeneutics of faith. Affirming that the Being question has been forgotten by the tradition, it puts an end to this same metaphysical movement which had made of God the supreme being whom man could master in representing it. The Heideggerian critique of onto-theology aims at deconstructing a representationalist thought, meaning a thought of 'duality' which ends up by doing away with all the biblical attributes of God. Yet the whole history of Christian theology is inseparable from the history of conceptions of being and of the

---

[8] *Die fröhliche Wissenschaft* (1982).

[9] See J. Granier, "La critique nietzschéenne du Dieu de la métaphysique", in J. Colette *et al.*, *Procès de l'objectivité de Dieu. Les présupposés philosophiques de la crise de l'objectivité de Dieu*, (Coll. *Cogitatio Fidei*, 41), Paris, 1969, pp. 65–86.

[10] Cp. G. Vattimo, *Introduzione a Heidegge*, Bari-Roma, 1971; about the Heideggerian critique of onto-theology, see C. Geffre, *Un nouvel âge de la théologoe*, (coll. *Cogitatio Fidei*, 68), Paris, 1972, pp. 71–75; *Heidegger et la question de Dieu*, Paris, 1980; P. Corset, "Heidegger et la question de Dieu", in Rev. *de l'Inst. cath. de Paris*, 1982, 1, pp. 57–76.

logos of human reason. Before the metaphysical God, man can no longer dance. Like theological *apophasis*, Heidegger denies any ascent to the cause, passing from the Being question to the question of the being in itself, to the *causa sui*, and recognizes man's powerlessness for knowing God in the field of metaphysics. Through his nihilism, Heidegger advances a more divine conception of God, but to attain this truly divine God, man must greet the mystery of being which dwells in him.

The nihilism of apophatic demythologization has its echo in Bultmannian hermeneutics as well: let us recall that the mode of representation in which what is not of the world, the divine, appears as being of the world is mythical, for example when the transcendence of God is thought as spatial remoteness. Yet, knowledge of God is only possible if we renounce the mythical language of symbols, received ideas and categories. Demythologization wishes to bring the myth back to its original intention.[11]

Finally, in Wittgenstein's *Tractatus logico-philosophicus* we rediscover a radical apophatism: language has a meaning, the world has a meaning, and yet this meaning is to be found outside of language and outside of the world. We cannot get out of language in order to express the fact that language expresses something. Thus language cannot express what makes it language, and consequently, "*of this about which one cannot speak, one must be silent*" (7).

Thus, here we measure both the modernity and universality of the apophatic attitude before truth.[12] The logical God is refused. Henceforth, a circle of silence must be drawn around the divine abyss. The speech of the Christian East is

[11]Cp. A. Malet, *Mythos et Logos. La pensée de Rudolf Bultmann*, Genève,1962, (Engl. trans., Dublin, 1969).

[12]See also E. Levinas, *Autrement qu'être ou au-delà de l'essence*, La Haye, 1974; J.-L. Marion, *L'idole et la distance*, Paris, 1977; ID., *Dieu sans l' Etre*, Paris, 1982.

not that of the rational ontology of the West, but a speech at the extremity of silence.

Theological Personalism[13]

Although God may be totally inaccessible and unknowable according to his Essence, he is not, for all that, impersonal. In fact, the divine energies manifest the divinity's mode of existence, which is personal. And this personal character of God is, indeed, the foundation of apophatism. God reveals Himself in his divine energies and through them offers the possibility of a participation in all of divinity. It is precisely this participation that is the sole way to knowledge of God.

Greek personalism is traditionally opposed to Latin essentialism. It is true that this contrast — which, for some, is considered to be at the basis of the schism between the Christian East and West — has essential repercussions on the way the mystery of the communion between God and man has been felt and expressed on both sides. Conceptions of the beatific vision and of mysticism, taken globally, are quite divergent here.

Theological personalism affirms that it is the Person of the Father that assures the common possession of the same substance by the Son and the Spirit. Thus their consubstantiality does not consist in their participation in an impersonal principle, but in their personal existence, received from the Father. May we underline from the outset that one must totally renounce the sociological or even the philosophical meaning of

---

[13]We refer the reader to some studies on the question: V. Lossky, "La notion théologique de la personne humaine", in *A l'image et à la ressemblance de Dieu*, Paris, 1967, pp.109–21, (Engl. trans., New York, 1974); A. de Halleux, " "Hypostase" et personne dans la formation du dogme trinitaire (ca 375–81)", in *Rev. Hist. eccl.*, 79 (1984), pp. 313–69; ID., "Personnalisme ou essentialisme trinitaire chez les Pères cappadociens? Une mauvaise controverse", in *Rev. théol. Louvain*, 17 (1986), pp. 129–55 and 265–92.

the concept of 'person' [in Greek, *hypostasis*] such as it is presented in trinitarian theology. Whereas in mundane reality, human beings tend to exist through the affirmation of self and mutual exclusion, in the theological sense the person is only fully a person to the extent that he/she is dispossessed of him/herself and is totally turned towards the other.

In the trinitarian mystery — which is the conceptual representation of this two-fold dimension of the divine aseity and of the procession of the divine towards the outside — there is no division of the one nature among the three Persons, each one including in himself the whole, the entire nature, for each one has nothing for himself. What we habitually call a human person ought rather to be understood as an individual. At the beginning of St. John's Prologue, the theological sense of person is given: "the Logos is towards God" [*ho logos en pros ton Theon*]. Sometimes this has been translated: the Logos is "with God". But '*pros*', in Greek, indicates a movement, an orientation: "the Logos is turned towards God". The concepts of Father, Son and Spirit which will be developed in later theology are but signs or symbols to guard against any anthropomorphic temptation. Here the Father is the fundament, the origin, the principle, totally inaccessible and unknowable according to his essence; the Son is in an intimate relation with this infinite origin; this intimate relation is 'pneumatic', spiritual — the Spirit or '*Pneuma*' means 'breath' —, it is a face-to-face relation. But this God "above everything and separated from everything", "descends towards everything".

Theological personalism cannot be separated from the Incarnation. The divine descent expresses itself in the theandric nature [*theos*, God; *aner/andros, man*] of Christ: in Him, it is the face of the living and personal God that is contemplated, it is the infinite compassion of God which re-establishes the possibility of man knowing God as a personal God, as an effusion of love for each human being. And it is as the image of

God [according to *Genesis* 1, 27], that man too is a personal being according to the same mode by which God exists as Being. Otherwise put, human nature can enter into a relationship with God identical to that which Christ maintains with the Father. The hypostatic union of the two natures, divine and human, in Christ, — such as it was defined by the Council of Chalcedon in the fifth century — is verified in every human being. Thus the Christian message can be summed up in this simple but fulgurating truth, which is the theandric or Christic nature of man. Christology is thus the good news announced to man that is the great antinomy of the Inaccessible who, through love, makes himself participatable.

As, for that matter, the Fathers and theologians of the Eastern Church have never ceased repeating: "*God became man in order that man might become god*". This formula is to be found for the first time in St. Irenaeus,[14] but comes up again in St. Athanasius,[15] St. Gregory of Nazianzus,[16] St. Gregory of Nyssa,[17] etc. Moreover, only this descent [in Greek *katabasis*] or this *kenosis* [from the Greek *kenôsis*, annihilation, abasement] of the Divine can convince man of God's mad love for him. If he accepts and welcomes this divine appeal, he becomes a "*participant in the divine nature*" according to St. Peter's expression.[18] Not only does man cease to be authentically and fully human outside of God, but the unique goal of his existence is this participation in God or deification [in Greek *theosis*].

The doctrine of the deification of man — or its corollary, the participation or personal communion of man in God —, is at the heart of the theology and the mysticism of the Chris-

---

[14] *Adv. Haer.*, 5, praef.(*PG* 7, 1120).
[15] *I Contr. Arian.*, 54(*PG* 25,192 B).
[16] *Poem. dogm.*, 10, 5–9 (*PG* 37, 465).
[17] *Or. cat. mag.*, 25 (*PG* 45, 65 D).
[18] 2 *Pt* 1, 4.

tian East.[19] It has been abundantly developed in the Patristic tradition, and particularly by St. Maximus the Confessor, who can be considered to be the real father of Byzantine theology.

We shall cite this short passage:

> God created us that we might become participants in the divine nature, that we might enter into eternity, that we might appear similar to him, being deified by the grace that produces all beings existent and makes exist everything which did not exist.[20]

This doctrine of deification which he makes the heart and aim of Christian spiritual life, was to be taken up much later in the synthesis of St. Gregory Palamas. It is important to evoke briefly the essential points of this palamite synthesis because it affords one of the most elaborated and most representative dogmatic foundations of mystical experience.[21]

In fact, Palamas is situated at the junction of numerous spiritual currents; notably the Hesychastic tradition with its apophatic critique of the naming of God, and the Jesus prayer which is the invocation of the name of Jesus. It deepens the Patristic distinction between 'theology' and 'economy' [*oikonomia*, in Greek], that is between God in Himself, beyond all affirmation and all negation, and the historical revelation of God.

But above all, Palamas was to emphasize the distinction

---

[19]Cp. M. Lot-Borodine, *La déification de l'homme selon la doctrine des Pères grecs,* (Coll. *Bibliothèque oecuménique*, 9), Paris, 1969.

[20]Epist. 43, *Ad Joannem cubicularium* (*PG* 91, 640 B.C).

[21]See J. Meyendorff, *A Study of Gregory Palamas,* (trans. from the French), Crestwood, 1974; A. de Halleux, "Palamisme et Scolastique", in Rev. *Théol. Louvain*, 4 (1973), pp. 409–22; ID., "Palamisme et tradition", in *Irénikon*, 48 (1975), pp. 479–93; G. Mantzaridis, *The Deification of Man. St Gregory Palamas and the Orthodox Tradition*, Crestwood, 1984.

between the inaccessible essence of God and the divine energies, uncreated and participatable. All of Palamas' theological work had as its goal resolving the antinomy of the knowable and the unknowable in God and, in so doing, he in fact surmounted neo-Platonism in his explanation of the relation of the infinite to the finite. Palamas wished to safeguard the essentialist metaphysics inherited from the Pseudo-Dionysius and, at the same time, to rediscover the existential personalism and immediate vision of God in the Scriptures and in the Fathers. But, the antinomy between positive and negative theologies has, precisely, a real foundation on the level of a distinction within the very being of God, between essence and energies. *Apophasis* transforms itself into antinomy and thereby man can realize deification. Besides, in distinguishing these energies of the divine essence, one averts any hint of an impersonal absorption or of pantheism.

Let us take up the Palamite antinomy again. Beings are the result of the divine will, but not of the essence. They do not proceed from the divine nature nor from anything which might be outside of it. They are linked to energies. In God these are constituted as the uncreated source of his action *ad extra*, understood as his face looking on the world. These divine energies ought not be confused with the essence nor with the hypostases or the divine persons, nor with created beings. Rather these eternal and uncreated energies in some way confer a personal character upon the divine essence. Thus they are in relation to "God for us" what the hypostases are in relation to "God in himself". Finally, they reveal two modes of the divine existence, within the essence and outside of the essence. If, then, the trinitarian God is incommunicable according to his essence, he at the same time comes to dwell in us according to the words of Christ told by St. John : "*We shall make our dwelling in him*".[22]

[22] Jn 14, 23.

The rapprochement is striking between the concept of deification in the Christian Eastern Tradition and that of realization in the supreme identity of the Ātman and of the Brahman according to the Advaita-Vedānta. We cannot study it here. We shall simply point out that deification by the uncreated energies makes man a full participant in the divine life, beyond all duality. This Advaitic experience rests upon a relationship personal from the outset through integration with Christ. In the same way, the Brahman with attributes is the visage of the Absolute and allows us to know the Absolute, because he is also the Brahman beyond any attributes. He who is *Śakti* is also Brahman.[23]

Let us recapitulate. Christian theology, especially in the East, thus in some way distinguishes four levels or four moments in reflection and in enunciation :

Firstly, the level of the deity, of the absolute divine essence, isolated in his aseity. This is totally unknowable. One can affirm nothing, unless it be unity. Thus one can only speak in terms of apophatic theology.

The second level is that of the deity inasmuch as it enters into an internal rapport: this is the eternal procession of the divine Persons of the Trinity. The Persons flow ceaselessly from the divine essence and eternally flow back into it. This procession of the Trinity *ad intra* also remains fundamentally unknowable. The only references that we have are only an extrapolation from what we have been able to know of God in his economy [in the Greek sense, *oikonomia*], meaning in creation and in Salvation History, in which He reveals Himself.

The third level is precisely that of the external relation of the Trinity with the creation, and particularly the cosmic

[23] Note of the Editor: This statement is more true regarding the Advaita of Kashmir Śaivism than of Vedānta. See the contributions in this Volume by H.N. Chakravarty, B.N. Pandit and J.N. Kaul.

event of the Christic Incarnation. It is here, at this properly historical and hermeneutical level, that theology will be the least apophatic and the least negative. It is here that it well extend itself as a discipline to sound the Mystery of God with language, all the while remaining incapable of making present what it seeks to represent. Thus it will limit itself to pointing out a direction, to indicating, to showing.

Finally, the fourth level is that in which *theologia* and *theoria* [contemplation, in Greek] merge. Here, theology is no longer a rational deduction from premises revealed through the Scriptures or through defined dogmas, but a vision. Not a vision of the divine essence, but, indeed, of the deifying Taboric Light which is Communication of God himself and participation in trinitarian life. This new knowledge, the most elevated possible, is founded on the distinction between the divine essence and the uncreated but participatable energies. Illuminated, transfigured or realized man transcends everything created, and reaches a sort of indistinction with God — otherwise called 'deification' — and surpasses any duality, without falling into a pantheistic type of identification — as some have suggested. Here theology will always be discursive, while experiential. It is no longer so much a language 'on' — even though it retains all the appearances — but a language 'from', a language flowing from within, whose expressions are surpassed by the excess or plenitude of a presence. This language freely and spontaneously flows from and expresses itself on the basis of the ineffable experience of the mystical union. Literature having this mystical union as its theme is no doubt abundant, but, paradoxically, deals with what one can neither say nor know. In the last analysis, the deification experience ends up expressing itself in the unsaid of language. Henceforth theology will be less a search for positive knowledge about the divine being than an experience of what is beyond all understanding.

These four movements or levels which we have distinguished in theology ought, in fact, to be reducible to only two: that of God *ad intra* — for one cannot dissociate the divine essence from its hypostases — and that of God *ad extra* knowable in His energies.

Transcendence, Language and Postmodernity

Is apophasis and personal participation in the Divine contradictory? They are in fact the two irreducible poles of one and the same experience which, such as it is formulated in the Eastern Christian Tradition — but also in part in Western apophatism — paradoxically corresponds to the status and responds to the demands of a postmodern theology.[24] Here, spiritual truth will henceforth bear the mark of the relation between the effacement of a particular significant event, and what they make possible, that is a dissemination of meaning in the field of interpretations. But, in short, these marks or words are bearers of a primary, original meaning allowing theology to effect a legibility in the real. But the significance of this theological discourse remains within language.

Going further, deconstructionist thought tears metaphysical status away from the sign, for there is nothing signified which is not already in the position of a signifier. As a consequence, scripture, or discourse, consists in a play of differences, of continual referrals, deconstructing the metaphysical notion of God or that of the subject's presence to self, thus depriving the question of the origin of meaning of all pertinence. Meaning is drawn into a process of dissemination, indefinite this time, barring the very possibility of the hermeneutical enterprise which postulates a meaning and a signifier-signified rapport. Every sign being always already inscribed within an interpretative network, there is no first

[24]Th. J.J. Altizer *et al.*, *Deconstruction and Theology*, New York, 1982; M.C. Taylor, *Erring. A Postmodern A/theology*, Chicago, 1984.

truth to interpret. This is the indefinite referral of signifier to signifier. Certitude is inaccessible given the perpetual instability of the sign. Meaning is formed and deformed in a continuous interweaving, in such a way that an interpretation never unveils a definitive meaning, but enlarges the text or speech in producing new meanings. Language possesses no definitive meaning but always remains transitional and erratic.

Thus, consciousness apprehends only signs disposed in a differential network. Transcendental signified disappears and makes the divine milieu possible, conceived as non-totalizable totality, where the finite is an interior dimension of infinitude, and reciprocally. The "death of God" in the secular city can henceforth be understood in terms of a radical christology, whose *Logos* is always necessarily *spermatikos*,[25] meaning in a perpetual motion of dissemination.

Modernity called the discursive and practical structures upon which traditional society rested into question. Deconstructive analysis calls into question the totality of the network of notions and concepts which founded philosophical and theological thought, such as the priority of the subject over predicates, as well as its alleged independence. But the subject is itself always already linked to a linguistic network and becomes a function of a given tongue.

This radical dispossession of the subject opens endless possibilities of overtures. Doesn't it seem to rejoin the theologico-mystical experience of the Christian East which also concludes to the radical incompletion of the tradition as an attempt at closure and mastery of meaning?

---

[25] Justin, *I Apol.*, 32, 8; *II Apol.*, 8, 1; 10, 2; 13, 3.

ŚAKTIPĀTA: GRACE IN KASHMIR ŚAIVISM

Jankinath Kaul 'Kamal'

yā kācidvai kvacidapi daśā
kiñcidabhyāsapūrād-
ānandākhya bhavabhayaharā
syāt subhaktasya sadyaḥ;
sidhissaiṣā surapitṛṛṇām
yasya bhaktyā bhavennu
taṃ svātmānaṃ vibhavavapuṣam
sadguruṃ vai prapadye.

That indescribable supreme state which is revealed in a spontaneous moment (of grace) regardless of time or place to an earnest devotee, while he has been absorbed continuously in spiritual practice for an unknown period, confers supreme joy (*ānanda*) that wipes off all doubt and fear whatsoever. That is verily the true accomplishment for celestials, for manes and for human beings. By whose grace this happens, to That Great Preceptor of supreme splendour who is my own Self, this prostration is made.

Rediscovery of the Śaiva faith was made around the ninth century AD in Kashmir, conspicuously by Vasugupta to whom the *Śiva-Sūtras* were revealed by Lord Śiva Himself. Vasugupta's *Spanda Kārikā*, a purport of the *Śiva-Sūtras*, was elaborated by his well-conducted disciple, Kallaṭa by name. Kallaṭa Bhaṭṭa is therefore known as the first *ācārya* of the Spanda order of Kashmir Śaivism, which is also called *Trika*

Śāstra (or *Śāsana*), because it evidently discusses the three modes of Reality viz. *Nara*, Śiva and the connecting link Śakti (*naraśaktiśivātmakaṃ trikam*, Abhinavagupta, *Parātrīśikā Vivaraṇa*) precisely known as *apara, para* and *parāpara*, an evidence of the monistic character of the Tantras. Later Somānandanātha's *Śiva Dṛṣṭi* and Utpaladeva's *Īśvarapratyabhijñā* respectively introduced and elucidated the *Pratyabhijñā* thought by which name Kashmir Śaiva Mysticism is known today.

Before this development, according to Swami Laksman Joo, the last exponent of Kashmir Śaivism, the Kula system, advocating the highest form of Śiva, had been introduced in Kashmir some time in the fourth century AD and the Krama system, connected with *rāja yoga* and *kuṇḍalinī yoga*, which stress the independence of vital airs and mind, had existed there even earlier, as is witnessed through *Yoga Vāsiṣṭha.* The Vedāntic thought of Gauḍapāda and Śaṅkarācārya through their *Māṇḍukya Kārikās* and *Prasthānatrayī* respectively had also influenced Kashmir simultaneously. The result was that Kashmir Śaiva Mysticism (i.e., Trika philosophy) developed with ideas relevant to the order from almost all schools of Indian philosophy. Kashmir Śaivism, in its entirety, was further elaborated in a systematic form by the great Master Abhinavaguptapāda in his *Tantrāloka.* Among his other important works, *Parātrīśikā Vivaraṇa* that explains the secret of Tantric mysticism, is the most outstanding one. Thus, Abhinavagupta gave clear dimensions to Śaivism that had developed with its different forms in Kashmir.

Consequently, there are different means suggested for attainment of supreme beatitude that every human being, celestials and manes aspire for directly or indirectly. But the most direct and easy way is to have the grace of a *guru* and the impact of his power, called *śaktipāta.* Even while the means are followed by aspirants in accordance with their individual capacities, levels of intellect or intensity in devotion, there arises need of one important thing for all and that is compassion (*kṛpā*) or favour (*anugraha*) which the Tantric Ācāryas called *śaktipāta*. To my mind it appears necessary to understand *śaktipāta* in three ways namely (i) what it is, (ii) when it happens and (iii) how it works.

What Śaktipāta Is

Śaktipāta is difficult to define, but it is certainly more than just the absence of desire. It reflects a state of consciousness, serene and taintless, and virtually constitutes the sovereign will of Lord Śiva. In English language we strictly call it 'grace' and not 'favour', because the latter is measurable against its opposite term 'disfavour'. Grace is immeasurable. It is an elegance of manner, a graciousness, which can only be a gift from God. It is not given .because we desire it. God gives this gift out of intense love for the devotee whom he chooses to be blessed. Grace does not descend even upon an aspirant who is actually alert for it or ever in *samādhi*. Sage Aṣṭāvakra said to Janaka: *ayameva hi te bandhaḥ samādhim avatiṣṭhasi* — "This is what binds you, because you always sit in *samādhi*".[1] Grace may descend in passive alertness which is actually 'choiceless awareness' of Divinity. *Śaktipāta*, therefore, may depend on the power of complete surrender to the Absolute — *Īśvara-praṇidhānād vā*[2] — according to the *Yoga Sūtra* of Patañjali. The aspirant says to himself:

> What have I to do with wishing,
> His will be done.
> To Him surrendered
> I have no wish of my own.

Pārvatī seems to have made such an utterance to herself when Śiva, in the guise of a *brahmacārī*, came to see the depth of

[1] *Aṣṭāvakra Gītā*.

[2] *Yoga Sūtra* I.23.

her faith that had led her to severe penance. No sooner did the *brahmacārī* want to deviate her mind from Lord Śiva than she wanted to turn away from his presence. But how far! She could neither go ahead nor keep back. This situation is beautifully expressed by Kālidāsa: *śailādhirājatanayā na yayau na tasthau.*[3] It was that divine ecstasy, that abrupt bloom of supreme consciousness where there is no 'coming in' or 'going out'. Pārvatī experienced perfect bliss on recognising the presence of Śiva Himself.

Śaktipāta, according to monistic mysticism, is unconditional and unhindered. *Nātra ko'pi ātmīya puruṣakāraḥ vidyate* — There is no human effort for earning *śaktipāta. Gale pādikayā nātha nīyate sadguruṃ prati* — "One is directed to the great preceptor as if tethered with a rope." The Upaniṣad also declares:

> *yamevaiṣa vṛṇute tena labhyas*
> *tasaiṣa ātmā vivṛṇute tanūṃ svām.*
>
> *Kaṭha Upaniṣad* II.23
>
> The *Ātman* can be realized only by him whom He favours and to him He reveals Himself.

Dattātreya's *Avadhūta Gītā* begins with the declaration: *īśvarānugrahādeva puṃsām advaita vāsanā.*[4] — "It is through the Lord's grace alone that one is led to monistic practices for self-realization." It is, therefore, by the independent will of Lord Śiva that *śaktipāta* or Divine grace may be granted to anyone at any place and even at any time. It is a transmission through *guru-śakti* through which the *śakti* in the person of the disciple is awakened and activated. "And that is natural", says M.P. Pandit.[5] Clarifying further "For this discipline revolves upon an axis of two ends, the *guru*

[3] *Kumārasambhava* V.85.
[4] *Anugraha* is synonymous with *śaktipāta* in this context.
[5] '*Śaktipata*' in M.P. Pandit, 'Traditions in Sadhana', pp. 129–30.

and the disciple. In the dynamics of this yogic *sādhanā* both have their parts to play. True, the major role is played by the power of the *guru* which initiates and works the *yoga*. But the disciple too has a responsibility. He has to contain and support the *śaktipāta* in its continued workings. Ceaseless purification and reorientation of one's energies of the body, life and mind so as to collaborate with the power set in operation by the *guru* is indispensable . . . Personal exertion, in some form or other, is necessary to equip and perfect the *ādhāra* in which the *guru* releases his *tapas-śakti*. At any rate, it is indispensable till the nature and the being of the disciple are completely surrendered to the higher will that is active and his *sādhanā* is entirely taken charge of by the *śakti*."

It is evident, therefore, that surrender (*prapatti*) and grace (*śaktipāta*) go together as is concretely expressed by Keśavamūrti of Sri Aurobindo Ashrama: "It looks as if in the scheme of manifestation, both man and God wait for some excuse — one to receive the grace and the other to bestow it, and at the end of the long journey both man and God fuse in a grand play — *Līlā*."[6]

Thus *śaktipāta* is an indefinite point of contact between *jīva* and *Īśvara*, where the former's individual age merges completely in the Supreme Reality, the monistic sovereignty that the wise call Eternal Joy and Perfect Bliss.

Divine grace is that light whose presence removes the darkness of ignorance with all its associated doubts. It changes a guessing game into a vivid and colourful experience of Supreme awakening where there is not an iota of duality — all self everywhere — '*sarvamidaṃ ahaṃ ca brahmaiva*'; says the *Śruti*. Utpaladeva prayed to Lord Śiva and pined to get firmly established in this super state:

anyavedyamaṇumātramasti na
svaprakāśamakhilaṃ vijṛmbhate,

---

[6] *Versatile Genius*, Edited by M.P. Pandit.

yatra nātha! bhavataḥ pure sthitiṃ
tatra me kuru sadā tavārcituḥ.

Śivastotrāvalī XIII.9

Where not even a trace
Of otherness exists,
Where self-luminosity is everywhere manifest,
There, in your city,
Let me reside
Forever as your worshipper.

(Tr. C. Rhodes-Bailly)

The Upaniṣad also tells about the favour granted to Brahmā among *devas*, to Sanaka among *ṛṣis* and to Śukadeva among human beings, who remain not even for a moment without the awareness of Supreme Consciousness.

kṣaṇārdhaṃ naiva tiṣṭhanti vṛttiṃ jñānamayīṃ vinā,
yathā tiṣṭhanti brahmādyāḥ sanakādyāḥ śukādayaḥ.

Abhinavagupta calls this state *jagadānanda*, universal bliss, imparted to him by his *guru* through *śaktipāta*:

yatra ko'pi vyavacchedo
nāsti yadviśvataḥ sphurat.
yadanāhatasaṃvitti paramāmṛta bṛṃhitam,
yatrāsti bhāvanādīnāṃ na mukhyā kāpi saṅgatiḥ.
tadeva jagadānandam asmabhyaṃ śambhurūcivān.

TĀ V.50–52

Where there is no gap of thought, no distraction,
Which is the universal gleam of consciousness,
Ever new, ever filled with increasing flow of divine nectar,

> Where there is no sitting for *samādhi* etc.
> That is *jagadānanda* as explained to me by Śaṃbhunātha.

Blessed with *śaktipāta*, the aspirant devotee witnesses no distinction between within and without, between the knower and the known. He has realized that Brahman is ever the same, residing in all things. In the words of Sri Aurobindo[7] ". . ., the highest emergence is the liberated man, who has realized the self and spirit within him, entered into the cosmic consciousness, passed into union with the eternal and so far as he still accepts life and action, acts by the light of energy of the Power within him working through his human instruments of Nature." After this state is revealed to an aspirant through *śaktipāta* of the utmost intensity — '*tīvrātitīvra*' as classed by Abhinavagupta — nothing can shake his sense of Reality. There is no pain above this and no joy beyond this for him as is endorsed by the *Bhagavad Gītā* itself:

> *yaṃ labdhvācāparaṃ lābhaṃ*
> *manyate nādhikaṃ tataḥ,*
> *yasmin sthito na duḥkhena guruṇāpi vicālyate*
>
> BG VI.22

> He wins a prize beyond all others — or so he thinks. Therein he (firmly) stands, unmoved by any suffering, however grievous it may be.
>
> (Tr. R.C. Zaehner)

When *śaktipāta* happens and the ego gets consumed in the fire of God's wisdom, the devotee gets dissolved in the ocean of His love. That *ānanda* of Para Brahman is knowable only in experience, when there is slow dawning of *Ṛtambharā Prajñā*[8] — consciousness full of Truth. Then there is the revelation of

---

[7] *Essays on the Gītā*.
[8] Patañjali, *Yoga Sūtra* I.48.

Para Brahman at the lucky moment of *śaktipāta*. It operates in every line of spiritual effort when the most pious relation of Preceptor-Disciple is recognized. *Śaktipāta* works in different forms at different levels of spiritual progress. Abhinavaguptapāda in his *Tantrāloka* has discussed at length the different levels of consciousness at which *śaktipāta* works in a systematic combination of its three basic forms, viz. *tīvra* (intense), *madhya* (middle) and *manda* (slow). *Śaktipāta*, being an integral part of the Indian spiritual tradition, is made to happen by the preceptor who has capacity and the higher sanction to effect the *pāta* in the disciple whom he chooses or is directed to choose. Such a *guru* is capable of regulating and, if necessary, checking this course of Power already released into action. In the latter case also there is an injunction prescribed in the Tantra:

> *viparīta pravṛtitvaṃ jñānaṃ tasmāt samāharet*
>
> Finding opposite or negative inclination in the disciple, the *guru* should draw back the infused power of knowledge from him.

To quote a few examples of positive inclinations: (i) Kākabhuṣaṇḍi[9] lived the long life of *yogi-jīvanmukta* on being established in the middle path of the two breaths, *prāṇa* and *apāna* — with perfect knowledge of self — as also evidenced in the *Netra Tantra*. His supreme consciousness had awakened through the grace of *prāṇa-kuṇḍalinī*. (ii) Queen Cuḍalā[10] is described to have worked grace on her husband Śikhidhvaja at the mental plane. She aroused his *cit-kuṇḍalinī* telling him "Recognize *kuṇḍalinī* in your self, that is the very life of mind which is called *puryaṣṭaka*." Such a grace is imparted like the scent of a flower, by means of touch. (iii) Hanumān, directed by king Sugrīva for spying, was chosen for *śaktipāta* through

---

[9] *Yoga Vāsiṣṭha, Nirvāṇa Prakaraṇa.*

[10] Ibid.

bodha-kuṇḍalinī, when he met Śrī Rāma, who had been wandering in the forest of Kiṣkindhā in search of Sītā. Hanumān recognized his divine preceptor in Rāma who graced him through mere sight. Both had met in their choiceless awareness. *Śaktipāta*, thus, takes place in a situation of desirelessness or *kāma-saṃnyāsa*, which the *Bhagavad-Gītā* calls *karma-saṃnyāsa* or *niṣkāma-karma-yoga.*[11] This may be possible only when the individual ego is not able to work for its limited ends and when actions are performed with detachment but devotion and to the best of one's ability. Then the endless chain of *karma* also ceases — *kṣīyante cāsya karmāṇi tasmin dṛṣṭe parāvare.*[12] — When the Supreme Reality is revealed, all *karmas*[13] (*āgāmī, sañcita* and *prārabdha*) are put to flight.

'God-realization', the wise say, is an over-all change in mental attitude of a *sādhaka.* It is spiritual entirety and that divine transformation comes in a moment when the grace of *śaktipāta* works through. It comes instantaneously, almost unaware. For that Brahmā-world is ever illumined.[14] The *sādhaka* blessed with very intense (*tīvra-tīvra*) *śaktipāta*, has not to strive or search for it. It comes spontaneously to him like a surprise gift. Among the thousand names of *Parā Śakti* listed in the 139 Sanskrit verses in *Bhavānīnāmasahasrastutiḥ*, there are names like '*nimeṣa, meghamālā*' and '*muhūrta*' extolling the deity, who is one with Para Śiva. The name '*nimeṣa*' connotes that *Parā Śakti* bestows grace of *śaktipāta* in a moment, like the high tension power of electricity, which is blissfully soothing and eternally sweet. *Parā Śakti* is named '*meghamālā*' as She acts like a streak of lightning in the clouds. The Divine Mother's grace

---

[11] *Bhagavad-Gītā* Ch. III.

[12] *Muṇḍaka Upaniṣad* II.2.9.

[13] According to plural form of Sanskrit grammar it means more than two or all the three kinds of *karma*.

[14] *Chāndogya Upaniṣad* VIII.4.2 — *sakṛdvibhāto hyevaiṣa brahmalokaḥ.*

may rise from anywhere or may get absorbed at any moment. Her grace accelerates the degree of awareness in an aspirant. The name '*muhūrta*' stands for the equinoctial point of grace. Śiva, according to Śaiva mysticism, is the great Guru. His grace remains always unlocked. Pārvatī or *śakti* is the power of His grace, known as '*guroranugrāhikā śakti*' in the Śaiva-Śākta way of thought. Śiva impels grace through His *śakti* who, with Her own free will, effects *śaktipāta* on a sincere and earnest devotee; the when-where-and-how of which cannot be known. It is an internal process concealed in the rarely catchable moment at the equinoctial point. The devotee who is passively aware of the Supreme Self, may benefit from this flowing grace. That moment is like the moment of passing colour shades of the setting sun — '*sandhyābhralekheva muhūrtaraṅga*'.[15] In yogic parlance that moment of grace is also termed '*viṣuvat*' and '*abhijit*', quite different from *uttara mārga* (higher path) and *dakṣiṇa mārga* (lower path), as referred to in the *Bhagavad-Gītā*, the *Bṛhadāraṇyaka Upaniṣad*, the *Pañcastavī*, etc. For an external illustration the two moments geographically correspond with summer equinox and winter equinox. But in the internal setting of the moment there is no taint of any thought whatsoever, as is beautifully put by Śrī Sāmba: "*tābhyāmanyā viṣuvadabhijin madhyamā kṛtyaśūnyā.*"[16] It is called *madhya mārga*, the middle path or royal path. This middle path of graceful character is *kṛtyaśūnya*, without any taint of action, for there is no egress or ingress of *prāṇa* and *apāna* for the period one can remain in the state. It is the state of 'perfect ease', termed *samādhi*, the state of bliss.

> *sukhamātyantikaṃ yat tadbuddhigrāhyamatīndriyam,*

---

[15] *Pañcatantra* I.194.

[16] *Sāmbapañcāśikā* v. 49.

> *vetti yatra na caivāyaṃ sthitaścalati tattvataḥ.*
> BG VI.21
>
> Nay, in which the soul experiences the eternal and super-sensuous joy which can be apprehended only through the subtle and purified intellect, and wherein established the said *yogī* moves not from Truth on any account.

It is then that *śaktipāta* may come to happen out of sovereign spontaneity.

How Śaktipāta Works

Śaktipāta affords what is called the 'waking *samādhi*' to the devotee *yogin* to whom effortless normal state of consciousness is revealed. Utpaladeva uses the phrase '*vyuthāne'pi samāhitaḥ*'[17] wherein, in his own words, there is spontaneous revelation of Supreme Reality — '*evameva śivābhāsaḥ syāt'!*[18] Aṣṭāvakra uses almost the same phrase to effect his grace upon Janaka. That is '*evameva sukhi bhava*'.[19] By this it becomes clear that *śaktipāta* is bestowed, not obtained. Lord Śiva, in the form of guru, gives the aspirant ammunition to fight the attraction towards petty enjoyments of the world. Otherwise, the search remains a mere intellectual exercise and the individual soul becomes an easy prey to confusion, doubt and frustration. Since the source of grace is the real Self, all beings can partake of it equally. But the veil of ego, even though unreal, blocks the light of grace as do the clouds which cover the sun and make its life-giving power ineffective. One has, therefore, to wait and watch with passive spontaneity as is said : 'Waiting for the word of the Master, watching His hissing sound'. One has only to be alert

[17] *Śivastotrāvalī.*
[18] Ibid.
[19] *Aṣṭāvakra Gītā.*

with purity of mind and sincerety of heart till *śaktipāta* is bestowed. Then how it works, is remarkably expressed in the *Sat Darśana Bhāṣya* of Sri Ramana Maharshi: "The Beyond takes hold of you. You can feel yourself one, with the One that exists, the whole body becomes a mere power, a force current; your life becomes a needle drawn to a huge mass of magnet and as you go deeper you become a mere centre and not even that, for you become mere consciousness. There are no thoughts and cares any longer; they are shattered at the threshold; it is an inundation, you are a mere straw; you are swallowed alive, but it is very delightful for you become the very thing that swallows you. This is the union of *jīva* with Brahman, the loss of ego in the real self, the destruction of ignorance, the attainment of Truth."

Śaktipāta worked on Śukadeva when king Janaka told him: "*mithilāyāṃ pradīptāyāṃ na me dahyati kiñcana.*" — 'Even if the whole of Mithilā burns, nothing is burnt to me'. *Śaktipāta* worked in Maitreyī when she posed a resounding question to sage Yājñyavalkya, her husband, while he was renouncing: "That which cannot give me immortality of what avail is that property to me?"[20] It worked in Nāmadeva[21] when he ran after the dog who had taken away his bread. The saint ran after the dog saying, "O my Gopāla! just stop and let me apply butter to the bread so that you swallow it with ease." This is how *śaktipāta* works.

In the end I again quote Ramana Maharshi, who gave a practically useful prescription for aspirants to follow: "Retreat ever within thine own self, seek the source whence the restless mind spins out an unceasing web of thoughts, brush aside the springing thought, concentrate at the root of thought and take repose in that stillness and quietude. So

---

[20] *Bṛhadāraṇyaka Upaniṣad* II.4.3 — *yenāhaṃ nāmṛtā syāṃ kimahaṃ tena kuryām?*

[21] A devotee of medieval age.

much is thy effort. What next is one for inner realization and does not admit of exposition in words".

The Nine Variations of Śaktipāta

Actually there are no classes of grace. These are, as Abhinavagupta himself says, only the variations between intensity and slow process.[22] The nine degrees of *śaktipāta* discussed in the *Tantrāloka* and *Tantrasāra*, are in brief:

I. *Tīvra-tīvra* or the grace of extreme intensity: This is spontaneous and sudden, infused with the great power — *mahāśaktiḥ samāviṣṭaḥ.*[23] Jayaratha, in his commentary of Tantrāloka, says that the person who happens to receive this degree of *śaktipāta* is fit for experiencing the wonderful Reality of Supreme consciousness.[24] It is impressed that such a soul cannot live in a body and that he is automatically liberated at once.[25]

II. *Madhya-tīvra* or the grace of middle intensity: With this degree of grace ignorance gets dissolved because the *yogin* himself knows the essence of liberation and bondage through his own wisdom and not from the (external) guru or *śāstra*:

> *madhyatīvrātpunaḥ sarvamajñānaṃ vinivartate.*
> *svayameva yato vetti bandhamokṣatayātmatām,*
> *tatprātibhaṃ mahājñānaṃ śāstrācāryānapekṣi yat.*
>
> TĀ XIII.131-32

His body remains but ignorance vanishes.[26] He has unflinching 'devotion to Rudra-Śiva': '*rudra bhaktiḥ sūniścalā*'.[27] This

---

[22] *Tantrāloka* XIII.210 — '*tatrāpi tāratamyādivaśācchīghraciräditaḥ*'.

[23] Ibid., XIII.211.

[24] Ibid., (comm) XIII.211 — '*parasaṃvit camatkārānubhavalābha bhājanaṃ bhavatītyarthaḥ*'.

[25] Ibid., XIII.130 — '*tīvratīvraḥ śaktipāto dehapātavaśāt svayaṃ mokṣaprada iti.*'

[26] Ibid., (comm.) — '*na dehasya nivṛttiḥ kintu ajñānasya*'.

[27] Ibid., XIII.214.

sign of the *yogi*, according to *Pūrvaśāstra*[28] is followed by *mantrasiddhiḥ* — 'accomplishment of the divine syllable'. The third sign is 'control over all the elements' — '*sarvatattva vaśitvam*'. The fourth sign is 'indifference towards the fruit of actions of previous birth' — '*prārabdhakāryaniṣpattiḥ*' and the fifth sign is 'perfection in knowledge and speech' — '*kavitvaṃ sarvaśāstrārthavettṛtvam*'.

III. *Manda-tīvra* or the grace of slow intensity: The *yogin* gets eager to meet his precepter who is perfect in every respect — '*saṃsiddhaḥ saṃskṛto'pi ca*'.[29] He becomes instantly liberated at the time when his preceptor initiates him into the Absolute and continues to live in the body as a *jīvanmukta* —

> *yasmin kāle tu guruṇā nirvikalpaṃ prakāśitam,*
> *tadaiva kila mukto'sau yantraṃ tiṣṭhati kevalaṃ'.*
> TĀ XIII.230-31

All doubt regarding pain and pleasure of the body goes off.[30]

IV. *Tīvra-madhya* or the grace of intense middle degree: When initiation does not become firm in the aspirant because of certain persisting impressions, these haunt the mind throughout his life, and so there is absence of comprehension of the Absolute. He knowingly asserts that he is Śiva but gets release only after leaving the mortal coil.[31] He is called *putraka sādhaka*.

V. *Madhya-madhya* or the grace of middle degree of middle intensity: The *yogin*, even being earnest to profit by attaining Śivahood '*śivalābhotsuko'pi san*'[32] enjoys yogic ac-

[28] *Mālinīvijaya Tantra* VIII.13.

[29] *Tantrāloka*, XIII.224.

[30] Ibid., XIII.231 — '*prārabdhakarmasambandhād-dehasya sukhiduḥkhite na viśaṅketa*'.

[31] *Tantrāloka* XIII.242 — '*vikalpāttu tanau sthitvā dehānte śivatāṃ vrajet*'.

[32] Ibid., XIII.242.

complishments in the same body and finally on its fall attains to Śiva.[33] Such an aspirant is known as *śivadharmī.*

VI. *Manda-madhya* or the grace of slowed middle intensity: This aspirant in the category of *śivadharmī*, enjoys yogic accomplishments in the following birth. After that he attains to Śiva through the slow degree of *śaktipāta.*[34]

VII. *Tīvra-manda* or the grace of slow but intense degree: The aspirant sustains with the power of initiation. He enjoys his desired accomplishments through some lives. In the long-run he takes to the path of *sakala* or *akala* (concrete or absolute) according to his capacity and finally attains Śivahood.

Such an aspirant is called *lokadharmī.*

VIII. *Madhya-manda* or the grace of slow-but-middle degree: The aspirant of this category enjoys his accomplishments through some more births and life experiences and finally gets initiation in the course of attainment of Śivahood.

IX. *Manda-manda* or the grace of slow, very slow degree: The aspirant, by and by passes through *sālekya* (seeing from near), *sāmīpya* (being near) and *sāyujya* (becoming one with) stages of spiritual development and only after enjoying the accomplished desires, receives initiation for proceeding towards the attainment of Śivahood. There is essential relation between *śaktipāta* and *kuṇḍalinī*: Awakening of *kuṇḍalinī śakti* takes place with corresponding variations of *śaktipāta.* In fact, it is the power of grace that brings about various blossoms on the tree of *kuṇḍalinī.* It is the sovereign will of lord Śiva that works through Śakti-Pārvatī, unconditioned by any human effort. It falls spontaneously on any seeker after truth in its own range of variety comprising intense (*tīvra*), middle (*madhya*) and slow (*manda*) degrees. This trichotomy of *śaktipāta*

---

[33] *Tantrasāra* XI — '*sa ca yogābhyāsalabdhamanenaiva dehena bhogaṃ bhuktvā dehānte śiva eva*'.

[34] *Tantrasāra* XI — '*nikṛṣṭa madhyāttu dehāntareṇa bhogaṃ bhuktvā śivatvameti*'.

apparently works through *kuṇḍalinī śakti* in various ways of its various states. It is therefore that this essential power is given the name *mahākuṇḍalinī.* The nine degrees of *śaktipāta* are described to set a standard for aspirants who have to comprehend the intricacies and subtleties within the limitations of their minds. According to different modes of the awakening of *kuṇḍalinī* the nine kinds of *śaktipāta* are classified under three heads: (i) *tīvra*, comprising *tīvra-tīvra, madhya-tīvra* and *manda-tīvra*, falls in the region of *bodha kuṇḍalinī*, which awakens through the grace of sudden and spontaneous revelation of Supreme knowledge. (ii) *Madhya* comprising *tīvra-madhya, madhya-madhya* and *manda-madhya*, is the range of *cit-kuṇḍalinī* or grace through *citta*, i.e. reflection, meditation, etc. (iii) *Manda* comprising *tīvra-manda, madhya-manda* and *manda-manda*, is the work of *prāṇa-kuṇḍalinī*, the grace initiating the right practice of *prāṇa* and *apāna* or simply called *prāṇāyāma* including *japa* and other modes of *saguṇa* worships. Awakening of *kuṇḍalinī* thus takes place in the corresponding degrees of *śaktipāta.*

Peace be to all
on this earth, in the sky and beyond.

HADEWIJCH OF ANTWERP AND HADEWIJCH II:

Mysticism of Being in the Thirteenth Century in Belgium

Odette Baumer-Despeigne

We still possess three fourteenth-century manuscripts of Hadewijch of Antwerp's writings which contain thirty-one *Letters*; forty-five *Poems in Stanzas*; sixteen *Poems in Couplets*; and fourteen *Visions* followed by a so-called "*List of Perfects.*" Of the three manuscripts, only one does not contain thirteen additional *Poems in Couplets* (Poems 17 through 29).[1] While Hadewijch of Antwerp's writings are thought to have been produced between 1220 and 1240, recent research attributes Poems 17 through 29 to another Béguine who wrote about a decade later. The Carthusian, Dom J. B. Porion dates these additional Poems at 1250, names the author 'Hadewijch II' and her lyrics "New Poems". Most certainly, says Porion, Hadewijch II belonged to the same circle of Béguines and is spiritually so near that she is called by the same name.[2] The present essay is based on Hadewijch of Antwerp's *Letters* and *Poems*. All quotations follow Mother

[1] Hadewijch of Antwerp and Hadewijch II's writings were circulating during the fourteenth century, then disappeared by the middle of the sixteenth. They were rediscovered only in 1867. J. Van Mierlo published them between 1908 and 1952. Abbreviations: *Letters*: L.; *Poems in Stanzas*: PS.; *Poems in Couplets*: PC.

[2] *Hadewijch d'Anvers, Poèmes des Béguines*, Traduits du Moyen-Néerlandais par Fr. J.B.Porion, Paris, Ed. du Seuil, 1954–85.

Columba Hart's translation, Hadewijch, The *Complete Works* (London: SPCK, 1981). The *Visions* are intentionally left out as we want to focus on her doctrinal work, *Letters* and *Poems*, written, so to say, from a waking state of consciousness, visionary literature being a theme in itself. For Hadewijch II we follow the only existing translation into a modern language, that by J.B. Porion, *Hadewijch d'Anvers, Ecrits mystiques des Béguines*[3], with additional references to the critical edition in Middle Dutch.[4]

From a historical point of view we do not know anything about Hadewijch of Antwerp, except the fact that her name designates her birthplace. Fortunately, we have an important testimony of Hadewijch's historical existence in the words of John of Leuuwen, the cook and disciple of the Dutch mystical writer John Ruusbroec who wrote a century after her death:

> We know of a saint and glorious woman called Hadewijch who was an authentic spiritual guide. The doctrine she expresses in her books is correct and inspired by God. ...but not useful for everyone, for many whose inner eye has not yet been opened by pure and silent love are not able to understand.[5]

This testimony proves that Hadewijch was known and considered by Ruusbroec himself to be an authority in spiritual matters. In fact he integrated many of her thoughts in his own theological works. Mother Hart says in her introduction to Hadewijch's complete works: "Ruusbroec took over the various elements of her mystical thought, deepened and enlarged

[3]See footnote 2.

[4]Hadewijch Mengeldichten opnieuw uitgiven door Dr J. Van mierlo, S.J. Antwerpen, Standard, 1952, (pp. 87–142).

[5]J. Van Leeuwen, qtd. by Heszler, *Stufen der Minne bei Hadewijch in: Frauenmystik im Mittelalter*, Schwaben Verlag, Stuttgart 1985, pp. 99ff.

them through his knowledge of theology and metaphysical psychology, and built from them his spiritual synthesis."[6] It is important to add that Ruusbroec indifferently quotes both Hadewijch of Antwerp and Hadewijch II.[7]

Hadewijch of Antwerp's importance is only fully understood in terms of her formation and life as a Béguine, and in terms of events which occurred in the Low Countries during the thirteenth century which influenced the emergence of new types of religious vocations, including the organization of six crusades, the advent of the bourgeoisie, the expansion of the cities and trade and the foundation of the first universities. During Hadewijch's life, dissolute behaviour and corruption of the clergy were widespread. Monastic life was not everywhere in a much better condition; in many monasteries the primitive rule was no longer observed.

In reaction to this situation a great fervor animated many layers of society zealously at work in religious renewal. In response to an intensified clericalization of the Church, a new mentality arose among lay men and women, who began to recognize the Gospel as their sole rule of conduct.[8] Spiritual life thus became an individual concern.[9] The view of Joachim of Flora (d.1202), in particular his foreseeing of a "renewal in the Holy Spirit with the coming of time" were widely spread and often repeated.

Within this context, the Béguinal movement represents a spontaneous upheaval at the turn of the twelfth century

---

[6] Hadewijch, *Complete Works*, 15.

[7] St Axters, *Hadewijchals voorloopster van de zalige Jan Ruusbroec*, in L.Reypens Album Ruusbroec Genoozschap, Antwerpen, 1964, pp. 57-72. G. Epinay-Burgard, *L'influence des Béguines sur Ruusbroec*, in Mediaevalia Lovaniensia I, Louvain 1984.

[8] J. Leclercq, *Histoire de la spiritualité chrétienne*, Paris, Aubier 1961, 315.

[9] C. Walker Bynum, *Jesus as Mother*, Berkely, California UP, 1982, pp. 82–109.

amongst spiritually minded lay women who wanted to lead a simple life dictated by the Gospel. They voluntarily practised chastity and poverty without joining any existing religious Order. The Béguines had neither a founder nor a foundress and were not an offshoot of monasticism. They wanted to remain independent and free from religious formalism.

The first group of Béguines emerged in the Duchy of Brabant. The oldest of those '*mulieres religiosae*' (pious women) was Mary of Oignies (1177-1213). In her biography, Magister Jacques de Vitry writes that Mary was a literate woman married to a rich merchant in Nivelles. Following their religious longings both decided to retire to a nearby leprosarium and take care of the sick. They stayed there twelve years. During that time Mary acquired such a great reputation for sanctity that she was overwhelmed with visitors, clerics and lay people. Feeling the need to lead a more solitary life, she went — with her husband's agreement — to Oignies and settled down as a lay sister in a little house next to the priory of the Augustinian canons.

In spite of her desire to remain unknown, she became the spiritual mother of the priory and again a multitude of visitors from far and near came to receive her advice. One visitor from Paris was her future biographer, Jacques de Vitry. With Mary's encouragement, he joined the Augustinians and became a popular wandering preacher. His sermons were so much the reflected image of Mary's zeal for the "cure of souls", that he could say of himself: "I was merely her instrument."[10] He ends his biography of her, saying that: "On her death-bed she praised the Trinity in Oneness and Oneness in the Trinity at length."[11]

As early as 1208 it is recorded that, inspired by Mary,

[10]E.W. McDonnell, *The Béguines and Beghards in Medieval Culture*, New York, Octagon, 1969, 23.

[11]McDonnell 381.

seven women were living together in Nivelles and consecrating their lives to prayer and charitable works. They were spiritually guided by Master John of Nivelles, in close connection with the Cistercian Abbey of Villers. This intense and fervent religious movement spread like wildfire, and groups of Béguines were formed in all cities of the Low Countries as well as in France and Germany.[12] Neither simple lay women nor nuns, the Béguines formed "pious associations" whose numbers went into the hundreds and even thousands. Everywhere they had the same aim: to fight silently against the sclerosis of the hierarchical Church and against the corruption of society, leading a contemplative life right in the middle of the cities. To become a Béguine meant to adopt a new style of religious life, a life of chastity and poverty without following any canonical rule or taking any vows. This new style of spirituality rendered the Béguines less dependent on the tutelage of the clergy.

Life as a Béguine was open to women of all classes in society, of all ages, and of all states. They were unmarried, married (if the husband consented) and widowed. However, most of them belonged to aristocratic or patrician families. Among them many were learned persons and highly gifted mystics. Lamprecht von Regensburg, a contemporary of Hadewijch, in his poem "Die Tochter Sione" speaks of pious women living in Brabant before 1250 whose meditation rendered them free of themselves and everything and led them to see God without intermediary, God as He is.[13]

In the early years of the movement the Béguines remained in their own houses, devoting their time to prayer and works of charity. As their number increased, they joined small

[12] H. Grundmann, *Religiöse Bewegungen im Mittelalter.* Darmstadt, 1961, pp. 431–52. J. Greven, *Die Anfänge der Béguinen*, Hrs. H. Finke, Münster, 1912, 47-53.

[13] Quoted by Porion, 49.

groups living in the house of one of their rich members. In their turn, small groups joined forces and built small houses next to each other in courtyard form, with a church in the center. From then on one can speak of a real Béguinage.[14] Each one was led by a 'great mistress' elected by the Béguines. The regulations were flexible enough to adapt to every type of spirituality, including ecstatic prayer, love mysticism or *Minnemystiek* and speculative mysticism or *Wesensmystik*. Each house's rules differed according to local conditions.

The main concern of the community was to participate daily in the liturgy, to recite the Hours together, to listen to spiritual instruction and to devote much time to private contemplation. Most Béguines' time was spent in silence in their own houses 'so that they never ceased to pray'.[15] Once a week they met in council and listened to the sermon of the "great mistress". New candidates were required to undergo a period of probation during which they were individually instructed by an older member. As regards the financial organization, the rich members provided for those who were less well off, donations were received and all of them were obliged to earn their livelihood by suitable work, such as teaching, or making lace, spinning, making embroidery. Béguines were also engaged in works of charity, maintaining hospitals and nursing the sick people outside the Béguinage.

Parish priests, Cistercians and, later, Franciscans or Dominicans took pastoral responsibility for them and provided them with religious "writings in the vernacular",[16] biblical translations and excerpts from classics of spirituality. But in 1242, the General Chapter of the Dominicans, afraid to see 'women' well versed in theological knowledge, forbad the dissemination of these translations. In spite of this interdiction,

---

[14] McDonnell, 126, 174, 479–83.
[15] Bethune, *Cartulaire*, quoted by McDonnell, 148.
[16] McDonnell, 402.

they remained extremely literate, for in some Béguinages they were able to maintain their own school of Liberal Arts.

As early as in 1216, Jacques de Vitry, now returned to his clerical state, obtained official recognition by the Papal Curia of the Béguines' new association, thus permitting them "to live in common and to perfect themselves in virtue by mutual assistance."[17] This recognition ensured their autonomy for the new life-style they had adopted, whose very essence was its voluntary, temporary and informal character. It also permitted the more gifted among them to teach and guide their sisters. Later, when the Brabant Béguines were suspected of heterodoxy by a hierarchy sensitive to possible anticlericalism, it is the same Jacques de Vitry who took up their defense. In the course of time, the ecclesiastical hierarchy attempted to institutionalize them, some groups did voluntarily submit to canonical constitutions and became monasteries. In 1311 Rome condemned the movement, declaring it should be abolished for ever from the Church. Nevertheless, in Brabant, many Béguinages did not submit and resisted the ecclesiastical ban. They were officially rehabilitated eight years later!

A Portrait of Hadewijch from her Writings

The only source of information concerning Hadewijch of Antwerp's personality is her writings, especially her *Letters* mostly addressed to young Béguines. In her we find the origin and the basis of Flemish mysticism as well as the first author to write on spiritual matters in the vernacular.[18] From the way she writes we can infer that she belonged to a patrician or even a noble family, for her works betray a refined education and the possession of a vast field of learning. According to the tradition in the upper classes of society of her time, she must

[17] McDonnell, 155.

[18] J. Van Mierlo, *Hadewijch une mystique du XIII siècle*, Revue d'Ascétique et de Mystique, Toulouse 1924, pp. 268–89.

have visited a school of Liberal Arts and acquired extended theological knowledge from another source. She was proficient in Latin, for she often quotes the Scripture; it is also evident that her theology is based on a deep acquaintance with the spiritual classics of masters such as St Augustin, St Bernard, William of St Thierry. Her use of French expressions reveals her knowledge of that language. Moreover she was a lyric genius as well as a perfect prose writer; her works stand among the Masterpieces of Flemish literature.

In the field of poetry she was well informed of the poetry of the *Trouvères*. Her poems are written in the language of courtly love or *Minne*.[19] She feels free to use the term *Minne* to express her love relationship with God, and at the same time transforms its meaning genially to a high spiritual level. "The austere service of love offered to the 'Lady' by the *Trouvères* becomes the service of love offered by the soul to God."[20]

If Hadewijch's writings reveal a very intensive affective life, she never becomes sentimental or childish in the way she expresses her love for God, even if she does it in passionate terms: "My soul melts away in the madness of love (*Orewoet*)."[21] In all circumstances she remains a well-balanced person full of common sense and humour. She writes to a young Béguine: "Always do remain humble in every way, yet not so humble that you become foolish" (L.23). To another disciple she says: "First be subject to your reason, and

---

[19] *Minne*, or spiritual love, is of feminine gender in Middle Dutch. The word *lieve* is used for carnal love. In fact, Hadewijch gives many different significations to the word *Minne*. It means either the spiritual love of men for God, for the person of Jesus, for the Holy Spirit, for the deity or for the Divine Essence. It may also designate the Person of the Father conceived as the origin of the Trinity. *Minne* is a word belonging to the language of courtly love.

[20] Hadewijch, *Complete Works*, 19.

[21] *Orewoet* or stormy longing, intense longing, rage of love as a re-action of God's touch at the root of the soul.

remain without singularities. Don't make a show of your spirituality." (L.13). Hadewijch is a "noble and fierce soul" who throughout her life and without fault, pursues her way unwaveringly, her whole being concentrated on her ideal. She plays the role of spiritual mother with self-conscious authority, convinced that she fulfills God's will and that she will be given the capacity for doing it.

Hadewijch is not a theoretician in mysticism. Her own experiences are the source of her writings. She has only to draw out of the plenitude of her interior maturity. Undoubtedly, she belongs to the mysticism of Love, the *Minnemystiek*, but we would like to demonstrate that she belongs simultaneously to the deepest current of speculative mysticism. A mysticism of Being not only underlies all her pursuit of Love but is the dominant element in her inmost quest.[22] In her own words:

> Love allures the soul and heart and makes the soul ascend out of itself and out of Love and into the essence of Love. (L.20)

According to Hadewijch of Antwerp and Hadewijch II divine love is paradoxical, for it implies at once a relationship with, and an 'absorption' in, the 'inaccessible' One.

Hadewijch's Pilgrimage to God

Hadewijch began her adventurous pilgrimage very early:

[22] Hadewijch, *Lettres spirituelles.* Martingay, Genève. 1972. Trad. Fr. J.B.M. Porion "Hadewijch sees everything in the light of Love which is simultaneously the means and the end of her spiritual life. It is along the lines of her triple tradition — Cistercian, Chivalrous, Beguinal — that we see how she attains a remarkable evolution in her experience as well as in her way of expressing it: the transformation from Minnemystiek's register to speculative Mysticism of Being, from the search of Love to the contemplation of the divine Essence." 20.

> Since I was ten years old I have been overwhelmed by such intense love that I should have died if God had not given me other forms of strength than people ordinarily receive, and if he had not renewed my nature with his own Being. (L.11)

Throughout her life, Hadewijch's main concern was to show the way to the depths. Her spirituality is experience-centered and emerges from her own personal contact with the 'Mystery' that lies at the heart of every human being. Her theological reflection is based on Augustinian Exemplarism: "We have to return from whence we come, to what we have not ceased to be in the Logos."[23] As she so uniquely says: "We have not yet become what we are." (L.6) Self-knowledge, in its deepest sense, is the aim for which Hadewijch strives. In L.18 we read:

> Understand the deepest essence of your soul, what 'soul' is ... Soul is a being that can be beheld by God and by which again God can be beheld.

It is on such metaphysical principles that her whole spirituality is grounded, while the motive power which propels her on the way — we could even say, her 'technique' — is ardent love of God. A love which is more than affective love, even more than a "stormy fiery longing" (*Orewoet*). It is a one-pointed, intense inner tension towards the yet Unknown, the Absolute, a readiness for total surrender of one's entire self to God. In her own words: "Give yourself to God to become what He is." (L.2).[24] Such is the real originality of Hadewijch's way that she proceeds simultaneously along the path of love and the path of knowledge whose end is 'Vacuity' in the

---

[23] St. Axters, *La spiritualité des Pays-Bas*, Paris, Vrin, 1948, p. 48.

[24] A thought probably inspired by William of Saint Thierry: "A will firmly strained towards God, this is love." *Epistola ad Fratres de Monte Dei*, p. 257 (SC 223 : 348).

undifferentiated Godhead beyond, or at the core of the Three Persons of the Trinity:

> In a divine clarity the soul sees, and it sees nothing. It sees a truth — Subsistent, Effusive, Total — which is God himself in eternity ... the Being of the Godhead in the Unity. (28)

These are certainly daring sayings. Dom Porion, commenting on this Letter, suggests to readers that they be seen as analogous. We would like to suggest that they somehow be taken more literally for what they are, an attempt at crystallizing the ineffable mystical experience which no human utterance can express:

> The soul that has stood so long with the God-Man that it understands such a wonder as God is in his Godhead, appears most of the time for those who are not acquainted with this experience to be ungodly through too much of godliness, ignorant through too much knowledge. (L.28)

Hadewijch's spiritual itinerary unfolds in three stages: the virtuous service of the beloved Lord, the new path which she denominates "Love's new school" and a dimension of consciousness which she calls "Nothingness in Love".

"*The noble service of the beloved Lord in all works of virtues.*" Speaking with all her authority, she says in L.30:

> He who wishes ... to be one with the Godhead must adorn himself with all the virtues with which God clothed and adorned himself when he lived as a Man.

Not only does she insist on practice, but she exhorts the novice:

> ... acquire a knowledge of all the virtues and learn them by exertion, in/by questioning study and earnest purpose. (L.24)

It is most remarkable how Hadewijch (in Letter 17) also preaches the practice of virtues in paradoxical terms akin to those of Zen koans,[25] translating them afterwards in terms of exemplarist theology:

> Be generous and zealous for every virtue
> But do not apply yourself to any virtue.

This she explains:

> The things I order you ...belong perfectly to the perfection of Love and belong perfectly and wholly in the Divinity ... for to be generous and zealous is the nature of the Holy Spirit... And not to apply oneself to a particular work is the Nature of the Father...This pouring out and keeping back is the pure Divinity and the entire Nature of Love.
> Fail not with regard to a multitude of things,
> But perform no particular work.
>
> The first of these verses expresses the power of the Father...The second verse expresses his just will, with which his justice works its unknown mighty works. These works are deep and dark, hidden for all who are below this Unity of the Godhead but nevertheless render service to each of the Three Persons.

And a few paragraphs further she adds:

---

[25] *Koan*: or a question which cannot be solved through logical reasoning or intellectual understanding.

> Have good will and compassion for every need,
> But take nothing under your protection ...

and explains:

> The first verse expresses what is proper to the Son, the second expresses the Nature of the Father[26] who engulfs him (the Son) in Himself; this terrible great work ever belongs to the Father. Yet it is the unity of purest Love in the Divinity.

This saying may be regarded as a commentary on 1 Cor. 15,28: "When everything is subjected to him, the Son himself will be subject in his turn to the One who subjected all things to him, so that God may be all in all", meaning that souls are engulfed in the Son and together with him in the Father. The letter ends with these words: "How you are to do or omit each of these things, may God, our Beloved teach you."

The new path or "Love's new school": Following the example of the *Trouvères*, she sings of a spiritual renewal through Love, under the vestment of the rebirth of nature in spring:

> "When March begins, we see
> All being live again
> And all plants spring up
> And in a short time turn green.
> It is the same with longing,
> Particularly that of the true lover" (of God).
> (PS.6)
> ... "They who come to Love's new school
> With new love,
> ... Love shall cause them to ascend
> To Love's highest mystery." (PS.7)

[26]The Father is taken here as the Principle of the Trinity. (Porion, 24, note 18).

But before one attains this "high mystery" which is to partake of and have fruition of[27] Love's Nature, Hadewijch knows only too well that one has to "risk many adventures", for the way which leads to such an experience is paved with trials and requires a long and patient asceticism. Poem 10 says it clearly:

> Lo! the day of love is dawning
> When men will never fear pain for Love's sake.

She goes so far as to say "Love has driven me to the verge of death ...for the fire of love burns to death everything it ever touches." (PS.16;PC.16) But the fierce Béguine does not ask for "any remedy" and goes on "questing the depthless depths of Love", sure that "Love always repays even though it often comes late." (PS.9) Hadewijch insists on this point, saying that Love requires a total abandonment of all self-centeredness and is a remorseless process of dying to oneself: "He who wants to remain faithful to Love must enter still living into death." (PC.10)

In another poem she explains that spiritual life is a dynamic existence for "Love is ever new, it causes the soul at all times to begin out of a new death."(PS.14). In Letter 19 she states precisely where this dynamism leads:

> When the soul is engulfed in God, and brought to nought...the soul becomes with Him all that He himself is.[28]

She thus summarizes the programme of Love's new school:

> If you wish to follow your being in which God created you, you should valiantly lay hold on the

[27] *Ghebruken*: to delight in.

[28] Even when the soul is so absorbed, the created individuality is not destroyed. Hadewijch compares the soul in that state with the rising sun. (L.19)

> best part — I mean the great totality of God —
> as your own good. (L.6)

These different quotations show how Hadewijch's love experience extends beyond affectivity, beyond emotiveness; how she discovered and realized on an experiential level the metaphysical basis of Love mysticism, and how it flows forth into a mysticism of Being:[29]

> In the light (of Love) we can learn
> How we shall love the God-Man
> In his Godhead and in his Manhood. (PC.16)

Thus "to live Christ as God and Man" is the most fascinating formulation. It means much more than to 'follow' Christ or live 'with' Christ: It is pregnant with a deep essential experience, which is to live in total accordance with Him as he lived in consequence of his being God-incarnate. It is experiencing Jesus as the supreme and unique paradigm of the God-man relationship, as well as the Man-God relationship.

In Letter 6 written to a 'dearly beloved', she explains:

> With the Humanity of God you must live here on earth, in the labors and sorrows of exile, while within your soul you love and rejoice with the omnipotent and eternal Divinity in sweet abandonment, for the truth of both the Humanity and the Divinity is one single fruition.

This last assertion springs out of Hadewijch's own experience. It echoes a spiritual attainment in which the two poles of inner life, the affective and the metaphysical are, at the deepest level, symbiotically joined. Hadewijch has reached the point

[29] "Mysticism of Being was wedded to mysticism of Love", Emilie Zum Brunn and Georgette Epinay-Burgard: *Women Mystics in Medieval Europe*, New York, Paragon, 1989.

where "dialectical oppositions become creative polarities", as Georges Vallin said.

To attain such a state Hadewijch suggests a special technique which is worth noticing (L.6):

> Love the Divinity not merely with devotion but with unspeakable desires (*Orewoet*), always standing before the *terrible and marvellous* countenance in which Love reveals herself and engulfed all works. (italics ours).

It is worth noticing the subtle difference made here between 'devotion', a personal and active approach of God and *Orewoet* the 'fury of love', which reduced the soul to inaction, to 'standing' in a kind of non-action, in which dialogue ends in silence.

"*Nothingness in Love*". Paradoxically enough, in Poem in Couplets 16 called 'Love's Seven Names', the highest name Hadewijch finds to give is 'Hell':

> Hell is the seventh name.
> For there is nothing love does not engulf and damn, . . .
> As Hell turns everything to ruin
> In Love nothing else is acquired
> But disquiet and torture without pity.
> . . . (the soul) is wholly devoured and engulfed
> In her unfathomable essence.

After passing such an ordeal, Hadewijch realizes that she has undergone a deep inner metamorphosis and can only stammer:

> What has happened to me now?
> I have given away all that I am.
> I am not mine:

> Love has engulfed the substance of my spirit.[30]
> PC.16)

What else could be added to such a statement? Love made her penetrate into a new dimension of consciousness. It has driven her out of her peripheral ego into a state of vacuity. If as she says, the 'substance of her spirit has been ruined', what remains? Only the most essential, which she was looking for from the beginning: 'She laid hold on her own good, which is God, and nothing less'. These daring sayings cannot be dismissed as being only verbal exaggerations. They have the flavour of lived experience, of authenticity. They are neither the fruits of beliefs or intellectual knowledge nor of affective excesses, but of events intuitively experienced. Henceforth only through paradoxical terms can she speak of her approach to the Divine Mystery. She confesses her inability to find adequate terms to speak of her experience in the depths of her being — "no words exist to express these things so far as I know" (L.17). "He who wishes to speak about these things must speak with his soul." (L.28), and she describes her experience of inner bareness (PS.38):

> To be reduced to nothingness in Love[31]
> Is the most desirable thing I know...
> Fighting Love with longing,
> Wholly without heart and without mind.

In such a state of bareness, in which there is "no more heart nor mind", how is it possible to express any 'longing'? These verses prove that every attempt to express her experience has

[30]This daring speculative saying finds its echo in Ruusbroec's last chapter of *The Spiritual Espousals*, (Trans. A. Wiseman, New York, Paulist, 1985) "Here there is a blissful crossing over and a self-transcending immersion into a state of essential bareness...where all the divine names and modes pass away into simple ineffability, ..." 152.

[31]What is 'reduced to nothingness' is the egoistic being.

failed. Her only choice is to take refuge in the ineffable, there where 'laisser-faire' and non-action is the only norm. "The soul has to remain in a blissful silence" (L.28). "I must then live out what I am." (PS.22)[32] Hadewijch does not mean here any kind of 'vanishing of consciousness', on the contrary she hints at an awakening which rises up out of the deep engulfment she has undergone. It is then that Nothingness explodes into Fullness, fullness of the experience of the Omnipresence of the "Deity Who is Love" (L.17). She makes a last attempt at "speaking with her soul" in L.28 in which we read:

> The soul sees how God is in his eternity. God through his own Divinity. In all this, it contemplates God in his Godhead, and in each of (its) attributes.

This difficult epistle ends with a no less difficult paragraph in which she relates anew her own experience:

> Thus spoke a soul in the liberty of God: I have understood all diversity in the pure Unity...I remained there standing above all things and I looked out above all things into the glory without end.[33]

In a text which is regarded as being a sermon but filed as L.22 we read:

> Those who follow this inner path penetrate within God from depth to depth. They walk outside all the ways open to the human mind.

---

[32] Porion suggests that this thought is based on St Bernard's Sermon on the Canticle LXXXIII: "naturae ingenuitatem servare."

[33] In this Hadewijch took inspiration from William of St Thierry who in *The Golden Epistle* "affirms"... man becomes 'non Deus, sed tamen quod est Deus: homo et gratia quod Deus et natura". p. 263 (SC 223: 354).

We will never be able to know exactly what Hadewijch meant by walking outside the way of representation. Could she have wanted to suggest through this ultimate metaphor 'the most inner secret of the One' which only the high fruition of Love can penetrate[34]? Or is this state the state of "enstasis" as Mircéa Eliade calls it, in which the ego explodes and the relational becomes changed over into the Transpersonal? By way of explanation, one can consider the question she asked in L.30 (which again is reminiscent of 1 Cor 5.28):

> What happens to those who have fully grown up and answered the fearful demand of the Unity (of the Godhead) when they make their ascent without returning...there, where the brilliant lightning flashes and the loud thunder resounds?

Listen to the answer which follows:

> Then the soul is brought to union out of the multiplicity of gifts, it becomes all that, that is (the Godhead)...united to the Unity of the Godhead.

This is an answer which is most paradoxical, for how can anything be united to Unicity? This is pure Exemplarism. It describes the ineffable return of the soul to her original being in the Godhead.

In less philosophical terms, Hadewijch exhorts her spiritual daughter to whom she addresses L.18 to come to full inner growth in these simple and beautiful terms, making use of the inner power of sight of her soul.

> This power of sight has two eyes, love and reason. Reason advances toward what God is, by means

[34] In his *Commentary on the Song of Songs*, William of St Thierry says: "love is knowledge: quoniam in hac re amor ipse intellectus est" ECC.57 (SC 82: 152).

> of what God is not. Love sets aside what God is not and rejoices that it fails in what God is.

This sentence shows clearly that for Hadewijch, love has the last word. "Love is knowledge."[35]

Hadewijch II: Her Specific Contribution

Unfortunately only thirteen poems from this unidentified Béguine have been preserved. They are contained in three of the four manuscripts (the fourth manuscript dates from the sixteenth century) of Hadewijch of Antwerp's works, they are filed as *Poems in Couplets* (*Mengeldichten*) 17 through 29.[36] Both Hadewijch of Antwerp and Hadewijch II belong to the same milieu and spiritual lineage; both are witnesses of mysticism of Being in Middle Dutch before Ruusbroec: it should be reiterated that both had a considerable influence on later mystical theology. Ruusbroec quotes both Hadewijchs without making any difference between them. He simply appropriates many of their texts, developing their themes in a more systematic way.[37]

---

[35]It is of interest to compare this text with a sixth-century one from Damascius, last of the Platonists, who spoke of a certain "unified knowledge" capable of approaching the ineffable One... "as long as knowledge is near the One, it draws some knowledge of It, thereafter closing the eyes, knowledge becomes union instead of knowledge." (*Des premiers principes*), quoted in Georges Vallin, *Lumière du non-dualisme*, Nancy, Press Universitaires, 1987, 93.

[36]These poems, says Dom Porion, "are one of the purest expressions of the spirituality current of which Master Eckhart together with Ruusbroec is the best known representative but not the initiator". *Hadewijch d'Anvers, Ecrits mystiques des Béguines*, 45.

[37]We can only mention the theme, for it needs treatment itself. "Often it is to these Béguines that we must turn to find the origin of expressions in the works of Eckhart and Ruusbroec that had been thought to be without precedent until the writings of these spiritual mistresses were rediscovered or brought to light again." E. Zum Brunn, XXXI.

The so-called Hadewijch II's style is more metaphysical, her vocabulary is nearer to that of the Rhineland mystics than that of Hadewijch of Antwerp and is therefore dated a short span of time later, apparently nearer the time of Meister Eckhart. Like her elder sister, Hadewijch II is not a theoretician of mysticism and her poems are the reflection of her own inner experience; they are 'Lived theology'.[38] The first two of her thirteen poems, *Poems in Couplets* 17 and 18, are a kind of digest of her spiritual itinerary.

Right at the beginning she warns those who want to follow her on her spiritual path that they will have to tread a solitary way, that is:

> ...To follow along a dark, unlaid and unmarked path, an altogether inner path.

This is a path on which:

> ...What we apprehend in high contemplation through naked understanding is certainly great, and yet compared to what escapes our grasp it becomes nothing.

With more precision she adds:

> Forward into this non-perceived depth, in this nescience must our desire strive.[39]

---

[38] Since mother Columba Hart did not include the poems of Hadewijch II in her *Hadewijch Complete Works*, the following analysis contains a first attempt at English translations of certain passages. After the completion of this article, Poems 17, 19 and 26 were published in *Women Mystics in Medieval Europe*, 132–39.

[39] As E. Zum Brunn writes, "In Dutch this ever-unattainable Transcendance is called *ontbliven* and means literally *what remains* above our reach..." Dom Porion has stressed the importance of this theme as a pre-Eckhartian testimony in Béguine mysticism, XXXIII.

The word 'desire' is very pale compared to its Dutch equivalent, *Minne*, which signifies a fiery will to dive into precisely that which escapes our faculties, that is this deficiency (*ontbliven*). 'Desire' then, needs qualification to suggest the strength of ardor, the fire of the high-mettled yearning which prompts her.

The Middle Dutch word, *ontbliven*, meaning deficiency, is in fact the central point of her thought and experience. She feels herself violently attracted by this 'beyond' understanding. Pursuing inexorably her quest, she plunges into the Unknown:

> Those whose desire penetrates deeper into the sublime, silent knowledge of pure love meet with an ever greater deficiency, their understanding finds a modeless renewal in the unclouded darkness, in the presence of absence.

To be able to perceive the divine presence without any mode (*sonder wise*) means that she has grown aware of a new inner depth dimension in which God's 'personal' absence is perceived as being his essential Presence.

Consistent with herself our Béguine does not hesitate in front of the abyss of the Unknown. On the contrary, she declares herself ready to risk her all (PC.18):

> The soul must be uprooted from herself by Love and hurled into the unfathomable abyss on High.
> There the soul abides in pure silence in her innermost recess.
> The soul must penetrate into the bareness of the One beyond reason,
> Where return is impossible, where there is no light to help her ...

> Where neither higher knowledge nor deep intuition can cast anchor ...
> There, something noble, neither this nor that, guides the soul into and absorbs her in her Origin. (PC.18)

Thus we see that the driving power which makes her fall into this abyss is Love (*Minne*). It is also Love which has, from the very first step on the contemplative path, monopolized all her energies and sustained her all the way through the 'wild desert'.

In poem 17, Hadewijch II has a few couplets which speak for themselves. Any commentary would take the bloom from their beauty:

> Understanding becomes isolated, within the shoreless eternity...and with quiet desire devote itself to a complete immersion in boundless totality, there something quite simple yet undisclosable is revealed — the Unalloyed, pure Void (*een bloet niet.*)
> The strong hold fast in that naked Void rich in their intuition yet faltering before the unknowable depths.
> ....To those inattainable depths they attribute a supreme value, in them they find their highest joy.
> I tell you, none can speak about it, save to say that he who desires inner understanding, and not just knowledge, must rid himself of reason's turmoil, of all forms and images.
> Those who do not divert themselves with other activities from those described here will find again unity in their first Beginnings — in their Principle. ...

> In the intimacy of the One these souls are interiorly pure and naked, without forms or images as though they were liberated from time, never created,[40] freed from their outward limits in silent space.
> Here I stop. I find neither end nor beginning nor any comparison which could justify the use of words.

The only thing to add after the full stop of Hadewijch is that, for her, God is not objectifiable and the Void is not empty!

In her other poems Hadewijch II tries to precise the inner transmutation she had to undergo in her depths once her soul 'had been established in this nakedness, in this passing away' (*overliden*):

> It is Love who teaches the soul this inmost transformation into Unity. (PC.22)

> It is the Unity of naked Truth which adapts the soul to the onefold nature of Eternity, of eternal Essence. (PC.29)

Another topic sung again and again by Hadewijch II is that of the immediacy of the divine presence in the soul in 'naked clarity' and 'inner freedom', as it is for example in Poem 23:

> (In contemplation) the soul dwells with you God,
> free and alone in Unity.
> She loses all images, forms and distinctions, when
> you nourish her with your wisdom and grant
> her knowledge of your fullness, which she cannot understand.[41]

[40]They have retraced their steps to what they are from all eternity in God.

[41]This is a state of the soul which Ruusbroec will call 'unknown knowledge' in *The Sparkling Stone*.

...and which scholarly knowledge can never penetrate.

This shows clearly that Hadewijch II's experience lies beyond all distinctions, all opposites; it may be called a non-dual experience of God. She meets God 'without intermediary' (*sonder middle*). She has discovered the 'point' of her rootedness in God, in the divine, in Truth.

The pure spark,
life of the life of our soul
which remains without end
united to the divine Source. (PC.27)

In Poem 24, the same exemplarist intuition serves as canvas to express this subtle knowledge that the Holy Spirit reveals in the twinkling of an eye:

Omnipotence attracts the soul,
Logos instructs her, Love leads her,
thus the Three sweep her off into the Unity,
where the saints find blessings and fullness
in their first Principle,
the pure deity. (*Gotheit*)

She then concludes with those daring verses:

In the Godhead,
no semblance of persons:
the Three in One
are pure Nakedness. (PC.20)[42]

Finally from the summit — or depths — of her spiritual pilgrimage, our Béguine develops her thoughts about the "life of the poor in spirit here on earth".[43] In Poem 26 she says:

[42]Ruusbroec will amplify this saying in *The Seven Rungs in the Ladder of Spiritual Love.* "There, where the divine Persons pass away in the Unity of their common Essence, in this groundless abyss of pure Beatitude there is no more Father, nor Son, nor Holy Spirit", Ch.14.

[43]Cp. Eckhart's sermon, "Beati pauperes spiritu".

It is not everything to withdraw from the world,
to go begging one's bread and all:
the poor in spirit must remain without thoughts
in the vast simplicity (of being)
which has neither end nor beginning, nor form, nor mode,
nor reason, nor senses, nor opinion, nor thought,
nor purpose, nor science: unencompassed, unlimited.

In this wild and solitary simplicity
the poor in spirit live in unity:
there they find nothing but silence
ever responding to Eternity's call.[44]

In reality this 'silence', this 'Void' in which she has been absorbed is not a Void in the negative sense of the word, on the contrary, it is the undifferentiated plenitude of the divine Essence, in her own words: "Unity and Trinity are one and single Omnipotence." (PC.22)

We end this chapter with the last words of her last poem (PC.29):

Those who never understood the Scriptures
cannot use reason to explain
what I have found in my inner being,
without any intermediary, without a veil,
beyond words.

Her explicit reference to the Scripture shows that Hadewijch II considered herself as being in conformity with Catholic orthodoxy. In his introduction to her Poems, Dom Porion

[44] Ruusbroec uses the same words in *A Mirror of Eternal Blessedness*: "He empties us of all images... There we find nothing other than a wild desert of imageless bareness, which always responds to the call of eternity."

underlines that as far as he knows, no theologian ever did suspect of heresy the boldness of her style.

An Attempt at Interpretation

There is scarcely any reason to comment on the significance of the astonishing statements of our Béguines. They do speak clearly for themselves. Their paradoxical terms, says Dom Porion "are transparent enigmas"! Nevertheless, we think it is expedient to add a few remarks, for the domain of mysticism of Being in the thirteenth century among women has been much too little studied so far. Chronologically speaking, the two Hadewijchs belong to the thirteenth century, but in reality they belong to a certain 'spiritual family' which has no historical boundaries, which is trans-historical and trans-cultural.

It seems necessary to emphasize the ease with which the Béguines, whenever they gathered and in spite of those troubled times, were able to find a kindly ear among clergy and monks, who indeed even encouraged them, taking on the function of chaplains. This was especially so in Brabant where they enjoyed, right from the beginning, close relations with the Cistercian monks at Villers — relations which were at once on individual and collective basis. Unfortunately, sermons given by the abbots or monks have not been preserved. It is only in hagiographical writings that we can get a glimpse of the different themes developed between monks and Béguines. It is known that some monks 'visited their spiritual daughters in the world', that others had a 'spiritual sister'. Many a time we have evidence of monks seeking spiritual advices by the *mulieres religiosae*, recluses and Béguines.

> The interaction between Cistercian and Béguines was about equal...however vast and complex these spiritual currents were in Belgium, the centre always remained the piety of the Béguines.

> Similarities with Bernardine piety are often less borrowings than points of contact in the emergence of the extraregular.[45]

If the Hadewijchs based their writings on Scripture and the authority of theological tradition, these writings contain no trace of reference to learning from a contemporary spiritual director. They contain only the reflection of the Béguines' personal experience. Moreover, neither Hadewijchs relates the experience of the highest states of consciousness to a life *post-mortem.* They insinuate that the highest states can be attained here on earth.[46] The freedom they demonstrate in their choice of theological terms is partly due to the fact that at the time when they were writing, Thomas Aquinas had not yet finished his *Summa.* This implies that they had not to conform to dialectical rules of Scholastics and could use freely a polyvalent vocabulary without having to make sharp distinction between the ontological and the intentional orders.

The ultimate aim of each Hadewijch's pilgrimage is in no way different, nor do their starting points on their path or their ways of getting there differ: for both the *Minne* thrusts the soul into another metaphysical dimension: "the abyss from On High" (Hadewijch II), the 'bottomless abyss' (Hadewijch of Antwerp). For both, it is precisely this leap into the Unknown that effects the existential opening to Transcendence which reveals itself as being the other face of Immanence.

It seems evident that both Béguines reached an extraordinary level of interior life. In a way they solved the squaring of the spiritual circle by an existential experience in the depths

---

[45] McDonnell, *Citeaux and Béguine Spirituality,* Ch. III. 320.

[46] Hadewijch of Antwerp: "Those who strive to content Love begin here on earth that eternal life" (L.12). Hadewijch II: "He who has been transformed... casts anchor in the beautiful Deity."

of their being simultaneously through personal union with the beloved Lord and transpersonal identification in inner vacuity to the undifferentiated, ultimate Reality.[47] In other words, they experienced the 'constitutive' spiritual dimension of the human being, as Hadewijch of Antwerp wished: 'to understand the deepest essence of the soul.

> Soul is a way for the passage of God from his depths into his liberty; and God is a way for the passage of the soul into its liberty that is into his inmost depths, which cannot be touched except by the soul's abyss. (L.18)

Finally it is important to recall that both, so to say, at the end of their itinerary, land in the pure Deity, beyond the Three Persons, for it is precisely here that we see the essential continuity between the two Béguines. Hadewijch of Antwerp spoke of "those who stay below the Unity of the Godhead", and Hadewijch II said "the Three in One are pure Nakedness."

Seven hundred years have passed, but the Hadewijchs have not lost anything of their actuality. One cannot but be fascinated by the personality of these women who, with no trace of inferiority complex, fearlessly and with great serenity follow their bold path, heartened by both creative genius and an independent spirit which they wisely displayed in an ecclesial framework. Thanks to them we rediscover today that dimension of deep interiority in the Christian tradition which unfortunately has been either eclipsed or misunderstood for whole centuries.

---

[47] As G. Epinay-Burgard has so concisely written: "Hadewijch's life reflects the fundamental experience of participation in the intra-Trinitarian mysteries. With their paradoxes Letters 17 and 18 show, at the same time, the consequences of union with the Trinity and the necessity of an overpassing into Unity." 110.

ENCLOSED IN GOD: THE JOYFUL SURPRISE OF ONE-ING

The Experience of Julian of Norwich

C. Murray Rogers

"It is all in a little thing, the size of a hazel nut. I hold it in the palm of my hand. I look at it with the eye of my understanding. "What can it be?", I ask. From somewhere the answer comes: "It is all that is made." How small it is, I say to myself, how easily it could disappear into nothingness, but then I hear it said: 'It lasts, and ever shall last, because God loves it; and in this way everything has its being by the love of God.' Yes, of this little thing there are three characteristics: the first is that God made it, the second is that God loves it, the third is that God keeps it. And then it dawns on me that I cannot tell the reality of him who is my maker, love and keeper, until I am one-ed to him, until I so adhere to him that there is absolutely no created thing between my God and me — until I am made so fast to Him that nothing separates my God and myself."[1]

The woman who experienced the heart of Reality in a "little thing, the size of a hazel nut", remains practically unknown, a fact that would certainly have pleased her. She lived in the fourteenth century in the thriving commercial centre and cathedral city of Norwich, in eastern England. Traumatic happenings such as the Black Death (when more than

[1] Paraphrase of ch. 5. of *The Revelations of Divine Love* by Julian of Norwich.

one-third of the population of England died), the Hundred Years' war with France, the Peasants' Revolt (a revolt of the poor and oppressed, brutally suppressed by both Church and State), and the defeat, abdication and execution of kings of England all happened in her day, while further afield in Europe popes were competing for power, the Great Schism tore the Catholic Church into three warring pieces — an echo of the corruption of the Church, among both clergy and bishops, as described in the writings and speeches of three contemporaries, John Wycliffe, William Langland and, the most famous, Geoffrey Chaucer.

We only know the date of Julian's birth because the event of her life, an event which consumed her energies of body, mind and spirit for the rest of her long life, happened, she tells us, when she was $30\frac{1}{2}$ years old, on Sunday, May 8th, 1373. In less than one week she experienced the sixteen revelations which were to be her sustenance for twenty years before she either committed them to writing herself or had them written down. That writing, *The Revelations of Divine Love*, the sharing of her spiritual experience, proved to be the first book written by a woman in the English language, a book which was largely ignored for 600 years, but has now, in the last fifty years, been re-discovered by many, including Thomas Merton, to be among the greatest of Christian mystical writings and its author to be "with John Newman the greatest English theologian."

We know nothing of her family or of the circumstances of her life; we do not know what led to her vocation to the life of an anchoress, a solitary, nor whether that decision came before or after the revelations which became the centre of her existence. We do know that her special calling was to contemplative silence, to solitude, and to recitation of the psalms and prayers of the church, in her anchorhold, a tiny house fixed to the outside wall of a church in Norwich. In this setting her long life pursued its course subsequent to her overwhelming experience of the Love of God. Her silence, however, did not prohibit her from being available to give comfort and advice to those who wished to come to her day by day. Her one room had two windows, one into the church where she could see the altar and could take part in the Eucharist, the central sacrament of Christian life, while through the other window which faced the busy street those in need could call to her and ask for the strength of her advice and prayers. Seated there between those two widows, she never ceased to dive deeper into the abyss of love which had opened up before her on that May day of 1373.

It was some years earlier, in the middle of that century, that a young woman week by week, even day by day, had stood at her devotions before the frescoes in certain of the churches of Norwich, frescoes in which the death of Christ on the Cross was depicted, not simply as physical suffering (as was common elsewhere in Europe) but as glorious triumph, with colours to match the glory. (These have in recent years been discovered and are in the cathedral of Norwich, revealing what Julian surely saw 600 years ago). It may well have been those times spent before the cross that led Julian to three longings, expressed in prayer, which she later saw as preparatory for the extraordinary revelations given to her in 1373.

Julian requested, firstly, that she be allowed to enter into "the mind of the passion", that the awareness of the sufferings of her Son which Mary, the Mother of Christ, had in its fullness, might be given to her also. In her own words: "I made this first petition so that after I would have a more true consciousness of the Passion of Christ." (ch. 2). The second request sprang from the first, and was a desire to participate in the suffering as far as is possible, even to the point of dying. She wished, as God's gift, for an illness which would bring her to the moment of dying when she herself and those around her would believe that her last hour had come, so that both the mercy of God and the terror of death might be hers, that eventually this experience of death might lead to a fuller living for the glory of God. She prayed that this might happen before she reached the age of thirty. She realised that these two prayers, for a deeper sharing in the Passion of Christ and for sickness to death, were uncommon prayers, so she added the condition: "Lord, you know what I want. If it is your will for me to have it, let me have it. If it is not your will, good Lord, do not be displeased, for I only want what you will."

The third gift which this young girl prayed for, a gift which sprang from a great longing, was for three "wounds" while she was still alive on this earth, the wound of true contrition, the wound of natural compassion and the wound of a full-hearted longing for God. She prayed this third prayer unconditionally, with the whole of herself. Then she adds, with her typical straight-forwardness, that she forgot all about the first two requests, while the third was always coming back to mind. Could it be that the "forgetting" of her first and second requests was a necessary pre-condition for their being answered?

Years later — how many, who knows? — illness struck. Julian in one week of high fever became desperately ill. The earlier request to become mortally ill had sunk so far into her unconscious that she found the illness most unwelcome and the thought of dying altogether distasteful, not because she was fearful but because she wanted to love God better and for a longer time before she tasted more fully the bliss of heaven. Nevertheless she was sinking...On the fourth night the family sent for the parish priest to anoint her with oil. For three more days and nights she lingered and then it became clear that she could not live until morning. Once more the priest came; he administered the last rites, her eyes became fixed, she grew delirious and her senses began to fade. The image of Christ on the cross was brought right up to her almost unseeing eyes; she had spoken her last, everything grew dark and a shortness of breath indicated the end.

Then it all began! Things previously known to her intellectually as a Christian became vividly real; they were totally present; the Lord was present, dying, living, speaking, loving. The past became the present: the relationship immediate. Certain onlookers, Julian's mother, her parish priest, a few friends, were present, at least at the beginning of the thirty hours or so of the "visions", but she alone "saw" and heard and at more than one point exclaimed (in ungrammatical Church-Latin): "Benedicite, domine! Benedicite, domine!" — "Bless, O Lord! Bless, O Lord!" even, on one occasion (ch.13) "Laughing loud and long"... "for I understood that we may laugh, comforting ourselves and rejoicing in God that the devil has been overcome."

Some long time after her full recovery, Julian was to record the Revelations as she had received them. She herself divided them into sixteen distinct "showings". Some she could see with her own eyes (she called them 'corporeal'); others were strong impressions on her mind, while the third type of teachings she called 'spiritual', in which she knew she was being taught but experienced no actual hearing.

These 'showings' or revelations are not shared with us in an orderly or systematic way. She was a theologian in the sense of the fourth century Desert Father who said: "He who really prays is a theologian and he who is a theologian really prays"! They came to her in that short period of days and it was in silence and prayer that she spent the next forty or fifty years, assimilating them. Many were surprises to her, others she puzzled over for years, asking questions and finding deeper levels of meaning as she lived with them. Indeed her work of feeding on this living Truth was never completed;

in the very last chapter, 86, she says: "this book has been begun by God's gift and his grace, but it has not yet been completed, as I see it." The same is true of more than the book; indeed we have a taste, a strong taste of fullness here, but there is always more "without end" — with which two words Julian concludes her account.

It is for this reason that every reader, every listener, to Julian's book, has his or her part to perform in the 'completing' of the book, in the giving of an active response. There is in the whole both a hub — a central truth — and the spokes, the unfolding of the truth in that same silence and prayer. Fifteen and more years was not a long enough time for Julian to reach the bottom of the abyss, for there was always more. "From the time of the showing (she wrote), I desired frequently to understand what our Lord's meaning was, and more than fifteen years afterward I was answered by a spiritual understanding that said, 'Do you want to understand your Lord's meaning in this experience? Understand it well: love was his meaning. Who showed it to you? Love. What did he show you? Love. Why did he show it? For love. Hold yourself in this truth and you shall understand and know more in the same vein. And you will never know or understand anything else in it forever."' (ch. 86)

Having turned to the end for a clue to enlighten the whole, we turn with Julian to the first experience that came to her at the point of her own near-dying and returning to life. This was the seeing of the crucifixion of Jesus, being present again at the dying of the Lord Jesus, finding the 'blessed Lady Mary' (the Mother of Jesus) present also, and being vividly aware of his great suffering and bloodshed, the discolouration of his face and the drying up of his flesh. Being aware of the agony of the passion of her Master, Julian became also, strangely, a sharer again and again in Joy. She inwardly knew that when Jesus appeared to her, the Blessed Trinity (whom she knew in Christian teaching from earliest childhood) was meant. "In this same showing (of the crucifixion), suddenly the Trinity completely filled my heart with the greatest joy. And so, understood it, will it be in heaven, without an end, for those who come there.... The Trinity is our everlasting lover. The Trinity is our endless joy and our bliss, through our Lord Jesus Christ and in our Lord Jesus Christ." (ch. 4) The suffering and joy of Lady Mary were inseparable and so it was and would be for Julian and for all who would discover the secret of Love. It was for Love that Jesus Christ suffered, the Love that He has for each person. Only when with Mary we recognise our nothingness, may we "love and have the uncreated God". (ch.5) Only there/here in Him do we find our being in God, almighty, all-wise, all good, and this is discovered when a simple soul comes to Him "nakedly, plainly and unpretentiously, for he is the natural dwelling of the soul touched by the holy Spirit." (ch. 5) We can understand why Julian found herself praying: "God, of your goodness, give me yourself, for you are enough for me. I can ask nothing less that is completely to your honour, and if I do ask anything less, I shall always be in want. Only in you I have all." (ch.5)

This life in God is our "natural will" and it is the good will of God "to have us". Until we have Him in the fullness of joy we fail to know who we are, for "our soul is so specially loved by him who is the highest that it goes far beyond the ability of any creature to realize it."

It is as she ponders this immeasurable love and her own littleness and poverty (greater even than Mary's) that she is overwhelmed with the courtesy and "great unassuming friendliness" of her God and Lord. He who is highest, mightiest, noblest and worthiest, "becomes lowest and meekest, friendliest and most courteous" and she adds... "This marvellous joy shall be shown us all when we see him." Julian's "humble God" was shown to her and it is in His humility,

His homeliness and courtesy that He relates to us in this life. No wonder that the crucifixion, so vivid and lifelike, hideous and dreadful, was also "sweet and lovely", a revelation of the compassionate courtesy with which God unceasing approaches His creation. She marvelled that this could be so and that she might be intimately related to such a God. Imagine Julian's astonishment when she "saw" the Lord "royally reigning in heaven", filling it with joy and mirth. She continues: "He himself endlessly gladdened and solaced his valued friends most modestly and courteously with the marvellous melody of endless love in his own fair, blessed face. This glorious countenance of the godhead completely fills all heaven with joy and bliss." The awareness that God thanks every man and woman for their years of service "especially for the years of those who deliberately and freely offer their youth to God" leaves her speechless. And she adds: "the more the loving soul sees this courtesy of God the more anxious it is to serve him all its life." (ch.14)

This "sharing in the divine laughter", God wanting our souls to be "merrily (cheerfully) occupied with his grace", brings her to see that "in us he delights without end, and in the same way we shall delight in him, with his grace."

But we would be very wrong if we imagined that Julian, in her awareness of the all-embracing love of God and of the joy that is its concomitant, was less than realistic in face of sin and evil. Both the vision of Christ's death and of his struggles with Evil, not to mention the cries of suffering and fear and brutality of her fourteenth century which were brought to her at the second of her windows, removed every temptation to minimise sin. The horror of evil is present and she is well aware that this pervades the world in which — then also — the poor and the oppressed were the ones to feel most crushingly its weight.

In face of this evil Julian knew — for she had seen it with

her own eyes — that there can be no wrath in God. True, in the Old Testament of the Christian Scriptures, she read of His wrath and anger as of a wrathful judge, against evil and the evil-doer. This wrath always implies blame, the blaming of others as of ourselves, which too speedily we attribute to God. Her experience of God's love in the Showings made her know that God never blames, that His goodness and love outweigh by far the awful evidence of the world's evil and the damnation thereafter which she was taught by the Church to be the destination of those refusing salvation. Julian longed to resolve this intolerable paradox, this impossible contradiction, and she learnt to do so (as Merton tells us) not by solving the contradiction but by "remaining in the midst of it, in peace" knowing that in God — in the final analysis, beyond our human comprehension — it is already solved.

Of the many places where this struggle continues in her, and between her and her Master (for she wrestles also with him in these matters which are beyond her),[2] she sees, as from "the other side", what evil means. In one place she writes: "Our failing is full of dread, our falling is full of shame, and our dying is full of sorrow. But still, in all this, the sweet eye of pity and love never departs from us, and the working of mercy does not cease. . . Grace brings about raising and rewarding, endlessly surpassing what our loving and our bitter labour deserve, as it spreads abroad and shows the noble, abundant largesse of God's royal lordship in his marvellous courtesy. This comes from the abundance of love." A little later she writes: "I saw no kind of wrath in God, neither for the short-term nor for the long, for truly, as I saw it, if God could be angry even a touch, we should never have life, nor place, nor being", "God cannot forgive" — because He already has!

However cruel and crazy the world might be — hers and ours — and however beyond her it was to understand with her

---

[2]Chapters 48 and 49.

mind the teaching of the Church as regards hell and damnation, the words — perhaps the most famous of the whole *Showings* — rang again and again in her, words spoken by "her good Lord" who said: "*All shall be well.*" — "You yourself shall see that all manner of things shall be well." And yet later, when she considered those millions "who die outside the faith of holy Church" and those who are "baptized christians and yet live unchristian lives and so die outside of charity", she confesses "it seemed to me impossible that all manner of things should be well, as our Lord had showed me." And the answer came: "What is impossible to you is not impossible to me. I shall have my word in all things,and I shall make all things well."

Those insistent questions of hers could only find fuller answer when in a spiritual teaching she learnt of the Lord's secret purposes. "It belongs", she heard "to royal lordship of God that he has his secret purposes in peace"; to us His servants belong obedience and reverence, not full knowledge of His purposes. The great secret, hidden in God, by which it will be seen how all things shall be well, is only known to Christ and to the Father; it is, Julian saw, "forever necessary for us to stop ourselves from speculating on what the great and secret deed shall be." By willing nothing but what God wills for us our way of faith is clear, for, "the more we busy ourselves to know his (God's) secrets, in that or anything else, the further away we shall be from knowing them." Enough for her that the "great deed", which will be known only when it is done, is safe in the loving will of God.

With that as background and foreground — the total and all-embracing love of God — how could Julian be anything but an optimist, full of invincible hope? She was clearly a theological optimist, diametrically opposed to the sin-centred pessimism of popular theology amidst the devastating collapse of cultural and spiritual values of her century. Perhaps at first reading her account of the *Showings of Love* which makes no reference to current affairs, nor to the human sufferings taking place around her, may seem a spiritual vision unrelated to the pains and agonies of humanity. It was, I believe, her optimism, founded on deep faith and absolute conviction, that constrained her to see every historical happening, however brutal and tragic, as contained in God's overriding purpose of love. What ground could there be for worry and despair when "our heavenly Mother Jesus can never allow us who are his children to perish."(ch. 61) At another time Julian says: "I saw with full certainty that God never changes his purpose in the slightest degree, and never shall forever." (ch. 11) Her unshakable optimism was able to transcend the twistedness of the world and of human actions and decisions, for this word rang in her: "See! I am God. See! I am in all things. See! I do all things. See! I never take my hands off my works, and never shall forever. See! I lead all things to the end I ordained for them from eternity, by the same might, wisdom and love by which I made them. How should anything be amiss?" (ch. 11) Those six words, "I shall make all things well" were to cover every eventuality; they will be shown to be conclusive when the "deed", the secret deed unknown to all creatures, is performed at the end of time, when "shall the same blessed Trinity make well all that is not well." (ch. 32) 'Can one need more assurance than this?', asks Julian of herself and of her readers.

The wonder of God, so near and real, brings Julian[3] to the insight: "Our Mother Jesus, He..." This was no grammatical error for she "saw" that "as truly as God is our Father, so truly is God our Mother." Maybe she knew that she was standing in a long succession of Christian mystics and theologians, such as Anselm, Aquinas, Bernard of Cluny, Mechtild of Magdeburg and a number of others for whom this was

[3]Ch. 59, 60, 61.

no new idea, but she makes no attempt to bolster her own witness by their names. Nor is she in any sense a feminist, many of whom today spring to use her words to support their own stance. Her mystical knowledge that sees God to be Mother springs direct from her awareness of God's love given to each of His creatures. "Our substance is in our Father, God Almighty. Our substance is in our Mother, God All-wisdom. And our substance is in our Lord God the Holy Spirit, All-goodness. For our substance is whole in each person of the Trinity, which is one God. Our sensuality is only in the Second Person, Christ Jesus..." (ch. 58) Far from Christ being "like our mother", he is the prototype of all motherhood and human motherhood is a reflection of his, "though it is true that our bodily bringing forth is very little, low and simple compared to our spiritual bringing forth, yet it is he (Christ) who does the mothering in the creatures by whom it is done." He it is who "borns" us! At every stage, birth, infancy, youth and age it is he, "our natural mother, our gracious mother", who himself "most humbly and most mildly" was born from Mary's womb and who in turn gives birth to us. And this is the truth underlying the "motherhood" of all things. There can be no doubt that Julian would find equality between the sexes — a matter with which we modern people in the west are so concerned — to be a corollary of the fact that both feminine and masculine are divine; there can be nothing and no one who stands apart from the fatherhood and motherhood of God. A true loving of God is the result of the "blessed love Christ works in us". It is our Mother Christ who says: "If I could suffer more (for love of all), I would suffer more...I am what you love." How, asks Julian, rhetorically, for she knows the answer, "can our heavenly mother, Jesus, allow any of us his children to perish?"

Where is one to find the solution, Julian asked herself, to the appalling dilemmas of her day, to the suffering and blatant evil, to the unrestrained love of self and of power, wellnigh as present in the life of the Church as in the life of society, in her century as in ours? Does the sociologist or the psychologist, or the philosopher or the technocrat or the politician or the theologian hold that answer? For this woman of Norwich there is only one place, only one way out, in which all ways are related, that is, in a mystical solution.

We may indeed find her mystical experience extraordinary. It was certainly a great marvel for her that God's unconditional love, a love utterly unqualified in its generosity, should be offered to her, a simple, unlettered, uneducated woman, and it was precisely her ordinariness which made her certain that this transcendent love of God was for everyone, everywhere. The extraordinary nature of this mystical experience was for the most ordinary of human beings, for it was for her, in no sense an élite specialist in spiritual matters. She would struggle for years to write an account of this experience that had come so miraculously to her, for how could she keep the marvel of God's all-embracing love to herself when so obviously, so clearly, it was the truth of every man, woman and child of the human race.

For her the daily life of each person was gifted with this secret of God; no high flights of strange heavenly powers, no extravagances in behaviour, no trances and levitations, no denial of human sense, no extreme asceticism, no spiritual emotions or striking signs and manifestations. Simply — and marvellously — the transformation of the daily reality of each person's 'world', for each finds Augustine speaking for him or herself: "Thou hast made us for thyself, O God, and our hearts are restless until they find their rest in thee."

In Julian's century and country there were only Catholic believers; she knew (but hardly as a part of her lived experience) that others existed elsewhere and that they too were included in Christ's word to her (already quoted): "What is impossible to you is not impossible to me." She knew, and shared with others her conviction, both at the window on to the road and in her sharing of her experience on paper, that her experience of union with God was as much for her neighbours in Norwich as for any who might chance upon her book of the *Showings of Divine Love*. If someone should see her as a mystic standing over against others, in a spiritually superior position to others, she would at once give the reply: "receiving the showing doesn't make me good, unless I love God better as a result" (ch. 9), "for in truth, it was not shown me that God loved me any better than he loves the last soul that is in grace." How can there be anything to be proud of when, in the light of God's 'I made it', 'I love it', 'I keep it' (of the small hazelnut), it is all from His side?

This led to Julian's emphasis on littleness, and nothingness. God is the "natural dwelling" of created beings and we human beings can only awake to this fact when we come "nakedly, plainly and unpretentiously". This leads to that increasingly single-minded desire and longing for God alone, without which one cannot be opened by the Spirit to the reality of the Great Lover of humankind and of all creation.

It was Julian's experience that once these truths are realised, that "only in you I have all", then prayer takes on "a new face." Becoming one with God, the awareness that one is "enclosed in God", far from being God's gift to us after death, is knowledge given in a life of prayer. She herself experienced the simplification of her prayer (ch. 6), "For as the body is clad in the clothes, and the flesh in the skin, and the bones in the flesh, and the heart in the whole, so are we, soul and body, clad and enclosed in the goodness of God. Yes, and more intimately than this, for all these may waste and wear away, but the goodness of God is ever whole and closer to us than any comparison can show." This awareness of being enclosed in God's love is beyond description, beyond words, but with His grace and His help we may stand in spirit "gazing with endless wonder at this lofty, unmeasurable love beyond human scope that Almighty God has for us of his goodness. And therefore we may ask our Love, with reverence, all that we will."

The result of this "mystical awareness" with which every person is endowed by creation is, Julian tells us from her own experience, a sense that one is becoming less in one's own sight, a sense of reverent awe at the marvel of one who is "enclosed in God", and a great sense of love toward one's fellows. Outwardly Julian, in common with any hermit or solitary, might appear to be endowed with personal, even individual spiritual maturity and growth. In fact it was her awareness of the Divine Mystery, the Holy Trinity, which imparted to her a love — His/Her Love — which embraces all.

This mystical inter-relatedness, including all persons and all matter (if such a dichotomy is allowed) has no boundaries. What has been called 'cosmic allurement' draws all that is into the Circle of Love, the Divine Mystery, and the photograph taken from space by an astronaut, the Planet Home, becomes as much the symbol of Julian's vision of inner space as of humanity's growing awareness of outer space. The universe is one. What for years we have described as 'inner' or 'outer' are but two facets of one whole; the new cosmic vision confirms Julian's intuition, the *Showings of Love* are yet to be completed and will be "without end". The lesson of love has now a cosmic dimension which leads to ever greater depths of silence and of worship of that permeating presence which enfolds all and from which nobody and nothing is excluded.

When Joseph Campbell was asked his advice to a young person setting out on his life's journey, he replied: "Follow your bliss." Would Julian, standing at that window looking on to the busy street of Norwich six centuries ago have answered differently? In truth, there is only one journey and "all shall be well".

References

Those well acquainted with Julian of Norwich will recognise that this paper owes much to the following works:

Christ our Mother , by Brant Pelphrey (London, Darton, Longman and Todd, 1989)

Julian Woman of our Day , edited by Robert Llewelyn (London, Darton, Longman and Todd, 1985)

A Lesson of Love , by John-Julian (New York, Walker and Co., 1988) Mother Julian's own book, *Revelations of Divine Love*, translated by M.L. Maestro (Doubleday, Image Books 1977).

THE ACTIVE MYSTICISM OF ST IGNATIUS LOYOLA

George Gispert-Sauch

From September 27th 1990 to 31st July 1991, Jesuits the world over celebrated the Ignatian year to mark the fifth centenary of the birth of the founder, Iñigo Ibañez de Loyola Sanchez (better known as Ignatius of Loyola), the last of the eleven legitimate children of a nobleman and feudal lord in a remote valley of the Basque country in northern Spain. As he has been an influential force not only in the Church but in European culture in general and at the same time a mystic of great depth, I thought an analysis of his type of mysticism would be appropriate in this Seminar.

A contemporary of Guru Nanak, although 22 years junior, Ignatius lived at a time of great social transformation in the European culture (1491-1556), right in the middle of the Renaissance signalling the birth of the modern Western world. During his life-time Columbus discovered the American continent for the Europeans, Vasco da Gama landed in Kozhikode, the first colonial empires were shaped. Luther, eight years older than Ignatius, protested against the power of the Church, and the religious unity of the European world was shattered even when the Muslim Empire had just been terminated on the Iberian soil. (In fact, the grandfather of Ignatius had fought one of the last battles against the Muslims in South Spain.)

Ignatius came from the small nobility of the Basque country, a part of the newly formed Spanish nation. His early service at the court of a subordinate lord led him to take part in the war against the French forces battling on Spanish soil. Then, in 1521, a canon ball seemed to shatter both his leg and his ambitions for a future in the court. It happened just one month after Martin Luther had defied Church and Empire in the Diet of Worms. The 30-year-old soldier managed to pass successfully through the trial and still hoped to rebuild a future. Convalescence from three operations was long and painful. To while away the long hours, he asked for some of the novels of the period, the stories of knights and their exploits which Cervantes would ridicule a century later. None were found in the austere ancestral home. But they did find two books. (We must remember that it was barely 70 years since printing had been invented in Europe.) One was the *Life of Christ* by the fourteenth-century Carthusian Ludolf of Saxonia, and the other the *Golden Legend*, a collection of lives of saints, by the thirteenth-century Jacopode Varazze (Voragine). These he read with avidity and interest: from the *Life of Christ* he extracted passages and quotations, specially the words of Jesus and his mother. The lives of saints set him adreaming of exploits he could do like theirs.

It may be of interest to note in passing that through this reading Ignatius came unknowingly into contact with the Indian tradition. The *Golden Legend* contained, among others, the life of St Josaphat, celebrated on 27th of November in the Latin and on 26th August in the Eastern churches. It has been now satisfactorily proved that this is a Christianised version of the conversion and renunciation of the Bodhisattva, popular at the time in Europe, deriving from the *Lalitavistara* through Syrian and Arabic Versions.

These readings started Ignatius on a journey of introspection and a life adventure that eventually made a mystic out of Iñigo the solider. The steps of the journey make for a fascinating, if well-known, reading: a renunciation of the ancestral home and of his status as a nobleman, changing his dress for that of a beggar and a pilgrim; several months of *sādhanā* in Manresa, discovering the mystery of the Divine and of himself, partly with the help of the Church, partly with his own spiritual experimentation; a pilgrimage to Holy Land (Palestine) to be at the place where he wanted to remain though the political situation did not permit him to do so. This may be the real turning point in Ignatius's spiritual quest. Circumstances did not permit him to follow the initial longing after his conversion to physically imitate Jesus in Jesus' own country and according to his life-style. Now he will search for a new form of spirituality: to help people of his own country and culture in their spiritual quest. He has discovered his vocation as a guru.

He returned to Spain and embarked at thirty into a belated period of studies in Spain and in Paris, a fellow student first of little children and later of young men ten or fifteen years younger than him. This stage resulted in the emergence of a group of dedicated friends that would become the Society of Jesus, sharing in Ignatius mystical outlook. The final stage of the Journey brought Ignatius' to Rome to place the group at the disposal of the Pope, head of the Church, the community of faith. Ignatius will from now on direct the growing group drawing much from his continued mystical experience, until he was called to the Further Shore in 1556. The special features of Ignatian mysticism would be kept alive in the spiritual practice and teaching of that Jesuit order (the Society of Jesus) and through it in the Church at large and beyond. The new mysticism of a Teilhard de Chardin, for instance, cannot be understood if one does not take into consideration his Jesuit roots. It was a mysticism of action.

Presuppositions

Perhaps it is important to pause a moment and bring out some of the theoretical presuppositions of this mysticism. It is true that mysticism is not a theory, but a lived experience and in a sense a way of life. But this does not deny that every form of mysticism grows in a particular culture with its frame of reference. It may or may not be in conflict with the dominant culture, but it cannot escape its influence.

The first cultural and philosophical presupposition of Ignatius is that being and action are correlative: *agere sequitur esse* was a traditional philosophical axiom. The ultimate root of action is not *prakṛti* or the realm of the *rajas*. Action is rather positively related to *sat*. It is therefore not necessary that the mystic should renounce activity once the deeper awareness of Being has been attained. In mystical life the transparency of Being in our consciousness finds expression in a more authentic activity. There had been indeed in the Christian tradition a mysticism of withdrawal into a life of *nirvṛtti*: the Desert Fathers, the anachoretes, the monasteries and other contemplative life styles. But this is one type of mysticism. Ignatius follows a different path: the experience of the divine creates an atmosphere or a level of awareness wherein he searches for the will of God for his own life. Later we shall point out that his mysticism includes also a further dimension.

The religious and theological world of Ignatius was different. Creation does not come from *rajas* or from *prakṛti*, but from the very heart of God, the ultimate Reality. Action does not stand in opposition to *sattva* but as the very expression of *sat*. The mystical life, the transparency of Being in our consciousness, finds expression also in authentic activity.

Another presupposition of the mysticism of Ignatius is a view of history as shot through with purpose, with a divine will. The world is not destined to be sublated even when it comes to an end, but to be resurrected, and history is not unrelated to eschatology. The mystical experience for Ignatius does not merely consist in the awareness of the divine at the heart of the universe in which he led his whole life, but rather in finding the thrust, the direction of the divine purpose and freely allowing himself to be taken into its movement. His military background may lead him to use military metaphors. But the more fundamental experience is the experience of purpose in action.

A third presupposition of Ignatian mysticism, consequent with what has been said, is that the Spirit, the Self, the Ultimate Reality of the Universe, is active. Activity is not a prerogative of matter: in fact Europeans tended then to see matter as of itself passive. For Ignatius God in His/Her/Its inner Self is active — or better pure act, and this is what the Trinity ultimately implies. God is also active in regard to the world that emerges from the Sovereign free will, and to which God is not a stranger.

Mysticism, therefore, in the Ignatian context cannot be identified with pure contemplation, with non-active life, even though some withdrawal from action has always been part of the mystical tradition. Much less could we identify mysticism with the paranormal phenomena attributed or found in mystics. Both the Indian and the Christian traditions are at one in discounting or giving little importance to the various *siddhis* said to be produced in the mystics by their intimate contact with the divine: visions, miracles, raptures, seeing in the distance, foretelling the future, acting on others, levitations, etc. Some of these may be phenomena consequent to the mystical state, but they cannot be identified with it.

The Path

The mystical path of Ignatius is perhaps best articulated in the little manual which he wrote, entitled *The Spiritual Exercises.* The title itself may make little sense in a traditional Indian context: exercises belong to the body, to matter, not to the Spirit. The Spirit is characterised by quiet, by luminosity ... However, we are not strangers to the concept of *sādhanās* and this could be the best translation of the idea of the spiritual exercises. They are a collection of reflections, a practical advice to help the master to lead the *sādhaka* to the goal which Ignatius would consider central to the mystical life.

Ignatius explains the purpose which he envisages in two simple words: *to order one's life*. Human life is definitely not what it should be. It is not only a question of suffering, nor even merely of sin and passion. It is also a question of disorientation. Our life needs enlightenment and orientation: *to order*. What will be the principle of order? Elsewhere in the book Ignatius spells this out as "to seek and find the will of God in the disposition of one's life"(1).[1] The presupposition here is clear: *there is* a will of God for each one, a direction to be given to one's life, a superior plan not perceptible in the course of ordinary daily consciousness, a plan which has been disturbed by sin or other interferences, but which can be found out with a spiritual method. One should note that it is not a question of discovering one's future life or knowing now what options we should take in the future. The exercises aim at ensuring the right decision *now*, for the orientation I need to give to my life today.

The method consists in negatively removing interferences, evil influences, forces that prevent the needle of one's life from pointing firmly and decisively to the North of God. Ignatius is quite realistic in his language: "to overcome oneself". The Exercises mean to be engaged in a battle not so much against external forces as against oneself — obviously in the area of what we in India call the *ahaṃkāra*; the superficial level where so many of our decisions are taken and so much of our lives lived. The idea is to stop us from taking decisions when,

[1] All numbers in brackets refer to that traditional sections of the book *The Spiritual Exercises*.

in his language, we are "determined (or influenced) by disorderly affections" — the *rāga-dveṣa* of the Gītā and other spiritual literature of India. Ignatius speaks of "removing all disordered affections" which in his language include all sinful decisions, even if only superficially sinful, or desires that are not expressions of absolutely right intention, and also all influences from wrong philosophies or cultural factors that often form part of our unconsciously accepted environment and could lead us astray from the right path. He finally tells us that we will progress in the mystical life in the measure in which we come out from the sphere of self-love, self-will and self-interest — again the word *self* expressing not the Indian *ātman* but the world of *ahaṃkāra*.

So far for the negative aspects of the *sādhanā*. One might think that the only requirement to achieve the ordering of one's life would be to achieve detachment from all *rāga-dveṣa* which alone can stand as an obstacle to the will of God. After that, it would only be a question of instruction on the way of perfection which such a duly prepared *sādhaka* would accept and assimilate without difficulty. Not so, Ignatius aims at a mystical life. The finding of God's will should be God's own revelation, God's direct (*aparokṣa*) contact with the *sādhaka* who has to prepare himself or herself for this. The ideal is to let one's whole life, at all levels of decision, be atune to the will of God under the inspiration of the life of Jesus Christ, the supreme model for the Christian; specially to perceive the will of God for one's concrete self here and how and not as a copy of any other life. Ignatius does not want to *teach* the *sādhaka about* the will of God. He does not know it. Only God knows it. The retreatant who has overcome the self, i.e., all false attachments, only prepares himself or herself to discover the divine direction in life. This direction can only be known by a mystical experience, a mystical level of consciousness. Ignatius says that the retreat is not a time for good advice or direct instruction by a guru — much as this may be laudable in other times and circumstances — but a time so to seek the Divine Reality that the Divine would itself reveal itself to the *sādhaka*, making him or her ablaze with the divine Presence, in love and adoration. The Creator will act directly on the creature, and the creature directly deal with the Creator (15).

Four Weeks, Three Mārgas

The *sādhanā* of the exercises is meant to last for about one month. The *sādhaka*, called the retreatant, is asked to renounce for this time all worldly activities and to devote the whole day — including part of the night — to prayer in a variety of methods, to reflection, to making oneself open and sensitive to the call of God. All the exercises, all the activities are oriented to the one thing: to order one's life by seeking and finding the divine purpose so as to act accordingly. The month is divided into four so-called weeks, varying in length according to the *adhikāra* of the retreatant.

St. Ignatius himself relates the four weeks to the traditional three ways or *mārgas* of the spiritual life as explained in Christian mystical theology (10). This classification is evidently different from the three *mārgas* of classical Hinduism. In the Christian context they represent successive stages of the spiritual or mystical growth, not alternative ways for different *adhikārins*. However, elements of the first and second stages continue to influence the third. The classification into the three ways, called the purgative, the illuminative and the unitive ways, was probably introduced into Christian literature by that great lover of triads, the Pseudo-Dyonisius, possibly a Syrian monk of aroud AD 500 who was deeply influenced by Greek thought. He called the three ways 'the purification of the uninitiated', 'the initiation of the purified' and 'the perfection of the initiated'. (A parallel but different division is at times found in Christian literature, that of "beginners, proficient and perfect".)

The first week of the Exercises corresponds obviously to the way of purification. The centre of the *sādhaka's* meditation is God's mercies on one's own sins and on the evil of the world, so that the meditation lead him or her to a new burst of gratitude and life and a decision to enter the good way in response to God's mercy and forgiveness. The aim is that the *sādhaka* comes to a clear frame of mind purified of the sinful past and rejecting whatever is imperfect, as far as he or she can, and of whatever may lead astray from God's path. Purification is the leitmotif. The strengthening of the will of the retreatant is the major thrust. But obviously the *sādhaka* alway counts on and prays for God's grace in this process of growth.

In the second week one enters into the period of illumination. The focus is the life and teachings of Jesus Christ which constitute the supreme model and inspiration for the Christian believer. But this contemplation on the life of Jesus is done from a specific perspective: what is the *purpose* of this life, what *orientation* does it show? At the heart of the week is the reflection and experience of the subtle ways in which Jesus, and therefore the retreatant too, can be tempted under the *ābhāsa* of goodness: the ways of triumphalism, of victory in God's name, the external show that so often accompanies religious attitudes and in fact corrupts them. Jesus is shown as overcoming these temptations and taking a different path, where he trod the ways of the poor, accepting the humiliations and the cross they brought, in love and without flinching. The *sādhaka* is now authentically free of attachments or fears to reflect on his or her own life and the orientation it has to take, not so much at the general level of opting for good, but at the concrete level of specific *choices*: how, in concrete, will my life be ordered so as to reflect fully the divine will for it? In *which way* has one to attain the good? Given the concrete possibilities in my life, what is the option most atune to the divine purpose?

To discover this and to embark upon it one cannot just rely on *tarka*, reason, even if it is rightly applied. One needs an illumination that raises us above the *vyavahārika* play of reason and of good resolutions. Underlying the method used here is the experience that first began at Loyola when Ignatius was a convalescing soldier and which coloured all his life and mysticism. While reading the life of Christ and of the saints Ignatius would dream of all sorts of exploits for Christ in the future of his life ahead of him. But Ignatius discovered then a new world. Let me quote Paramananda Divarkar who possibly better than anybody else has analyzed the conversion experience of Ignatius:

> What made all the difference, and eventually brought about a thorough transformation, was his growing awareness of something that was taking place at a level more profound than thought or feeling, in an area of his being whose very existence was a surprising revelation to him, where he was most truly himself and closest to God. This is how it happened: It dawned on him that though he derived great pleasure both from his pious considerations and from his sentimental reveries, yet deep down, the former brought him peace and contentment, whilst the latter did not. He came to recognize the first as godly — that is, as leading to God and presumably coming from God — whereas the others were not. A marginal note added to the text of the Autobiography tells us that *this was first reflection on the things of God; and later, when he composed the Exercises, it was from this experience that he began to clarify his ideas with regard to the diversity of spirits.* Ignatius' religious experience had from the start

> two marked characteristics: it was the awareness of a *happening* rather than of an idea, of *an active God* who not so much said as did something; and it occurred at the depth of his personality which became his base, so to speak, for responding to God and for assessing the worth of all his reactions to reality.[2]

This will be the method that he proposes to the *sādhakas* in the Exercises. He wants them to reach the depth of the personality, underneath the *vṛttis* activated by meditation and contemplation, to the level underlying the surface activity, where God is most actively present. Perhaps we could speak of a descent from the *manas* level to the *buddhi*, where true wisdom resides, or deeper to the reality of the *ātman*.

One might ask here why Ignatius does not follow the way of *quieting* the *vṛttis* through shutting out all the doors of thought and affectivity. He rather uses the *vṛttis* as passages that lead him to the deeper level where the divine is directly experienced.

The contrast need not be exaggerated. In the Upaniṣads, at any rate, *śravaṇa* and *manana* are also means to reach the *brahmabodha*. However this is not so in the way of Yoga or in the Buddhist Vipassana meditation where the ideal is to suppress all movements and activity of the mind.

On the other hand, although we do not find the ways of Patañjali Yoga in the method of Ignatius, still he does tell his *sādhaka* that the mental activity should lead to the deeper levels, and that one should stop and rest wherever one finds spiritual fruit and satisfaction (76), because "much knowledge does not fill and satisfy a person but to *internally experience* and taste reality" (2). We think we have here the principle of

---

[2] "Ignatius of Loyola, the Inside Story" in *Vidyajyoti Journal* 54 (1990, p. 435).

inwardness, of reaching the deeper levels of being well beyond the world of the *vṛttis*.

In spite of this convergence, I think that there are differences in the spiritual discipline of the two paths, and they are rooted in the different perceptions of the meaning of action. The Yoga tradition hopes to see the deeper levels of the waters after achieving perfect *prasāda* or quiet, serenity, because the absence of ripples enables us to see the depth. The Ignatian tradition seeks to perceive the divine in the power underlying the movement of the waves. Action is the transparent epiphany of Being provided we are able to see it. And Being is dynamic.

The exercitant or retreatant is taught by God the way Ignatius was. We remember that he experienced the different emotions during his readings at Loyola and how he sort of detached himself from the first level or *vṛttis* and could see the underlying forces that were moving him, and so reach the deeper levels where God was speaking to him. With patience the *sādhaka* will be able to know with the certainty and depth of the mystic, the purpose of God in his or her life, the orientation he or she should give to the life itself. It is interesting to notice that one of the signs that Ignatius gives to discern the authentic touch of God in the flow of one's *vṛttis* as distinguishable from inauthentic human or devilish influences, is peace and deep joy. The *Nārada Bhakti Sūtra* also speaks in a similar context of discernment of *śāntiparamānandarūpatvāt*. This is the effect of the divine touch in the depths of the self.

If the second week is the period of illumination regarding one's life and one's future, the third and fourth weeks together represent the unitive way. Their purpose is to seal the awareness of God's self-communication to the *sādhaka* with a deeper personal experience of His presence, in some ways similar to the *abheda* or *advaita* experience of the Indian tradition, although probably not identically the same.

The retreatant contemplates the passion and death of Jesus (third week) and his risen life after the resurrection (fourth week) as given in the Gospel accounts and other New Testament texts. He or she sees him as the Lord who continues invisibly present to the world and to the *sādhaka* and who guides the exercitant and the community to which he or she belongs. The level of union with the Lord is now much more than merely knowing the direction of one's life and God's will to be accomplished. It is a union at the deeper levels of the person where the emotional and affective are rooted so that the retreatant shares in the suffering and the joy of the Lord. This sharing is not so much at the levels of *harṣa-śoka* as the deep level of *nirvāṇa* and *ānanda*, or perhaps better, the level of love in its purest and deepest form, both as suffering love and joyful love. The retreatant achieves not only sympathy for the Lord, a vibration of his emotions in reaction to the Lord's emotions, but a union, a real share in the very reality of the death and new life of Jesus.

The Supreme Goal Beyond the Purpose

The goal of the Exercises of Ignatius is perhaps best expressed in the last contemplation of the book that reflects his type of mysticism. The purpose of this *sādhana* is summarised in one phrase: to have such an experience of the divine that one enters into a new consciousness, a new basic attitude wherein one is able '*ever to love and to serve*'. It is at this level that one could speak of an Ignatian *abhedabhāva* because one is able to find God in all things and all things in God. The isolation of the individual, his false autonomy, his metaphysical distance from the Creator is overcome in a vision of union. But this union is not static, solitary, a bath of the mystic in pure being, alone with the alone, but a union with a being that eternally manifests itself in action — or perhaps action, *karma*, is not the right term, rather love, a dynamic and saving power, the *śakti* which underlies the universe. Ignatius hopes that the *sādhaka* will enter into a new consciousness of the divine reality as operative within the whole universe and renounce his or her autonomy and independence and surrender to the power of love that surrounds the world.

The final goal of the *sādhaka* is perhaps best expressed in the characteristic prayer which Ignatius asks the *sādhaka* to pray repeatedly during this contemplation:

> Take, Lord, and receive all my liberty, my memory, my understanding, and my will — all that I have and possess. You, Lord, have given all that to me. I now give it back to you, O Lord. All of it is yours. Dispose of it according to your will. Give me love of yourself along with your grace, for that is enough for me. (234)

Here we seem to go beyond the scope of the *sādhanā* of the Exercises. We are no longer seeking the ways along which we have to express our commitments. That was a necessary step and orientation that was needed, the immediate issue of the *sādhana*. But not the ultimate goal. The end is surrender of everything to the Lord, letting the Lord take over, so to speak, and live himself and act in the *sādhaka*. The *sādhaka* needs only the infusion of a superior degree of love which can only be God's gift of grace. This is enough.

This dimension of Ignatian mysticism appears at first sight to go deeper and beyond the mysticism of action. We have a glimpse of it in the life and specially in the spiritual Diary of Ignatius, a small portion of which (1544–45) has been kept. It reveals a life of intimate communion with the Trinity — the God he had known from his infancy, from the Church and from his theological studies. The diary and other words of Ignatius show him in intimate union in the life of God. He lives an intense awareness of the Father, the Son and the Spirit, the foci of the Divine Unity.

It would appear at first sight that the Incarnation is somewhat lost sight of in this kind of writing. The active commitment is not mentioned in the Contemplation for Obtaining Love. Only total surrender, the Divine taking hold of the creature, and love as the one thing that lasts. Yet this apparent transcendence of the experience of love is never quite remote from concrete options: the contemplation is part of the Exercises which are oriented to find the right option in life. The Diary of Ignatius is written at the time of the inner deliberation regarding concrete ways in which the Jesuits would have to live in the Church and the world. This discernment is essential to the Diary. The mystical includes and embraces the concrete active options one takes, even if it overflows into the realm of the absolute Mystery.

It is interesting to note that the contemplation sees the divine reality as Source, as immanently active and as giving out its own energy for the love of the whole created world. The final vision is one of all things descending from that Supreme Reality like the rays from the sun, the waters from spring. We are not far away from the *bimba-pratibimbavāda*, even if interpreted in a Christian context, the dynamism of all things being integrated into a unitary vision.

Thus we are introduced in the mystical reality of Ignatius: 'finding God in all things and all things in God' an expression reminiscent of a *śloka* of the Gītā. His mysticism is not only contemplative: it is one of surrender to the divine power of love. All descends from above but, more important, all is an expression of an active love that leads all things to a final consummation. This would be the Ignatian *abheda-bhāva*, nonseparation (or is it *bhedābheda*?). The words have, of course, different meanings in different contexts, but there is a harmony of mystics.

This mysticism was marked by two important and strong experiences Ignatius had at the beginning of his new life and when he entered into its last phase. At the beginning, at the side of a river the Cardoner, at Manresa, near Barcelona, an evocative setting, he had an experience of illumination, a synthetic and unified perception of the universe. According to his own testimony, recorded by one of his faithful disciples, while sitting at a chapel facing the river "the eyes of his understanding began to be opened; not that he saw any vision, but he *understood and learnt* many things, both spiritual matters and matters of faith and of scholarship and this was with so great an enlightenment that everything seemed new to him", to which the scribe comments at the margin, "this left his understanding so very enlightened that he felt as if he were another man with another mind". Ignatius continues the narrative to his reporter: "The details of that he understood then, though they were many, cannot be stated, but only that he experienced a *great clarity in his understanding.* This was such that in the whole course of his life, after completing sixty-two years, even if he gathered up all the various helps he may have had from God and all the various things he has known, even adding them all together, he does not think he had got as much as at that one time"(30).[3] We must remember that in between he had spent a dozen years at the university and taken a Master's degree in theology! Are we reminded of the illumination under the Bo-Tree?

If the first great experience was clearly illuminative, the second was clearly unitive in an Ignatian sense. As he enters the last period of his life Ignatius, now forty seven years old, walks towards Rome to find out the concrete service required of him and his companions. But he desires that this service be not his own decision and action or theirs, but God's own action through them. God acts in his Son Jesus and Ignatius wanted to be integrated into that saving action. As he approaches Rome he enters a church to pray and "he experi-

[3]See *Ablaze with God*, presented by P. Divarkar, pp. 57-58.

ences such an inward change and saw so clearly that God the Father placed him *with Christ his Son* that he would not dare to doubt it — that God the Father had placed him *with his Son*" (96). A companion of that period recalls that the Son was the Son who carried *the cross*.

This experience tells us symbolically important elements of Ignatian mysticism:

(a) It comes from God: it is not the result of a *sādhanā*. It has to be received. He is not worthy of it, he cannot make himself into a companion of Jesus.

(b) The experience which characterised his whole life, places him in intimate union with Jesus: this is why he insists that his group be called 'company of Jesus'. Jesus is at the centre of the Ignatian *sādhanā*. His life is an association with Jesus. And Jesus means for Ignatius an active presence of God in our history — the Jesus of the Gospels, working the salvation by preaching, healing, forgiving, suffering, choosing the poor and the unimportant people. It is therefore a mysticism of dedication to the Reign of God's saving power in history.

(c) Specifically it is Jesus with *the cross*. In his vision of life and of history Ignatius saw that the fear of suffering, specially the fear of being humiliated, of losing power, of losing control of life, is the great block for people to live the authentic religion of love which Jesus had preached and to come into deep union with God. Ignatius faces this fear of *duḥkha* in a frontal attack. He fixed his eyes on Jesus on the cross and develops in himself and wants to develop in his followers '*a relish of the cross*' even the most unnerving and humiliating aspects of it, because of the memory of Jesus on it: not, of course, a cross where suffering is glorified, but a cross where suffering is lovingly accepted when it comes as result of seeking the rule of God's love in our midst. If we tend to prostitute our deepest values because of the fear of suffering, the memory of Jesus on the cross enables Ignatius the mystic to use even suffering and humiliation as a means of love. The problem of suffering is solved not by an analysis of its causes but by the acceptance of its effect when pervaded by love. It is a mysticism centred on the person and history of Jesus, on the mystery of the cross as the supreme expression of love and salvation.

(d) The mysticism centered on Jesus goes beyond Jesus: Jesus actually leads Ignatius to the Father and to the Mystery of God whom he knows as triune. There love translates itself less in activity and more in total surrender. Passivity, or rather letting the Divine Presence be operative. Its reflection in the human spirit can only be described as unqualified love.

The Depths

The title of this essay speaks of an active mysticism. We may indeed describe the mysticism of Ignatius as active, as expressing itself in service, but it would be wrong to see it as a mere spirituality of activity, a mere inspiration for devoting our life to good works for God. It is deeper than that. We are dealing here with a mysticism which operates at the depth of the personality, not merely at the level of action and day-to-day decision. In the early experiences of Loyola and Manresa Ignatius learns to discover this depth dimension. The mind and the senses are not renounced, but the core of the person is elsewhere.

> The ultimate reality in every human being, or that which each individual most truly is, has been variously designated: the unique person, the transcendent self, the apex of the soul, the heart which God alone can directly reach, the spirit that has a mysterious kinship with the divine spirit, the *ātman* that illumines one's most intimate psychological processes ... whatever it be, this is where

> Ignatius takes his stand; it becomes his base, so to speak, from where to respond to God and to all reality; and to scrutinize, in the light of this response, his other reactions at other levels of his being, and to distinguish in them what is authentic and what is not.[4]

It is from this depth, where distance between creature and Creator has been, so to speak, shortened, where the veil of *māyā* that affirms autonomy drops, where the resistance of sensual nature to suffering and the cross is overcome, where God is in direct touch with the human personality and the person is totally free to allow himself or herself to become part of the divine action of love in the world, that the mysticism of action springs. This is the level Ignatius discovered and wanted his *sādhaka* to discover. Here he becomes, and his followers would want to become, channels or expressions of God's own active and saving love. Beyond this there is only the final resurrection in union with Jesus Christ and when Jesus Christ, the Son, "will also be subjected to him who put all things under him, that God may be everything to everyone." (1 Cor 15:28).

[4] P. Divarkar, *Ablaze with God*, p. 135.

AESTHETICS OF MYSTICISM OR MYSTICISM OF AESTHETICS?

The Approach of Kashmir Śaivism

Bettina Bäumer

naraśaktiśivātmakaṃ trikaṃ
hṛdaye yā vinidhāya bhāsayet
praṇamāmi parām anuttarām
nijabhāsāṃ pratibhācamatkṛtim.

Abhinavagupta
Maṅgalaśloka 3
Parātrīśikā Vivaraṇa

I offer homage to the supreme and
Unsurpassable (Deity Consciousness),
the Wonder of ever new Insight,
shining in its own light,
Who reveals the trinity of the created
beings,
Divine Energy and Śiva,
holding them in Her Heart.

We begin this reflection on the relationship between aesthetics and mysticism in the so-called 'Kashmir Śaivism', and especially in Abhinavagupta, by invoking the great Goddess Consciousness, in the words of the third Maṅgalaśloka of Abhinavagupta's *Parātrīśikā Vivaraṇa*.[1] Whether we understand *hṛdaya* as the heart of the Supreme Consciousness

[1] Abhinavagupta, *Parātrīśikā-Vivaraṇa. The Secret of Tantric Mysticism.* Trans. by Jaideva Singh. Delhi (Motilal Banarsidass), 1988.

Herself, in which even the trinity (*trika*) is contained and revealed (Jaideva Singh), or as the heart of the author (Abhinavagupta), in which She places the Three, *nara*, Śakti and Śiva (R. Gnoli), this verse reveals the wonderful nature of Goddess Consciousness. She is herself of the nature of *pratibhā-camatkṛti*, the sudden, intuitive delight or wonder of (at the same time aesthetic and mystical) experience. It implies that the trinity or *trika* would not be known unless the flash of this intuition is realized in the heart — and ultimately the heart of the Goddess Consciousness (*devī svātma saṃvitti*, v. 2) is not different from the heart of the devotee or *sādhaka*, hence the ambivalence.

Much has been said and written about the unity and yet difference of the aesthetic and the mystical experience in Abhinavagupta and his predecessors as well as followers, and I should not repeat well-known facts. But on the background of all this I want to focus on the question expressed in the title of this paper: *Mysticism of Aesthetics or Aesthetics of Mysticism*? The aesthetic experience has to do with the senses (*indriya, karaṇa*), whereas the mystical experience transcends the senses and reaches to the Unsurpassable, Absolute (*anuttara*).

There are three levels where this question can be discussed: on the metaphysical level, on the level of aesthetic or mystical experience, and on the level of artistic or spiritual practice. Obviously, the last is meant to lead to the second and ultimately get merged in the reality expressed by the first. One could start either from 'above', from the theoretical, or 'below', from the experiential, and the result reached would be the same. In fact, the three levels are totally interdependent: *sarvaṃ sarvātmakam.*[2]

Obviously, it is not possible to deal with all the three levels in all the traditions and texts, and here we can only throw

[2]Cp. *Parātrīśikā Vivaraṇa*, op. cit., p. 91 and passim.

light on some aspects which may have received less attention in the study of aesthetics. All the points raised in this paper have to be placed in the context of the great *maṇḍala* of the Trika system. Like in a *maṇḍala*, we have first to draw the lines, and then place the coloured powder in the various compartments.

Metaphysical

Since we are expressing ideas which have been conceived in Sanskrit through the medium of a foreign language which has been imprinted by a different tradition, we have to be careful in using certain concepts. The very words 'aesthetics' and 'mysticism' have a history of their own in the European tradition which cannot be ignored when using them.[3] But a conscious use of such terms can also lead to a mutual enrichment of traditions and to a clarification, as we can see in many works of A.K. Coomaraswamy, for instance.

'Aesthetics' has to do with beauty. But what do we understand by beauty?[4] One of the basic definitions of beauty in the European tradition is 'harmony'. Its opposite, ugliness, is disharmony, dissonance. Harmony is an agreement of the beautiful thing and the source of Beauty, God and hence the beautiful (thing) is a 'reflection' of the 'original'. For the definition of these basic concepts we may quote Thomas Aquinas:[5]

> In existing things, the beautiful and the beauty are distinguished ..." ... for the beautiful is

[3]Cp. the article by Alois Haas in this volume.

[4]Cp. D.H.H. Ingalls, "Words for Beauty in Classical Sanskrit Poetry", in: *Indological Studies in Honor of W. Norman Brown*, ed. by E. Bender, American Oriental Series 47, New Haven, Conn., AOS, 1962, pp. 87–107; A.K. Coomaraswamy, "The Mediaeval Theory of Beauty", in: *Selected Papers I, Traditional Art and Symbolism*, ed. by R. Lipsey, Princeton University Press, 1977, pp. 189–228.

[5]In the translation of A.K. Coomaraswamy, art. cit. pp. 212–13.

> what participates in beauty, and beauty is the participation of the First Cause, which makes all things beautiful. The creature's beauty is naught else but a likeness (*similitudo*) of divine beauty participated in by all things.

Coomaraswamy, in his note, relates this 'likeness' to the idea of 'reflection', but he does not elaborate. In the context of Kashmir Śaivism, the conception of the world as *ābhāsa* or *pratibimba* of the Divine Original (*bimba*) would be the first starting point in a metaphysics of beauty. As for the difference between 'participation' and 'reflection', the latter is never understood in the sense of an illusory appearance by Abhinavagupta. It is interesting to note that in the context of the four *upāyas*, the theory of *pratibimba* is used in the highest, *śāmbhavopāya*, where everything is related to and every means leads to a full 'participation' in the Divine Reality. The description Abhinavagupta gives in his *Tantrasāra* III of *pratibimba* is far from a simple theory of reflection as appearance. Besides the example from which the very word is derived, i.e. a reflection in the mirror, where the reflection is the entire world and the mirror is pure consciousness, he also uses comparisons from sense-experience (smell, taste, touch and sound). Let us consider the example of sound: *pratibimba* is compared to echo resounding in space. This echo is not the original sound, because the one who has produced it hears it as if it were the voice of somebody else, but in fact it is his own voice. What Abhinavagupta wants to say in all these examples is that the *pratibimba* is in reality not different from *bimba*, the original. But this *advaita* is not illusionistic, it allows for a difference which makes the aesthetic experience possible. It comes closer to 'participation' in the scholastic sense.

Abhinavagupta summarizes his idea of *pratibimba* thus:

> Just as all this appears like a reflection, in the

> same way the universe appears in the light of the Supreme Lord.
> (If you ask:) What is the (original) image (that is reflected here)?
> (I answer:) It is nothing.
> (You further ask:) Has then the reflection no cause?
> Are you asking for a cause and how it is reflected? This cause is nothing but the Energy of the Supreme Lord, called 'Freedom'. Ultimately it is the Lord who contains in Himself all the reflected reality and whose Self is the All, because the universe is of the nature of Consciousness, it is the locus of the revelation of Consciousness.[6] Since the universe is reflected in Consciousness, this is the cause of all reflections.
>
> *Tantrasāra* III

Thus the first connotation of beauty is related to 'reflection', 'likeness' and 'participation' in the original, perfect image of pure Consciousness — but not in a static sense, because manifestation is produced by the very *svātantryaśakti* of the Lord. What this means in the field of mystical experience will be seen later.

Another aspect of beauty as harmony in the Western tradition is called *consonantia* in Latin — note the musical implication of the term. Let us first consider the scholastic definition by Thomas Aquinas, who is elaborating on Dionysius the Areopagite:

> Again, he explains the other part, viz. that God is the cause of the 'harmony' (*consonantia*) that is in things. But this harmony in things is of two sorts. The first as regards the order of creatures

[6] *saṃvinmayaṃ hi viśvaṃ caitanyasya vyaktisthānam iti.*

> to God, and he touches upon this when he says that God is the cause of harmony "for that it summons all things to itself," inasmuch as He (or it) turns about all things toward Himself (or itself), as being their end, as was said above; wherefore in the Greek, beauty is called *kālòs*, which is derived from . . . "to summon." And second, harmony is in creatures accordingly as they are ordered to one another; and he touches upon when he says that it gathers together all in all to be one and same. Which may be understood in the sense of the Platonists, viz. that higher things are in the lower by participation, the lower in the higher eminently . . ., and thus all things are in all. And since all things are thus found in all according to some order, it follows that all are ordered to one and the same last end.[7]

We need not simply identify these concepts, because each carries with it its own associations, but similarly *samatā* or *sāmya* is the central concept of 'harmony' in Kashmir Śaivism. Again, *samatā* is not a static identity or sameness, it implies a harmony, balance, equilibrium, and also a sense of proportionality (according to the meaning of *sama*). It implies the same inter-relatedness of all things, high and low (*sarvaṃ sarvātmakam*). The goal of Śaiva Yoga is this very *samatā*, which has all these implications, ranging from the supreme, mystical level to the level of social equality.[8]

The very first verse of the *Parātrīśikā* opens with the

---

[7] Art. cit., p. 213.

[8] Cp. B. Bäumer, "Cosmic Harmony: *Samatā* in Kashmir Śaivism", in: *Universal Responsibility. Felicitation Volume in Honour of H.H. The 14th Dalai Lama, Tenzin Gyatso on His 60th Birthday*, ed. by R.C. Tiwari and Krishna Nath. New Delhi, The Foundation for Universal Responsibility, 1995, pp. 111–19.

question of the Devī addressed to Bhairava:

> *anuttaraṃ kathaṃ deva*
> *sadyaḥ kaulikasiddhidam,*
> *yena vijñāta mātreṇa*
> *khecarī-samatāṃ vrajet.*

It would be worthwhile to comment on Abhinavagupta's exposition of the word *khecarī-samatā* in his *Vivaraṇa.* After stating the metaphysical meaning, he comes down to the sense-experience and the aesthetic experience.[9] The metaphysical meaning is clear:

> Therefore, homogeneousness (*sāmya* or *samatā*) of the *khecarī-śakti* constitutes liberation. This homogeneousness (sameness) of the *khecarī-śakti* is due to the awareness of the essential nature of the *anuttara* (i.e. the unsurpassable Absolute Reality) which is constantly present and which arises from the bliss of the recognition of the completion of the union of the divine Śakti with Śiva, and acquires stability by the realization of the consciousness of bliss of both (*ubhayavimarśānandarūḍhi*).
>
> PTV, Tr. Jaideva Singh, p. 42

Abhinavagupta then elaborates on the process of creativity as well as the sensual experience which brings about this state of *khecarī-samatā.* It is interesting that he not only describes the process in the case of a pleasurable experience, such as love, or hearing of sweet music, but also in the case of grief or suffering. If the heart is attuned to the oneness of *khecarī* (*sahṛdayatā*), even painful experiences can lead to the same

[9]Cp. K.D. Tripathi, "From Sensuous to Supersensuous – An Inquiry into some terms of Indian Aesthetics", in: B. Bäumer (Ed.), *Prakṛti III: The Āgamic Tradition and the Arts*, New Delhi (IGNCA and D.K. Printworld) 1994.

state of harmony. Harmony is always between two or more entities, and here the ultimate state of *samatā* is that between Śiva and Śakti, representing all the polarities in the universe, which is experientially achieved in the consciousness of the yogin or *sādhaka*.[10] What Abhinavagupta describes in this context is a process of integration of sense-experience (it may be erotic, aesthetic, or an intense experience of pain) with the supreme and unalterable Divine Consciousness (*nistaraṅga, dhruvapada*). Thus it also implies the integration of a fleeting emotion with a permanent state of mystical identification. Here it is not a question of a clear-cut distinction between the aesthetical and the mystical, but, on the basis of an ongoing spiritual practice,[11] the sense-experience triggers the mystical realization described as *kaulikasiddhi* and *khecarī-samatā* (*Parātrīśikā* v. 1).

We have mentioned two essential characteristics of beauty: reflection or participation, and harmony. The third quality which is universally valid is that beauty has to do with light, clarity or transparency. Things are beautiful insofar as they radiate or reflect light, both in a physical as well as metaphysical sense. Pure beauty is always transparent, and allows an intelligibility of its own, depending on the medium. This is a very vast subject which I can only hint at without elaborating. Again, to quote Thomas Aquinas, who comments on Dionysius saying that God "is the cause of harmony and lucidity":

> Applying the same principle proportionately in other beings, we see that any of them is called beautiful according as it has its own generic lucidity (*claritatem sui generis*), spiritual or bodily as the case may be, and according as it is consti-

[10] Cp. PTV, trans. p. 44.

[11] Abhinavagupta declares that this text is meant for advanced disciples and not for beginners.

> tuted with due proportion.
>
> How God is the cause of this lucidity he shows, saying that God sends out upon each creature, together with a certain flashing (*quodam fulgore*), a distribution of his luminous 'raying' (*radii*) which is the font of all light; which flashing "distributions (*traditiones*) are to be understood as a participation of likeness; and these distributions are beautifying", that is to say, are the makers of the beauty that is in things.[12]

Now, light, *prakāśa*, is the main characteristic of the Divine nature in Kashmir Śaivism, as in most Indian systems. But this pure Light-of-Consciousness is not experienced without its reflection, *vimarśa*. It is in this dynamic relationship of *prakāśa* and *vimarśa* that the aesthetic experience is to be placed, where, just as we have seen in the case of *khecarī-samatā*, the beauty of the reflection is thrown back onto the source of beauty, the source of Light: *prakāśa*. The entire manifestation is nothing but an expansion of the original Light appearing in all the forms of the universe:

> Similarly Bhairava who is of the nature of light (i.e. spiritual light of consciousness) is self-proved, beginningless, primal, the ultimate in all respects, and present in everything. What else is to be said regarding Him? He displays His Light identically (*svaprakāśaṃ prakāśayati*) in the expansion of all the categories of existence (e.g. the 36 *tattvas*), all the objective phenomena (*bhāvas*), and views them all as Himself (*tathaiva ca vimarśati*) in His self-delight (*camatkāratve*) which never vanishes (*anapeta*). That which is this perception in that way (i.e. as identical with Himself), makes His

[12] Coomaraswamy, art. cit., p. 213.

> self-revelation (*bhāsana*) evident in lakhs, crores, ten crores (*arbuda*), ten *arbudas* of endless future (*bhāvī*) manifestations and absorptions to be brought about by *māyā* and thus he appears in those very forms (*tathārūpaṃ eva bhavati*).
>
> PTV, pp. 111–12

Metaphors

To show that these are not abstract ideas, we could analyze here the use of artistic metaphors, which are not accidental but central to Kashmir Śaivism. Every *darśana* has a set of basic metaphors which serve to illustrate the philosophical truths. Not by chance the two frequently used metaphors are taken from painting on the one hand, and drama on the other. Music does not serve as a metaphor, though it pervades a lot of Abhinavagupta's speculations on the power of the Word (*vāk, mantra*), etc. The metaphor of painting illustrates the idea of *ābhāsa* and of the world as an image (*jagaccitra*) created by the Divine Artist.[13] It does not have illusionistic overtones, as the same image has in Vedānta.[14] The image is real, and yet entirely dependent on the freedom of the creator. Here the *svātantrya-śakti* is the main characteristic of the Divine as well as human artist. Art can only be created by a spirit of freedom. The implication of the metaphor of painting is obviously the beauty of the work of art which produces a sense of wonder (*camatkāra*) and leads the observer to a state of identification.[15] The entire *bimba-pratibimba-vāda* is related, not only to an image in a mirror, but to the metaphor

---

[13]Cp. Bettina Bäumer, "The Divine Artist", in: *The Indian Theosophist, Thakur Jaideva Singh Felicitation Number*, Oct.–Nov. 1985, Vol. 82, 10–11, pp. 79–86.

[14]Cp. Dakṣiṇāmūrti Stotra.

[15]It is interesting to note that sculpture is not used as an important metaphor in Kashmir Śaivism, as it is in Southern Śaiva Siddhānta, esp. the figure of Śiva Naṭarāja.

of painting.

The second artistic metaphor used is that of drama: *jagannāṭya.*[16] Leaving aside here the *Abhinava Bhāratī*, we may reflect on the *Śiva-Sūtras* which elaborate on this simile, starting from the Sūtra *nartaka ātmā*, "The Self is an actor/dancer" (III.9 and ff.).

According to the commentator, Kṣemarāja, this is said of the self-realized yogin who becomes one with the Lord. Kṣemarāja explains his action as being *svaparispanda līlayā*, "playful by his own inner vibration", which manifests itself in movements of dance, a dance that is far from being a merely external movement, for "it is based on his being established in his innermost hidden essential nature" (*antarvigūhitasvasvarūpāvastambhamūlam*). Now all the terms used assume a double meaning, a yogic meaning and a technical meaning of the elements of drama. Thus the various parts played by an actor are the stages of consciousness like waking, dream, etc., i.e. *bhūmikā* (*tattajjāgarādinānābhūmikāprapañcam*).

In this context Kṣemarāja quotes a verse of Bhaṭṭa Nārāyaṇa's *Stavacintāmaṇi* (59):

> O Śiva, you have produced the drama of the three worlds containing the real seed of all creation and the germ within it. Having performed its prelude, is there any other artist but you who is capable of bringing it to its conclusion?

Śiva is here the artist (*kavi*), both author and stage-director of the universal drama in which he is also the actor. All the parts of a Sanskrit drama are also parts of the world-drama. For instance, *bīja*, the 'seed', is in drama the source

[16]Cp. Bettina Bäumer, "The Play of the Three Worlds: The Trika Concept of *Līlā*", in: William Sax (ed.), *The Gods at Play. Līlā in South Asia.* OUP, New York, 1994.

of the plot contained in some allusion, while in the world the seed is *māyā*, the source of manifestation. *Garbha*, 'germ' or 'womb' is the schema of the dramatic action, while in the created world *garbha* corresponds to *prakṛti*, the womb of all existence. *Prastāva* is the introductory part of the play corresponding to creation, and *saṃhāra* its completion, corresponding to the reabsorption or dissolution of the universe.

Adding another quotation from Utpaladeva's *Īśvara-pratyabhijñā* (probably *Vivṛti*, since it is not traceable), Kṣemarāja concludes by saying that the Lord is the producer of the world-drama who remains awake even when the whole world is asleep, i.e. at the stage of *saṃhāra*. The verse of *Stavacintāmaṇi* following the one quoted by Kṣemarāja (v. 60) adds to the meaning of the divine actor and stage-director, for there Śiva is praised as the one who makes the real unreal and the unreal real, being both, free and unfree.[17]

The *Śiva Sūtra* further identifies the stage of the (inner or outer) drama with the inner Self or individual soul: *raṅgo'antarātmā* (ŚSū III.10), because: "The place where the self takes delight with the intention of exhibiting the play of the world drama is the stage, i.e. the place where the Self adopts the various roles."[18] The three levels of meaning are here the external theatre stage, the universal stage of the world-drama, and the yogic stage of the inner Self (*bhūmikā* again in the meaning of stages in yoga and roles of the actor). The purport of the simile is the spiritual or yogic level, as also in the following Sūtra, where the senses are called the spectators: *prekṣakāṇīndriyāṇi* (III.11). Kṣemarāja comments: "The senses like eyes, etc. of the yogi witness inwardly their inmost Self full of the delight in exhibiting the world drama. By the

---

[17] *namaḥ sadastāṃ kartum asattvaṃ sattvam eva vā,*
svatantrāyāsvatantrāya vyayaiśvaryaikśāline, v. 60.

[18] *rajyate'smin jagannāṭya krīḍāpradarśanāśayenātmanā iti raṅgaḥ, tattadbhūmikā grahaṇasthānam*, Kṣemarāja on the above.

development of the performance of the drama, they provide to the yogi fullness of aesthetic rapture in which the sense of difference has disappeared".[19]

Here it becomes clear that the simile is not merely a pretext for explaining the inexplicable (as in *Vedānta*), because the play is a real play of delight even for the yogin. The senses are here not denied, but they assume the role of spectators of the world drama that is reflected in the inner consciousness, on the interior stage. Interiority (*antarmukhatā*) is not opposed to playful manifestation, it is rather the condition for the fullness of aesthetic delight (*camatkāra-rasasaṃpūrṇatā*). Since the world-drama is really enacted by the Lord himself, the yogin can enjoy its beauty and, instead of being distracted by external multiplicity, dissolve any sense of separateness due to this experience of joy (*vigalita vibhāgān*). Here the aesthetical and the mystical rapture become identical, the yogin being able to enjoy things more fully due to his rootedness in interiority.

Aesthetical/Mystical Experience

On this background we come now to the main question that this paper wants to raise, i.e. the mutual enlightenment of the aesthetical and the mystical. One of the key terms in both is *camatkāra/camatkṛti* or *vismaya*, the wonder or surprise of a delightful experience, an unexpected overwhelming of joy. *Camatkṛti* cannot be the outcome of any deliberate effort, it is always spontaneous, even if it is preceded by an effort of artistic expression on the one hand, and of spiritual practice on the other. Lilian Silburn describes *camatkāra* as "the rapture proper to the *sahṛdaya* who appreciates the drama and to the mystic who, at a much higher degree, enjoys divine bliss. But in both cases the impression is spontaneous,

[19] III.11, tr. Jaideva Singh.

it does not depend on any effort. The *guru* in the case of the second or the actor in the case of the first do nothing but lifting the veil and removing the obstacle, so that the inner ecstasy wells up immediately."[20]

As in the *maṅgalaśloka* cited in the beginning, *pratibhā* and *camatkṛti* are intimately related. Abhinavagupta has an interesting passage in the *Tantrāloka*:[21]

> In the measure in which the uncreated reality exceeds, to the same degree the wonder of delight (*camatkāra*) increases . . .
>
> Those who rest in the intuitive consciousness (*pratibhā*) consisting in the fullness of the first letters, certainly attain poetic and rhetoric gifts. But he who rests in pure Consciousness in its highest form, devoid of any limitations of conventions, what is it that he does not know? What is it that he is not able to do?
>
> *Tantrāloka* XI.76–80

Here it is the same illuminating power of *pratibhā*, an aspect of pure consciousness, which leads to poetic creation in the field of expression, and to unlimited knowledge and activity in the spiritual field. Both share in the same wonder of delight. Abhinavagupta develops this idea more extensively in his *Parātrīśikā Vivaraṇa*,[22] in the context of the phonemes of language, and of musical sound. At the end of a very revealing passage on the effect of sounds, he summarizes his views, starting with the identification of *camatkāra* with the supreme Śakti:

[20] L. Silburn, *Śiva-Sūtra et Vimarśinī de Kṣemarāja*, Paris (De Boccard) 1980, p. 172.

[21] Quoted in R. Gnoli, *The Aesthetic Experience According to Abhinavagupta*, Varanasi (Chowkhamba Sanskrit Series Office), 1968, p. LI, note.

[22] J. Singh, op. cit., pp. 188ff. (translation), pp. 70–72 of the Skt. text.

> *svātantryaikarasāveśacamatkāraikalakṣaṇā,*
> *parā bhagavatī nityaṃ bhāsate bhairavī svayam.*
>
> The Supreme Power, who is Bhairavī, whose characteristic is wondrous delight issuing from her unique autonomy, shines externally by herself.

Any experience of *camatkāra*, whether aesthetical or mystical, is therefore a participation in the Śakti who is characterized as 'being immersed (*āveśa*) in the one *rasa* of absolute freedom (*svātantrya*).'

The difference and/or unity of the aesthetical and the mystical can be observed clearly in the case of spiritual practices (*dhāraṇā*) which use the aesthetic experience for a mystical end. We may see examples from the *Vijñāna Bhairava* and, in the context of *bhakti*, from the *Śivastotrāvalī* of Utpaladeva.

The sound of instrumental music can induce a state of absorption and identification with the supreme void of space, the condition of all sound:

> *tantryādivādyaśabdeṣu dīrgheṣu kramasaṃsthiteḥ,*
> *ananyacetāḥ pratyante paravyomavapur bhavet.*
>
> ViBhai v. 41
>
> If one listens with undivided attention to the sounds of string instruments and others which are played successively and are prolonged, then one becomes absorbed in the supreme ether of consciousness.

Jaideva Singh adds the following Notes:

1. The resonance of musical notes lasts for a long time and being melodious it attracts the attention of the listener. Even when it stops, it still reverberates in the mind of the listener. The listener becomes greatly engrossed in it. A musical note, if properly produced, appears to arise out of eternity and finally to disappear in it.

2. When the music stops, it still vibrates in the memory. If the yogin does not allow his mind to wander to something else, but concentrates on the echo of the music, he will be absorbed in the source of all sound, viz. *parā-vāk* and thus will acquire the nature of *Bhairava.*

Obviously, the same music can be experienced at different levels by different listeners, depending on their state of consciousness. As Abhinavagupta says in his *Tantrāloka*, the insensitive (*ahṛdaya*) are unable to get merged or identified with the object of aesthetic enjoyment, in this case musical sound, which is ultimately Consciousness itself.[23] Jayaratha comments briefly on the two terms: "In the world those are called 'sensitive' (*sahṛdaya*) who experience a sense of wonder by identifying themselves with exceedingly beautiful music etc.; others are known to have their heart somewhere else, they are insensitive (*ahṛdaya*)."[24] In the case of a sensitive person, the state of absorption may happen spontaneously.

Another instance of music is given after the example of other sensual joys, such as sexual joy and the pleasure of eating and drinking (ViBhai vv. 69–72) which are expressions or ways of reaching a state of bliss.

> *gītādiviṣayāsvādāsamasaukhyaikatātmanaḥ,*
> *yoginastanmayatvena manorūḍhes tadātmatā.*
>
> ViBhai v. 73
>
> When the mind of a yogī is one with the unparalleled joy of music and other (aesthetic delights), then he is identified with it due to the expansion of his mind which has merged in it.

The difference between the yogin and the aesthete listening to music is that the mind of the first has already been firmly

[23] TĀ III.240b–241a: *yeṣāṃ na tanmayībhūtiste dehādinimajjanam, avidanto magnasaṃvinmānāstvahṛdayā iti.*

[24] Jayaratha on the above.

concentrated, and he hears the totality of sound, not the individual sounds. This leads to a state of identification with the source of sound. There are examples of other art forms which have different implications, i.e. the contemplation of the universe as a painting which brings about joy (not disillusionment, cp. v.102). The intense experience of dancing or of walking leads to a mystical state at the moment of the cessation of movement:

> *bhrāntvā bhrāntvā śarīreṇa tvaritaṃ bhuvi pātanāt,*
> *kṣobhaśaktivirāmeṇa parā saṃjāyate daśā.*
>
> ViBhai v.111
>
> If one moves round and round with the body and suddenly falls on the ground, then, when the energy of agitation comes to an end, the supreme state arises.

Most of the practices of *Vijñāna Bhairava* are directed to the experience of the void, *śūnya*, and the aesthetic experiences are no exception. It is not the particularity of the beauty of sound, nature, of an image etc., which produces a state of wonder and of identification, it is rather the emptying of the mind of all *vikalpas* produced by an absorbing experience. The senses themselves are to be meditated upon as voids:

> *śikhipakṣaiś citrarūpair maṇḍalaiḥ śūnyapañcakam,*
> *dhyāyato'nuttare śūnye praveśo hṛdaye bhavet.*
>
> ViBhai v.32
>
> By meditating on the five voids of the senses which are like the various colours of the peacock's feathers, the yogin enters in the Heart of the absolute Void.

Finally, Utpaladeva's *Śivastotrāvalī* can throw a different light on the question raised in the title of this article. Its basic *rasa* is *bhakti*. There is no attempt at any systematic presentation, since its verses are a spontaneous outpouring of non-dual devotion. And yet there is a consistency in agreement with Utpala's theology.

First of all, God is the exceedingly beautiful One (*vitata lāvaṇya*, II.21). Kṣemarāja explains the unsurpassed Divine Beauty as being due to the intensity of supreme bliss.[25] It is that Divine Beauty which is the unending source of attraction in all other, created beauty. The senses themselves are enlivened by the divine consciousness (X.18–19). Therefore the very contact with the beautiful objects creates a sense of wonder and delight:

> *yatsamastasubhagārthavastuṣu*
> *sparśamātravidhinā camatkṛtim,*
> *tāṃ samarpayati tena te vapuḥ*
> *pūjayantyacalabhaktiśālinaḥ.*
>
> XIII.14

> That which bestows on all objects of beauty
> The property of giving wonder at the mere touch
> By that very principle do those endowed with
> Unwavering devotion
> Worship your form.

Kṣemarāja explains this act of worship as a resting in the Divine (*tvayyeva viśrāmyanti*). Thus the three main phases of this aesthetic-mystical experience are: (1) the 'touch' of the beautiful object; (2) the sense of wonder and delight (*camatkṛti*); (3) the worship of the Divine Form (*vapuḥ*), i.e. seeing the body of pure Consciousness in all things[26] which implies a state of merging or rest (*viśrānti*). The Divine Itself

---

[25] *paramānandaghanatvena atispṛhaṇīyatvāt*, on the above.

[26] Cp. Kṣemarāja: *te vapuḥ – cinmayaṃ svarūpam.*

is the source of all this experience of beauty, as the very next verse says:

> Being self-luminous
> You cause everything to shine;
> Delighting in your form
> You fill the universe with delight;
> Reeling with your own bliss
> You make the whole world dance with joy.
>
> XIII.15

Whether the approach is through *bhakti* as in the *Śivastotrāvalī*, or through a piercing of the senses to reach a state of void, as in the *Vijñāna Bhairava*, one condition is the sensitivity or *sahṛdayatā*, both aesthetic and mystical, and another condition is the intensity of the experience. Kṣemarāja makes it clear in his Vimarśinī on *Śiva Sūtra* I.12, *vismayo yogabhūmikāḥ*:

> As a person is struck with wonder by seeing something extraordinary, even so there is a pleasant surprise for the great *yogī* who notices in mute wonder an expansion (in the power) of his entire complex of senses, as they come fully under the infiuence of the inner Self which is a mass of consciousness and full of unique, pre-eminent and ever-new delight of I-consciousness which blossoms forth in the experience of the various objects of perception. The *yogī* has this experience in himself that is full of uninterrupted joy — a joy with which he never feels satiated.
>
> (Tr. J. Singh, p. 52)[27]

[27] Comm.: *yathā sātiśayavastudarśane kasyacit vismayo bhavati tathā*

This *yathā-tathā* is not a simple comparison, it actually implies that the same state of ecstasy or wonder can be reached, either triggered by an external extraordinary experience, or attained by an inner process of stages of Yoga, without any external cause. The first is mediated by the senses, the second needs no mediation. These differences are then related to the four *upāyas*, depending on the level of consciousness of the one undergoing the experience. Generally, *āṇavopāya* and *śāktopāya* would be mediated by some external or mental means, whereas *śāmbhavopāya* and *anupāya* do not require any cause or means. But in every stage of the *upāyas* the experience would be one of *vismaya*, the joy of astonishment.

Coming back to the question raised in the title, we can draw some general conclusions:

1. Based on the metaphysical insights of Trika, on the doctrines of *prakāśa-vimarśa, ābhāsa, bimba-pratibimba, pratyabhijñā* etc., the mystical experience is no doubt also aesthetical. First of all, it does not deny the positive role of the senses and of their objects in the realization of the Divine. And the goal of all the *upāyas* being a state of harmony, *samatā*, beauty is an essential part of this harmony. Finally, the Divine itself, Śiva, is Beauty and Delight, being ever united with the Śakti who is Herself *pratibhā* and *camatkṛti*.

2. On the other hand, the aesthetic experience has all the potential of being or becoming mystical, depending on the purity and sensitivity of the one undergoing it. In essence it can be nothing else, because the very source of beauty is the Divine, Śiva, and the very cause for the wonder of delight is Śakti. Any real aesthetic experience is a spark of recognition, or it is nothing. A difference remains as to the degree of fullness: in the case of the mystical experience, the 'I' (*aham*) is fully realized, in the case of the aesthetic experience it may be only a glimpse. The difference lies in the degree of merg-

ing or identification — *tanmayībhāva* — and in the relative permanence of the identification.

The sense-experience serves thus as a door of entrance to the ultimate experience. This is the unique contribution of Kashmir Śaivism to an integral mysticism which does not exclude any human dimension but embraces every possible experience and at the same time pierces through it to the Absolute — *anuttara.*

APPENDIX

1. Bibliography R. Panikkar

ABHISHIKTANANDA, Svāmī 1986 — *La montée au fond du coeur*, Paris (O.E.I.L.).

AKHILANANDA, Svāmī 1949 — *Hindu View of Christ*, Boston (Branden).

AUGSTEIN, Rudolf 1972 — *Jesus Menschensohn*, München (Bertelsmann).

BAIRD, William 1977 — *The Quest of the Christ of Faith* — Reflections on the Bultmann Era, Waco, Texas (Word Books).

BARR, James 1970 — "The Symbolism of Names in the Old Testament", in *Bulletin of the John Ryland Library* 52 (1969–70) pp. 11–29.

— 1976 — "Story and History in Biblical Theology" in *The Journal of Religion* 56/1, pp. 1–17.

BAYART, Julian 1966 — "Cosmic Christ and Our Evaluation of other Religions", in *Clergy Monthly Supplement.*

BELLET, Maurice 1990 — *Christ*, Paris (Desclée).

BEN-CHORIN, Schalom 1967 — *Der Nazarener in jüdischer Sicht*, München (List).

BENEDIKT, B. & SOBEL, A. 1992 — *Der Streit um Drewermann*, Wiesbaden (Sobel).

BENJAMIN, Roger 1971 — *Notion de personne et personnalisme chrétien*, Paris (Mouton).

BOTTERWECK, G.J.; RINGGREN, H. (eds.) 1973 — *Theologisches Wörterbuch zum Alten Testament*, Stuttgart (Kohlhammer).

BOULGAKOV, Serge 1982 — *Du Verbe Incarné -L'Agneau de Dieu*, Lausanne (L'Age d'Homme) [trad. du russe (1933) par C. Anronikof].

BOUYER, Louis 1978 — "The Eternal Son: a Theology of the Word of God and Christology", in *Our Sunday Visitor* (Huntigton, IN).

BUECHNER, Frederick , *et al.* (eds.) 1974 — *The Faces of Jesus*, New York (Rinerwood-Simon & Schuster).

CABA, José 1977 — *El Jesús de los Evangelios*, Madrid (BAC).

CABADA-CASTRO, Manuel 1975 — "La vivencia previa del absoluto como presupuesto del acceso teorético a Dios" en VARGAS-MACHUCA, (1975) 65–88.

COBB, John B. 1975 — *Christ in a Pluralistic Age*, Philadelphia (Westminster).

CROSSAN, John Dominic 1991 — *The Historical Jesus*. The Life of a Mediterranean Jewish Peasant, San Francisco (Harper & Collins).

DANESE, Attilio 1984 — *Unità e pluralità*. Mounier e il ritorno alla persona, Roma (Città Nuova Editrice).

DANESE, Attilio (ed.) 1986 — *La questione personalista*. Mounier e Maritain nel dibattito per un nuovo umanesimo, Roma (Città Nuova).

DANIELOU, Jean 1986 — *La Trinité et le mystère de l'existence* Paris (Desclée).

DE SMET, R. 1976 — "The Discovery of the Person", in *Indian Philosophical Quarterly* IV.1, pp. 1–23.

DI NICOLA, Giulia Paola 1991 — *Reciprocidad hombre/mujer*, Madrid (Narcea).

DODD, C.H. — *The Founder of Christianity*, New York (Macmillan) 1970.

DORÉ, J. 1984 — "Jésus-Christ" in *Dictionnaire des religions*, POUPARD (1984) pp. 847–58.

DREWERMANN, Eugen 1984/1985 — *Tiefenpsychologie und Exegese* (2 Vols.), Olten-Freiburg (Walter).

— 1987/1988 — *Das Markus-Evangelium* (2 crols.), Olten-Freiburg (Walter).

DUPUIS, James 1966 — "The Cosmic Christ in the Early Fathers", *Indian Journal of Theology*, pp. 106–20.

— 1977 — *Jesus Christ and His Spirit* — Theological Approaches, Bangalore (T.P.I.).

— 1989 — *Jésus-Christ à la rencontre des religions*, Paris (Desclée).

DUQUOC, Chr. 1972 — *Christologie.* II-Le Messie, Paris (Cerf).

FEINER, Johannes/LOEHRER, Magnus (eds.) 1970 — *Mysterium Salutis.* Grundriss heilsgeschichtlicher Dogmatik. Vol. 3, Köln (Benziger).

FLUSSER, David 1968 — *Jesus in Selbstzeugnissen und Bilddokumenten*, Reinbek bei Hamburg (Rowohlt).

FREI, Hans W. 1975 — *The Identity of Jesus Christ* — The Hermeneutical Bases of Dogmatic Theology, Philadelphia (Fortress).

FRIEDLI, Richard 1989 — *Le Christ dans les cultures*, Fribourg, Paris (Ed. Universitaires, Cerf).

FRIES, Heinrich (ed.) 1962 — *Handbuch theologischer Grundbegriffe*, München (Kösel).

FRIES, Heinrich *et al.* (eds.) 1981 — *Jesus in den Weltreligionen*, St Ottilien (Eos).

GALTIER, Paul 1939 — *L'unité du Christ — Etre... Personne.... Conscience*, Paris (Beauchesne).

— 1947 -*Les deux Adam*, Paris (Beauchesne).

— 1954 *La conscience humaine du Christ*, Roma (Gregorianum).

GARRIGOU-LAGRANGE, R. 1953 — "-La possibilité de l'Incarnation sans aucune déviation panthéiste", in *Angelicum* (XXX, 4) pp. 337–346.

GEISELMANN 1962 — "Jesus Christus", in *Handbuch theologischer Grundbegriffe*, FRIES (1962), Bd. I. pp. 739–70.

GONZALEZ DE CARDENAL, Olegario 1975 — "Un problema teológico fundamental: La preexistencia de Cristo. Historia y hermenéutica." in *Teología y mundo contemporáneo*, VARGAS MACHUCA (1975), pp. 179–221.

— *Jesús de Nazaret. Aproximación a la Cristología*, Madrid (BAC).

GONZÁLEZ FAUS, José I. 1984 — *La humanidad nueva. Ensayo de Cristologia*, (6th edition) Santander (Sal Terrae).

GRIFFIN, David R. 1973 — *A Process Christology*, Philadelphia (Westminster).

GRILLMEIER, Alois 1975 — *Christologische Forschungen und Perfektionen*, Freiburg (Herder).

— *Mit ihm und in ihm*, Freiburg (Herder).

GRILLMEIER, Alois/SCHMAUS, Michael (eds.) 1965.

— *Handbuch der Dogmengeschichte*. Band III. Faszikel Ia. Freiburg (Herder).

GUARDINI, Romano 1939 — *Welt und Person. Versuche zur christlichen Lehre vom Menschen*. Würzburg.

— 1958 — *Die menschliche Wirklichkeit des Herrn*, Würzburg (Werkbund).

HAAS, Alois M. 1971 — *Nim din selbes war -Studien zur Lehre von der Selbsterkenntnis bei Meister Eckhart, Johannes Tauler und Heinrich Seuse*, Freiburg (Universitätsverlag).

HAMERTON-KELLY, R.G. 1973 — *Pre-existence, Wisdom and the Son of Man*. A Study of the Idea of Preexistence in the New Testament, Cambridge (University Press).

HAUSHERR, Irénée 1955 — *Direction spirituelle en Orient autrefois*, Roma (Pont. Inst. Orientalium Studiorum).

HEILER, Friedrich 1961 — *Erscheinungsformen und Wesen der Religion*, Stuttgart (Kohlhammer).

HODGSON, Peter C. 1971 — *Jesus — Word and Presence*: An Essay in Christology, Philadelphia (Fortress).

ISAAC, Augustine 1974 — *Jesus the Rebel*, Mangalore (Sallak Publications).

KAHLEFELD, Heinrich 1981 — *Die Gestalt Jesu in den synoptischen Evangelien*, Frankfurt am Main (Knecht).

KASPER, Walter 1974 — *Jesus der Christus*, Mainz (Grünewald). English translation: *Jesus the Christ*, London (Burns, Oates), New York (Paulist) 1976.

KENDALL, Daniel/ O'COLLINS, Gerald 1992 -"The Faith of Jesus", in *Theological Studies*, 53, pp. 403–23.

KITTEL, G./FRIEDRICH G. (eds.) 1964–74 — *Theological Dictionary of the New Testament* [Trans. and edited by G.W. Bromiley], Grand Rapids, Mich. (Eerdmans).

KITTEL, Gisela 1989, 1990 — *Ders Name über alle Namen* I — Biblische Theologie AT; II Biblische Theologie NT Göttingen (Vandenhoeck & Ruprecht) (2 vols.).

KRÖGER, Athanasius 1967 — *Mensch und Person*: Moderne Personbegriffe in der katholischen Theologie, Recklinghausen (Paulus).

LIEBAERT, Jacques 1965 — "Christologie. Von der Apostolischen Zeit bis zum Konzil von Chalcedon" in *Handbuch der Dogmengeschichte*, SCHMAUS (1965) Bd. III, F. Ia, pp. 19–127.

LIMONE, Giuseppe 1988 — *Tempo della persona e sapienza del possibile*. Valori, politica, diritto in Emmanuel .Mounier. (2 vols.), Napoli-Roma (Edizione Scientifiche Italiane).

LOEHRER, Magnus/FEINER, Johannes (eds.) 1970 — *Mysterium Salutis. Grundriss heilsgeschichtlicher Dogmatik.* Bd. 3 Köln (Benziger).

MAISCH; VÖGTLE A. 1969 — *Jesus Christ.* I Biblical in *Sacramentum Mundi*, RAHNER (1969) 174–83.

MARTIN, R.P. 1967 — *Carmen Christi.* Philippicum II 5–11 in Recent Interpretations and in the Setting of Early Christian Worship, Cambridge (Univ. Press).

MC GINN, Bernard 1992 — *The Foundations of Mysticism*, New York (Crossroad).

MONTEFIORE, H.W. 1966 — "Towards a Christology for Today" in *Soundings* ed. by A.R. Vidler, Cambridge (University Press).

MOUNIER, Emmanuel 1936 -*Manifeste au service du personalisme.*

— 1950 — *Feu la Chrétienté.* Carnets de route, Paris (Seuil).

— 1952 — *Personalism*, London (Routledge & Kegan Paul).

MOUNT SAVIOUR MONASTERY 1972 — *On the Experience of God.* 15 Papers by several monks o.s.b., *Monastic Studies* 9 (Autum).

MOUROUX, Jean 1952 — *L'expérience chrétienne. Introduction à la Théologie*, Paris (Aubier).

— 1955 — *The Christian Experience*, London (Sheed and Word).

NEDONCELLE, Maurice 1942 — *La réciprocité des consciences*, Paris.

— 1944 — *La personne humaine et la nature*, Paris (Presses Univ. de France).

— 1970 — *Explorations Personnalistes*, Paris (Aubier).

NEWBIGIN, Lesslie 1978 — "Christ and Cultures" in *Scottish Journal of Theology* (Edinburgh) XXXI, 1 pp. 1–22.

NOLAN, Albert 1976 — *Jesus before Christianity.* The Gospel of Liberation, London (D.L.T.).

O'COLLINS, Gerald, KENDALL, Daniel 1992 -"The Faith of Jesus", in *Theological Studies,* 53, pp. 403–23.

ORBE, Antonio 1985 — *Il Cristo*. Vol I. Testi teologiche e spirituali del I al IV secolo. A cura di..., Italia (Mondadori & Fondazione Lorenzó Valla).

ORTEGA, Augusto Andrés 1970 — "Cristo: su conciencia humana y su persona divina" in *Homenaje a Xavier Zubiri*. Vol I, ZUBIRI 1970, pp. 91–119.

PANIKKAR, Raimon 1972/6 — *Salvation in Christ: Concreteness and Universality, the Supername*. Inaugural Lecture at the Ecumenical Institute of Advanced Theological Study, Tantur, Jerusalem, pp. 1–81.

— 1972/14 — "Super hanc petram" due principi ecclesiologici: la roccia e le chiavi. in *Legge e Vangelo. Discussione su una legge fondamentale per la Chiesa*, Brescia (Paideia) pp. 135–145.

— 1975/1 -"El presente tempiterno. Una apostilla a la historia de la salvación y a la teología de la liberación." in *Teología y mundo contemporáneo*, VARGAS-MACHUCA (1975), pp. 133–75.

— 1977/3 — "Verstehen als Überzeugtsein" in *Neue Anthropologie* VII, *Philosophische Antropologie*. Hrsg. von H.G. Gadamer & P. Vogler. Stuttgart (Thieme) pp. 132–167.

— 1977/XXV — *The Vedic Experience. Mantramañjarī*. An Anthology of the Vedas for Modern Man and Contemporary Celebration. Los Angeles, Berkeley (University of California Press) & London (DLT) 1977 [2nd edn., Pondicherry (All India Books) 1983; 2nd Indian edn. New Delhi (Motilal Banarsidass) 1989].

— 1983/XXVII – *Myth, Faith and Hermeneutics*. Bangalore (ATC) 2nd. edn.

— 1986/10 — "The Threefold Linguistic Intrasubjectivity" in *Intersoggettività Socialità Religione*. Ed. M.M. Olivetti. *Archivio di Filosofia* (Roma) LIV, 1/3, pp. 593–606.

— 1992/34 — "A Christophany for our Times", *Theology Digest* (Sant Louis, MI) Spring, pp. 3–21.

PARENTE, Pietro 1951 — *L'io di Cristo*, Brescia (Morcelliana).

PELIKAN, Jaroslav 1965 — *The Finality of Jesus Christ in an Age of Universal History.* A Dilemma of the Third Century, Richmond, Virginia (John Knox).

— 1987 — *Jesus through the Centuries.* His Place in the History of Culture, New York (Harper & Row).

POUPARD, P., *et al.*, (eds.) 1984 — *Dictionnaire des Religions*, Paris (PUF).

QUELL, Gottfried 1967 — "Pater" in *Theological Dictionary of the New Testament*, Kittel, Friedrich, ed., [transl. and ed. Bromiley] Grand Rapids, Mich., (Eerdmans) vol. V; pp. 959–974.

RAHNER, K. [et al.] eds., 1969 — *Sacramentum Mundi. An Encyclopedia of Theology*, Freiburg (Herder) [English Translation Montreal (Palm) 1969].

RAHNER, K.; THÜSING, W. 1972 -*Christologie.* Systematisch und exegetisch, Freiburg (Herder).

RAVINDRA, Ravi 1990 — *The Yoga of the Christ in the Gospel according to St John*, Longmead (Element Books).

RENWART, Lion 1993 — "Image, de Dieu, image de l'homme". Chronique de Christologie, *Nouvelle Revue Theologique*, 115, pp. 85–104.

RINGGREN, H. 1973 — *Theologisches Wörterbuch zum Alten Testament*, Botterweck, Ringgren eds., Stuttgart (Kohlhammer), vol. I, cols. 1–19.

ROSENBERG, Alfons 1986 — *Jesus der Mensch.* Ein Fragment, München (Kösel).

ROVIRA BELLOSO, J.M. 1984 — *La humanitat de Déu. Aproximació a l'essència del cristianisme*, Barcelona (Edicions 62).

RUPP, George 1973 — "Religious Pluralism in the Context of an Emerging World Culture", in *Harvard Theological Review* LXVI, pp. 207–18.

— 1974 -*Christologies and Cultures.* Toward a Typology of Religious Worldviews, The Hague, Paris (Mouton).

SANTIAGO-OTERO, Horacio 1990 — *El conocimiento de Cristo en cuanto hombre*, Pamplona (Universidad de Navaera).

SCHILLEBEECKX, Edward 1963 — *Christ*: the Sacrament of the Encounter with God, New York (Sheed & Word).

— 1985 — *The Schillebeeck Reader*, New York (Crossroad).

SCHMAUS, Michael/GRILLMEIER, Alois (eds.) 1965 -*Handbuch der Dogmengeschichte.* Band. III. Faszikel Ia. Freiburg (Herder).

SCHNACKENBURG, Rudolf 1970 — *Christologie des Neuen Testaments* in *Mysterium salutis* FRINER (1970), Bd. 3, pp. 227–388.

SCHOONENBERG, Piet 1971 -*The Christ. A Study of the God-Man Relationship in the Whole of Creation and in Jesus Christ*, New York (Seabury).

SCHREITER, Robert (ed.) 1985 — *The Schillebeeckx Reader*, New York (Crossroad).

SCHRENK, Gottlob 1967 — "Pater" in *Theological Dictionary of the New Testament,* KITTEL (1967), vol. V; pp. 945–59, 974–1022.

SIMONSON, Conrad 1972 — *The Christology of the Faith and Order Movement*, Leiden, Köln (Brill).

SMITH, Huston 1992 — "Is There a Perennial Philosophy ?" in J. OGILVY (editor) *Revisioning Philosophy*, Albany (SUNY) pp. 247–62.

SOBRINO, Jan 1976 — *Cristologia desde America Latina*, Mexico DF (Centro de reflexión teologica). English translation: *Christology at the Crossroads*, Maryknoll, N.Y. (Orbis) 1978.

STOCKLI, T. (ed.) 1991 — *Wege zur Christus-erfahrung*, Dornach (Verlag am Goetheanum).

SUGIRTHARAJAH, R.S. (ed.) 1993 — *Asian Faces of Jesus*, Maryknoll, N.Y. (Orbis Books).

SWIDLER, Leonard 1988 — *Jeshua.* A Model for Moderns, Kansas City (Sheed & Ward).

THIBAUT, René 1942 — *Le sens de l'Homme-Dieu*, Paris (Desclée de Brouwer).

THISELTON, C.A. 1974 — "The Supposed Power of Words in the Biblical Writings", *Journal of Theological Studies* 25, pp. 183–299.

THRESMONTANT, Claude 1983 — *Le Christ hébreu. La langue et l'âge des Evangiles*, Paris (O.E.I.L.).

THOMPSON, William M. 1985 — *The Jesus Debate. A Survey and Synthesis*, New York (Paulist).

VAN DER LEEUW 1956 — *Phänomenologie der Religion*, Tübingen (Paul Siebeck).

VARGAS-MACHUCA, Antonio (ed.) 1975 — *Teologia y mundo contemporáneo* (Homenaje a K. Rahner), Madrid (Cristiandad).

— 1992 — "Jesus Fundador del Cristianismo? Biblia y Fe, 54 (1992) pp. 301–12.

WARE, Robert C. 1974 — "Christology in Historical Perspective", *The Heythrop Journal* XV/1, pp. 53–69.

WHITHERINGTON, Ben 1990 — *The Christology of Jesus*, Mineapolis (Fortress).

XIBERTA, Bartholomeus 1954 — *Tractatus de Verbo Incarnato* (2 vols.), Matriti (CSIC).

ZUBIRI, Xavier 1970 — *Homenaje a Xavier Zubiri* (2 vol.), Madrid (EMC).

— 1975 — "El problema teologal del hombre" in *Teologia y Mundo contemporáneo*, VARGAS-MACHUCA (1975), Madrid (Cristiandad) pp. 55–64.

2. Abbreviations and Bibliography Kashmir Śaivism

BG *Bhagavad Gītā*: with *Gītārthasaṃgraha* commentary of Abhinavagupta, ed. by Pt. Lakshman Raina, Srinagar, KSTS, 1933.

ĪPK *Īśvarapratyabhijñā Kārikā* of Utpaladeva: with the comm. of Abhinavagupta, Vol. I, ed. by Mukund Ram Shastri, Srinagar, KSTS No. XXII, 1918.

ĪPV *Īśvarapratyabhijñā Kārikā* of Utpaladeva: with the Vimarśinī of Abhinavagupta Vol. II, ed. by Madhusudan Kaul Shastri, Srinagar, KSTS No. XXXIII, 1921.

ĪPVVim *Īśvarapratyabhijñā Vivṛti Vimarśinī* of Abhinavagupta: 3 Vols., ed. by Pt. Madhusudan Kaul Shastri, Srinagar, KSTS, 1938–41.

KS *Kumārasambhava* of Kālidāsa: ed. & tr. by M.R. Kale, Delhi, MLBD, 1995.

KSTS Kashmir Series of Texts and Studies, Srinagar.

MVT *Mālinīvijayottara Tantra*, ed. by Pt. Madhusudan Kaul Shastri, Srinagar, KSTS No. XXXVII, 1922.

— *Pañcastavī*: The Pentad of hymns of Kuṇḍalinīyoga, ed. & tr. by Jankinath Kaul, Srinagar, Sri Ramakrishna Ashrama, 1996.

PTV *Parātrīśikā Vivaraṇa* of Abhinavagupta: The Secret of Tantric Mysticism, tr. by Jaideva Singh, Sans. text ed. by Swami Lakshmanjee, ed. by Bettina Bäumer, Delhi, MLBD, 1988.

— *Sāmbapañcāśikā*, ed. by Swami Lakshmanjee, Iśvara Ashrama, Guptagaṅgā, Srinagar, 1976.

— *Śivadṛṣṭi* of Sri Somānanda Nātha: with the Vṛtti of Utpaladeva, ed. by Madhusudan Kaul Shastri, Srinagar, KSTS No. LIV, 1934.

— *Śivastotrāvalī* of Utpaladeva: with the comm. of Kṣemarāja, ed. by Rājānaka Lakṣmaṇa, Varanasi, Chowkhamba Sanskrit Series Office, 1964.

— *Śaiva Devotional Songs of Kashmir*: A Translation and Study of Utpaladeva's Śivastotrāvalī by C. Rhodes Bailly. State University of New York Press, Albany, 1987.

SpKā *Spanda Kārikās*: The Divine Creative Pulsation, ed. & tr. by Jaideva Singh, Delhi, MLBD, 1980.

ŚSū *Śiva Sūtras*: The Yoga of Supreme Identity with the comm. Vimarśinī of Kṣemarāja, ed. & tr. by Jaideva Singh, Delhi, MLBD, 1979 (reprint 1995).

TĀ *Tantrāloka* of Abhinavagupta: with the comm. of Jayaratha, ed. by R.C. Dwivedi and Navajivan Rastogi, Vols. I–VIII, Delhi, MLBD, 1987.

— *Tantrasāra* of Abhinavagupta: KSTS, 1918.

ViBhai *Vijñānabhairava*: Divine Consciousness, A Treasury of 112 types of Yoga, ed. & tr. by Jaideva Singh, Delhi, MLBD, 1979 (reprint 1993).

ABOUT THE CONTRIBUTORS

Alois M. Hass is (retired) Professor of German Literature (Medieval) at the University of Zürich, Switzerland, and one of the most eminent scholars on German mysticism, especially Meister Eckhart. He is author of a number of books and articles on mysticism.

Swami Nityananda Giri is a disciple of Sri Gnanananda and a leading Swami in his Ashram Sri Gnanananda Thapovanam in Tamil Nadu. His fields are Vedānta and Śaiva Siddhānta, and he is deeply involved in Hindu-Christian dialogue.

Raimon Panikkar is Emeritus Professor of the University of California, Santa Barbara (U.S.A.) in Religious Studies and comparative Philosophy. He has lectured in India, Europe and America, and is the author of about 40 books and a number of articles. He is a leading figure in interreligious studies and intercultural thought.

Hemendra Nath Chakravarty is a traditional Pandit living and teaching in Varanasi. He is a disciple of Pandit Gopinath Kaviraj and an authority on Tantra and Kashmir Śaivism.

Sr. Brigitte (Late) is an Anglican Sister of German origin. For some years she was Prioress of a convent in England, and she also lived as a hermit. Since about 20 years she is living in Christa Prema Seva Ashram, Pune, where she is at present Acharya, teaching and guiding seekers.

Baljinath Pandit is a retired Professor of Sanskrit from Jammu and a renowned scholar in Kashmir Śaivism. He has authored several books on Kashmir Śaivism.

Serge Descy is a Belgian theologian and political scientist. As a priest, he belongs to the Eastern Christian Tradition (Greek-Melkite Catholic Church). He was a lecturer at the *Institute Catholique des Hautes Etudes Commerciales* in Brussels, and associate professor at the *Saint Paul Institute of Philosophy and Theology* in Harissa, Lebanon. He was also in charge of two organizations for interreligious dialogue in the Middle East and for co-operation in development in Asia. He lived as a hermit in Lebanon and now as Swami Atmananda in Rishikesh.

Jankinath Kaul ('Kamal') (Late) is a Pandit from Srinagar, Kashmir, where he was lecturer in a College; and later Editor of Sri Ramakrishna Ashrama in Srinagar. He is a scholar of Vedānta and Kashmir Śaivism, being a disciple of Swami Lakshman Joo. He has translated and commented upon several Sanskrit texts and composed Sanskrit poetry.

Odette Baumer-Despeigne (Late), originally from Belgium and living in Switzerland, studied religion at the University of Louvain, Belgium. She was in correspondence with Swami Abhishiktananda (Henri Le Saux), and edited several of his books in French, with her introductions. She also deciphered and copied his spiritual diary in French. She was advisor of the Monastic Interreligious Dialogue (M.I.D. and D.I.M.).

Murray Rogers, an Anglican priest, whose life and that of his small community, Jyotiniketan, has been lived largely in India 1946–1971, the Old City of Jerusalem 1971–1980 and Hong Kong 1980–1989, and at present in Canada. He has been much involved in the Gandhian Movement and also in questions of indigenisation of the Church and in Interfaith Dialogue.

George Gispert-Sauch, a Jesuit from Spain, did his doctorate in Indology in Paris. He lives in India for about 30 years, teaching at the Jesuit College, in Kurseong, and now in Vidyajyoti College in Delhi. He writes and is co-editor of "Vidyajyoti" Journal.

Bettina Bäumer born in Austria, after her studies in Indology, Philosophy and Religion she lived in Varanasi, India, since 1967, researching in Sanskrit, Hinduism and Indian art and teaching. She was Research Director of Alice Boner Foundation, Varanasi, and Visiting Professor in Religious Studies in Vienna Universtiy. She has edited and authored a number of books and articles in the field of Hinduism, Indian aesthetics and comparative mysticism. She is president of the Abhishiktananda Society since 1988.